The Ionian Islands

written and researched by

Nick Edwards and John Gill

ROUGH
GUIDES

NEW YORK • LONDON • DELHI

www.roughguides.com

Contents

Architecture on Corfu
insert following p.112

**Ionian beaches and
costline insert** following
p.224

3

◄◄ View of Ionian Sea from Ithakí ◄ Ássos, Kefalloniá

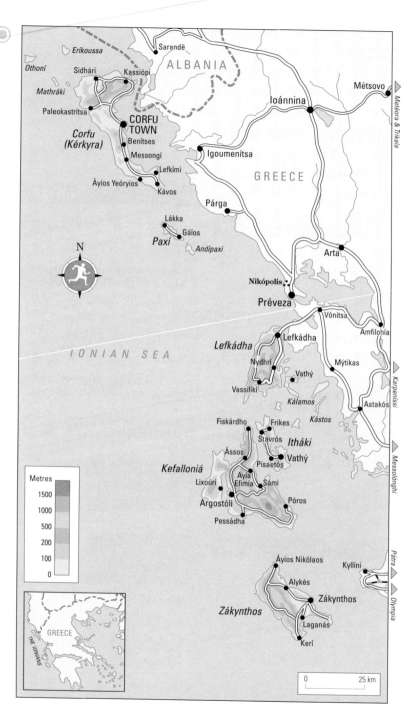

Introduction to

The Ionian Islands

Tracing a ragged line down the west coast of Greece, the Ionian islands are no more than 30km from the mainland, yet this has been far enough to exclude them from many of the key events in Greek history, most notably occupation by the Ottoman Turks. However, their position at the south of the Adriatic instead put them at the mercy of northerly invaders, primarily the Venetians and, later, the British, whose cultures fused with those of the islands. The Venetians, who first arrived in the archipelago in the late fourteenth century, imported language, art, music, law and architecture; the British turned up in the eighteenth century and unpacked local government, education, civil engineering, cricket and ginger beer. To a lesser or greater degree, all these influences can still be found in the islands, and the Italians and British remain the region's main summer visitors.

 The Ionian islands comprise a **core group** of six – Corfu (Kérkyra), Paxí (Paxos), Lefkádha (Lefkas), Itháki (Ithaca), Kefalloniá (Cephallonia) and Zákynthos (Zante). Kýthira, isolated at the foot of the Peloponnese, along with its satellite Andikýthira, is officially part of the Ionian group, completing the ancient Heptanese, but the duo are not covered in this Guide, as they bear few similarities to the core group of islands and share no transport connections with them.

As the big narrative happened elsewhere, the Ionian has no major archeological sites – though Olympia, just two hours' drive from Pátra on the

5

Fact file

• The **Ionian Islands** form the northwesternmost part of Greece. Kefalloniá is the largest island with a surface area of 904 square kilometres, followed by Corfu, around two thirds of the size. Paxí is the smallest of the major islands at only 25 square kilometres. The **terrain** is mostly rugged and mountainous; the highest mountain is **Mount Énos**, on Kefalloniá at 1628m.

• The total **population** of the islands is about 210,000 with just over half of that number living in Corfu. Itháki and Paxí by contrast only have around 3000 inhabitants each. **Corfu Town** is the largest city in the island group, with around 40,000 inhabitants, and is also the regional capital. The population is almost exclusively **Greek-speaking** and Greek Orthodox.

• The Ionians are divided into five **prefectures** (*nomi*), which send representatives to the 300-seat, single-chamber parliament in Athens. Greece has been a **parliamentary republic** since 1974, with a president elected for a five-year term. The **party** currently in power is the right-centrist Néa Dhimokratía, which finally wrestled power from the socialist PASOK in early 2004, although PASOK retained the five Ionian seats. Greece is also a member of the EU and NATO.

• The Ionian Islands' main foreign currency earner is **tourism**, while their biggest exports are **agricultural products**, such as olives, olive oil, wine and honey.

Peloponnesian mainland, is accessible from the southern islands. However, there are some spectacular medieval **fortresses**, and **museums** on the larger islands that trace the archipelago's cultures back to the Paleolithic era. Itháki (if not one of the other Ionian islands) is considered to be the site of the home of Odysseus and even has scattered remains to show for it, with neighbouring islands also laying claim to other locations and events from the *Odyssey*.

The major feature that distinguishes the Ionians from the mainland and the central swarm of Greek islands in the Aegean is **climate**: a reliable rainfall pattern has allowed centuries of fairly stable agriculture and has nurtured olive trees, vineyards, rich fruit and vegetable crops, and even wheat and cereal farming on some islands. The Ionian islands display similar geographical characteristics, too: all are mountainous (even tiny Paxí has a noticeable ridge), with their east coasts tending to comprise gently

▼ Áno Perithia, Corfu

dipping slopes above flat, sometimes reclaimed, farm land. The **west coasts** are invariably rocky, with cliffs up to 200 metres high. This geology conspires against tourism, placing most of the best beaches on the less accessible west coasts, and the worst on the handy east coasts – where lazy developers

▲ Café-life, Argostóli, Kefalloniá

have tended to concentrate their attentions. With the exception of Corfu's southwest and north coasts, the south coast of Kefalloniá, southern Zákynthos and pockets of western Lefkádha, most beaches are pebbly, usually shelving into sand.

Island-hopping through the Ionian is not as tricky as you might imagine and, with a month on your hands, you could easily get a decent taste of all six major islands, though you would be unable to see them all in depth. There is certainly not the abundance of ferry and hydrofoil lines weaving through the group that the Aegean is blessed with, but most of the islands have at least one connection with their nearest neighbour. The chain breaks down, though, between the northern duo, Corfu and Paxí, and the southern quartet: apart from a sporadic summer service between Corfu and Kefalloniá, there are no direct boats between the two groups, forcing you to travel via the mainland, though that in itself can be a pleasurable experience and allows you to glimpse a different side of Greece. Full details of all the possible inter-island connections are given throughout the Guide.

Venetian influence

The Venetians ruled over the Ionian Islands for more than four hundred years, leaving a profound influence on the culture. Two of the more visible legacies of their rule are the extensive olive-tree plantations and exquisite architecture found all over the islands, especially the graceful free-standing campaniles that accompany many churches. The cultural influence of the Venetians is also visible in the Italianate style of the Ionian school of painting, while many Italian words have been absorbed into the language and Hellenized over time.

Where to go

For those with less time to play with, **Corfu** and **Zákynthos** are the easiest of the islands to visit: both have busy international airports, and a developed structure of package and independent tourism. Over the years, however, they have acquired a reputation (not entirely undeserved) as sleazepits, the blame for some of which can be laid at the door of unscrupulous Greek and British tourism operators. The tackier resorts on Corfu tend to be on its east coast – Ípsos and Kávos are currently given over to booze, bonking and bungee-jumping – though dwindling tourism in recent years has had the effect of places like

> **Kefalloniá boasts some of the best unspoilt beaches and wildest mountainscapes in the Ionians.**

Benítses reinventing themselves as family resorts. On Zákynthos, Laganás is located on one of the island's finest beaches and is now reaching levels of excess to rival anything on Corfu. However, such large-scale tourist developments take up only a small proportion of each island, and most locals and visitors remain quite undisturbed by the overblown commerce and razzmatazz.

Kefalloniá's airport has yet to attract the volume of traffic of either Corfu or Zákynthos, and yet the island boasts some of the best unspoilt beaches and wildest mountainscapes in the Ionians. Despite the publicity generated by *Captain Corelli's Mandolin*, much of the island remains relatively undiscovered: resorts like chic Fiskárdho and popular Skála are very busy throughout the season, but others, such as Ayía Efimía, never seem to fill, and some remote beaches can be quiet even in August. Its northerly neighbour **Lefkádha**

has two notable pockets of development – Nydhrí and the windsurfers' paradise, Vassilikí – but the rest of the heavily indented coastline and the handsome, mountainous interior are largely unspoilt by tourism. It's not necessarily true any more that the further you travel from an airport, or an island with an airport, the more you'll distance yourself from the crowds. Many landing at Corfu head at great speed for **Paxí**, barely 12km long and covered in olive trees, only to find its three busy fishing village resorts, two of them tiny, completely full in high season; those who touch down on Kefalloniá and hop over to small and mountainous **Itháki**, the most unspoilt of the core islands, should have better luck, but limited infrastructure means space is still tight in August.

▲ Vegetable market

The **satellite islands**, such as the Dhiapóndia islets off northwest Corfu, Meganíssi off Lefkádha, and even Andípaxi south of Paxí, are becoming more accessible to adventurous travellers each year. But if it's solitude that you are seeking, you also have opportunities on the main islands. On Corfu, consider the areas around Korissíon lagoon or Mount Pandokrátor; on Lefkádha, aim for the hills around Karyá or the southwest coast, especially Atháni; try the Lixoúri peninsula or Ássos on Kefalloniá; or the northeast of Zákynthos. On the other hand, if you want to live as the Greeks do, try the island capitals: Corfu Town has transformed itself in recent years, Lefkádha Town has a lively buzz to it, and Argostóli retains a spacious charm despite being razed by the 1953 earthquake. The other seismic victim, Zákynthos Town, also has a certain class and lovely setting, despite busy traffic. Secondary towns like Lefkími on Corfu or

◀ Dusk on Corfu

Lixoúri on Kefalloniá are even less influenced by tourism and, of course, some mountain villages still see hardly any outsiders at all.

It's worth noting that nobody ever came to the Ionian islands looking for cordon bleu food or Scandinavian plumbing (but the same can be said for just about the whole of Greece). In all but the smartest **accommodation**, bathrooms are haphazard, though almost never insanitary. And while there are excellent **tavernas** on many islands, most, over the decades, have been content to reach a happy medium with their foreign customers. They still generally serve meals lukewarm, however, following the Greek nostrum that hot food is bad for the system, and on the smaller islands certain vegetables can be hard to come by. These shortcomings seem almost to be celebrated by the thousands who return, regardless, to the islands year after year. One of the reasons they return – beyond some of the finest swimming and watersports in the Mediterranean, the landscape, sunshine and balmy nights out under the Milky Way – is the **welcome** that all but the largest resorts still manage to extend. Despite the pressure of tourism, the islanders remain a disarmingly friendly people, and reserved Britons are often embarrassed by their astonishing kindness. The traditional quality of

Homer's Odyssey

The Ionian Islands form the backdrop to what is often described as the first romance in the history of Western literature: the magical, tear-jerking 24-book epic poem, *The Odyssey*, authored by the semi-mythical blind poet Homer, and telling the tale of the delayed return of the Greek hero  Odysseus to his kingdom in Ithaca (usually, though not always, identified with the modern island of Itháki).

The story opens with Odysseus, alone, stranded on an island belonging to the nymph Calypso, while his wife Penelope, far away, at home in Ithaca, is beset by unattractive suitors who are demanding that she re-marry. She, desperate to put off the evil hour, dispatches her son Telemachus to get news of Odysseus from two other Greek kings, Nestor and Menelaus. Slowly we learn how Odysseus is released by Calypso at the behest of Zeus but how a Poseidon-induced storm then washes him up on the shores of Phaeacia, where kindly maiden Nausicaa introduces him to the king. At a banquet in his honour, Odysseus tells of his hardships and adventures with, among others, the Lotus-eaters, Cyclops, the witch Circe and the Sirens. The Phaeacian king pities him and sends him home to Ithaca, where, on arrival, he disguises himself as an old beggar. Having secretly surveyed the situation, he reveals his identity to his son Telemachus, and then proceeds to rout the suitors before being recognised and accepted by his loyal wife Penelope.

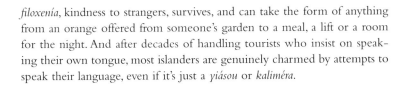

Petani Beach, Kefaloniá

filoxenía, kindness to strangers, survives, and can take the form of anything from an orange offered from someone's garden to a meal, a lift or a room for the night. And after decades of handling tourists who insist on speaking their own tongue, most islanders are genuinely charmed by attempts to speak their language, even if it's just a *yiásou* or *kaliméra*.

When to go

f you can, it's best to avoid the islands in late July and most of August, when holidaying Greeks and Italians descend en masse, accommodation is scarce, and prices soar along with the temperatures. June and early September are just as good for those concerned about fine weather – in fact, recent years have seen a number of fairly unstable high summers, with rainy Augusts followed by stunning Septembers and Octobers. In June, the sea is usually warm enough for swimming to be a joy; in September it can be as warm as a bath.

May, September and October are the times for bargain flights and packages, and, though you may risk short spells of inclement weather, are probably the best times to visit. In May and early June, many spring flowers are still in bloom, and villages and villagers are fresh from the winter. In late September and early October you can be blessed with fine weather, warm seas and almost no other visitors. However, bargain package deals in these low-season periods should be carefully scrutinized: some remote resorts

Biking at Vassilikí, Lefkádha

11

▲ Listón, Corfu Town

(noted in the Guide) close early, leaving those without the wherewithal to rent transport with precious little choice in food and entertainment.

Early May and late October mark the beginning and end of charter flights to the islands, although there's a mini winter season around Christmas and New Year. Outside these times you have to come by ferry, or fly via Athens, but, with the exception of Paxí, every island capital has hotels open year-round, and most local accommodation companies can rustle up somewhere suitable to stay. When the rafts of knick-knacks are packed away until next season, even the most developed resorts resume their prelapsarian charm, and major towns − in particular, Corfu Town − are to be seen at their best. The only bars or tavernas will be those the Greeks themselves use, which is usually the best recommendation at any time of the year. The winter months, November especially, see spectacular storms in the Ionians, yet it is possible to get sunburnt on Christmas Day. Off-season travel is also the only way to catch the two biggest festivals of the year: pre-Lenten carnival, a Venetian tradition maintained with parades, parties and mischief; and Orthodox Easter, which is celebrated for a full week and can be an extremely moving experience.

Prevailing northwesterly winds affect all the Ionian islands, commonly rising in the afternoon, occasionally developing into the *maéstro* − the Ionian equivalent of the Aegean *meltémi* − which can blow for three days or more. These winds make the Ionians ideal for yachting holidays and watersports, but can make beaches at exposed resorts hellish. The climate figures given below are official averages for Corfu − if any generalizations about Ionian weather can be made in advance, they can be made only about the region as a whole − although the record wet summer of 2002 washed the zero rainfall figures down the drain. The archipelago has any number of micro-climates: Lefkádha's valleys are like little lost Shangri-Las of meteorology, and Paxí gets only a fraction of the storms that gang up on nearby Corfu's Mount Pandokrátor.

Average temperatures and rainfall in Corfu

	Jan	Feb	Mar	Apr	May	Jun	Jul	Aug	Sep	Oct	Nov	Dec
Daily temperatures (°C)												
	13	14	16	19	23	28	30	31	28	23	18	15
Average rainfall (cm)												
	15	14	10	6	4	1	0	0	1	15	20	18

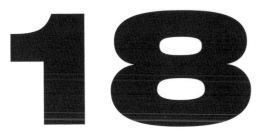

18
things not to miss

It's not possible to see everything The Ionian Islands have to offer in one trip – and we don't suggest you try. What follows is a selective taste of the islands' highlights: superb beaches, ancient ruins and colourful festivals. They're arranged in five colour-coded categories, which you can browse through to find the very best things to see and experience. All highlights have a page reference to take you straight into the Guide, where you can find out more.

01 Pórto Katsíki and Egremní beaches, Lefkádha Page **169** • If you really want to get away from it, these two wild, west-coast beaches offer the perfect opportunity.

02 Áyios Spyrídhon church, Corfu Town Page **82** • The atmospheric church of the island's patron saint contains his relics and important works of art.

03 Korissíon lagoon, Corfu
Page 117 • This quiet backwater in the south of the island is a haven for waterfowl and is bordered by a deserted beach.

05 Vathý, Itháki
Page 182 • A bay within a bay, Vathý enjoys one of the most idyllic settings in the archipelago.

07 Shipwreck Bay, Zákynthos
Page 256 • Take a boat trip to one of the island's most beautiful beaches, with a sunken ship as a unique centrepiece.

04 Andípaxi
Page 142 • Take a day-trip for swimming and some of the best snorkelling in the Ionian Sea at the coves on Paxí's smaller sister.

06 Robola wine
Page 209 • Taste wine at Rombola's locally renowned winery near Frangáta in Kefalloniá; look out too for their festival in August.

08 Melissáni cave, Kefalloniá
Page 218 • The boat trip into the eerie blue light of the underground lake near Sámi is an unforgettable experience.

09 **Tavernas at Fríkes, Itháki** Page **191** • Choose from a quartet of quality restaurants at this relaxed mini-resort in the north of the island.

10 **Churches in Lefkádha Town** Page **154** • The island capital boasts a fine selection of churches, several centuries old and displaying works by Ionian artists.

12 **Petaní beach, Kefalloniá** Page **212** • One of the finest beaches in the archipelago is tucked away on the remote west coast of the Lixoúri peninsula.

11 **Loggerhead turtles** Page **249** • Learn about the efforts to protect this endangered species in one of its major breeding grounds at Laganás Bay, Zákynthos.

13 **Windsurfing in Vassilikí, Lefkádha** Page **165** • The bay off the island's southernmost resort is a magnet for windsurfers from all over Europe and holds regular competitions.

14 **Easter Procession, Corfu** Page **59** • Easter is a great time to be in Corfu, both for its beautiful religious ceremonies and for the days of feasting and celebration that follow.

15 **Skála, Kefalloniá** Page **214** • Don't miss this pair of perfectly preserved mosaics in an excavated Roman villa.

16 **Angelókastro, Corfu** Page **105** • Stunning 360-degree views can be enjoyed from this precipitous castle near Paleokastrítsa.

17 **Hike the Corfu Trail** Page **122** • If you don't have time to walk all of it, try to cover at least some of the island's 200-kilometre-long designated scenic route.

18 **Cricket** Page **80** • Watch cricket being played in an unlikely setting on Corfu Town's Spianádha, while sipping a drink in one of the Listón's many cafés.

Basics

Basics

Getting there

At roughly 2000km and three hours by air from London, Corfu is the nearest Greek island to the UK and Ireland; its southerly siblings Kefalloniá and Zákynthos are barely half an hour's flight further. For most visitors, flying is the only viable option for getting to the Ionians unless your visit is part of a longer overland trip through Europe.

Only a few carriers fly direct to Greece **from North America**, and none offers direct flights to Corfu and the Ionians, so all arrangements are routed at least through Athens. If you have time, you may discover it cheaper to arrange your final Greece-bound leg of the journey in the UK (see p.20), in which case your only criterion will be finding a suitable and good-value North America–Europe flight.

There are no direct flights **from Australia and New Zealand** to the Ionian islands, so your best option is to fly to either Athens or London. From Athens you can get a connecting flight with Olympic Airlines, or continue your journey overland; from London it's possible to pick up a cheap charter flight (see p.20). Alternatively, you might choose to include Athens on a RTW ticket, usually valid for one year, as part of a longer trip. The same conditions apply from **South Africa**.

You can often cut costs by going through a **specialist flight agent** – either a consolidator, who buys up blocks of tickets from the airlines and sells them at a discount, or a **discount agent**, who in addition to dealing with discounted flights may also offer special student and youth fares and a range of other travel-related services such as travel insurance, rail passes, car rentals, tours and the like. Some agents specialize in **charter flights**, which may be cheaper than anything available on a scheduled flight – but departure dates are fixed and withdrawal penalties are high. You may even find it cheaper to pick up a bargain **package deal** from one of the tour operators listed on the following pages and then find your own accommodation when you get there.

Booking flights online

Many airlines and discount travel websites offer you the opportunity to book your tickets online, cutting out the costs of agents and middlemen. Good deals can also be found through discount or auction sites, as well as through the airlines' own websites.

Online booking websites

Ⓦ **www.travel.yahoo.com** Booking facilities as well as Rough Guide material incorporated in its general coverage.

Ⓦ **www.cheapflights.com** Flight deals, travel agents, plus links to other travel sites.

Ⓦ **www.cheaptickets.com** Discount flight specialists (US only).

Ⓦ **www.expedia.com** Discount airfares, all-airline search engine and daily deals (US only; for the UK, Ⓦ www.expedia.co.uk; for Canada, Ⓦ www .expedia.ca).

Ⓦ **www.gaytravel.com** Gay online travel agent, offering accommodation, cruises, tours and more.

Ⓦ **www.hotwire.com** Bookings from the US only. Last-minute savings of up to forty percent on regular published fares. Travellers must be at least 18 and there are no refunds, transfers or changes allowed. Log-in required.

Ⓦ **www.lastminute.com** Offers good last-minute holiday package and flight-only deals. (UK only; for Australia, Ⓦ www.lastminute.com.au).

Ⓦ **www.priceline.com** Name-your-own-price website that has deals at around forty percent off standard fares. You cannot specify flight times (although you do specify dates) and the tickets are non-refundable, non-transferable and non-changeable (US only; for the UK, Ⓦ www.priceline .co.uk).

Ⓦ **www.travelocity.com** Destination guides, hot Web fares and best deals for car rental, accommodation and lodging as well as flights. Provides access to the travel agent system SABRE, the most comprehensive central reservations system in the US.

ⓦ**www.travelshop.com.au** Australian website offering discounted flights, packages, insurance, and online bookings.

Flights from the UK and Ireland

There are no direct scheduled flights to the Ionian islands, but Corfu is well connected by **summer charter flights** with UK and Ireland airports: Gatwick, Manchester, Birmingham, Belfast, Bristol, Cardiff, East Midlands, Edinburgh, Glasgow, Luton, Newcastle, Norwich, Stansted, Belfast and Dublin all have charter flights to Corfu at least once a week in summer. More and more British airports are also developing seasonal charter connections with the region's three other airports: **Zákynthos** (the busiest and most accessible after Corfu), **Kefailoniá** and **Préveza**. Island-hoppers aiming for the hopper-friendly triangle of Lefkádha, Itháki and Kefallonía should consider either Préveza or Kefallo-niá airports: both offer good access to the islands, and Préveza, though on the mainland, is only thirty minutes by regular bus from Lefkádha Town. **Routing via Athens** is generally only a useful option if you're travelling **out of season** (when there are only a few obscure charters into the Ionians around Christmas or Easter), or if you're planning to stay longer than a charter would allow and need a **scheduled ticket**. The cheapest option of all, especially out of season, can be to book a cheap flight on Ryanair from London Stansted to **Brindisi** in Italy, and then catch a ferry from there direct to Corfu.

In addition to the websites listed on p.19, good sources when **shopping around for flights** are the classified ads in national papers – the *Guardian*, *Independent*, *Observer*, *Sunday Times* – and Teletext. Local newspapers and listings magazines also carry ads for companies selling budget flights. Among travel agents, high-street branches of the major chains tend to be geared to selling you a package holiday rather than a bargain flight, but this can be an extremely cheap way of holidaying in the destination of your choice if you don't mind being restricted to staying in the busy resorts.

Charter flights

Most UK and Irish travellers to the Ionian islands will arrive by direct **charter flight**, either with a package holiday or on a flight-only deal. These flights have fixed and unchangeable outward and return dates, and are usually for one or two weeks, although most operators can offer three- or four-week flights for a nominal extra fee. The cheapest charter flights tend to be those **into Corfu**, with those **from London** slightly cheaper than provincial airports. Flight-only deals from Gatwick to Corfu generally **cost** between £120 and £220, depending on the season and departure/arrival times. Flights **from major provincial airports** such as Manchester and Birmingham tend to be £10–20 higher, those from Glasgow and smaller airports like Bristol £30–40 higher. Flights **from Ireland** are more again: in high season, a charter flight from Dublin to Corfu currently costs over €350, including taxes, and from Belfast around £260.

Time zones

Greece is in the same time zone as much of the Middle East, two hours ahead of GMT. Greek daylight saving time falls in line with the rest of the EU, beginning at 2am on the last Sunday in March, when the clocks go forward one hour, and ending at 2am the last Sunday in October, when they go back. For North America, the difference is seven hours ahead of Eastern Standard Time, ten hours for Pacific Standard Time, with an extra hour plus or minus for those weeks in April when one place is on daylight savings and the other isn't. Greece is between five and nine hours behind Australia, depending on your location down under and respective daylight savings, and between nine and eleven hours behind New Zealand. The time is the same in South Africa, except during the summer when Greece jumps forward an hour. A recorded time message (in Greek) is available locally by dialling ☎141.

Fly less – stay longer! Travel and climate change

Climate change is a serious threat to the ecosystems that humans rely upon, and air travel is the fastest-growing contributor to the problem. Rough Guides regard travel, overall, as a global benefit, and feel strongly that the advantages to developing economies are important, as is the opportunity of greater contact and awareness among peoples. But we all have a responsibility to limit our personal impact on global warming, and that means giving thought to how often we fly, and what we can do to redress the harm that our trips create.

Flying and climate change

Pretty much every form of motorized travel generates CO_2 (the main cause of human-induced climate change) but planes are far and away the worst offenders, not just because of the sheer distances they allow us to travel, but because they release a selection of greenhouse gases high into the atmosphere. The statistics are frightening: two people taking a return flight between Europe and the US will contribute as much to climate change as an average household's gas and electricity over a whole year.

Fuel-cell and other less harmful types of plane may emerge eventually. But until then, there are really just two options for concerned travellers: to reduce the amount we travel by air (take fewer trips – stay for longer!), and to make the trips we do take "climate neutral" via a carbon offset scheme.

Carbon offset schemes

Offset schemes run by climatecare.org, carbonneutral.com and others allow you to make up for some or all of the greenhouse gases that you are responsible for releasing. To do this, they provide "carbon calculators" for working out the global-warming contribution of a specific flight (or even your entire existence), and then let you contribute an appropriate amount of money to fund offsetting measures. These include rainforest and other indigenous reforestation, and initiatives to reduce future energy demand – often run in conjunction with sustainable development schemes.

Rough Guides, together with Lonely Planet and other concerned partners in the travel industry, are supporting a carbon offset scheme run by climatecare.org. Please take the time to view our website and see how you can help to make your trip climate neutral.

Ⓦwww.roughguides.com/climatechange

Flights to **Zákynthos and Kefalloniá** are limited to Gatwick and the major provincial airports, costing between £150 and £240 depending on season. Préveza's small, semi-military airport is the worst served, with only one or two flights from the major airports per week, at prices also starting from around £150. **Charter flights to Athens** are worth investigating in low season, when they can go for as little as £100.

Different regulations concerning charter tickets apply to EU nationals and those from outside the EU. **Non-EU nationals** flying charter must purchase a return ticket, valid for no fewer than three days and no more than four weeks. They should also have an accommodation voucher – a hangover from the days when flight-only deals were not meant to be sold – which should be issued by the ticketing agency but which will not actually get you accommodation.

Student/youth charters are sold as one-way flights only and are available to both EU and non-EU nationals. By combining two one-way charters you can stay for over a month. Student/youth charter tickets are available to anyone under 26, and to all card-carrying full-time students under 32.

Scheduled flights

Getting from the UK and Ireland to the Ionian islands using **scheduled flights** is a roundabout process. The Greek national carrier Olympic Airlines (1–2 daily) and British Airways (2 daily) have non-stop flights **from London Heathrow to Athens**, which with advance booking can cost under £200, but usually over £200 in August. Keep an eye open for British Airway's special World Offer deals. British Airways also has one daily flight (except Tues) from March to October from Gatwick. The budget airline EasyJet (direct booking only) has one daily flight to Athens from both London Luton and Gatwick, which can cost under £40 one way, if you book well in advance. **From Dublin** scheduled flights via London are operated by British Airways, Aer Lingus and British Midland/ Olympic, and cost around €400. Scheduled flights from British regional airports route via Heathrow in the first instance.

From Athens, there are daily internal flights on Olympic to Préveza and all the Ionian island airports (AegeanCronus also serves Corfu, costing from around £40 one-way and averaging 45 minutes' flying time). If you fly to Athens on Olympic, you can get a reduction on the domestic leg of your journey as part of an inclusive deal. For more information on internal flights, see p.28. Bus and ferry connections from Athens are cheaper and more frequent than flights, but take between seven and eleven hours to reach the islands.

Consolidators for London–Athens flights on **eastern European airlines** may have cheaper discount flights than Olympic, BA and Virgin, but flights are routed via the airlines' capital cities, where you may have to spend several hours.

Travellers **from Ireland** might also consider buying a **flight to London** and a charter ticket or package from there to the Ionians – a rather cumbersome itinerary, but possibly cheaper. Companies such as Ryanair offer high-season returns often under €100 to Gatwick, Luton or Stansted, which all have charter connections to the Ionian islands.

If you want to stay a long time or are uncertain of your return date, you might consider flying on two separate **one-way tickets** (but check p.29 regarding any visa restrictions that might affect you). Outside high season, island travel agents often advertise one-way tickets back to Britain. However, avoid coming back on national holidays and,

crucially, at the end of the season, when travel companies are looking for the cheapest way to get their guest workers home.

Scheduled airlines

Aer Lingus ☎0818/365 000, ⊛www.aerlingus.ie.
British Airways UK ☎0870/850 9850, Ireland ☎1890/626 747; ⊛www.ba.com.
British Midland ☎0870/607 0555, ⊛www.flybmi.com.
CSA Czech Airlines ☎0870/444 3747, ⊛www.csa.cz/en.
EasyJet ☎0870/600 0000, ⊛www.easyjet.com.
LOT Polish Airlines ☎0845/601 0949, ⊛www.lot.com.
Malév Hungarian Airlines Danube Travel ☎0870/909 0577, ⊛www.malev.hu.
Olympic Airlines UK ☎0870/606 0460, ⊛www.olympicairlines.com.
Ryanair UK ☎0906/270 5656, Ireland ☎01/609 7800; ⊛www.ryanair.com.

Packages and specialist tours

The vast majority of UK and Irish visitors to the Ionians are on **package holidays**, comprising flights, transfers and accommodation. Corfu and Zákynthos are the most developed, and so will probably have the cheapest deals, but comparing like with like, there is little difference between the islands. The other islands are less developed and can offer some surprisingly good-value package deals, especially if you shop around. Some package bargains are even worth taking for the flight alone, leaving you to use the accommodation as you see fit.

For a more low-key and genuinely "Greek" holiday, it's best to travel with one of the smaller **specialist agencies** listed below. Most of these are more expensive than the mainstream package companies, but they tend to have found the best accommodation in the best areas, and you're also paying for a much higher standard of attention from resort staff. Best of all, however, is to contact a **local accommodation agency**, some of whom can arrange flights and even transfers. As well as plugging you into the local community, it also plugs your money into the local economy. Ask the Greek Tourist Office for a copy of their monthly *GTP Travel-Tourism Guide* or look them up online at ⊛www.gtpnet.com.

Specialist tour operators

Club Vassiliki ☎01920/484121, ✆www
.clubvass.com. Windsurfing packages to Vassilikí in
Lefkádha, including flights, accommodation, beginner
instruction and insurance.

Corfu à la Carte ☎01635/210250, ✆www
.travelalacarte.co.uk. Traditional villas on Corfu (the
quieter northeast coast) and at Longós and Gáïos
on Paxí.

CV Travel ☎0870/606 0013, ✆www.cvtravel
.co.uk. One of the big three (along with Greek Islands
Club, and Simply Ionian), with some of the islands'
most luxurious (and expensive) properties on Corfu
and Paxí on its books.

Direct Greece ☎0870/191 9244, ✆www
.directgreece.co.uk. Villas and apartments on
Corfu, Lefkádha and Zákynthos (and at Párga on the
mainland).

First Choice ☎0870/850 3999, ✆www
.firstchoice.co.uk. Standard package operator with
resorts all over the Ionians, and branches all over
the UK.

Go Holidays Dublin ☎01/874 4126, ✆www
.goholidays.ie. Package-tour specialists with
branches in other parts of the country.

Greek Islands Club ☎020/8232 9780, ✆www
.greekislandsclub.com. One of the longest-
established villa and apartment companies in the

Ionian, with prime properties on most of the islands,
including Andípaxi. Also offers specialist holidays,
such as painting and cultural tours.

Island Wandering ☎0870/777 9944, ✆www
.islandwandering.com. Tailor-made holidays to Corfu,
Lefkádha, Itháki, Kefalloniá, Zákynthos and on the
mainland.

Kosmar Villa Holidays ☎0870/700 0747,
✆www.kosmar.com. Best operator in the 2005
British Travel Awards. Hotels and apartments in Corfu,
Lefkádha, Kefalloniá, Paxí, Párga and Zákynthos.

Manos Holidays ☎0870/753 0530, ✆www
.manos.co.uk. One of the biggest package companies
specializing in the Ionians, with a wide range of
apartments and hotels on Corfu, Lefkádha, Kefalloniá,
Zákynthos, Paxí, Meganíssi and Párga.

Neilson ☎0870/333 3356, ✆www.neilson.co.uk.
Watersport and flotilla holidays based in Nydhrí and
Vassilikí on Lefkádha, as well as windsurfing at the
latter.

Planos Holidays ☎01373/814 200, ✆www
.planos.co.uk. Now the biggest single operator
on Paxí, Planos offers bonded flight–transfer–
accommodation package deals, using some of the
best properties on the island, many of them in and
around Lákka.

Sailing Holidays Ltd ☎020/8459 8787, ✆www
.sailingholidays.com. Popular and competitive
company that organizes yachting flotillas in the Ionians.

Simply Ionian ☎020/8541 2202, ✆www
.simply-travel.com. Fastest-growing of the big three,
with select properties on Corfu, Paxí, Kefalloniá, Itháki,
Lefkádha, Meganíssi and Zákynthos. Specializes in
village and country villas, as well as specialist interest
holidays, including sailing, painting and walking.

STA Travel ☎0870/160 0599, ✆www.statravel
.co.uk. High street and campus branches all over the
UK. Very good rates with Olympic via Athens to the
Ionian islands.

Sunvil Holidays ☎020/8568 4499, ✆www
.sunvil.co.uk. Specializes in upmarket, out-of-the-
way villas and apartments on Corfu and Lefkádha.
Also activity holidays: walking, painting, cycling and
watersports.

Tapestry ☎020/8235 7800, ✆www
.tapestryholidays.com. The most upmarket operator
of them all, with exclusive villas on all the islands
except Zákynthos. Some exceed £2000 per person
for a week.

Flights from North America

The Greek national airline, Olympic Airlines,
flies to Athens out of New York (JFK),
Boston, Montréal and Toronto and offers

reasonably priced add-on flights to the Ionian airports. Delta is the only US carrier currently offering a direct service to Athens from New York and Atlanta, although American Airlines and US Airways have code-sharing arrangements with Olympic, allowing them to quote through fares from Chicago, Dallas, Denver, LA, Miami, Ottawa, Quebec, SF, Seattle, Vancouver and Washington DC, as well as some smaller cities. A number of European airlines, listed below, can arrange connections to Athens or Corfu via their gateway cities, which can be considerably cheaper than the direct flights.

In general there just isn't enough traffic between North America and Athens to make for very cheap fares: **APEX** tickets usually constitute the best deal but they must be bought at least twenty-one days in advance and allow a maximum thirty-day stay. Other deals to keep an eye open for are special airline **Eurosavers** off-season and youth/ student fares.

Regardless of where you buy your ticket, fares will depend on the **season** and are highest from May to September, when the weather is best; they drop during the "shoulder" seasons – September/October and March/ April – and you'll get the best prices during the low season, November to March (excluding Christmas and New Year, when prices are hiked up and seats are at a premium). Note also that flying on weekends ordinarily adds $50 to the round-trip fare; price ranges quoted below assume midweek travel.

Non-stop Olympic Airlines flights **from New York** or **Boston** to Athens start at around $600 return in winter and rise to $1600 in high season if booked at short notice but you should pay more like $1200 if you book well in advance. Delta's round trips from New York and Atlanta are very similar in price. **Indirect flights** from the East Coast with American or European airlines should be available for between $500 and $1500, depending on the season. Common-rating and marketing arrangements between airlines mean that prices to Athens from the **Mid-West**, **Deep South** or **West Coast** are not much higher, especially off-season, ranging from $700 to $1700.

From Canada, APEX return fares to Athens on the non-stop Olympic flights from Montréal and Toronto rise from around CDN$1500 in winter to nearly CDN$3000 in summer. Indirect flights on Air Canada, British Airways, Air France, KLM or Swiss cost around CDN$500 less in summer but are hardly any different in winter; some Eastern European carriers like Czech Airlines often have better deals. From Calgary or Vancouver there are no direct flights and you can expect to pay around CDN$1500 in winter, CDN$2800–3000 in summer.

Airlines in the US and Canada

Air Canada ☎1-888/247-2262, ⊛www .aircanada.ca.
Air France US ☎1-800/237-2747, ⊛www .airfrance.com; Canada ☎1-800/667-2747, ⊛www.airfrance.ca.
Alitalia US ☎1-800/223-5730, Canada ☎1-800/361-8336; ⊛www.alitalia.com.
American Airlines ☎1-800/433-7300, ⊛www .aa.com.
British Airways ☎1-800/247-9297, ⊛www .british-airways.com.
Czech Airlines US ☎1-877/359-6629 or 212/765-6022, Canada ☎416/363-3174; ⊛www .czechairlines.com.
Delta Air Lines ☎1-800/241-4141, ⊛www .delta.com.
Lufthansa US ☎1-800/645-3880, Canada ☎1-800/563-5954; ⊛www.lufthansa.com.
Northwest/KLM Airlines ☎1-800/447-4747, ⊛www.nwa.com, ⊛www.klm.com.
Olympic Airlines ☎1-800/223-1226 or 718/896-7393, ⊛www.olympicairlines.com.
Swiss ☎1-877/359-7947, ⊛www.swiss.com.
US Airways ☎1-800/622 1015, ⊛www .usairways.com.

Specialist tour operators in the US and Canada

Very few North American operators book group tours specifically for Corfu and the Ionians; at most, they might include one or two nights on Corfu. You can, however, get a tour operator to book you a tailor-made, independent package trip.

Adventures Abroad ☎1-800/665-3998 or 360/775-9926, ⊛www.adventures-abroad.com. General operator, offering group and individual tours and cruises.
Cosmos ☎1-800/276-1241, ⊛www .cosmosvacations.com. Planned vacation packages with an independent focus and good discounts.

Hellenic Adventures ☏1-800/851-6349 or 612/827-0937, ⓦwww.hellenicadventures.com. A vast range of small group and independent tours: cultural, historical, horseback riding, hiking, culinary and family-oriented.

Homeric Tours ☏1-800/223-5570, ⓦwww .homerictours.com. General Hellenic tour operator, with packages to Corfu via Athens and winter break specials.

STA Travel ☏1-800/781-4040, ⓦwww.statravel .com. Worldwide specialists in independent travel; also student IDs, travel insurance, car rental, rail passes, etc.

Valef Yachts ☏1-800/223-3845 or 215/641-1624, ⓦwww.valefyachts.com. Yachting trips and charters.

Flights from Australia and New Zealand

With the huge Greek diaspora in **Australia**, Olympic Airlines has several **direct flights** a week to Athens from Sydney and Melbourne via Bangkok. Slightly cheaper, however, are the **single-connection** routeings run by carriers like Qantas and British Airways, while **multi-stop** deals with various Asian airlines are cheaper still, but obviously take a lot longer. From **New Zealand** you will have to make at least one connection, likelier two or more, in Australia, Asia or Europe.

For both Greece and London, most airlines operate the following fare **seasons** (with some slight variations): **low** January 16–end February; **high** May 16–July 31 and December 11–23; and **shoulder** the rest of the year. Fares from the major Australian cities are common-rated, and A$200–400 more if you go via Canada or the US. Flying from Christchurch and Wellington costs NZ$150–300 more than from Auckland.

Tickets purchased direct from the airlines tend to be expensive, so it's best to head for a **travel agent** (STA, which offers fare reductions for ISIC card holders and those under 26, and Flight Centre generally offer the lowest fares), or check out one of the **online booking** websites (see p.19). Depending on the airline and routeing, simple return trips from any major Australian city **to Athens** will cost A$1500–1700 in low season, up to A$1800–2200 in high season. Returns to Athens from New Zealand tend to be in excess of NZ$3000 at any time of year, making RTW tickets an attractive option. The lowest fares **to London** are with Britannia

during their charter season from November to March (from around A$1400/NZ$1900). At other times, airlines like Garuda are very competitive, with prices such as A$1300–1750/NZ$1700–2200 from the respective countries. Finally, for a **RTW ticket** with half a dozen stopovers, including Athens, you can expect to pay A$2200–2600 and NZ$3500–4000, depending on the season.

Airlines in Australia and New Zealand

Air New Zealand Australia ☏13 24 76, New Zealand ☏0800/737 000; ⓦwww.airnz.com.

Alitalia Australia ☏02/9244 2445, New Zealand ☏09/308 3357; ⓦwww.alitalia.com.

Britannia Airways Australia ☏02/9247-4833, New Zealand ☏09/308-3360; ⓦwww .britanniaairways.com.

British Airways Australia ☏02/8904 8800, New Zealand ☏0800/274 847 or 09/357 8950; ⓦwww .britishairways.com.

Garuda Indonesia Australia ☏02/9334 9970, New Zealand ☏09/366 1862; ⓦwww .garuda-indonesia.com.

Olympic Airlines Australia ☏02/9251-2044; ⓦwww.olympic-airways.gr.

Qantas Australia ☏13 13 13, ⓦwww.qantas.com .au; New Zealand ☏09/357 8900, ⓦwww.qantas .co.nz.

Royal Jordanian Australia ☏02/9244 2701, New Zealand ☏03/365 3910; ⓦwww.rja.com.jo.

Singapore Airlines Australia ☏13 10 11, New Zealand ☏09/303 2129; ⓦwww.singaporeair.com.

Thai Airways Australia ☏1300/651 960, New Zealand ☏09/377 0268; ⓦwww.thaiair.com.

Specialist tour operators in Australia and New Zealand

Since the Ionians are not a major destination for Australians and New Zealanders, there are no pre-packaged holidays, but the following agents can put together a holiday to suit your needs.

Eurolynx Level 3, 20 Fort St, Auckland ☏09/379-9716, ⓦwww.eurolynx.co.nz. Individually tailored travel itineraries.

Grecian Tours Australia ☏03/9663 3711, ⓦwww .greciantours.com.au. Package tours, discounted flights, rail passes and car rental.

Greece and Mediterranean Travel Centre Australia ☏02/9313 4633, ⓦwww .greecemedtravel.com.au. Can book travel, accommodation and hire cars throughout Greece, including Corfu.

Kyrenia Travel Services Australia ☎ 02/9283-2144. Greek holidays, accommodation, tours and cruises.

STA Travel Australia ☎ 1300/733 035, ⓦ www.statravel.com.au; New Zealand ☎ 0508/782 872, ⓦ www.statravel.co.nz. Good for arranging budget deals to the islands, especially for students and under 26.

Sun Island Tours Australia ☎ 1300/665 673, ⓦ www.sunislandtours.com.au. Package holidays to Greece, including Corfu.

Flights from South Africa

There are no direct flights from South Africa to the Ionians and the only non-stop flights from between South Africa and Greece is Olympic's thrice weekly Johannesburg–Athens route. Otherwise, the most popular routeing is with any of the other major European airlines, including BA, KLM, Air France or Lufthansa (often in partnership with South Africa Airways), who will cover the leg between Johannesburg or Cape Town and the respective hubs in Europe. These airlines will often allow a stopover at little or no extra cost. Sometimes good deals can also be had with airlines from countries in north Africa or the Gulf that serve Athens, such as Egyptair or Emirates.

The **cost** of tickets depends on the season, with the most expensive periods being July–September and over the Christmas and New Year holidays. The cheapest times to fly are from March to May and again in November, with the rest of the year considered "shoulder season". Whether you fly direct or indirect, you'll get the best deal if you book well in advance, especially for the busy periods. In general terms, the best deals for a **return ticket** from Johannesburg in low season start at around 4500 rand, rising sharply to as much as 12,000 rand if booked at short notice in high season. Flights from Cape Town usually cost 50–200 rand extra and connecting flights from smaller airports around South Africa will incur the usual add-ons. **RTW tickets** are another option, if your visit to Greece is part of a longer trip, but they cost much more than their Antipodean counterparts at around 18–20,000 rand.

Airlines in South Africa

Air France ☎ 0860/340 340, ⓦ www.airfrance.com.

British Airways ☎ 011/441 8600, ⓦ www.british-airways.com.

Egyptair ☎ 011/390 2202, ⓦ www.egyptair.com.eg.

Emirates Airlines ☎ 011/883 8420, ⓦ www.emirates.com.

KLM Airlines ☎ 0860/247 747, ⓦ www.klm.com.

Lufthansa ☎ 0861/266 554; ⓦ www.lufthansa.com.

Olympic Airways ☎ 011/860 1614, ⓦ www.olympicairways.gr.

South African Airways ☎ 0861/359 722, ⓦ www.flysaa.com.

Virgin Atlantic ☎ 011/340 3400, ⓦ www.virgin-atlantic.com.

Specialist tour operators in South Africa

South African operators are unlikely to book **group tours** specifically for Corfu and the Ionians, though you might find a tour that includes Corfu at least. Otherwise you can ask one of the tour operators below to book you a tailor-made, **independent package** trip. Many agents will help you find a cheap flight and perhaps accommodation.

STA Travel ☎ 011/447 5414, ⓦ www.statravel.co.za. Worldwide specialists in independent travel; also student IDs, travel insurance, car rental, rail passes, etc.

Thompsons Tours ☎ 011/770 7677 or 021/408 9555, ⓦ www.thompsons.co.za. Does group and customized travel arrangements all over the world.

Wide Horizons Travel ☎ 021/683 3153, ⓦ www.co.za. Offers worldwide packages and can help put together a holiday in the Ionians.

Wynberg Executive Travel ☎ 021/659 2220, ⓔ wynbergtravel@galileosa.co.za. Agency that can tailor trips worldwide, including Greece and the Ionians.

Flights and ferries from mainland Greece and Italy

The Ionian islands have a wide choice of **ferry connections** with mainland Greek and Italian ports, as well as scheduled **flights** between Athens and Corfu, Préveza (for Lefkádha), Keffaloniá and Zákynthos. The links with Italy are particularly useful if you're working your way across Europe and want to bypass the former Yugoslavia.

Besides the long-distance sea connections with Italy and the larger Greek ports

Ferries from Italy to the Ionians and mainland Greece

Routes

From the Italian ports, most ferries depart in the afternoon or evening, though there are occasional high-season morning departures. All voyage durations given are approximate. Superfast, Minoan and Med Link have the fastest crossings of the regular ferries, but the new high-speed catamarans run by companies such as SNAV and Italian Ferries cover the distance in under half that time. The companies with the most frequent crossings are given below.

From Ancona ANEK (1 daily) and Minoan (1 daily) via Igoumenítsa (15–19hr) to Pátra (22–26hr).

From Bari Superfast (3–4 weekly) to Corfu (8hr); Ventouris (1 daily) and Marlines (4 weekly) to Igoumenítsa (11–13hr), some via Corfu (2–3 weekly; 10hr). Superfast (daily) to Igoumenítsa (9hr) and Pátra (15hr 30 min).

From Brindisi Agoudimos (April–Dec 4 weekly–1 daily to Igoumenítsa (9hr), some via Corfu. Fragline (Apr–Oct almost daily) via Corfu (7–8hr) to Igoumenítsa (9–11hr). Hellenic Mediterranean Lines (May–Sep 4–7 weekly) direct to Pátra (15hr) and in high season to Kefalloniá (3–4 weekly; 11hr) and Zákynthos (1–2 weekly; 12hr); SNAV (early July–early sep 6 weekly) to Corfu (4hr) and Paxí (5hr).

From Venice Minoan (April–Oct 6–7 weekly) and ANEK (4–6 weekly) go via Corfu (25hr) and Igoumenítsa (26hr) to Pátra (33hr).

Sample Fares

Prices below are one-way high/low season fares; port taxes (€7–12 per person in each direction) are not included. High-speed ferries and catamarans cost about double.

Corfu/Igoumenítsa from Ancona: deck class €66/42; vehicle from €98/54.

Corfu/Igoumenítsa from Bari or Brindisi: deck class €46/24; vehicle from €50/22.

Corfu/Igoumenítsa from Venice: deck class €75/55; vehicle from €121/74.

Pátra from Ancona: deck class €68/39; vehicle from €95/50.

Pátra from Bari or Brindisi: deck class €48/32; vehicle from €50/30.

Pátra from Venice: deck class €80/60; vehicle from €130/80.

Agents in Italy

The dialling code for Italy is ☏39, and is followed by the area code including the first zero, then the number. Note that advance bookings can also be made online.

Agoudimos Brindisi: ☏0831/529 091, ⓦwww.agoudimos-lines.com.

ANEK Ancona: ☏071/205 959, ⓦwww.anek.gr.

Blue Star Brindisi: ☏0831/562 200; Ancona: ☏071/2071068; Venice: ☏041/277 0559, ⓦwww.bluestarferries.com.

Fragline Brindisi: ☏0831/590 196, ⓦwww.fragline.gr.

Marlines Bari: ☏080/523 1824, ⓦwww.marlines.com.

Minoan Lines Ancona: ☏071/201 708; Venice: ☏041/271 2345, ⓦwww.minoan.gr.

SNAV Brindisi: ☏0831/525 492, ⓦwww.snav.it.

Superfast Ferries Ancona: ☏071/202 033; Bari: ☏080/521 1416, ⓦwww.superfast .com.

Ventouris Bari: ☏080/521 7118; Brindisi: ☏0831/521 2614, ⓦwww.ventouris.gr.

Viamare Travel UK ☏020/7431 4560. A UK agent for ANEK, Blue Star, Fragline, Marlines, and Ventouris.

described above, the Ionian islands are served by a variety of local ferries from the Greek mainland (Lefkádha, which has a land link and direct bus connections with the mainland, is the exception). Full details of each island's local ferry services are given in the "Travel details" at the end of the relevant chapter, and the more significant mainland ports are described in the Guide – Igoumenítsa on p.71, Párga on p.132, Préveza on p.150 and Pátra on p.198. Information about routes between the islands and general advice on Greek ferries can be found on pp.27–36. If you're travelling direct to the Ionians from Athens, flying is the most convenient mode of transport, given the length of the bus and train journeys to the ports (8hr 30min, for example, to Igoumenítsa), but costs about three times as much.

Flights from Athens

Olympic Airlines operates daily **flights from Athens** to all the Ionian island airports: Corfu (3–6 daily), Kefalloniá (1–3 daily) and Zákynthos (1–2 daily), as well as Préveza (3–5 weekly) on the mainland (for Lefkádha bus connections). Current standard one-way **prices** are Corfu €92, Kefalloniá €90, Zákynthos €90 and Préveza €83. Return prices are exactly double those of single tickets. AegeanCronus runs similarly-priced flights from Athens to Corfu only (1–2 daily).

Island flights are often full in peak season; if they're an essential part of your plans, it is worth trying to make a **reservation** at least a week in advance. As travel agents cannot give discounts on domestic flights, it is best to book direct with the airlines: Olympic Airlines in Athens ☎210/926 9111, in Thessaloniki ☎2310/368 311, ⓦwww .olympicairlines.com; AegeanCronus in Athens ☎210/998 8350, ⓦwww.aegeanair .com (see Corfu Town Listings p.90 for local contacts). Domestic air tickets are non-refundable, but you can change your flight, space permitting, without penalty up to a few hours before your original departure.

Size restrictions mean that the fifteen-kilo **baggage weight limit** is fairly strictly enforced; if, however, you've just arrived from overseas or purchased your ticket outside Greece, you are allowed the 23-kilo standard international limit.

Ferries from Italy

Ferries operated by a variety of companies connect four of Italy's Adriatic ports – frequently from **Ancona**, **Bari** and **Brindisi**, with fewer from **Venice** – to some or all of Greece's main Ionian Sea ports (Igoumenítsa, Corfu, Sámi on Kefalloniá, Zákynthos Town and Pátra). Some of these ferries call at more than one port en route; you can stop over at no extra charge if you get these stops specified on your ticket. All the ferries detailed below also run in the opposite direction, with similar frequencies and durations.

Ferries have several classes of ticket, from deck through aircraft-style seats and shared cabins to deluxe. In summer, it's essential to **book tickets** a few days ahead, especially in the peak July/August period – and certainly if you are taking a car across. During the winter you can usually just turn up at the ports, but it's still wise to book in advance if possible. Substantial reductions apply on many lines for both InterRail or Eurail pass holders, and for those under 26. Rail pass holders should check if there are free crossings on particular lines in any given year. Slight discounts are usually available on return fares for all travellers. For those with camper vans, many companies allow you to sleep in your van on board, sparing you the cost of a cabin berth; ask about reduced "camping" fares. Bicycles go free, motorbikes cost €15–60, but are free from Brindisi.

Visas and red tape

UK, Irish and all other EU nationals need only a valid passport for entry to Greece; you are not stamped in on arrival or out upon departure, and in theory enjoy the same civil rights as Greek citizens (see "Living in the Ionians", p.60). US, Australian, New Zealand, Canadian and most non-EU Europeans receive entry and exit stamps, effectively a "tourist visa", in their passports and can stay, as tourists, for ninety days. If you are a non-EU citizen arriving on a busy charter from an EU country, especially in the dead of night, make sure your passport does get stamped to avoid awkward questions on departure.

Non-EU citizens who wish to remain in Greece for longer than three months should officially apply for an **extension**. This can be done in Corfu Town at the *Ipiresía Allodhapón* (Aliens' Bureau) at Alexandhrás 19 (☎26610/39 277); brace yourself for a web of bureaucracy. In other locations you visit the local police station, where staff are usually more co-operative.

In theory, if you are an **EU national**, you can stay indefinitely and have the same employment rights as any Greek; as your passport is never stamped, nobody knows or cares how long you have been in the country, and the equal rights theory is only likely to be tested if you fall foul of the authorities. Unless of Greek descent, visitors from **non-EU countries** are currently allowed only one six-month extension to the basic tourist visa, for which a hefty fee of €450 is charged. If you do bite the bullet, the procedure should be set in motion a couple of weeks before your time runs out. If you don't have a work permit, you will be required to present pink, personalized **bank exchange receipts** (ask the bank for these when you exchange money) totalling at least €1500 for the preceding three months, as proof that you have sufficient funds to support yourself without working. Possession of unexpired credit cards, a Greek savings account passbook or travellers' cheques can to some extent substitute for this requirement.

Some non-EU resident individuals get around the law by leaving Greece every three months and re-entering a few days later but a new official rule states you must leave for a non-EU country and stay out for ninety days, so you will have to rely on the unpredictable chances that your passport will not be scrutinized too closely.

If you **overstay** your time and are caught, you will be fined and deported. Those who have not already been caught will be given €450 on-the-spot fines when they attempt to leave the country; no excuses will be entertained except perhaps a doctor's certificate stating that you were immobilized in hospital. It cannot be overemphasized just how exigent Greek immigration officials often are on these issues.

Greek embassies and consulates abroad

Australia 9 Turrana St, Yarralumla, Canberra, ACT 2600 ☎02/6273 3011, ⓦ www.greekembassy .org.au.
Canada 80 Maclaren St, Ottawa, ON K2P 0K6 ☎613/238 6271.
Ireland 1 Upper Pembroke St, Dublin 2 ☎01/676 7254.
New Zealand 5–7 Willeston St, Wellington ☎04/473 7775.
South Africa 995 Pretorius St, Arcadia-Pretoria 0083 ☎012/437 252.
UK 1a Holland Park, London W11 ☎020/7221 6467, ⓦ www.greekembassy.org.uk.
USA 2221 Massachusetts Ave NW, Washington, DC 20008 ☎202/939-5800, ⓦ www.greekembassy.org.

Insurance

UK and other EU nationals are, officially at least, entitled to free medical care in Greece (see "Health matters", p.31), upon presentation of an E111 form, available from most post offices. In practice, the E111 is rarely demanded, nor is proof of nationality. "Free", however, means just admittance to the lowest grade of state hospital (known as a *yenikó nosokomío*), and does not include nursing care or the cost of medication. For prolonged treatment you may well be better off with private care, as expensive as anywhere else in Europe, and in remote parts of the islands that is likely to be your only option.

Some form of **travel insurance** is therefore advisable – indeed essential for North Americans, Australians and New Zealanders, whose countries have no formal healthcare agreements with Greece (other than allowing for free emergency treatment). For **medical claims**, keep receipts, including those from pharmacies. You will have to pay for all private medical care on the spot (insurance claims can be processed if you have hospital treatment), but it can all be claimed back eventually. Travel insurance usually provides cover for the **loss of baggage, money and tickets**, too. If you're thinking of **renting a moped** or motorbike on the islands (many people do), make sure the policy covers motorbike accidents. Some policies exclude rented bike or car accidents, others will cover such events but only if you were acting within local traffic laws when the accident happened. Check whether any policy excludes **"risky" pastimes**, which may include hang gliding, mountaineering, scuba-diving and even trekking.

Before paying for a whole new policy, it's worth checking if you're **already covered**: some all-risks homeowners' or renters' insurance policies may cover your possessions when overseas and many private medical schemes (such as BUPA or PPP in the UK) offer coverage extensions abroad. In Canada, provincial health plans usually provide partial cover for medical costs overseas, while holders of official student/teacher/youth cards in Canada and the US are entitled to meagre accident coverage and hospital in-patient benefits. Students will often find that their health coverage extends to the vacations and for one term beyond the date of last enrolment. Most credit-card

Rough Guides travel insurance

Rough Guides offers its own travel insurance, customized for our readers by a leading UK broker and backed by a Lloyd's underwriter. It's available for anyone, of any nationality and any age, travelling anywhere in the world.

There are two main Rough Guide insurance plans: **Essential**, for basic, no-frills cover; and **Premier** – with more generous and extensive benefits. Alternatively, you can take out **annual multi-trip insurance**, which covers you for any number of trips throughout the year (with a maximum of 60 days for any one trip). Unlike many policies, the Rough Guides schemes are calculated by the day, so if you're travelling for 27 days rather than a month, that's all you pay for. If you intend to be away for the whole year, the **Adventurer** policy will cover you for 365 days. Each plan can be supplemented with a "Hazardous Activities Premium" if you plan to indulge in sports considered dangerous, such as skiing, scuba-diving or trekking.

For a policy quote, call ☏0870/033 9988 from the UK or log onto ⓦ**www .roughguidesinsurance.com** from wherever you are.

issuers also offer some sort of vacation insurance, which is often automatic if you pay for the holiday with their card. However, it's vital to check just what these policies cover – frequently only death or dismemberment in the UK.

Health matters

There are no required inoculations for Greece, though it's wise to ensure that you are up to date on tetanus and polio. Don't forget to take out travel insurance (see p.30), so that you're covered in case of serious illness or accidents.

Water quality is variable in the Ionian islands and, although the larger hotels have a good drinking water supply, that cannot be said of smaller and more out-of-the-way places. In such cases, it is invariably a matter of taste rather than safety, although some villa and apartment companies warn you to boil tap water before drinking it. On smaller islands such as Paxí, many properties use undrinkable *glýpha*, desalinated seawater, in bathrooms. Bottled water is widely available if you're uncertain. On the other hand, in some places, especially in the mountains, you will find springs with cool, clear water, high in mineral content.

Specific hazards

The main health problems experienced by visitors have to do with **over-exposure to the sun** and the odd nasty from the sea. To combat the former, don't spend too long in the sun, cover up and wear a hat, use high-factor sunblock (preferably not the waterproof variety: this simply bastes you) and drink plenty of fluids in the hot months to avoid any danger of sunstroke. Remember that even a hazy sun can burn. For sea wear, goggles or a diving mask are useful, as well as footwear for walking over slippery rocks.

Hazards of the deep

In the sea, you may have the bad luck to meet an armada of **jellyfish** (*tsoúkhtres*), especially in late summer; they come in various colours and sizes, from tiny purple ones to some the size of a large pizza. Various over-the-counter remedies are sold in resort pharmacies; baking soda or diluted ammonia also help to lessen the sting. The welts and burning usually subside of their own accord within a few hours; there are no deadly man-of-war species in Greek waters.

Less venomous but more common are black, spiky **sea urchins** (*ahini*), which infest rocky shorelines year-round; if you step on or graze one, a sewing needle (you can crudely sterilize it by heat from a cigarette lighter) and olive oil are effective for removing spines from your anatomy; if you don't extract them, they'll fester.

The worst maritime danger – fortunately very rare – is the **weever fish** (*dhrákena*), which buries itself in tidal zone sand with just its poisonous dorsal and gill spines protruding. If you tread on one, the sudden pain is excruciating, and the exceptionally potent venom can cause permanent paralysis of the affected area. The imperative first aid is to immerse your foot in water as hot as you can stand, which degrades the toxin and relieves the swelling of joints and attendant pain, but you should still seek medical attention as soon as possible.

Somewhat more common are **stingrays** (Greek names include *platý*, *seláhi*, *vátos* or *trígona*), which mainly frequent bays with sandy bottoms, against which they can camouflage themselves. Though shy, they can give you a nasty lash with their tail if trodden on, so shuffle your feet a bit on entering the water.

Sandflies, mosquitoes, snakes, scorpions

If you are sleeping on or near a beach, a wise precaution is to use insect repellent, either lotion or wrist/ankle bands, and/or a tent with a screen to guard against **sandflies**. Their bites are potentially dangerous, as the flies spread visceral leishmaniasis, a rare parasitic infection characterized by chronic fever, listlessness and weight loss.

Mosquitoes (*kounoúpia*) in Greece carry nothing worse than a vicious bite, but they can be infuriating. The best solution is to burn pyrethrum incense coils (*spíres* or *fidhákia*), which are widely and cheaply available. Better, if you can get them, are the small electrical devices (trade name *Vape-Net*) that vaporize an odourless insecticide tablet; many "rooms" proprietors supply them routinely. Insect repellents, such as Autan, are available from most general stores and kiosks on the islands.

Adders (*ohiés*) and **scorpions** (*skorpii*) are found throughout the Ionians; both species are shy, and the latter usually quite small and harmless, but take care when climbing over dry-stone walls where snakes like to sun themselves, and don't put hands or feet in places (eg shoes) where you haven't looked first.

Pharmacies and drugs

For **minor complaints** it's easiest to go to the local pharmacy (**farmakío**). Greek pharmacists are highly trained and dispense a number of medicines that elsewhere could only be prescribed by a doctor. In the larger towns and resorts there'll usually be one who speaks good English. Pharmacies are usually closed evenings and Saturday mornings, but are supposed to have a sign on their door referring you to the nearest one that's open. **Homeopathic and herbal remedies** are quite widely available, too, and the larger island towns have dedicated homeopathic pharmacies, delineated by the green cross sign.

If you regularly use any form of **prescription drug**, you should take a copy of the prescription together with the generic name of the drug – this will help should you need to replace it and also avoid possible problems with customs officials. In this regard, it's worth pointing out that codeine is banned in Greece. If you import any you might find yourself in serious trouble, so check labels carefully; it's the core ingredient of Panadeine, Veganin, Solpadeine, Codis and Empirin-Codeine, to name just a few compounds.

Contraceptive pills are now widely available, but don't count on getting them outside of a few large island towns (over the counter from *farmakía*). **Condoms**, however, are inexpensive and ubiquitous – just ask for *profylaktiká* (the vulgar term *kapótes* is equally understood but not recommended) at any pharmacy or corner *períptero* (kiosk). It's also quite common to find them prominently displayed in supermarkets, sometimes with the blunt legend "Anti-AIDS".

Lastly, **hay fever** sufferers should be prepared for the early Greek pollen season, at its height from April to June. If you are taken by surprise, pharmacists stock tablets and creams, but it's cheaper to travel prepared: commercial antihistamines such as Triludan are difficult if not impossible to find in the islands, and local brands can cost around €18 for a pack of ten.

Doctors and hospitals

For **serious medical attention**, phone ☎166 for an ambulance. You'll find English-speaking doctors in any of the bigger towns or resorts; travel agencies or hotel staff should be able to come up with some names if you have any difficulty.

In **emergencies** – for cuts, broken bones etc – treatment is given free in **state hospitals**, though you will only get the most basic level of nursing care. Greek hospitals expect patients' families to feed and care for them in hospital, so as a tourist you'll be at a severe disadvantage. Somewhat better are the ordinary state-run **out-patient clinics** (*iatría*) attached to most public hospitals and also found in rural locales; these operate on a first-come, first-served basis, so go early – hours are usually 8am to noon.

Don't forget to obtain **receipts** for the cost of all drugs and medical treatment; without them you won't be able to claim back the money on your travel insurance.

Costs, money and banks

The cost of living in Greece has spiralled during the years of EU membership: the days of renting an island house for a pittance are gone forever, and food prices now differ little from those of other member countries. However, outside the established resorts, travel between and around the islands remains reasonably priced, with the cost of restaurant meals, short-term accommodation and public transport still cheaper than anywhere in northern or western Europe except Portugal.

Prices depend on where and when you go. The towns and larger tourist resorts are more expensive, and costs everywhere increase sharply in July, August and at Easter. **Students** with an International Student Identity Card (ISIC) can get discounted admission fees at many museums, though these, and other occasional discounts, are sometimes limited to EU students.

Currency

Since 2002, Greece has belonged to the single EU currency, the **euro** (€). The euro is split into 100 cents. There are seven euro **notes** – in denominations of 500, 200, 100, 50, 20, 10, and 5 euros, each a different colour and size – and eight different **coin** denominations, including 2 and 1 euros, then 50, 20, 10, 5, 2, and 1 cents. Euro coins feature a common EU design on one face, but different country-specific designs on the other. No matter what the design, all euro coins and notes can be used in any of the twelve member states (Austria, Belgium, Finland, France, Germany, Greece, Ireland, Italy, Luxembourg, Portugal, Spain and The Netherlands). At the time of writing the euro was worth about US$1.20 and £0.68 sterling.

Some basic costs

In most parts of the Ionian islands a **daily budget** of €40–60 (£27–40/US$48–72) per person will get you basic accommodation, breakfast, picnic lunch and a simple evening meal, if you're one of a couple. Camping would cut costs considerably. On €70–100 (£46–68/US$84–120) a day you could be living quite well, plus treating yourself and sharing vehicle rental.

Inter-island **ferries** are reasonably priced, subsidized by the government in an effort to preserve island communities. A deck-class ticket between any of the southerly islands and the mainland costs about €12, while between Corfu or Paxí and the mainland or Paxí the ticket can be as little as €6. Long-distance journeys, such as between Corfu and Pátra, start at around €30.

The simplest double **room** generally costs around €20–25 a night, depending on the location and the plumbing arrangements. Organized **campsites** are little more than €4 per person, with similar charges per tent. With discretion, you can camp for free in the more remote, rural areas and close to the smaller resorts; places are detailed in the text.

A basic **meal** out with local wine can still sometimes be had for €10 a head. Add a pricier bottle of wine, seafood or more careful cooking, and it could be up to €25 a head – but you'll rarely have to pay more than that, except in smarter or overtly touristy restaurants or for non-Greek cuisine. Sharing seafood, Greek salads and dips is a good way to keep costs down in the better restaurants, and sharing is quite common, as is sticking to just one or two starters. Even in the most developed resorts, with inflated "international" menus, more earthy but decent tavernas where the locals eat are detailed in the text. **Bars** and **cafés** tend to be comparatively expensive, so a fondness for coffee or cocktails can easily lead to overspending.

Banks and exchange

Greek **banks** are normally open Monday to Thursday from 8.30am to 2.30pm, Friday 8.30am to 2pm. Certain branches in larger island towns or tourist centres are open extra hours in the evenings and on Saturday mornings for **exchanging money**. Outside these times, the larger hotels and travel agencies can often provide this service – though with hefty commission of two to three percent. In the busier centres **exchange bureaux** with lower commission and longer hours are cropping up in increasing numbers. Always take your passport with you as proof of identity, and be prepared for a bit of a wait, although exchange procedures have been streamlined.

The safest way to carry money is in **travellers' cheques**, since you'll be refunded if they're stolen or lost. They can be obtained from banks (even if you don't have an account) or from offices of Thomas Cook and American Express; you'll pay a commission of between one and two percent. You can cash the cheques at most banks, and (at poorer rates) at quite a number of hotels, travel agencies and tourist shops. Each transaction in Greece will incur a **commission** charge of €1.20–2.40, so you won't want to change too many small amounts.

Finally, there is no need to purchase lots of euros **before arrival**. Airport arrival lounges will usually – though not always – have an exchange booth open for passengers on incoming international flights. If you're travelling independently, it's wise to bring a small stash of euros with you, for taxis, drinks or meals. If you're stuck, remember that hotel-owners rarely expect payment up front and will usually accept your passport as surety.

Credit cards and cash dispensers

Major **credit cards**, though still not as widely used as in many countries, are gradually being accepted by an increasing number of the more upmarket hotels, and to a lesser extent, tavernas. Although they can be used for withdrawing money from

cash dispensers (ATMs), provided you have a PIN number, **debit cards** linked to current accounts via the Cirrus/Plus/Maestro systems incur lower fees than those using credit cards. ATMs are now found in all large ports, resorts and island capitals, and in an increasing number of smaller resorts, though not yet on any of the satellite islands. Be aware too that your card issuer will charge a fee for each withdrawal.

Emergency cash

If you don't have access to cash via a credit or debit card and need money in an emergency you could have **money wired** to you, though it's not very convenient or cheap, and should be considered a last resort. It's also possible to have money wired directly from a bank in your home country to a bank in Greece, although this is somewhat less reliable because it involves two separate institutions. If you go down this route, your home bank will need the address of the branch bank where you want to pick up the money and the address and telex number of the Athens head office, which will act as the clearing house; money wired this way normally takes two working days to arrive, and costs around €40 (£27/$48) per transaction.

Money-wiring companies

Thomas Cook US ☎1-800/287-7362, Canada ☎1-888/823-4732, UK ☎01733/318 922, Republic of Ireland ☎01/677 1721; ⊛www .thomascook.com.
Travelers Express Moneygram US ☎1-800/926-3947, Canada ☎1-800/933-3278; ⊛www.moneygram.com.
Western Union US and Canada ☎1-800/325-6000, Australia ☎1800/501 500, New Zealand ☎09/270 0050, UK ☎0800/833 833, Republic of Ireland ☎1800/395 395; ⊛www.westernunion .com.

Information

The National Tourist Organization of Greece (Ellinikós Organismós Tourismoú or EOT; GNTO abroad) has offices in most European capitals, and major cities in Australia and North America (see below for details). It publishes an impressive array of free, glossy, regional pamphlets that are good for getting an idea of where you want to go, even if the text is usually in brochure-speak. The EOT also has a reasonable map of Greece, and brochures on special interests and festivals.

Tourist offices

EOT offices in the Ionians are actually in very short supply; only Corfu and Argostóli now have offices, though both are friendly and keen to help. They keep lists of rooms and other accommodation, can advise on trips to island sights, and may know certain tricks about buses and ferries that don't appear on the timetables. Elsewhere, local travel companies, hotels and other businesses are usually happy to help with information. Outside of Greece, EOT is known as GNTO and their website (ⓦwww.gnto.gr) contains a good deal of useful information, as well as contact details for their offices in many countries worldwide not listed below. Note that there are no Greek tourist offices in Ireland, New Zealand or South Africa. In these countries, apply to the embassy for assistance.

Greek national tourist offices abroad

Australia 51 Pitt St, Sydney, NSW 2000 ☎02/9241 1663.
Canada 91 Scollard St, 2nd floor, Toronto, ON M5R 1GR ☎416/968-2220; 1233 rue de la Montagne, H3G 1Z2 Montréal, Québec ☎514/871-1535.
UK 4 Conduit St, London W1R 0DJ ☎020/7734 5997.
US 645 Fifth Ave, New York, NY 10022 ☎212/421-5777.

The Ionians on the Internet

Among the growing number of **websites** with material relating to the Ionian islands the following URLs are worth surfing for information relating to the Ionian islands in general:

ⓦ**www.foi.org.uk** Beautifully designed site of the Friends of the Ionian, with practical information on all the islands, message boards and an emphasis on the environment, walks, and the natural splendour of the archipelago.

ⓦ**www.ionian-islands.com** This developing website has plenty of practical info on agencies, shops, tavernas and accommodation, including limited online booking links. Corfu, Kefalloniá and Zákynthos complete at time of writing.

ⓦ**www.ionion.com** Website with practical information, news and visuals on Kefalloniá and Itháki.

Getting around

Island-hopping isn't as easy in the Ionians as it is in parts of the Aegean, although there are ferry connections throughout the archipelago. Particularly well served are Lefkádha, Itháki and Kefalloniá, within an hour's voyage of each other and with regular ferries to a choice of destinations on each island daily. Zákynthos is also connected to Kefalloniá, and to Kyllíni on the mainland.

The only regular **inter-island flights** are Olympic's once-weekly Corfu–Preveza–Kefalloniá–Zákynthos route, which runs in summer only, and the new seaplane service between Corfu and Paxí. For getting around the islands themselves, there are basic bus services, which many tourists choose to supplement at some stage with moped, motorbike or car rental.

Ferries

Shuttle **ferries** from the islands **to the nearest mainland ports** – which, except in the case of Lefkádha, are the islands' primary links with the outside world – are usually relatively stable. However, apart from the Four Islands line services between Lefkádha, Itháki, Kefalloniá and Zákynthos, **inter-island ferries** cannot be trusted from one year to the next. Corfu–Itháki and Corfu–Kefalloniá links have been discontinued in recent years, so most people wanting to travel between Corfu or Paxí and the southern Ionian islands go via the mainland and bus. Each island's ferry connections with the mainland and neighbouring islands is listed in "Travel Details" at the end of each chapter.

Ferry services are drastically reduced in the **off season**, but with the exception of Paxí, each island has at least one daily connection to a neighbouring island or mainland port. Only the worst weather conditions – a force six upwards, which few would want to sail in anyway – prevent large ships leaving. The **types of ferries** you'll encounter vary enormously, from the landing-craft lookalikes that shuttle between Corfu and Igoumenítsa, or Argostóli and Lixoúri, which have little more than a cabin, snack bar, toilet and open upper decks, to the comparatively luxurious vessels that ply international routes, and

between the southerly islands and mainland, which have restaurants, shops and cinemas.

If you're planning to travel on any of the long-distance ferries, it is advisable to check availability with more than one ferry company – some agents will tell you theirs is the only ferry available, despite the fairly sizeable evidence to the contrary moored perhaps only a few metres from their office. Tickets are **deck class** unless you request otherwise, and allow you use of bars, restaurants and public seating areas. Pullman or aeroplane-type seating, allowing you to sleep, costs slightly more. **Cabins**, worth considering in high season, bad weather or particularly if you're travelling in a group of two to four people, cost between double and quadruple the price of a basic ticket. **Motorbikes and cars** are issued extra tickets; slightly less than the cost of a deck ticket for the former, up to three or four times that for the latter. Pets and bicycles commonly travel free. Technically, written permission is required to take rental vehicles on ferries, although this is rarely, if ever, policed.

It's common to pay on board most inter-island ferries, although a few years back the larger ferries introduced computerized **ticketing**, which often requires pre-purchase at a quayside ticket agency. Most ferries run their own ticketing systems, and your ticket will probably commit you to a specific sailing on a named vessel, although on journeys such as Igoumenítsa–Corfu, it's easy to transfer tickets at the dockside ticket offices. If you're uncertain whether you'll make a specified departure, check if the ticket is transferable.

The only **hydrofoil** services in the Ionians are in the north of the archipelago, linking Corfu with Igoumenítsa and Paxí during the summer months only.

As independent fishing is gradually elbowed out by factory fishing, so the romantic notion of renting a **kaḯki** also sails off into the sunset, although some tourist *kaḯkia* issue one-way tickets, as on the Parga–Paxí route. Otherwise, as with **sea taxis**, which command around €100 for an hour's journey one-way between islands, *kaḯkia*, when available, tend to be very expensive. It is still possible, however, especially in smaller ports and at quieter times of the season, so ask around.

Buses

The mythical boneshakers you had to share with livestock have for the most part been replaced by the modern cream-and-green **buses** of the national company, **KTEL** (Kratikó Tamío Ellinikón Leoforíon). On small islands like Paxí, one island bus trundles back and forth from end to end; larger islands such as Corfu and Kefalloniá are served by fleets of buses based in the capital. Note that almost all routes radiate out from the capital, and there are few, if any, connections between outlying towns and villages except along the radial routes. In some places, however, there are weekday early morning and early afternoon services connecting outlying communities to collect or drop off students attending schools and colleges in larger towns. These are not always advertised on timetables, so it's worth asking, particularly if you've spotted a bus where the timetable said there wasn't a service.

Bus services on the islands are not as unreliable as popular myth would have it, and when printed **timetables** are available, they are usually adhered to surprisingly well, at least from the originating terminal. Most buses turn round immediately or after a short break, and can often be flagged down anywhere along the road, although on busy built-up stretches they will only pull up at designated stops.

You **pay** on board nearly all buses in the Ionians. Exceptions include those originating in Lefkádha Town which, like the mainland bus stations, has a computerized ticketing system, with numbered seats. Corfu's suburban blue bus system is a confusing mix of pay-on-board and pre-pay (from the ticket kiosk by the bus ranks in Platía Saróko). Pre-pay buses are those with *horís ispráktor* (without conductor) signs on the driver's window. **Prices** on island buses are good value – an hour's journey the length of an island will probably cost little over €3 – although mainland bus journeys are slightly more expensive.

There are no **airport bus** services in the Ionians.

Car rental

Car rental in the Ionians costs a minimum of €200 a week in high season for the smallest, Group A vehicle, including unlimited mileage and insurance; prices on the smaller islands are usually higher. Outside peak season, at the smaller local outfits in less popular resorts, you can often get terms of about €25 per day, all inclusive, with better rates for a rental of three days or more. Shopping around agencies in the larger resorts – particularly on Corfu – can yield a variation in quotes of up to 30 percent for the same conditions over a four- to seven-day period; a common hidden catch, however, is to charge extra for kilometres in excess of 100 per day. Open **jeeps**, an increasingly popular extravagance, begin at about €50 per day, rising to as much as €70 at busy times and places.

Many basic-rate rental prices in Greece don't include tax, collision damage waiver (CDW) and personal insurance, so check the fine print on your contract. Be careful of the hammering that cars get on minor roads; tyres, windscreen and the underside of the vehicle are almost always excluded from even supplementary insurance policies. All agencies will want either a credit card or a large cash deposit up front; minimum age requirements vary from 21 to 25. In theory an **International Driving Licence** is also needed, but in practice European, Australian, New Zealand and North American ones are honoured.

In peak season only you may get a better price (and, more importantly, better vehicle condition) by booking through one of the **international companies**, rather than arranging the rental once you're in Greece; this may also be the only way to get hold of a car at such times. In the Ionians, Avis

(Corfu, Kefalloniá, Zákynthos), Budget (Corfu, Lefkádha, Kefalloniá, Zákynthos), Europcar/National (Corfu, Lefkádha, Kefalloniá) and Hertz (Corfu, Lefkádha, Kefalloniá, Zákynthos) all have outlets, mainly in island capitals, airports or major resorts.

International car rental agencies

UK and Ireland

Avis Britain ☎0870/606 0100, Northern Ireland ☎028/9024 0404, Republic of Ireland ☎01/605 7500; ⓦwww.avis.com.
Budget UK ☎0800/181 181, ⓦwww.budget .co.uk; Republic of Ireland ☎0903/277 11, ⓦwww.budget.ie.
Europcar Britain ☎0845/722 2525, Northern Ireland ☎028/9442 3444, Republic of Ireland ☎01/614 2888; ⓦwww.europcar.com.
Hertz UK ☎0870/844 8844, ⓦwww.hertz.co.uk; Republic of Ireland ☎01/676 7476, ⓦwww.hertz.ie.

North America

Avis ☎1-800/331-1084, ⓦwww.avis.com.
Budget ☎1-800/527-0700, ⓦwww.budget.com.
Hertz US ☎1-800/654-3001, Canada ☎1-800/263-0600; ⓦwww.hertz.com.
National ☎1-800/227-7368, ⓦwww.nationalcar .com.
Thrifty ☎1-800/367–2277, ⓦwww.thrifty.com.

Australia and New Zealand

Avis Australia ☎13 63 33, NZ ☎09/526 2847; ⓦwww.avis.com.au.
Budget Australia ☎1300/362 848, ⓦwww .budget.com.au; NZ ☎09/976 2222, ⓦwww .budget.co.nz.
Hertz Australia ☎13 30 39, NZ ☎0800/654 321; ⓦwww.hertz.com.au.

South Africa

Avis ☎0861/113 748, ⓦwww.avis.co.za.
Budget ☎0861/016 622, ⓦwww.budget.co.za.
Europcar ☎011/574 4457, ⓦwww.europcar .co.za.
Hertz Australia ☎044/801 4710, ⓦwww.hertz .co.za.

Driving in Greece

Greece has the highest **accident rate** in Europe after Portugal, and many of the roads can be quite perilous: asphalt can turn into a one-lane surface or a dirt track without

warning on secondary routes, and you're heavily dependent on magnifying mirrors at blind intersections in congested villages. Uphill drivers insist on their right of way, as do those who approach a one-lane bridge – **flashed headlights** mean the opposite to what they do in the UK or North America, here signifying that the driver is coming through or overtaking.

Wearing a **seatbelt** is compulsory, and children under the age of 10 are not allowed to sit in the front seats. It's illegal to drive away from any kind of accident, and you can be held at a police station for up to 24 hours. If this happens, you have the right to ring your consulate immediately to summon a lawyer; don't make a statement to anyone who doesn't speak, and write, very good English.

Tourists with proof of membership of their home-motoring organization are given free **road assistance** from ELPA, the Greek equivalent, which runs breakdown services on the larger islands (not Paxí or Itháki); in an emergency ring their road assistance service on ☎104. Many car rental companies have an agreement with ELPA's equally widespread competitors Hellas Service and Express Service, but they're prohibitively expensive to summon on your own – over €100 to enrol as an "instant member".

Buying fuel

Fuel currently costs around €0.85–0.95 a litre for regular unleaded (*amólivdhi*), €0.95–1.05 for super unleaded. Note that many stations in island towns and rural areas close at 7pm sharp. Nearly as many are shut all weekend, and though there will always be at least one pump per district open, it's not always apparent which that is. Filling stations run by international companies (BP, Mobil and Shell) usually take **credit cards**; Greek chains like EKO, Mamidhakis and Elinoil don't.

Incidentally, the smallest grade of motor **scooters** (Vespa, Piaggio, Suzuki) consume "mix", a red- or green-tinted fuel dispensed from a transparent cylindrical device. This contains a minimum of three-percent two-stroke oil by volume; if this mix is unavailable, you brew it up yourself by adding to "super" grade fuel the necessary amount of separately bottled two-stroke oil (*ládhi dhío trohón*). It's wise to err on the side of excess (say five percent by volume); otherwise you risk the engine seizing up.

Motorbikes, mopeds – and safety

The cult of the **motorcycle** is highly developed in the Greek islands, presided over by a jealous deity apparently requiring regular human sacrifice. **Accidents** among both foreign and local motorbikers are common, and some package companies have taken to warning clients in print against renting motorbikes or mopeds. However, with a bit of caution and common sense riding a bike on holiday should be a lot less hazardous than, say, dodging traffic in central London or New York.

Many tourists come to grief on rutted dirt tracks or astride mechanically dodgy machines. In many cases accidents are due to attempts to cut corners, in all senses, by riding two to an underpowered scooter. Don't be tempted by this apparent economy – and bear in mind, too, that you're likely to be charged an exorbitant sum for any repairs if you do have a wipeout.

One precaution is to wear a **crash helmet** (*krános*); many rental outfits will offer you one, and may make you sign a waiver of liability if you refuse it. Helmet-wearing is in fact required by law, and though very few people comply, there are occasional police blitzes, especially in island capitals. Above all, make sure your travel **insurance policy** covers motorcycle accidents. Reputable establishments require a full **motorcycle driving licence** for any machine over 75cc, and you will usually be required to leave a passport as security.

True **mopeds** (which you start with a pedal) are almost non-existent these days and the once-common semi-automatic **motorbikes**, known in Greek as *papákia* (little ducks) after their characteristic noise, are increasingly being phased out in favour of fully automatic **scooters**. These smaller bikes are generally rented out for €15–20 a day. Larger **trail bikes** are available for experienced riders for around €20 a day. Rates can be bargained down out of season, or if you negotiate for a longer period of rental. Before riding off,

make sure you check the bike's mechanical state, since many are only cosmetically maintained. Bad brakes and worn spark plugs are the most common defects; dealers often keep the front brake far too loose, with the commendable intention of preventing you going over the handlebars. If you have a breakdown most reputable places will come and rescue you, so it's worth taking down the phone number of the rental agency in case the bike gives out and you can't get it back, or if you lose the ignition key.

Cycling

Cycling on the Ionian islands is not such hard going as you might imagine, unless you're planning to traverse island hill or mountain ranges, in which case a mountain bike and a mountain biker's stamina are essential. Away from the busier resorts and arterial roads, which are hellish for cyclists and pedestrians alike, cycling is an ideal form of transport. Virtually every resort will have bikes for rent, at around €5–8 a day.

If you have your own mountain or touring bike, you might consider bringing it with you: bikes fly free on most airlines, if they're within your twenty-kilo luggage limit, and are free on most ferries. Any spare parts you might need, however, are best brought along, since there are no specialist bike shops in the islands beyond rental agencies, and parts are difficult to obtain.

Hitching

Hitching on the Ionian islands is a hit-and-miss affair, and carries the usual risks and dangers, particularly for solo women travellers. However, Greece is in general one of the safest places to hitch. These days, though, the key question is whether you'll find anyone prepared to stop. On the larger islands and in larger resorts, especially, it's almost taken for granted (not unreasonably) that foreigners should rent or pay for their own transport. In Greece's increasingly car-mad culture, the idea of not driving anywhere baffles most islanders under donkey-owning age. That noted, hitching is a great way to meet islanders and see the landscape, particularly in outlying areas, where it's not uncommon for villagers to stop and offer lifts unasked. Just don't expect to get very far very fast.

Taxis

Greek **taxis** and tariffs are a law unto themselves. Most vehicles in the Ionians are fitted with meters, and there are various regulations on metering, but for most visitors the back of a cab is hardly the place to start arguing the toss about Greek transport law. Always request and negotiate a price beforehand, ideally in Greek, however basic your Greek is. Expect to be overcharged on journeys from airports to capitals (around €6 at Corfu, €10 at Kefalloniá). Apart from airport rides, taxis are still roughly half the price paid to cover a similar distance in Britain. In rural areas, taxis respond to hailing, and will even return to collect you if full. Taxi-sharing is common, though if you board a taxi that already has a passenger (whom you don't know) inside, you are each expected to pay your full share.

Hiking

Greeks are just becoming used to the notion that anyone should want to **walk** for pleasure or as a means of getting from A to B, yet if you have the time and stamina it is probably the best way to see many of the islands. This Guide includes tips on good bases and routes; for advice on maps see p.289. The newly opened Corfu Trail is a particularly well-organized and impressive route – see p.122 for details.

Accommodation

There are a great number of beds available for tourists in the Ionian islands. At most times of the year you can rely on turning up anywhere and finding a room – if not in a hotel, then in a private house or block of rooms (the standard island accommodation). All the larger islands have at least two basic, inexpensive campsites too.

However, from late July to early September, when large numbers of Greeks and Italian visitors arrive in the islands, you may well experience problems if you haven't booked accommodation in advance. The first three weeks of August constitute the peak of high season, when rooms are like gold dust almost everywhere. Some resorts can literally fill up, and in busy periods room owners, and even hoteliers, are less inclined to rent for one or just a few nights; some won't even contemplate stays of less than a week. At these times, it's worth looking away from the obvious tourist areas, turning up at each new place early in the day, and taking whatever is available in the hope of exchanging it for something better later on.

Out of season, there's a different problem: rooms close from November to March (campsites even earlier), leaving hotels your only option, probably in the island's main town or port; there'll be very little life outside these places, anyway, with all the seasonal bars and restaurants closed. Just one hotel, the *Mentor*, stays open on Itháki; there are none on Paxí. If you're set on travelling out of season, local travel companies can sometimes help to find suitable accommodation, often at bargain prices.

Private rooms, apartments and studios

The most common form of island accommodation is privately let **rooms** – *dhomátia*. These are regulated and officially classified by the local tourist police, who divide them into three classes (A down to C), according to their facilities. These days the bulk of them are in new, purpose-built low-rise buildings; scarcely any remain in people's

Accommodation price codes

Rooms and hotels listed in this book have been price-coded according to the scale outlined below. The rates quoted represent the cheapest available double room in high season. Out of season, rates can drop by as much as fifty percent or more, especially if you negotiate for a stay of three or more nights. Single rooms, where available, cost around seventy percent of the price of a double. In hotels from code ❹ upwards, breakfast is often included.

❶ up to €30
❷ €31–40
❸ €41–50

❹ €51–70
❺ €71–90
❻ €91–120

❼ €121–150
❽ over €150

homes, where guests used to be treated with disarming hospitality. The accommodation in these purpose-built blocks usually consists of **apartments** (*dhiamerísmata*) or **studios** (*garsoniéres*), though there seems to be little distinction between the two, and both will often have kitchen facilities.

Rooms are almost always scrupulously clean, whatever their other qualities. At their simplest, you'll get a bare, concrete or wood room, with basic furnishing and shared toilet facilities (cold water only). At the fancier end of the scale, you'll find modern, purpose-built and fully furnished rooms with a smart, modern bathroom attached and a fully equipped kitchen. Sometimes there's a choice of rooms at various prices – owners will usually show you the most expensive first. Room **prices** and standards are not necessarily directly linked, so always ask to see the room before agreeing to take it and settling on the price. Consequently, it is not easy to generalize, but simpler rooms usually come under our codes ❶–❷, which can often be en-suite these days. Those with better furnishings and more facilities are in codes ❸–❹, while the top of the range are usually in code 5 and even sometimes ❻. Areas to look for rooms, along with recommendations of the best places, are included in the Guide. One practice not so common in the Ionians any longer is that of room-owners meeting ferries. In smaller places you'll often see rooms advertised, usually in English but sometimes in German (*Zimmer*) or Italian (*camare*). The Greek signs to look out for are *Enoikiázonte dhomátia/dhiamerísmata* or *Enoikiazómena dhomátia/dhiamerísmata* – "Rooms/apartments to let". If you can't find rooms or, as is sometimes the case,

there are no signs for them, ask in a shop, *kafenío* or taverna: if they don't have rooms themselves, they'll often know someone who does. Even in small villages, there is often someone prepared to earn some money by putting you up.

Room owners still occasionally ask to keep your passport – ostensibly "for the tourist police", but in reality to prevent you departing without paying. Some owners will be satisfied with taking your passport details, or simply ask you to pay in advance. They'll usually return the documents once they've got to know you, or if you need them for another purpose (to change money, for example).

Hotels

There are **hotels**, from basic to luxury, in most island towns, ports and resorts in the Ionians. In the larger resorts, however, many are block-booked by package holiday companies.

Like private rooms, hotels are **categorized** by the tourist police. They range from Luxury down to E-class, and all except the top category have to keep within set price limits. Letter ratings are supposed to correspond to facilities available, though in practice categorization often depends on location and other, less obvious criteria (some decent hotels in quieter areas, because they are away from the main resorts, receive a relatively low categorization, and are therefore surprisingly good value). D-class usually have attached baths, while in C-class this is mandatory, along with a bar or breakfast area. The additional presence of a pool and/or tennis court will attract a B-class rating, while A-category hotels must have a restaurant, bar and extensive common areas. Luxury hotels are in effect self-contained holiday villages; both they and A-class outfits usually back a private beach. **Prices** have to be displayed in the room, although outside the high season you will normally find yourself paying less than the advertised price. Again there are no hard and fast rules, but D- and E-class hotels usually correspond to our codes ❷–❸, C–class to codes ❹–❺, B–class and A-class to codes ❻–❼, while the luxury hotels will invariably fall into the top code ❽ or perhaps the upper end of code ❼.

In terms of **food**, C-class hotels are required only to provide the most rudimentary of continental breakfasts – in practice, most now let you choose whether to take a room with or without breakfast – while B-class and above will usually offer some sort of buffet breakfast including cheese, cold cuts, sausages, eggs, etc. With some outstanding exceptions, noted in the Guide, lunch or supper at hotel-affiliated restaurants is bland and poor value. This proviso might make you think twice about the rare hotels whose rates include mandatory half- or even full-board.

Villas and long-term rentals

The easiest – and usually most reliable – way to arrange a **villa rental** is through one of the package holiday companies detailed in the "Getting there" section on pp.22–26. They can offer some superb places, from simple to luxury, and costs can be very reasonable, especially if shared between four or more people. Several of the companies we list will arrange "multi-centre" stays on two or more islands.

On the islands, a few local travel agents arrange villa rentals, mostly places not booked or listed by the overseas companies, and sometimes representing excellent value. **Out of season**, you can sometimes get a good deal on villa or apartment rental for a month or more by asking around locally, though in these days of EU convergence and the increasing desirability of the islands as year-round residences, "good deal" means anything under €250 per month for a large studio or small one-bedroom flat.

Accommodation practicalities

Electricity runs on 220 volt AC throughout the country. Wall outlets take double round-pin plugs as in the rest of continental Europe. Three- to two-pin adaptors should be purchased beforehand in the UK, as they can be difficult to find in Greece; the standard five-amp design will allow use of a hair-dryer. North American appliances will require both a step-down transformer and a plug adapter.

Laundries (*plindíria*) are rare in the Ionians, except in main towns, but they are beginning to crop up in some of the main resort towns; sometimes an attended service wash is available for little or no extra charge over the basic cost of €5–6 per wash and dry. Otherwise, ask room owners for a *skáfi* (laundry trough), a bucket (*kouvás*) or the special laundry area; they may freak out if they catch you using bathroom washbasins (Greek plumbing and wall mounting being what they are). Dry cleaning costs around €1 an item, more for large ones like coats.

The other infamous drawback of Greek plumbing is that it generally cannot cope with **toilet paper** so you have to drop your waste in the basket provided rather than flush it unless you have specifically been told it is OK. More likely, you will find a large handwritten plea not to flush any paper.

Camping

Officially recognized **campsites** in the Ionians are restricted to Corfu (ten), Lefkádha (seven), Kefalloniá (two) and Zákynthos (seven); see the Guide for full descriptions. Most places cost €4–5.50 a night per person, roughly the same fee per tent, and €6–8 per camper van, but at the fanciest sites, rates for two people plus a tent can almost add up to the price of a basic room. Generally, you don't have to worry about leaving tents or baggage unattended at campsites; the Greeks are one of the most honest nationalities in Europe. The main risk comes from other campers. Although most Greek campsites are reasonably well lit, don't forget to take a torch (flashlight) with you.

Freelance camping – outside authorized campsites – is such an established element of Greek travel that few people realize that it's officially illegal. Since 1977 it has actually been forbidden by a law originally enacted to harass gypsies, and regulations are increasingly enforced. If you do camp rough, it's vital to exercise sensitivity and discretion. Police will crack down on people camping (and especially littering) around popular tourist beaches, particularly when a large community of campers develops. Off the beaten track, however, nobody is very bothered, though it is always best to ask permission locally in the village taverna or café. During high season, when everything may be full, attitudes towards freelance camping are more relaxed. At such times the best strategy is to find a sympathetic taverna, which in exchange for regular patronage will probably be willing to guard small valuables and let you use their facilities.

Eating and drinking

Greeks tend to socialize mostly outside their homes, and sharing a meal is one of the chief ways of doing it. The atmosphere is always relaxed and informal, with an accent on celebration, usually with children, grandparents, other relatives and friends in tow. Greeks are not big drinkers – what drinking they do is mainly to accompany food, as an appetizer or digestif – though in the resorts a whole range of bars, pubs and cocktail joints have sprung up principally to cater for tourists.

Breakfast, snacks and picnic fare

Greeks don't generally eat **breakfast**, but the resorts cater for tourists, with anything from a basic continental to a full cooked breakfast in the more Anglo-centric places. The price can vary considerably (€4–8), depending on what you choose and the competition. The continental breakfasts usually offer a choice of *méli me voútiro* (honey poured over a pat of butter), or jam (all kinds are called *marmeládha* in Greek; ask for *portokáli* – orange – if you want proper marmalade), with fresh bread or *friganiés* (melba-toast-type slivers) and orange juice. More indigenous and cheaper alternatives are available from bakers' and street stalls, including *tyrópites* (cheese pies) and *spanakópites* (spinach pies), or *kouloúria* (crispy pretzel rings sprinkled with sesame seeds) and *voutímata* (heavy biscuits rich in honey or cinnamon).

Traditional **snacks** can be one of the distinctive pleasures of Greek eating, though they are being increasingly edged out by an obsession with *tóst* (toasted sandwiches) and pizzas. However, savoury pies with sausages (*loukánika*), and sweet ones with cream (*kréma*), fruit (*froúta*) or chocolate (*sokoláta*) are an excellent source of cheap fuel food at any mealtime. Small kebabs (*souvlákia*) are widely available too, and in most larger resorts you'll find *yíros* – doner kebab with garnish in thick, doughy *píta* bread that's closer to Indian nan bread, often with *patátes* (the Greek equivalent of chips) and *tzatzíki* or a spicy sauce.

Picnic fare is good, cheap and easily available at bakeries and *manávika* (fruit-and-veg stalls). **Bread** is often of minimal nutritional value and inedible within a day of purchase. It's worth paying extra at the bakery (*foúrnos*) for *olikís* (wholemeal), *sikalísio* (rye bread), *oktásporo* (eight-grain), or even *enneásporo* (nine-grain) which are particular specialities of wheat-growing Lefkádha. Although the Ionian archipelago is an olive-producing region, local **olives**

are hard to find; they take forty days of daily rinsing with salted water before they leach natural poisons and become edible, so don't try tasting one off a tree. Local **olive oil** is, however, available – and delicious – usually from oil-pressing factories or the older shops. However, it rarely makes it into tavernas or restaurants.

Féta cheese is ubiquitous – often, these days, imported from Holland or Denmark, though local brands are usually better and not much more expensive. The goat's milk variety can be very dry and salty, so ask for a taste before buying; if you have a fridge, leaving the cheese in water overnight will solve both problems. This sampling advice goes for other indigenous cheeses as well, the most palatable of which are the expensive Gruyère-type *graviéra*.

Despite the presence of farmland and the rainy winters, **fruit and vegetables** are fairly basic in the islands: potatoes, carrots, onions, courgettes and aubergine form the staple in shops on small islands such as Paxí, with little variation on the larger islands. Salad vegetables are more widely available, although lettuces are as rare as hen's teeth on some islands, hence the ubiquity of *horiátiki* (peasant) salad: cucumber, onion, tomato, olives and féta cheese. Apples, pears, peaches, bananas, grapes and mountains of various melons are also plentiful and usually cheap. Useful **phrases** for shopping are *éna tétarto* (250g) and *misó kiló* (500g). If you're self-catering and know your herbs by sight or smell, they're often available for free in the open countryside, in particular thyme, rosemary and oregano. Cheap local red wines are unbeatable with oil in salad dressings.

Restaurants

Greek cuisine and **restaurants** are simple and straightforward. There's no snobbery about eating out; everyone does it, and it's still reasonable – around €12–15 per person for a substantial meal with a fair measure of house wine in an authentic Greek establishment. The increasing number of restaurants serving international and ethnic cuisine are likely to work out more expensive, nearer €25 per person, occasionally more in a really flashy joint.

In choosing a restaurant, the best strategy is to go where the Greeks go. They eat late: 2pm to 3pm for **lunch**, 9pm to 11pm or even later for **dinner**. You can eat earlier, but you're likely to get indifferent service and cuisine if you frequent establishments catering to tourist timetables. Chic appearance is not a good guide to quality; often the more ramshackle, traditional outfits represent the best value – one good omen is the waiter bringing a carafe of refrigerated water, unbidden, rather than pushing you to order bottled stuff.

In resort areas, it's wise to keep a wary eye on the **waiters**, who are inclined to urge you to order more than you want, then bring things you haven't ordered. They may never actually write anything down when you order, and may work out the **bill** by examining your empty plates. Although cash-register receipts are now officially required in all establishments, these are often only for the grand total, and even if the accompanying handwritten bill is itemized, it will probably be illegible. Where prices are printed on menus, the figure is inclusive of all taxes and **service charge** – for advice on tipping see p.59.

Bread costs extra but consumption is not obligatory unless it is part of the **cover charge** (€0.90–1.50), as it often is; you'll be considered deviant, however, for refusing as Greeks always accompany their meal with it. If you do like the bread, you will not be charged for ordering more. **Children** are normally very welcome at restaurants and tavernas, day or night, and owners have a high tolerance of children playing around tables, although this may not be the case with neighbouring tables. Feeding the inevitable crowd of mendicant cats is frowned on, and unhygienic anyway.

Estiatória

There are two basic types of restaurant: the **estiatório** and the taverna. Distinctions between the two are minimal, though the former is more commonly found in town centres and tends to have the slightly more complicated dishes, termed **mayireftá** (literally, "cooked"). An *estiatório* will generally feature a variety of oven-baked casserole dishes: *moussakás*, *pastítsio*, stews like *stifádho*, *yemistá* (stuffed tomatoes or peppers), the oily vegetable casseroles called *ladherá* and oven-baked meat or fish. Choosing these dishes is commonly done by going back to the kitchen and pointing at the desired trays.

Batches are cooked in the morning and then left to stand, which is why the food is often lukewarm or even cold. Greeks don't mind this and, in fact, most believe that hot food is bad for you. If you do mind, ask for it *zestó* (hot). Some meals actually benefit from being allowed to marinate in their own juices before warming again. Similarly, you have to specify if you want your food with little or no oil (*horís ládhi*), but once again you will be considered a little strange, since Greeks regard good olive oil as essential to digestion. A sure sign of a primarily touristic restaurant is if the salad comes without a good lashing of oil on it.

Desserts (*epidhórpia* in formal Greek) of the pudding-and-pie variety don't exist at *estiatória*, and yoghurts only occasionally. Fruit is always available in season – watermelons and melons are the summer standards, grapes come in towards the end of summer, while apples and oranges fulfil the role during winter. Autumn treats worth asking after include *kydhóni* or *akhládhi stó foúrno*, baked quince or pear with some sort of syrup or nut topping.

Tavernas

Tavernas range from the smart and fashionable to rough-and-ready huts set up behind a beach, under a reed awning. Basic tavernas have a very limited menu, but the more established will offer some of the main *estiatório* dishes mentioned opposite, as well as the standard taverna fare. This essentially means *mezédhes* (hors d'oeuvres) and *tís óras* (meat and fish, fried or grilled to order). Increasingly, under the influence of tourism, tavernas serve up more adventurous international cuisine.

Since the idea of courses is foreign to Greek cuisine, starters, main dishes and salads often arrive together unless you request otherwise. The best thing is to order a selection of *mezédhes* and salads to share, in true Greek fashion. Waiters encourage you to take the *horiátiki* **salad** – the so-called "Greek salad" with *féta* cheese – because

it is the most expensive. If you only want tomato, or tomato and cucumber, ask for *domatosaláta* or *angourodomáta*. *Láhano* (cabbage) and *maroúli* (lettuce) are the typical winter and spring salads.

The most interesting **mezédhes** are *tzatzíki* (yoghurt, garlic and cucumber dip), *melitzano-saláta* (aubergine/eggplant dip), *kopanistí* (spicy cheese dip), *kolokythákia tiganitá* (courgette/zucchini slices fried in batter) or *melitzánes tiganités* (aubergine/eggplant slices fried in batter), *yígandes* (white haricot beans in vinaigrette or hot tomato sauce), *tyropitákia* or *spanakopitákia* (small cheese and/or spinach pies) and *okhtapódhi* (octopus).

Among **meats**, *souvláki* (shish kebab) and *brizóles* (chops) are reliable choices. In both cases, especially the latter, pork (*hirini*) is usually better and cheaper than veal (*moskharísia*). The best *souvláki*, though not often available, is lamb (*arnísio*). The small lamb cutlets called *païdhákia* are very tasty, as is roast lamb (*arní psitó*) and roast kid (*katsíki stó fournó*) when obtainable. *Keftédhes* (meatballs), *biftékia* (a sort of hamburger) and the homemade sausages called *loukánika* are cheap and good. *Kotópoulo* (chicken) is also always a safe bet.

Seafood dishes such as *kalamarákia* (fried baby squid) and *okhtapódhi* (octopus) are a summer staple of most seaside tavernas, and in some places *mýdhia* (mussels) and *garídhes* (small prawns) will be on offer at reasonable prices; *mýdhia saganáki* (mussels fried in a cheese and tomato sauce) is a particular treat. Keep an eye out, however, for freshness and season – mussels in particular are a common cause of stomach upsets in midsummer. Seaside tavernas also offer **fish**, though the choicer varieties, such as *barboúni* (red mullet), *tsipoúra* (gilt-head bream), or *fangrí* (common bream), are expensive. The price is usually quoted by the kilo, which should be not much more than double the street market rate – eg if squid is €8 a kilo at the fishmongers, that sum should fetch you two 250-gramme portions. It is procedure to go over to the cooler and pick your own, but if this isn't an option you should always specify how little or much you want.

As in *estiatória*, traditional tavernas offer fruit rather than **desserts**, though nowadays these are often available, along with coffee, in tavernas frequented by foreigners.

Specialist tavernas and vegetarians

Some tavernas specialize. **Psarotavérnes**, for example, feature mainly fish and seafood, while **psistariés** serve spit-roasted lamb, pork or goat (generically termed *kondosoúvli*), grilled chicken (*kotópoulo skáras*) or *kokorétsi* (grilled offal).

If you are **vegetarian**, you may be in for a hard time, and will often have to assemble a meal from various *mezédhes*. Even the excellent standbys of yoghurt and honey, *tzatzíki* and Greek salad begin to pall after a while, and many of the supposed "vegetable" dishes on the menu are cooked in stock or have pieces of meat added to liven them up. Where restaurants do serve an above average range of vegetable dishes, we've mentioned this in the Guide.

Wines

Both *estiatória* and tavernas will usually offer you a choice of bottled **wines**, and many have their own house variety kept in barrels, sold in bulk by the quarter-, half- or full litre and served either in glass flagons or brightly coloured tin "monkey-cups". Similarly, most tavernas stock their own wine, but don't always advertise it to foreigners so always ask whether they have wine *varelísio* or *hýma* – respectively meaning "**from the barrel**" and "**bulk**". Non-resinated bulk wine is almost always more than decent. **Retsina** – pine-resinated wine, a slightly acquired taste – is also usually better, and startlingly cheap, straight from the barrel but is becoming harder to come by. Some of the older village shops stock it as well as some tavernas. Kourtaki retsina in the small tin-top bottles is the most basic, and best served extra-chilled, as is the preferable Malamatina brand.

Among the more common bottled wines, Calliga, Boutari and Lac de Roches are good, inexpensive whites, while Boutari Nemea is perhaps the best mid-range red. If you want something better but still moderately priced, Tsantali Agioritiko is an excellent white or red, and Boutari has a fine "Special Reserve" red. Local bottled wines of note, such as Kefalloniá's fine Robola range, are mentioned in the relevant chapters.

The kafenío

The **kafenío** is the traditional Greek coffee shop or café, found in every town, village and hamlet in the country. Although its main business is Greek coffee – prepared *skéto* or *pikró* (unsweetened), *métrio* (medium) or *glykó* (sweet) – it also serves spirits such as *oúzo* (see opposite), brandy (Metaxa or Botrys brand, in three grades), beer and soft drinks. Another refreshing drink sold in cafés is *kafés frappé*, a sort of iced instant coffee with or without milk and sugar – uniquely Greek despite its French-sounding name. Like Greek coffee, it is always accompanied by a welcome glass of cold water. Standard fizzy soft drinks are also sold in all *kafenía*.

Like tavernas, *kafenía* range from the plastic and sophisticated to the old-fashioned, spit-on-the-floor variety, with marble or brightly painted metal tables and straw-bottomed chairs. An important institution anywhere in Greece, they are the focus of life in more remote villages. You get the impression that many men spend most of their waking hours there. Greek women are rarely to be seen in the more traditional places – and foreign women may sometimes feel uneasy or unwelcome in these establishments. Even in holiday resorts, you will usually find there is at least one coffee house that the local men have kept intact for themselves. Some *kafenía* close at siesta time, but many remain open from early in the morning until late at night. The chief socializing time is 6–8pm, immediately after the siesta. This is the time to take your pre-dinner *oúzo*, as the sun begins to sink and the air cools down.

Increasingly, the *kafenío* is making way for more European-style **cafeterias** with padded seats and attempts at chic decor, more to please the trendy younger generation of Greeks than tourists. In these places you are more likely to find "proper" tea (*evropaïkó*) and non-Greek coffee. *Nescafé* has become the generic term for all instant coffee, regardless of brand; it's generally pretty vile, and in resort areas smart proprietors have taken to offering genuine filter coffee, dubbed *gallikós* (French), cappucino or expresso. Another new favourite is *fréddo*, like *frappé* but made with cappucino.

Oúzo and mezédhes

Oúzo is a simple spirit of up to 48 percent alcohol, distilled from the grape-mash residue left over from wine-making, and then flavoured with herbs such as anise or fennel. It's comparable to a very rough schnapps, aqua vit or genever. When you order, you will be served two glasses: one with the *oúzo*, and one full of water that you tip into the former until it turns a milky white. You can drink it straight, but the strong, burning taste is hardly refreshing. It is becoming increasingly common to add ice cubes.

Until not long ago, every *oúzo* you ordered was automatically accompanied by a small plate of **mezédhes**, on the house: bits of cheese, cucumber, tomato, a few olives, sometimes octopus or even a couple of small fish. Unfortunately these days you usually have to ask, and pay, for them.

Sweets and desserts

Similar to the *kafenío* is the *zaharoplastío*, a cross between café and patisserie, which serves coffee, alcohol, yoghurt with honey, and sticky cakes.

The better establishments offer an amazing variety of pastries, cream and chocolate confections, honey-soaked Greco-Turkish sweets like *baklavás*, *kataïfí* (honey-drenched "shredded wheat"), *galaktoboúreko* (custard pie), and so on. The latter is something of a rarity nowadays, and when encountered should be tried.

If you want a stronger slant towards the dairy products and away from the pure sugar, seek out a **galaktopolío**, where you'll often find *rizógalo* (rice pudding – rather better than the English school-dinner variety), *kréma* (custard) and homemade or at least locally made *yiaoúrti* (yoghurt), best if it's *próvio* (from sheep's milk). These establishments, however, are definitely on the decline.

Ice cream, sold principally at the *gelaterias* which have carpeted Greece of late, can be very good and almost indistinguishable from their Italian prototypes. A scoop (*baláki*) costs €1–1.50; you'll be asked if you want it in a cup (*kýpello*) or a cone (*konáki*), or with *sandiyí* (whipped cream) on top. By contrast, mass-produced stuff like Delta or Evga brand is pretty trashy, with the honourable exception of Mars and Opal Fruit ices and Dove Bars.

Bars and beer

Bars (*barákia*), once confined to towns, cities and holiday resorts, are now found all over Greece. They range from clones of Parisian cafés to seaside cocktail bars, by way of imitation English pubs, with satellite channels offering Premier League football, MTV-type videos or even soaps running all day. Most bars close at about 2am or 3am during the week and 4am at weekends, depending on the municipality, but in the busier resorts some still stay open till dawn.

Drinks are invariably more expensive than in a café, costing around €4–8. Bars are, however, most likely to stock a range of **beers**, all foreign labels made locally under licence or imported, with the exception of the new Greek brew Mythos. Kronenbourg and Kaiser are also commonly found, with the former available in both light and dark; since 1993 a tidal wave of even pricier, imported German beers, such as Bitburger and Warstein, has washed over the fancier resorts. Amstel is the ubiquitous cheapie, rather bland but inoffensive; the Dutch themselves claim that it is better than the Amstel available in Holland. A possible compromise in both taste and expense is the sharper-tasting Heineken, universally referred to as a *prássini* by bar and taverna staff after its green bottle. Increasingly, tourist bars are serving draught beer, which in British-biased resorts may be Boddingtons or Youngs, as well as the standard lagers; Guinness and Strongbow cider are also not uncommon these days.

Communications

Postal services

Most **post offices** are open Monday to Friday from about 7.30am to 2pm, though in certain large towns – for example Corfu, Lefkádha and Argostóli – they also have evening and weekend hours.

Airmail **letters** from the islands take three to seven days to reach the rest of Europe, five to twelve days to North America and a little longer to Australia and New Zealand. Generally, the larger the island (and the planes serving its airport, if it has one), the quicker the service. Aerograms are slightly faster, and for a modest fee you can further cut delivery time to any destination by using the express (*katepígonda*) service. Registered (*sistiméno*) delivery is also available, but it is quite slow unless coupled with express service. If you are sending large purchases home, note that **parcels** should, and often can only, be handled in the main island capitals.

For a simple letter or card, **stamps** (*grammatósima*) can also be purchased at a *períptero* (kiosk). However, the proprietors charge ten percent commission on the cost of the stamp, and never seem to know the current international rates. At the time of writing, a stamp for a postcard or letter up to 20gm, costs €0.65 to anywhere in the world. Ordinary **postboxes** are bright yellow, with the hunting horn logo, and express boxes dark red; if you are confronted by two slots, *esoterikó* is for domestic mail, *exoterikó* for overseas.

Receiving mail

The **poste restante** system is reasonably efficient, especially at the post offices of larger towns. Mail should be clearly addressed and marked "poste restante", with your surname underlined, to the main post office of whichever town you choose. It will be held for a month, and you'll need your passport to collect it.

Telephones

Telephone calls are relatively straightforward. Street-corner call boxes work only with **phone cards**; the most common basic one, available from *períptera* (kiosks), OTE offices (*Organismós Tilepikinoníon tis Elládhos*) and newsagents, costs €4. You will have to go to OTE for the higher denomination cards, which, unsurprisingly, are the best value. It's easy enough to use up any remaining phone card units with a quick call home.

Very occasionally you come across a chunky coin-operated phone at a *períptero*. While local calls are reasonable (€0.20 for the first six minutes), long-distance ones have some of the most expensive rates in the EU – and definitely the worst connections, although the situation is gradually improving as exchanges are being digitalized. Other options for local calls are from a *kafenío* or bar (same charge as at kiosks), but you won't be allowed to use these for trunk or overseas calls.

For inter-island or **international** (*exoterikó*) **calls**, it's better to use either card phones with OTE cards or the better value **pre-paid cards** (usually €5 or €10), which give access via a freephone number and have a scratch-off PIN code. Apart from the cheaper rates, these cards have the advantage of being usable from any keypad phone, including those at hotels, which do not usually charge as no units are registered on their switchboard. Otherwise, **avoid** making long-distance calls from a hotel, as they slap a fifty-percent surcharge onto the already outrageous rates. Unfortunately, the pre-paid cards are a relatively new phenomenon and hard to come by on the islands, even in their capitals – if you travel via Athens or Pátra, pick one or two up there.

Calls on a €4 card get you about fifteen minutes to all EU countries and much of the rest of Europe, and around ten to North America, Australia or New Zealand. Pre-paid cards can get you up to four times as

Useful phone codes and numbers

To call Greece from abroad, you dial the international access code + 30 (country code) + full area code + number. The full area code should also be dialled if you're phoning from within Greece, as it's now an integral part of the number, even when calling locally.

Phoning abroad from Greece
Dial the country code (given below) + area code (minus any initial 0) + number
Australia ☎0061
Canada ☎001
Ireland ☎00353
New Zealand ☎0064
South Africa ☎0027
UK ☎0044
US ☎001

Useful Greek telephone numbers
ELPA Road Service ☎104
Fire brigade ☎199
Medical emergencies ☎166
Operator (domestic) ☎132

Operator (international) ☎161
Police/Emergency ☎100
Speaking clock ☎141
Tourist police ☎171

Phone credit card operator access numbers from Greece
AT&T USA Direct ☎00 800 1311
Australia ☎00 800 61 11; (Optus) ☎00 800 6121
British Telecom ☎00 800 4411
Canada Direct ☎00 800 1611
MCI ☎00 800 1211
NTL (ex-Cable & Wireless) ☎00 800 4422
Sprint ☎00 800 1411
Verizon ☎00 800 1511

long. **Cheap rates**, a reduction of ten to fifty percent depending on call distance, apply from 10pm to 8am daily, plus all day Sunday, for calls **within Greece**; calling **internationally**, cheap rates take effect from 10pm to 6am for Europe, 11pm to 8am for North America and 8pm to 6am for Australia. Discounts for other destinations are minimal.

Mobile phones are an essential fashion accessory in Greece, with the highest per-capita use in Europe outside of Italy. There are four networks at present: Panafon, Telestet, CosmOTE and Q-Telecom. Ringing any of them from Britain, you will find that costs are exactly the same as calling a fixed phone, though of course such numbers are pricey when rung locally. Coverage country-wide is fairly good, though there are a number of "dead" zones in the shadows of mountains and on really remote islets. **Pay-as-you-go**, contract-free plans are being heavily promoted in Greece (such as Telestet B-Free and Panafon À La Carte), and if you're going to be around for a while – for example, working a season in the tourist industry – an outlay of €100 or less will see you to a decent apparatus and your first calling card, which lasts six months rather

than the sixty-day norm in Britain. Before you take your own mobile phone with you, check with your provider that it will work in Greece and whether you can insert a Greek SIM-card into it once there.

British Telecom, as well as North American long-distance companies like AT&T, MCI and Sprint, provide **credit card call** services from Greece, but only back to the home country. There are now local-dial numbers with some cards, such as BT, which enable you to connect to the international system for the price of a one-unit local call, then charge the international call to your home phone – cheaper than the alternatives. **Faxes** are best sent from post offices and some travel agencies – at a price; receiving a fax may also incur a small charge.

Internet and email

Email and **Internet** use has caught on in a big way in Greece; electronic addresses or websites are given in the Guide for those travel companies and hotels that have them. Your own email needs will be well catered for by the various Internet cafés which have sprung up in the larger towns and resorts. Rates vary between around €2 and €6 per hour.

One of the best ways to keep in touch while travelling is to sign up for a free Internet **email address** that can be accessed from anywhere. Once you've set up an account, you can use these sites to pick up and send mail from any Internet café, or hotel with Internet access.

Ⓦwww.kropla.com is a useful website giving details of how to plug a **lap-top** in when abroad, phone codes around the world, and information about electrical systems in different countries.

The media

Since the fall of the junta in 1974, Greece has prided itself on upholding freedom of speech and the press. Consequently, there is a bewildering array of national and local daily newspapers, as well as a constantly growing number of TV channels. Publications and programmes in English are not uncommon and the most easily accessible are outlined below.

English-language publications

British **newspapers** are fairly widely available in Greece at a cost of €1.75–2.50 for dailies, or €4 or up for Sunday editions. You'll find day-old copies of *The Independent* and *The Guardian*'s European edition, plus a few of the tabloids, in all the resorts as well as in major towns. American and international alternatives include the turgid *USA Today* and the more readable *International Herald Tribune*, the latter including as a major bonus a free, complete English translation of the respected Greek daily *Kathemerini*. *Time* and *Newsweek* are also widely available, as are popular publications in other European languages. In the busier resorts, you'll find a wider range of the better known music, sport and women's magazines too.

Greek publications

Although you will probably be excluded from the **Greek print media** by the double incomprehensibilities of alphabet and language, you can learn a fair bit about your Greek fellow-travellers by their choice of broadsheet, so a quick survey of Greek magazines and newspapers won't go amiss.

Many papers are funded by **political groups**, which tends to decrease the already

low quality of Greek dailies. Among these, only the centrist *Kathemerini* – whose former proprietor Helen Vlahos attained heroic status for her defiance of the junta – and the now daily *Vima* approach the standards of a major European newspaper. *Eleftherotypia*, once a **PASOK** mouthpiece, now aspires to more independence, and has editorial links with Britain's *Guardian*; *Avriani* has now taken its place as the PASOK cheerleading section; *Ta Nea* is mostly noted for its extensive small ads. On the **far left**, *Avyi* is the Eurocommunist forum with literary leanings, while *Rizospastis* acts as the organ of the KKE (unreconstructed Communists). *Ethnos* was also shown some years back to have received covert funding from the KGB to act as a disinformation bulletin. At the other end of the political spectrum, *Apoyevmatini* and *Eleftheros Typos* generally support the **centre-right** Néa Dhimokratía party, while *Estia*'s no-photo format and reactionary politics are both stuck somewhere at the turn of the last century. The **nationalist**, lunatic fringe is staked out by paranoid *Stohos* ("Our Goal: Greater Greece; Our Capital: Constantinople"), while *Eleftheri Ora* still harps on about the unjust treatment received by the surviving colonels of the junta. Given the generally low level of journalism, there is little need for a soft-porn or gutter press, unlike in Germany or the UK.

Among **magazines** that are not merely translations of overseas titles, *Tahydhromos* is the respectable news-and-features weekly; *Ena* is more sensationalist, *Klik* a crass rip-off of *The Face* and *To Pondiki* (The Mouse) a satirical weekly revue in the same vein as Britain's *Private Eye* or *Spy*; its famous covers are spot-on, and accessible to anyone with minimal Greek. More specialized niches are occupied by low-circulation titles such as *Adhesmatos Typos* (a muck-raking journal) and *Andi*, an intelligent biweekly somewhat in the mould of Britain's *New Statesman*.

Radio

If you have a **radio**, playing dial roulette can be rewarding. As the government's former monopoly of wavelengths has ended, regional stations have mushroomed and the airwaves are now positively cluttered. On Corfu, for example, frequencies around 100 FM play host to a variety of local radio stations that vary greatly in quality. If you're lucky you'll hit upon a station from the mainland playing wild folk music such as *ipirótika*. The **BBC World Service** broadcasts on short wave throughout Greece; 9.41, 15.07 and 12.09 MHz are the most common frequencies. The websites for **Radio Canada** (ⓦ www.rcinet.ca) and **Voice of America** (ⓦ www.voa.gov) list their world service frequencies in Greece and around the globe.

TV

Greece's three government-owned **TV stations**, ET1, NET and (from Thessaloníki) ET3 nowadays lag behind private, mostly right-wing channels – Mega, Alpha, Antenna, Star and Skai – in the ratings, although their quality is far superior. They are the only ones to provide a decent range of educational programmes such as documentaries, along with current affairs, sport and quality cinema, including works from around Europe and

further afield, not just America. On NET, news summaries in English are broadcast daily at 6pm. Programming on the private channels tends to be a mix of soaps (especially American, Italian, Spanish and Latin American), game shows, Hollywood movies of varying quality and more sports.

Local stations in the Ionians, as elsewhere in Greece, offer little more than regional news and sporting events, plus second-rate serials and foreign movies, unless they spring into life with a belting display of folk music from a recent festival. It should also be noted that Greek censors have a high tolerance level when it comes to sex, and the private channels can get pretty raunchy late at night; if your hotel subscribes to Filmnet, then you will be in for an eyeful of hardcore porn after midnight. Whatever the channel, all foreign films and serials are broadcast in their original language, with Greek subtitles. Most private channels now have programming round the clock. Numerous **cable and satellite** channels are received, including Sky, BBC World, CNN, MTV, Super Channel, French Canal Cinque, German Sat and Italian Rai Uno or Due. The range available depends on the area (and hotel) you're in.

Cinema

Greek **cinemas** show a large number of American and British movies, always in the **original language**, with Greek subtitles. They are highly affordable, currently €7–9 depending on location and plushness of facilities. In the Ionians, however, there are only indoor cinemas on Corfu and Lefkádha, with occasional showings in town halls on Zákynthos and elsewhere. An outdoor movie in summer at the more numerous garden cinemas is worth catching at least once for the experience alone, though it's best to opt for the earlier screening (approximately 9pm) since the soundtrack on the later show tends to be turned down to avoid complaints from adjacent residences.

Opening hours and public holidays

The one constant about Greek opening hours is change. Hours may alter for reasons that elude those who happily alter them. The traditional timetable starts at a relatively civilized hour, with shops opening between 8.30 and 9.30am, then runs through until lunchtime, when there is a long break for the hottest part of the day. Businesses (but not banks) may then reopen in the mid- to late afternoon.

Tourist areas tend to adopt a slightly more northern timetable, with shops and offices, as well as the most important archeological sites and museums, usually open throughout the day but until much later at night in the case of shops.

Business and shopping hours

Most **government agencies** are open to the public on weekdays from 8am to 2pm. In general, however, you'd be optimistic to show up after 1pm expecting to be served the same day. Private businesses, or anyone providing a service, frequently operate a 9am–6pm schedule. If someone is actually selling something, then they are more likely to follow a split shift as detailed below.

Shopping hours during the hottest months are theoretically from approximately 9am to 2.30pm, and from 6 to 9pm. During the cooler months the morning schedule may start and finish slightly later, the evening trade a half-hour or even a full hour earlier. There are so many exceptions to these rules, though, that you can't count on getting anything done except from Monday to Friday, between 9.30am and 1pm. It's worth noting that delis and **butchers** are not allowed to sell fresh meat during summer afternoons (though some flout this rule); similarly, **fish-mongers** are only open in the morning, as are **pharmacies**, which additionally are shut on Saturday, except for the duty rota. Tourist shops and minimarkets, especially in the busier resorts, tend to be

---

Public holidays

January 1
January 6
March 25
First Monday of Lent (*Katharí Dheftéra,* Feb/March; see below)
Easter weekend (according to the Orthodox festival calendar; see below)
May 1
Whit Monday/Pentecost (*Áyio Pnévma*, 50 days after Easter, usually in June)
August 15
October 28
December 25 & 26

There are also a large number of local holidays, which result in the closure of shops and businesses, though not government agencies.

Variable religious feasts

	Lent Monday	Easter Sunday	Whit Monday
2006	March 6	April 23	June 12
2007	February 20	April 8	May 28
2008	March 10	April 27	June 16

open all day until quite late in the evening as long as there are people around.

All of the above opening hours will be regularly thrown out of sync by the numerous **public holidays and festivals**. The most important, when almost everything will be closed, are listed in the box.

Ancient sites, museums and monasteries

Opening hours of **ancient sites** and **museums** vary considerably. As far as possible, individual times are quoted in the text, but bear in mind that these change with exasperating frequency and at smaller sites may be subject to the whim of a local keeper. The times quoted are generally summer hours, which operate from around late April to the end of September. Reckon on similar days but later opening and earlier closing in winter. Reductions on entry fees of approximately 25 percent often apply to senior citizens, 50 percent to students with proper identification. In addition, entrance to all state-run sites and museums is **free** to all EU nationals on Sundays and public holidays from

November to March – non-EU nationals are unlikely to be detected as such unless they go out of the way to advertise the fact.

Smaller sites tend to close for a long lunch and siesta (even where they're not supposed to), as do **monasteries**. The latter are generally open from about 9am to 1pm and 5 to 8pm (3.30–6.30pm in winter) for limited visits. For advice on dress codes see p.59. It's free to take **photos** of open-air sites, though the rules on museum photography vary and the use of videos or tripods anywhere requires an extra fee and written permit. This usually has to be arranged in writing from the nearest Department of Antiquities (*Eforía Arheotíton*). It's also worth knowing that Classical studies students can get a free three-year pass to all Greek museums and sites by presenting themselves at the office on the rear corner (Tossítsa/Bouboulínas) of the National Archeological Museum in Athens – take documentation, two passport-sized photographs and be prepared to say you're a teacher (anyone with a university degree in Greece is automatically regarded as a teacher of that subject).

Festivals

Many of the big Greek festivals (see the box on pp.54–55) have a religious basis, and are observed in accordance with the Orthodox calendar. Give or take a few saints, this is similar to the regular Catholic liturgical year, except for Easter, which can fall as much as three weeks on either side of the Western festival.

Easter

Easter is by far the most important festival of the Greek year – infinitely more so than Christmas – and taken much more seriously than in western Europe. The festival is an excellent time to be in Greece, both for its beautiful religious ceremonies and for the days of feasting and celebration that follow. Corfu, in particular, is a good place to be, but each village celebrates the event, and in the smaller villages you're more likely to

find yourself invited to join in. Similarly, each island and village has its own variations on the main ceremonies. Corfu continues its tradition of pottery-smashing from windows around the old town on Easter Saturday morning (Lefkádha and Zákynthos have a similar tradition), and the spectacular firework display at midnight over the Spianádha. Each town and village parades its saints' icons in great panoply and, on Paxí, islanders strew the country lanes with flowers from

January 1

New Year's Day (*Protokhroniá*) in Greece is the feast day of Áyios Vassílios (St Basil), and is celebrated with church services and the making of a special loaf, *vassilópitta*, in which a coin is baked and which brings its finder good luck throughout the year. The traditional New Year greeting is *Kalí Khroniá*.

January 6

Epiphany (*Áyia Theofánia*, or *Ta Fóta* for short), when the *kalikántzari* (hobgoblins) who run riot on earth during the twelve days of Christmas are banished back to the nether world by various rites of the Church. The most important of these is the blessing of baptismal fonts and all outdoor bodies of water.

Pre-Lenten carnivals

This period, known as *Apókries* throughout Greece, spans three weeks, climaxing during the seventh weekend before Easter and finishing on *Katharí Dheftéra* (Clean Monday), the start of Lent. See p.52 for upcoming dates. All the islands in this Guide have elaborate festivities, parties and parades, usually based around the capital towns; in the Ionians, the tradition harks back to the Venetian era, and is dubbed *Karnaváli* (Carnival).

March 25

Independence Day and the Feast of the Annunciation (*Evangelismós*) is both a religious and a national holiday, with, on the one hand, military parades and dancing to celebrate the beginning of the revolt against Turkish rule in 1821 and, on the other, church services to honour the news being given to Mary that she was to become the Mother of Christ. There are major festivities at any place with a monastery or church named *Evangelístria* or *Evangelismós*.

April 23

The feast of **St George** (*Áyios Yeóryios*), the patron of shepherds, is a big rural celebration, with much dancing and feasting at associated shrines and towns. If April 23 falls before Easter, ie during Lent, the festivities are postponed until the Monday after Easter.

May 1

May Day is the great urban holiday when townspeople traditionally make for the countryside for picnics and return with bunches of wild flowers. Wreaths are hung on their doorways or balconies until they are burnt on Midsummer's eve. There are also large demonstrations by the Left, claiming the *Ergatikí Protomayiá* (Working Class First of May) as their own.

May 21

Ionian Day is the anniversary of the islands' union with Greece in 1864, celebrated on Corfu with marches, wreath-laying, flybys and much military pageant. Also the saints' days of **Áyios Konstandínos** and **Ayía Eléni**, therefore the most celebrated name day in Greece.

Late June to early September

Lefkádha Festival of Language and Arts. Launched in a postwar atmosphere of internationalism, this aims to bring together disparate cultures to enhance understanding. Spread out over a three-week period, the festival mixes music and dance from South America, Europe and the Mediterranean countries.

June 29

The **Holy Apostles** (*Áyii Apóstoli*), Petros and Pavlos (Peter and Paul). Two of the more widely celebrated name days.

July 26

Ayía Paraskeví is celebrated in the

many parishes and villages bearing that name.

August 11
Áyios Spyrídhon. The one fixed date of the Corfiot patron saint's four festival days, remembering the saint's intervention when disaster threatened the island. The gold casket containing the saint's remains is paraded around the centre of the town. (The other days, floating in the calendar, are Palm Sunday, Easter Saturday and the first Sunday in November.) The saint's day is also a major celebration in Karyá on Lefkádha.

August 15
Apokímisis tis Panayías (Assumption or Dormition of the Blessed Virgin Mary). This is the day when people traditionally return to their home village, and in many places there will be no accommodation available on any terms. Even some Greeks will resort to sleeping in the streets. There are major festivities throughout the islands – strangest of all is the ritual **snake-handling** at the village of Markópoulo on Kefalloniá.

August 24
Áyios Dhionýsios. One of two days (the other is the visitor-unfriendly December 24) for the saint, with major celebrations held around Áyios Dhionýsios churches, notably in Zákynthos Town.

September 8
Yénisis tis Panayías (Birth of the Virgin Mary) sees special services in churches dedicated to the event.

September 14
A last major summer festival, the **Ýpsosis tou Stavroú** (Exaltation of the Cross).

October 26
The feast of **Áyios Dhimítrios**, another popular name day. New wine is traditionally tapped on this day, a good excuse for general inebriation.

October 28
Óhi Day, the year's major patriotic shindig – a national holiday with parades, folk-dancing and speechifying to commemorate Metaxas's apocryphal one-word reply to Mussolini's 1940 ultimatum: *óhi!* ("No!").

November 8
Another popular name day, the feast of the **Archangels Michael and Gabriel** (Mihaíl and Gavriíl, or the Taxiarhón), marked by rites at the numerous churches named after them, particularly at the rural monastery of Taxiárhis on Itháki.

December 6
The feast of **Áyios Nikólaos**, the patron of seafarers, consequently a big favourite on all islands, with many chapels dedicated to him.

December 25
A much less festive occasion than Greek Easter, **Christmas** (*Khristoúyenna*) is still an important religious feast. In recent years it has acquired all of the commercial trappings of the Western Christmas, with decorations, trees and gifts. December 26 is not Boxing Day as in England, but the **Sýnaxis tis Panayías** (Meeting of the Virgin's Entourage), a legal holiday.

December 31
New Year's Eve (*Paramoní Protokhroniás*), when, as on the other twelve days of Christmas, children go door to door singing the traditional *kálanda* (carols), receiving money in return. Adults tend to play cards, often for money. The *vassilópitta* is cut at midnight (see January 1).

their gardens. Zákynthos has a tradition dating from the Middle Ages of practical jokes played on shop-owners through the Easter period.

The first great public ceremony takes place on **Good Friday** evening as the Descent from the Cross is lamented in church. At dusk the *Epitáfios*, Christ's funeral bier, lavishly decorated with flowers by the women of the parish, leaves the sanctuary and is paraded solemnly through the streets.

Late Saturday evening sees the climax in a majestic *Anástasis* Mass to celebrate Christ's triumphant return. At the stroke of midnight all lights in each crowded church are extinguished, plunging the congregation into the darkness that envelops Christ as he passes through the underworld. Then there's a faint glimmer of light behind the altar screen before the priest appears, holding aloft a lighted taper and chanting *Avtó to Fos* ("This is the Light of the World"). Stepping down to the level of the parishioners, he touches his flame to the unlit candle of the nearest worshipper, intoning *Dhévte, lávete Fos* ("Come, take the Light"). Those at the front of the congregation and on the aisles do the same for their neighbours until the entire church is ablaze with burning candles and the miracle reaffirmed.

Even the most committed agnostic is likely to find this moving. The traditional greeting, as an arsenal's worth of **fireworks** explode around you in the street, is *Khristós anésti* ("Christ is risen"), to which the response is *Alithós anésti* ("Truly He is risen"). In the week up to Easter Sunday you should wish people a Happy Easter: *Kaló Páskha*; after the day, you say *Khrónia pollá* ("Many Happy Returns", or literally "Many Years"). Worshippers then take the burning **candles** home, and it brings good fortune on the house if they arrive still lit. On reaching the front door it is common practice to make the sign of the cross on the lintel with the flame, leaving a black smudge visible for the rest of the year. The **Lenten fast** is traditionally broken early on **Sunday** morning (usually just after midnight) with a meal of *mayirítsa*, a soup made from lamb tripe, rice and lemon. The rest of the lamb will be roasted on spits for Sunday lunch, and festivities often take place through the rest of the day.

The Greek equivalent of **Easter eggs** are hard-boiled eggs (painted red on Holy Thursday), which are baked whole inside twisted, sweet bread-loaves (*tsourékia*) or distributed on Easter Sunday. People rap their eggs against their friends', and the owner of the last uncracked one is considered lucky.

The festival calendar

Most of the other Greek festivals are in honour of one or another of a multitude of **saints**. The most important are detailed in the box on pp.54–55: a village or church bearing one of the saint's names mentioned here is a sure sign of celebrations – sometimes right across the town or island, sometimes quiet, local and consisting of little more than a special liturgy and banners adorning the chapel in question. Saints' days are also celebrated as **name days**; if it's a friend's name day, you wish them *Khrónia pollá* ("Many Happy Returns"). Also detailed are a few more **secular holidays**, most enjoyable of which are the pre-Lenten carnivals.

In addition to the specific dates mentioned, there are literally scores of **local festivals** (**paniyíria**) celebrating the patron saint of the village church. With hundreds of possible name-saints' days (liturgical calendars list two or three, however arcane, for each day) you're unlikely to travel around Greece for long without stumbling on something. Those that fall in the warmer months are usually lively outdoor events lasting most of the night. Apart from the general list above, the location and date of many specific ones are mentioned in the course of the Guide.

It is important to remember the concept of the **paramoní**, or eve of the festival. Most of the events listed above are celebrated on the night before, so if you show up on the morning of the date given you will very probably have missed any music, dancing or drinking.

Watersports

The Ionian islands can claim some of the finest watersports facilities in the Mediterranean. Watersport equipment – from the humble pedalo to top-of-the-range competitive windsurf boards and sails – can be rented out in most resorts, and larger resorts have waterskiing and parasailing facilities.

The last few years have seen a massive growth in the popularity of **windsurfing** in Greece. The country's bays and coves are ideal for beginners, and boards can be rented in literally hundreds of resorts. Because of the shared geography and prevailing winds of the Ionian islands, it is typically the sandy or pebbly parts of the west coasts, often inaccessible except by boat, that provide the best conditions. Only Paxí and Zákynthos are exceptions to this rule, with west coasts dominated by high, hostile cliffs. Morning winds are gentle, ideal for novices, and the afternoon winds will test even the most experienced. Rentals start from around €12 an hour. Fully inclusive windsurf holidays on islands such as Lefkádha start at around €600 a week.

Waterskiing is available at a number of the larger resorts, and even on the smaller islands. By the rental standards of the ritzier parts of the Mediterranean, it is a bargain, with twenty minutes' instruction often available for around €15–20. At many resorts, **parasailing** (*parapént*) is also possible; rates start at around €25 a go.

A combination of steady winds, appealing seascapes and numerous natural harbours has long made the Greek islands a tremendous place for **sailing**. Holiday companies offer all sorts of packaged and tailor-made cruises and there are some specialists in yacht and bareboat charters (see the "Getting there" sections). Locally, small boats and dinghies are rented out by the day at many resorts from around €50 and upwards, depending on the size and power. Larger craft can be chartered by the week or longer, either bareboat or with skipper, from marinas on Corfu and bases in most of the islands. Where the Aegean has its notorious *meltémi*, the Ionian has its equivalent **maéstro**, which can blow for up to three days and make for pretty nauseating sailing, most often at either end of the season, but sometimes at points during it. For more details on all aspects of sailing, contact the Hellenic Yachting Federation at Pireás (T210/41 37 351, W www.eio.gr).

Scuba-diving is still a minority sport in the Ionian, but growing fast because of its popularity among north European visitors. Many schools are in fact run by visitors from Germany and the Nordic countries, with some Brits now muscling in on the act and an increasing number of Greeks catching on. The average charge for a single tank dive is €40–50, usually with a discount for multiple dives. Instruction for PADI courses (from around €320) and guided introductory dives are available at most schools so you do not have to have any previous experience. We list diving schools where they arise in the Guide and more extensive information can be obtained in Britain from the British Sub-Aqua Club (T020/7723 8336, W www.bsac.com) or from GNTO offices in other countries. In Greece you can contact the Union of Greek Diving Centres in Athens (T210/92 29 532 or 41 18 909).

Culture and etiquette

Greece is by no means as conservative a society as it used to be and the Greeks are renowned for a fairly relaxed attitude towards the behaviour of foreign visitors. Still, there are a few issues worth mentioning to help you make the most of your stay without causing offence. This section also covers attitudes towards women, gay travellers and children.

Sexual behaviour and nudity

Attitudes in Greece are much as they are throughout the rest of the Mediterranean when it comes to **public displays of affection**. Nobody is going to get too upset at kissing couples, as long as the display does not spill into the pornographic. Similarly, it is common for women to bathe **topless** on most beaches and many Greek females do it themselves. It is still frowned upon at certain family beaches, however, so the best rule of thumb is to see what other people are doing and follow suite. Full **nudity** is officially illegal almost everywhere and certainly not tolerated except on certain, usually isolated strands, where it has become the norm and is ignored by the authorities. Any such beaches are mentioned throughout the text.

Women travellers

Most women find that travelling solo or with other female companions is fairly **hassle-free** in Greece, especially when compared to nearby countries like Italy. The most common source of annoyance comes in the form of unwanted attention by cruising **kamákia** (little harpoons). These are the macho young males who spend a fair chunk of their summers "fishing" for foreign females. Different women find different tactics the best way to rid themselves of these pests, varying from silent ignoring to a few choice words directed at the offender. Any softness or display of interest is likely to make the pursuer harder to shake off though. Other than that, instances of serious crime (see p.62) are low and women should feel comfortable about activities like walking alone at night and camping. For guide-lines on appropriate dress in churches etc, see opposite.

Gay travellers

Male homosexuality is **legal** over the age of 17 in Greece, but still very covert. Male bisexuality is common but rarely admitted. Out gay Greeks are rare, and out lesbians rarer still: they can suffer harassment from peers, although thanks to the culture of *filoxénia* (hospitality) gay visitors will encounter few, if any, problems. Most Greeks regard **same-sex couples** with bemusement, although a very few younger males have adopted the homophobia of some British visitors. Gay and lesbian tourists are discreetly visible on virtually all the Ionian islands. There are gay-owned/run bars and businesses in the islands, but they rarely advertise the fact. Greek men are terrible flirts – cruising them is a semiotic minefield and definitely at your own risk (references in gay guides to male cruising grounds should be regarded with great caution). Native lesbians are virtually invisible in Greece, and are unusually absent from Lefkádha, despite its claim to a major role in queer history – proto-dyke Sappho is said to have committed suicide by throwing herself from the cliffs of Cape Lefkátas (see p.169).

Travelling with children

Kids are worshipped and indulged throughout Greece, and present few problems when travelling. There is no problem, for example, taking toddlers to tavernas till all hours just as the locals do, other than breaking your own routines. International **baby food** and **nappy** (diaper) brands are ubiquitous and reasonably priced, and concessions are offered on most forms of transport. Private rooms and luxury hotels are more likely to offer some kind of babysitting service than the mid-range hotels. **Child seats** are always available when renting cars as well. The Ionians do not, however, present many attractions designed specifically for kids, other than the few water amusement parks and odd mini-zoo dotted about.

Gestures

As is the case in most countries, there are a few Greek **gestures** which either do not exist elsewhere, or mean something different from their English equivalents. The most common one to baffle foreign visitors is the Greek version of "**No**" or "I don't know": instead of shaking their heads, they tip them sharply backwards, accompanied by a raising of the eyebrows. Often the raised eyebrows alone do the job and there may or may not be a verbal "tut" as well. Likewise, but less confusing, the Greek sign for "**Yes**" is not so much a complete nod of the head as a gentle tilt of it down and to one side. When somebody beckons you to come in their direction the hand movement is basically the same but with the fingers pointing downwards rather than up. The Greek equivalent of sticking two fingers up at someone (or one in the USA) is to stretch out the hand quickly with all the digits splayed in the object's direction. This is literally "putting the evil eye" on the person and, although it is often used in jest, it can cause offence and so the motion is best avoided – be careful when waving to a waiter that you want five of something, for example.

Religion

The Orthodox Church by no means exerts the **influence** over Greek society that it used to, even if the regular sight of black-robed priests and the number of churches and festivals suggests the contrary. This is especially true among the younger generations, who have become disillusioned with the various scandals that have gripped the Church, whilst embracing global materialism with gusto. If you do visit any churches or monasteries to get a taste of the country's religious heritage, however, it is best to be sensitive about your manner of dress. Small seaside places of worship may be more relaxed but most operate a fairly strict **dress code** for visitors; shorts on either sex are unacceptable, and women are often expected to cover their arms and wear skirts – wraps are sometimes provided on the spot.

Bargaining and tipping

Bargaining isn't a regular feature of life, though you'll find it possible with private rooms and some hotels out of season. Similarly, you may be able to negotiate discounted rates for vehicle rental, especially for longer periods. Services such as shoe, watch and camera repair don't have iron-clad rates, so use common sense when assessing charges (advance estimates are not routine). Most **shops** have fixed prices but in tourist areas where they tend to over-charge in the first place, a little bartering, especially if you can manage some Greek, is likely to lead to a reduction.

Tipping is not expected in most establishments other than the top luxury-style hotels. In most tavernas a simple rounding-up of the bill or a €0.50–1 coin for the waiter is appreciated but not *de rigueur*. Again, a tiny rounding-up is all that taxi drivers expect and if the journey has not been metered, you can bank on the fact that a healthy "tip" has already been built into the agreed price.

Living in the Ionians

Since Greece's full accession to the European Union in early 1993, a citizen of any EU state has the right to live and work in Greece, in theory at least. In practice, however, there can be a number of bureaucratic hurdles to overcome. So far only a small, if growing, number of Brits and other northern Europeans have chosen Greece as a retirement location, or a place to set up a second home in the sun. For most people, living here also means working and the opportunities are definitely limited when it comes to making a living.

In the Ionian islands the availability of teaching posts in the private **language schools** (*frondistíria*) was always limited, in comparison to on the mainland, and increased restrictions on the number of such positions for non-Greeks (see below) have made matters more difficult, so you may stand more chance in a commercial or leisure-orientated trade, most likely in the field of tourism.

Despite the theoretical freedom of employment, you may find yourself involved in a bureaucratic process if you plan to work for someone else. You first have to visit the nearest Department of Employment and collect two forms: one an **employment application** which you fill in, the other is to be filled in as the formal offer of work by your prospective employer. Once these are vetted, and revenue stamps (*hartósima*, purchased at kiosks) applied, you take them to the Aliens' Bureau (*Ipiresía Allodhapón*) or, in its absence, the central police station, to support your application for a **residence permit** (*ádhia paramonís*). For this, you will also need to bring your passport, two photographs, more *hartósima* and a stable address (not a hotel). Permits are given for terms of three or six months (white cards), one year (green triptych booklets), or even five years (blue booklets) if they've become well acquainted with you. For one- or five-year permits, a **health examination** at the nearest public hospital is required, to screen for TB, syphilis and HIV. The situation is constantly evolving, so check with your employer if all this is necessary; just don't presume that he or she will know the current official policy. If you're intent on setting up your own business, you won't

be surprised to hear there are yet more hurdles to jump, including setting yourself up with the TEVE **insurance** scheme for the self-employed and obtaining a tax number (*foroloyikó mitróo*, usually abbreviated to *af-fi-mí*) from the local tax office (*eforía*).

The reality is that an EU passport and the unwillingness of the Greek government to be taken to the European Court of Justice make you pretty safe from prosecution for ignoring any regulations, and it is easy to pick up **casual work**. As fruit-picking and manual labour is now the exclusive domain of illegal and underpaid Albanian refugees, your best chance is in tourism-related jobs. Most women and some men working casually in Greece find jobs in **bars** or **restaurants** around the main resorts. Men, unless they are "trained" chefs, will be edged out by Albanians even when it comes to washing up.

If you're waiting or serving, most of your wages will probably have to come from tips, but you may well be able to get a deal that includes free food and lodging; evening-only hours can be a good shift, leaving you a lot of free time. The main drawback may be the chauvinist attitudes of your employer; ads in the local press for "girl bar staff" are certainly to be treated with caution. The large resorts of Corfu and Zákynthos are the easiest places in the Ionians to find bar work.

On a similar, unofficial level you might be able to get a sales job in **tourist shops** anywhere with a high concentration of foreigners or (if you've the expertise) helping out at one of the many **windsurfing** or less numerous **scuba-diving** schools that have sprung up all around the coasts. **Yacht** marinas can also prove good hunting-grounds, though less for the romantic business of crewing, than for scrubbing down and repainting. The best possibilities are likely to be on Corfu or Lefkádha.

Perhaps the best type of tourism-related work, though, is that of courier/greeter/group coordinator for a **package holiday company**. With such a British tour operator presence as there is in the Ionians, there are plenty of opportunities and, although some knowledge of Greek is an advantage for dealing with local room owners and the like, it is not a requirement, as your main mandate is to keep the punters happy. Many such staff are recruited through ads in newspapers outside Greece, but it's by no means unheard of to be hired on the spot in April or May. Advantages of this kind of work are that you're usually guaranteed about six months of steady employment, and that if things work out you may be re-employed the following season with a contract and foreign-currency wages from the home company, rather than from the local affiliate.

You may do even better by working for yourself, as long as you are discreet. Travellers have reported rich pickings during the tourist season from **selling jewellery** on island beaches, or on boats – trinkets from Asia are especially popular with Greeks (though you will first have to persuade customs officials that all those trinkets you are bringing in are presents for friends). Roadside **cosmetic** enterprises like putting in coloured hair braids or doing henna tattoos are also

becoming more common. Finally, **busking** is a well-established occupation that can also be quite lucrative, though it doesn't seem as common in the Ionians as in other parts of Greece; playing on a shady street corner, however, can make you around €5 per hour, more if you're lucky.

At the present time, all **non-EU nationals** who wish to work in Greece do so surreptitiously, unless employed by their government or a multinational company, with the ever-present risk of denunciation to the police and instant deportation. Having been forced to accept large numbers of EU citizens looking for jobs in a climate of rising unemployment, Greek immigration authorities are cracking down hard on any suitable targets, be they Albanian, African, Swiss or North American. That old foreigners' stand-by, teaching English, is now officially available only to TEFL certificate-holders, preferably Greek, non-EU nationals of Greek descent, or EU nationals – in that order. Many *frondistíria*, however, still employ teachers without worrying about the paperwork. If you are a non-EU foreign national of Greek descent, you are termed *omólogos* (returned Greek diaspora member) and in fact have tremendous employment and residence rights – you can, for example, open your very own *frondistírio* with minimum qualifications (something painfully evident in the often appalling quality of English instruction in Greece). The downside, if you are male and under 40, is that you may find yourself being drafted into military service.

Trouble and the police

Greece has traditionally been one of Europe's safest countries, with a low crime rate and an almost unrivalled reputation for honesty. However, in recent years there has been a noticeable increase in theft and crimes, usually blamed on Albanians and other immigrants, but often perpetrated by tourists, particularly in the cities and resorts, so it's wise to lock things up and treat Greece like any other European destination. Below are a few pointers on offences that might get you into trouble locally, crimes you may fall foul of, and an introduction to Greek police.

Offences

The most common brushes that tourists have with the authorities are caused by nude sunbathing and camping outside authorized sites.

Nude bathing is legal on only a very few beaches, and is deeply offensive to the more traditional Greeks. Generally, though, if a beach has become fairly established as naturist, or is well secluded, it's highly unlikely that the police are going to intervene. Where they do get bothered is if they feel a place is turning into a "hippie beach" or nudity is getting too overt on mainstream tourist stretches. Most of the time, the only action will be a warning, but you can officially be arrested without warning – facing up to three days in jail and a stiff fine.

Very similar guidelines apply to **freelance camping**, though for this you're still unlikely to incur anything more than a warning to move on. The only real risk of arrest is if you are told to move on and fail to do so. In either of the above cases, even if the police do take any action against you, it's more likely to be a brief spell in their cells than any official prosecution.

Drug offences are treated as major crimes, which may not be surprising in view of the growing local use and addiction problem, even on the smaller islands. The

maximum penalty for "causing the use of drugs by someone under 18", for example, is life imprisonment and an astronomical fine. Theory is by no means practice, but foreigners caught in possession of even small amounts of grass do get long jail sentences if there's evidence that they've been supplying the drug to others. Even if you are ultimately acquitted of any offence, you may be in jail for at least a year awaiting trial, with little or no chance of making bail.

If you are arrested for any offence, you have a right to contact your **consulate**, which will arrange a lawyer for your defence. Beyond this, there is little they can or (in most cases) will do. In the meantime, do not sign any statements unless they have been clearly and reliably translated into English.

Crime

Violent crime is still extremely rare in Greece, even more so on the islands than in large mainland cities. So your chances of being mugged or, in the case of women, raped are very low indeed. This does not mean you should let your guard down completely, and it is sensible to take the usual precautions concerning your possessions and personal safety. If you do get into a crisis situation, call one of the numbers in the box opposite immediately.

The crime from which you are most likely to suffer is petty **theft**. Either a bag goes missing while you are on the beach or in a crowded bar, or, less likely, something disappears from your accommodation. If you do suffer a theft and you intend to claim on

> In an **emergency**, dial ☎100 for the police; ☎171 for the tourist police; ☎166 for an ambulance; ☎199 for the fire brigade.

your insurance when you return home, then you are obliged to obtain a police statement, which will normally be a time-consuming and frustrating affair at best.

That said, the vast majority of visitors to the Ionians will suffer from nothing worse than the odd unscrupulous taxi driver.

The police

Aside of a few special units that you are most unlikely to encounter, the three most common branches of the Greek constabulary are the **regular police** (*astynomía*), the **traffic police** (*trohéa*) and the **tourist police** (*touristikí astynomía*). There are no dramatically distinguishing features in their appearance apart from the diagonal white band usually worn over the uniform by the traffic police.

The tourist police, as their name suggests, exist to help foreigners: but this "help" may consist of nothing more than handing out brochures from their offices (listed in the Guide) and pointing you on your way. You are far more likely to spot them sipping coffee or cruising round in their cars with friends than pounding the beat. This can be advantageous insofar as it reduces your chances of being stopped for any minor transgression such as not wearing a motorbike helmet; but it is a disadvantage when you need their help. Nor are you likely to find the average traffic policeman much more useful when it comes to asking for directions. It goes without saying that it is best for you to remain calm and polite, even in the face of official apathy, so as not to end up on the wrong side of the law.

Travellers with special needs

Lightweight wheelchairs are not an uncommon sight on beaches in the Ionians, proving that wheelchair users, at least, do holiday here. With planning, wheelchair users and those who have difficulty in seeing or walking (or any other disability) can enjoy an inexpensive and trauma-free holiday in even the smallest of island resorts.

It has to be admitted, though, that little in Greece – from the roads and the buses to public and private buildings – is designed with the disabled in mind. Very few public buildings have **ramps** or **special toilet cubicles**, for example, and accommodation or restaurants usually only have steps to access the different levels.

The first thing to do when planning for your holiday is to spend some time gathering **information** about your choice of destination, and options for travel and accommodation. Addresses of contact organizations in Greece are published below, and the Greek National Tourist Organization (see p.35 for contact details) is a good place to address specific questions. They publish a useful questionnaire which you can send

to hotels or apartment/villa owners. Where possible, try to double-check all information, as things in Greece have a habit of changing suddenly.

Planning a holiday

There are **organized tours and holidays** designed specifically for people with disabilities, and most tour operators will advise on the suitability of holidays advertised in their brochures. Travelling more independently is also perfectly possible, provided that you plan for the worst and don't assume that assistance will always be immediately at hand. If you're not entirely confident you can manage alone, try to travel with an able-bodied friend (or two).

Read your travel **insurance** small print carefully to make sure that people with a pre-existing medical condition are not excluded. And use your travel agent to make your journey simpler: airlines can cope better if they are expecting you, with a wheelchair provided at airports and staff primed to help. A medical certificate of your fitness to travel, provided by your doctor, is also extremely useful; some airlines or insurance companies may insist on it.

Shopping

As you might expect, the resorts in the Ionians are as crammed with shops selling typical tourist souvenirs as anywhere else on the planet where holidaymakers gather en masse. Indeed, it is a sign of increasing globalization that you are just as likely to find jewellery or carvings from Asia and Africa as local crafts in many shops. There are, however, a few items which are more genuine mementoes of specific islands.

The most characteristic craftwork to be found on Corfu is carved **olive wood**. These items may take the shape of natural logs, boxes, or woodwind pipes; they can also come in the form of larger items like furniture. Outlets are plentiful, especially in Corfu Town and all over the north of the island. Prices depend on the size and complexity of the piece, ranging from just a few euros to several hundred.

Lefkádha's main artisitic produce is the traditional **lace embroidery** centred on the mountain village of Karyá. Much of the work is very intricate and it is all done by hand, meaning that the larger pieces made of the best quality material are expensive, often running to several hundred euros. Smaller items like handkerchiefs and table runners can be purchased for around €10–25.

The other noted Ionian handicraft is the cotton and woollen **rug-weaving** at Volímes on Zakynthos. You'll have all sorts of colours and designs to choose from, the famous loggerhead turtle being a favourite motif. Prices start at around €15 and can rise sharply for the most exquisite work.

Finally, you might choose to bring home something to **eat** or **drink** as a souvenir from your Ionian holiday. Favoured options include the sticky Corfiot liqueur *kumquat*, quality olive oil from Paxí, fine Kefallonian wine or sweet nougat *mandoláto* from Zákynthos. None of these items will set you back more than about €10 a portion.

The períptero

Most shops in the Ionians are fairly recognisable from their English counterparts. But one unique establishment to be found throughout Greece is the streetside kiosk, known in Greek as **períptero.** They can vary in size but sell everything from pens to disposable razors, stationery to soap, sweets to condoms, cigarettes to plastic crucifixes – and are often open when nothing else is.

Guide

Guide

1

Corfu (Kérkyra)

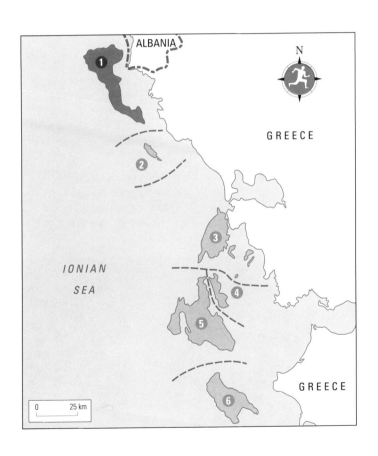

CHAPTER 1 # Highlights

* **The Listón, Corfu Town** The capital's colonnaded main strip with its cafés is the place to be seen; you might even catch a game of cricket being played here. See p.80

* **Áyios Spyrídhon church, Corfu Town** Corfu's most venerated place of worship contains some superb artwork. See p.82

* **Paleópolis, Corfu Town** These archeological remains are little visited and make for an atmospheric wander. See p.85

* **Kassiópi** The most attractive resort in the north offers a scenic harbour and Angevin fortress, as well as beaches and a dazzling array of restaurants and bars. See p.98

* **Myrtiótissa** A visually stunning beach, part nudist, and a Durrell favourite. See p.109

* **Sinarádhes** Sample the atmosphere of traditional Corfu in this sleepy mountain village. See p.111

* **The Korissíon lagoon** This isolated patch of wetlands in the south is home to a variety of waterfowl, and boasts some of Corfu's most deserted strips of sand. See p.117

* **The Corfu Trail** The newly designated 200-kilometre-long walking route covers the length of the island. See p.122

△ Corfu Town seen from Vídhos

Corfu (Kérkyra)

angling between the southern tip of Italy and the west coast of mainland Greece, at the point where the Adriatic meets the Ionian Sea, the lush green sickle of **Corfu (KÉRKYRA)** was one of the first Greek islands to attract mass tourism in the 1960s. Since then it has acquired the sleaziest reputation among the islands, although much of this is exaggerated and due more to snobbery than actual fact. It's true that indiscriminate exploitation by package-tour operators and their willing Corfiot partners turned parts of Corfu into eyesores, but many of the island's resorts have developed a more moderate form of tourism and, even in the most overrun places, unspoilt parts of the coast and interior are often only a few minutes away on foot. Anyway, recent years have seen a decline in tourism, a source of worry to those dependent on it, but a distinct advantage to the paying customer. One positive result is a better balance between mass and individual tourism than on some of the smaller islands. This benefits both the independent traveller, by offering more availability at lower prices, and the small-time local operator, by allowing more chance to compete with the big boys. The island authorities have also taken steps – a little late in the day, some would say – to reverse its image as overdeveloped and tacky. The island has some of the best beaches in the whole archipelago – no fewer than 33 of them were awarded blue flags in 2005 – and idyllic bays that still resemble the "delectable landscape" Lawrence Durrell described in *Prospero's Cell*.

The main settlement, **Corfu (Kérkyra) Town**, for many years a mess of collapsing tenements and traffic congestion, was renovated in the 1990s and is now one of the most elegant island capitals in the whole of Greece, with indubitable charm and a number of cultural attractions. Tourist development tends to be confined to the coasts, concentrated in resorts that you can either easily avoid or use as a base for exploring the surrounding area. There are no high-rise hotels here in the Spanish mould: **accommodation** tends to be in apartments, rooms, villas and small hotels, while the larger resort hotels are horizontal rather than vertical, never more than five storeys high. Transport on the island's **bus** system is cheap, reliable and will get you to almost every village or resort. The island-wide green buses stop between 6 and 8pm, and restricted services run on Sundays, while the blue suburban buses that run within a ten-kilometre radius of Corfu Town operate till around 10pm. Both systems radiate out from Corfu Town, and around €3 will get you to the furthermost points of the island inside an hour and a half.

The island's finest scenery is on the north coast. The northeast is served by a single mountain road with turnings leading down to small pebbly bays and clear blue water, while the northwest is characterized by towering cliffs and

wide sandy bays. The region is dominated by the bulk of **Mount Pandokrátor** and neighbouring peaks, whose foothills and summits offer great walks and even better views – though the mountain attracts more than its fair share of bad weather, particularly in low and shoulder seasons. The centre and south are less hilly and more verdant: the lush farmland of the **Rópa plain** which extends south from just below the resort of Paleokastrítsa, is the island's fruit (and veg) basket. The south has two distinct sides: narrow, stony beaches and a few hidden beauty spots face the mainland, while the southwest-facing coast is backed by verdant countryside and features some of the best sandy beaches on the island.

If you want to see the whole island, it's probably best to head south first; apart from a handful of beauty spots detailed below, it doesn't have the scenery and variety found elsewhere, and although the north has more overall development

IGOUMENÍTSA, the third busiest passenger port in Greece and increasingly important as a commercial port with the impending completion of the cross-country Via Egnatia, is Corfu's major link with the mainland. Boats also ply daily to Paxí, and it's a key stop on ferry routes between Italy and Pátra. The town is an important crossroads for mainland **bus services**, with connections to Athens and Thessaloníki, inland to Ioánnina and south to Párga and Préveza; the **bus station** is at Kýprou 47, the main shopping street, a short walk away from the southeast corner of the town's main square, Platía Dimarhíou, which stands two blocks back and a few blocks east of the port. There's little in this busy industrial port to detain you, and most people travelling in either direction will find connections onwards: **ferries** to Corfu Town's New Port run every 15 minutes to one hour from 4.30am to 10pm daily year round, with at least one crossing daily to Paxí. Buses to Athens stop at 6pm and to Ioánnina at 8pm, while the one Thessaloníki bus leaves at 11.45am (Mon–Sat).

Should bad connections or a tiring journey force you to **stay** in Igoumenítsa, you'll find that hotels are plentiful, though not particularly appealing; most are to be found either on or just back from the seafront. The nearest budget hotel to the port is the *Acropolis* at Ethnikís Andístasis 58A (℡26650/22 342; ❷), although the *Stavrodhromi* (℡26650/22 343; ❶) at Soulíou 14, the street leading diagonally uphill and northeast from the Platía Dimarhíou, is better value; neither has en-suite rooms. A smarter seafront option close to the port is *Oscar*, Ayíon Apostólon 149 (℡26650/23 338; ❹), while a cheaper but comfortable choice with en-suite rooms is the *Egnatia*, Eleftherías 1 (℡26650/23 648; ❸), in the southeast corner of Platía Dimarhíou – ask for a rear room facing the pine grove. The closest **campsite** is the *Drepano* (℡26650/24 442; April–Oct), out at Dhrépano beach, 5km west.

A short walk away from the Corfu dock west along the seafront will bring you to a marina used by visiting yachts and fringed with an elegant promenade. Here on Antístasis, you'll find some stylish **bars**, catering to high-spending Greeks who hang out at nightspots like *Art* and *Memphis*. Also nearby are some of the better **restaurants**, such as the *Petros* and *Emilios psistariés*. Another direction to head in search of food is the north end of the front, where several fish tavernas and *ouzerís* come to life in the evening, as does the *Psarotaverna O Timios*, just south of the new port. Next to the large, open-air *Traffic Bar*, there's a **cinema**, Pame, which sometimes screens English-language films.

There are **banks** and 24-hour ATMs opposite the ferry docks on Apostólon, as well as **international ferry offices**, and a **post office** on Evangelístrias, just behind the north end of the seafront. **Corfu ferries** dock at the open quay north of the secured international terminal; different boats operate their own ticketing systems, with the name of the ferry posted on one of two ticket kiosks opposite the loading ramps. If you miss or skip a sailing, your ticket may not be valid for a later one, though usually you can change it. Crossing times depend on the boat: the regular open-topped ferries take around 1hr 15min; a couple of larger boats also operate – these are slightly more expensive, but cut the journey time to an hour.

these days, the southern resorts have fewer redeeming factors, and there is little of interest away from them. Hardened **beach** nuts go west, to Myrtiótissa and other strands to the south. If you want scenery and unspoilt bays, head for the northeast coast between Nissáki and Kassiópi. Resorts noted for **nightlife** include Kassiópi, Sidhári, Ípsos and, notoriously, **Kávos**, a favourite with young ravers, in the south. If you're on a tight schedule, spend a day in Corfu Town, move north to Kalámi, Koulóura and Áyios Stéfanos, and then head for the west coast.

Some history

Although important defensive structures were built at outposts such as Kassiópi and Paleokastrítsa during the Middle Ages, the island's history is essentially that of its main town. Indeed, the name "Corfu" is an Italian corruption of the ancient Greek word *koryphai*, the "hills" on which the town's two forts were built.

Archeological finds carbon-dated to the middle Paleolithic – when the island was still part of the mainland, and much of the Adriatic was dry land covered by vast forests – indicate that there's been a settlement of sorts on the site of the town for over fifty thousand years. Much of prehistoric Corfu has been discovered around the sites of two ancient natural harbours: one at the opposite end of Garítsa Bay to the town centre, near the Mon Repos estate; and the other in the Hyllaic Harbour, now the Halikópoulou lagoon, bisected by the airport runway. The latter is also thought to have been the site of settlements of **Eretrians**, mainland Greeks who arrived here via Albania in 750BC. They were soon followed, and displaced, by invaders from **Corinth**, who made Corfu Town (which they called Corcyra, from which modern Greek Kérkyra is derived) one of the most powerful forces in ancient Greece, turning it into a mighty walled city and a major sea power in the region. During the Persian Wars of the fifth century BC, Corfu provided the second largest naval force after Athens. Along with other Ionian islands, it fought alongside Athens against the Spartans in the Peloponnesian War.

Much to the relief of the inhabitants, who had been overrun by Illyrian pirates, the city was taken over by the **Romans** in 229 BC. It remained under Rome's rule, supplying men and ships in its wars, and after the division of the empire in 395 AD both city and island came under the control of the eastern or **Byzantine Empire**. Corfu was nominally Byzantine for over eight centuries, but as one of the most distant outposts of the empire, it was prone to raids by Vandals, Goths, Saracens, Normans and others. It was seized, briefly, by the Venetians in 1205, who were followed by the Despots of Epirus and the fortress-building Angevins. After further suffering at the hands of pirates, the islanders asked for help from **Venice** in 1386, under whose rule they then remained until 1797. The Venetians imposed their own laws, language, art and architecture, and began the construction of the town as it is seen now, including structures on both the Paleó and Néo Froúrio hills.

Following Napoleon Bonaparte's defeat of the Republic of Venice in 1797, Corfu and the other Ionian islands were acquired by **France**. The French began what was proposed as an extensive plan of development, which resulted in the construction of the famous Listón, modelled on the Rue de Rivoli in Paris. Bonaparte's true legacy to the islanders, however, was a taste for independence and republicanism, which was vigorously and even violently discouraged when the city and island were taken by the **British** in 1814. The British began the last notable stage of civic construction, building the Palace of SS George and Michael, as well as various public amenities, under lords Guildford and Maitland. Despite these efforts, the British rulers were not liked by the general populace; Maitland, in particular, was despised for his arrogant attitude towards the islanders, who nicknamed him "The Abortion". The Ionian islands were finally offered to Greece by Queen Victoria in her speech at the opening of Parliament in 1864 (Victoria's great-great-great-nephew Prince Philip would be born in the Mon Repos estate in Garítsa Bay some sixty years later).

During **World War II**, Corfu was occupied by the Italians and Germans between 1941 and 1944, and was heavily bombarded by Nazi planes. Over a quarter of Corfu Town was destroyed, including the library, parliament and numerous churches. Most, if not all, of the town's Jewish population, who had found refuge here over the centuries after pogroms elsewhere in Europe, were arrested and shipped off to the Nazi death camps. The elegant Listón makes a haunting appearance in Claud Lanzmann's epic Holocaust documentary, *Shoah*, as the place where Corfu's Jews were rounded up.

Corfu Town

Corfu Town (Kérkyra in Greek) is the place where the island's heritage and commerce collide with an almighty bang. In high summer it can seem hellish, with a seemingly endless stream of tour coaches dumping even more tourists on a town that's already overflowing with its own hotel guests and a native population of around 45,000. It's not a place to come for peace and quiet, and certainly not a place to arrive without checking on accommodation beforehand; even in the depths of winter some hotels are fully booked. Yet if you intend to see much of the island by bus, it's the only place to base yourself, and renovations of its older buildings since the mid-nineties, plus the appearance of new restaurants, galleries and other attractions, have made Corfu Town more attractive than it has been for a long time.

Behind the bustle there remains a beautiful city in miniature, fortified in Byzantine times, developed by the Venetians, added to by the French – and, some would say, desecrated by the British. It's one of the most attractive towns in all the Greek islands, and certainly in the Ionian. When the crowds subside, at siesta time and in low season, it's well worth ambling around its elegant arcades, boulevards and squares. If you're just visiting on a day-trip, you shouldn't miss, first of all, the two **forts**, the **palace**, the warren of alleys in the **Campiello** and the old streets behind the **Listón**, including exquisite **Áyios Spyrídhon** church. Visitors based here a little longer can choose from a number of trips to nearby sights. The most popular is to the tiny islet of **Pondikoníssi**, which can however get rather overrun in summer. More enjoyable perhaps are the newly excavated **Doric temples** in the recently opened Mon Repos estate, the **British cemetery** or a boat ride to **Vídhos islet**.

Arrival, information and getting around

Most visitors arrive at Corfu's **airport**, 2km south of the centre of the town. There are no airport buses, and taxis have a tradition of overcharging (expect to pay around €6), but with a pack or other manageable bag it's not a long walk into town. Car rental agencies at the airport are listed on p.89.

Corfu has two distinct ports, though they're near to each other on the same straight seafront. The **New Port** (**Néo Limáni**), several hundred metres west of Platía Athinágora in the old town, serves most of the passenger vessels – the major ferry and hydrofoil links with Brindisi, Bari and Ancona in Italy, with Paxí, and with Igoumenítsa and Pátra on the Greek mainland, all moor here. Only excursion boats, the shuttle across to Vídhos and private craft use the **Old Port** (**Paleó Limáni**), right by the Platía Athinágora. Neither port is much more than ten minutes' walk from the heart of the town, and the island-wide bus station is also a short walk away. Taxis are readily available at the ports, bus stations and main squares at all times.

Buses from Athens and the island's outlying towns and communities arrive at the main bus station on Avramíou, behind the agricultural co-operative building; the suburban bus station is in Platía Yioryíou Theotóki, universally known

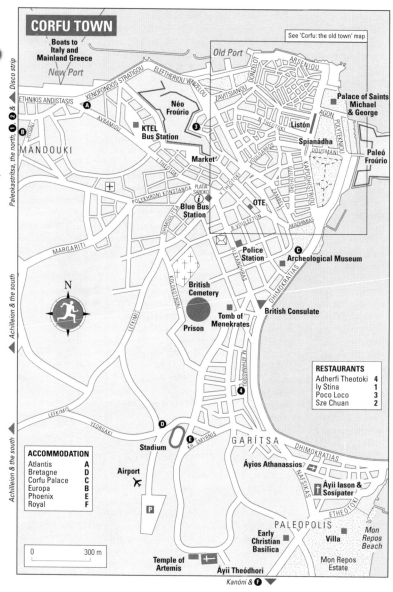

CORFU TOWN

See 'Corfu: the old town' map

Boats to Italy and Mainland Greece

New Port

Old Port

Disco strip

Paleokastritsa, the north, **1 2 &**

ETHNIKIS ANDISTASIS **A**

B

MANDOUKI

Achilleion & the south

Achilleion & the south

XENOFONDOS STRATIGOU

ELEFTHERIOU VENIZELOU

AVRAMIOU

ARSENIOU

DONZELOT

ZAVITSIANOU

AGON

N. THEOTOKI

POLYTEKNOU

KAPODHISTRIOU

Palace of Saints Michael & George

Listón

Spianádha

DOUSMANI

Paleó Froúrio

Néo Froúrio

KTEL Bus Station

3

Market

THEOTOKI

PLATIA SAROKO

i

Blue Bus Station

OTE

GUILFORD

ZAMBELI

AKADHIMIAS

R. VOULEFTON

POLYKHRONI KONSTANDA

DHIMOULITSA

MARGARITI

LEFKIMIS

KOLOSTROU

LEFKIMIS

YEORGAKI

N

British Cemetery

Prison

Tomb of Menekrates

ALEXANDRAS

Police Station

DHIMOKRATIAS

C Archeological Museum

British Consulate

M. ATHANASSIOU

4

D

Stadium

E KN. SMYRNIS

Airport

P

GARÍTSA

DHIMOKRATIAS

NAFSIKAS

Áyios Athanassios

Áyii Iason & Sosípater

ETHEOTOKI

PALEOPOLIS

Early Christian Basilica

Villa

Mon Repos Estate

Mon Repos Beach

Temple of Artemis

Áyii Theódhori

Kanóni & **F**

| 0 | 300 m |

RESTAURANTS
Adherfi Theotoki	4
Iy Stina	1
Poco Loco	3
Sze Chuan	2

ACCOMMODATION
Atlantis	A
Bretagne	D
Corfu Palace	C
Europa	B
Phoenix	E
Royal	F

as Platía Saróko, and sometimes anglicized to San Rocco. **Car-drivers** should note that a new one-way system has been introduced, with an anticlockwise flow around the arterial road that runs along the seafront. Much of the centre is inaccessible by car, and poor for **parking**. The best official car park (€1.50 per day) is at the Old Port, and some streets in the vicinity operate a pay-and-display system (€1.50 tickets available from kiosks). Otherwise, it's best to park

Tours and trips from Corfu Town

Various trips and cruises are available from Corfu Town, perhaps the most interesting being the day-trip to nearby **Albania**. These tours (Tues, Thurs, Fri & Sun depart 9.30am) cross by hydrofoil from the Old Port to **Sarand'**, where an optional coach transfer takes you on to the extensive ancient ruins of **Butrint**, which has impressive structures from the Hellenistic, Roman, Byzantine and Venetian eras; later you return for a meal and shopping. Tours are much cheaper if booked directly through the operating agent in Corfu Town, Petrakis (☎26610/25 155 or 38 690, ⓦwww .ionian-cruises.com) at Ethnikís Andístasis 4, in the New Port. Prices direct from Petrakis are €30 to Sarand', plus €9 port taxes, and an extra €18.50 for the coach trip and buffet lunch.

Other enjoyable **boat cruises** include those to the satellite islands, Paxí and the mainland resort of Párga, as well as further afield to other Ionians. Prices vary but again they are considerably cheaper booked through an operating agent in Corfu Town than in the resorts. Apart from Petrakis (see above) the other main tour operator is Sarris at Venizélou 13 (☎26610/25 317, Ⓔsarriscruises@aias.gr), also in the New Port.

Though designed as a scheduled service rather than for day-trips, the most exciting recent development in Corfu tourism is the new **seaplane** service (ⓦwww .airsealines.com) to Paxí, which actually departs from the marina at Gouvia. It now also flies to Yiánnina on the mainland and hopes to expand to other islands and even to Brindisi in the near future.

---

outside the centre – there are quieter side streets in the Garítsa and Mandoúki districts, for example.

Corfu Town is best explored on foot, but if you're flagging, you might consider catching the theme park-style **miniature train** (€3.50), which runs from the far end of the Listón down the Garítsa seafront to the Mon Repos area (see p.85). The cute-looking horse-and-traps that you'll see touting for custom can be a fun way to get around, but cost a stiff €30 for a half-hour ride around the old town.

The **tourist office** (Mon–Fri 8am–2pm; ☎26610/37 520 or 37 638, ⒺE.O.T.corfu@otenet.gr) has been housed temporarily inside the Customs Building at the New Port. It is friendly and provides information on accommodation and transport; when they move to a new location, their telephone numbers will remain the same. A new **municipality kiosk** in the middle of Platía Saróko distributes free maps and brochures. Several publications provide useful **listings** information: the free monthly *Liston* magazine (bilingual Greek/English) includes a detailed calendar and entertainment suggestions; the monthly English-language *Corfiot* newspaper (€2) has interesting articles, as well as info on events, eating out and ferry and bus timetables; and, if your Greek is up to it, try the monthly *Exit stin Kérkyra* magazine (€2.50), which has cultural features, a great music section and nightlife tips. You should be able to find these publications in any bookshop or *períptero*.

Interesting Corfu-specific websites include the entertaining ⓦwww .corfuonline.gr (with a mailing list and message boards), and ⓦwww .corfuxenos.gr, which offers good historical and cultural sections, as well as practical information.

Accommodation

Accommodation in Corfu Town can be rather hard to come by, and when found, expensive and cramped – it's cold comfort to know that, because of the town's topography, even well-to-do apartments in the old town tend to be tiny. The surrounding bluffs hinder further construction, and the airport and adjacent farmland prevent much more expansion, so new accommodation developments have been squeezed north to Kondókali and beyond, and south to Pérama and further. Even in mid-winter the hotels can fill up with business-people; at least, unlike the resorts, the capital's hotels do remain open year round. At any time of year, it's best to call ahead.

Private rooms tend to be in the old town, and the Mandoúki area, near the two ports (though room owners much less frequently meet major ferry arrivals in the New Port than they used to). If you want to book in advance, the best place to contact is the Room Owners' Association, whose office is round the corner from the OTE office at D. Theotóki 2a, on the corner with Polylá (Mon–Fri 9am–1.30pm, plus Tues, Thurs & Fri 6–8pm; ☎26610/26 133, Ⓔoitkcrf@otenet.gr). A number of agencies near the Néo Froúrio also offer rooms in the Mandoúki area, including the seafront Katsaros Travel, Andhréa Kálvou 6 (☎26610/27 002, Ⓕ42 413). Budget travellers might be advised to head straight for a **campsite**, although the nearest one is 7km north towards Dhassiá (see p.91).

Inexpensive to moderate hotels

Astron Dónzelot 15 ☎26610/39 505 or 39 986, Ⓔhotel–astron@hol.gr. This long-standing travellers' favourite was completely renovated several years ago but has recently pegged back its prices, making it the best value hotel in the Old Port, with all mod cons. ❹

Atlantis Xenofóndos Stratigoú 48 ☎26610/35 560, Ⓔatlanker@mail.otenet.gr. Large and spacious air-con hotel in the New Port; its functional 1960s ambience rather lacks character. ❹

Bretagne Yeorgáki 27 ☎26610/30 724 or 35 690, ⓦwww.hotelbretagne.gr. Barely 100m from the airport runway, this is not the place for a quiet night, but it's useful if you're arriving late or leaving early. The rooms, all en-suite, are comfortable and modern, and there's a restaurant and bar. ❹

Europa Yitsiáli 10 ☎26610/39 304, Ⓕ26610/26 786. A small hotel one block back from the New

Port quay; handy if you're arriving by ferry, though rather shabby and disorganized. The cheaper rooms are with shared baths. ❸

Hermes Markorá 14 ☎26610/39 268 or 39 321, Ⓕ31 747. A hotel with average rooms, some with shared baths, and friendly staff. Its main drawback is that it overlooks a lively street market. ❸

🏃 **Phoenix** Khris. Smýrnis 2, Garítsa ☎26610/42 290, Ⓕ42 990. A small, stylish, good-value hotel between the airport and the seafront. Handy for flights at awkward hours. Breakfast included. ❸

Royal Kanóni ☎26610/37 512, ⓦwww.hotelroyal .gr. A huge, classically decorated hotel up on Kanóni hill with smart air-con rooms. Pool, bar and room balconies all offer views of the bay. Surprisingly good value. ❹

Upmarket hotels

Arcadion Kapodhistríou 44 ☎26610/37 670, ⓦwww.arcadionhotel.com. Upgraded but very overpriced hotel in a central setting, with en-suite rooms with balconies and views over the Listón and Spiánadha. Street noise can be a problem, especially at weekends. ❼

🏃 **Bella Venezia** N. Zambéli 4 ☎26610/46 500 or 44 290, ⓦwww.bellaveneziahotel .com. Best of the posher hotels: lovely, colourful Neoclassical building close to the *Cavalieri*, with all the *Cavalieri's* comforts but cheaper. ❻

Cavalieri Kapodhistríou 4 ☎26610/39 041 or 39

336, ⓦwww.cavalieri-hotel.com. Smart, plush and friendly, with great views and a roof bar open to the public. ❼

Corfu Palace Hotel Dhimokratías 2 ☎26610/39 485-7, ⓦwww.corfupalace.com. Luxury hotel with pools, landscaped gardens and magnificent rooms: but the bed linen is stiffly starched and the restaurant operates a dress code. ❽

Konstantinoupolis Zavitsiánou 1 ☎26610/48 716–7, ⓦwww.konstantinoupolis.com. Classy hotel in the Old Port, with tasteful decoration and comfortable rooms. ❻

The Town

Despite its modest size, Corfu Town is actually a collection of quite different areas, each with a distinct character. The compact **historic centre** – the area enclosed by the Old Port and the two forts – consists of several smaller districts: **Campiello**, the oldest, sits on the hill above the harbour; **Kofinéta** stretches towards the Spianádha (Esplanade); **Áyii Apóstoli** runs west of the Mitrópolis (Orthodox) cathedral; while tucked in beside the Néo Froúrio are **Ténedhos**, what remains of the old **Jewish quarter** ("Evraïkí" in Greek) and **Spiliá**. These districts form the core of the old town, and their tall, narrow alleys conceal some of Corfu's most beautiful architecture.

The town's main **commercial area** lies inland from the **Spianádha** (Esplanade), roughly between Y. Theotóki, Alexándhras and Kapodhistríou

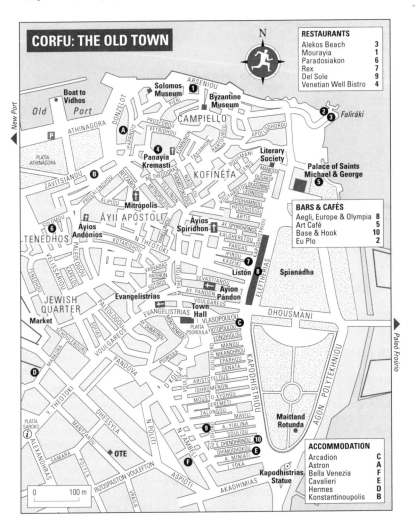

CORFU: THE OLD TOWN

N

RESTAURANTS
Alekos Beach	3
Mourayia	1
Paradosiakon	6
Rex	7
Del Sole	9
Venetian Well Bistro	4

BARS & CAFÉS
Aegli, Europe & Olympia	8
Art Café	5
Base & Hook	10
Eu Plo	2

ACCOMMODATION
Arcadion	C
Astron	A
Bella Venezia	F
Cavalieri	E
Hermes	D
Konstantinoupolis	B

0   100 m

If you're planning to visit more than just a couple of Corfu Town's sights, it's worth investing in a **combined ticket**, costing €8, which allows entry into the Paleó Froúrio and the Archeological, Asiatic and Byzantine museums, all described below.

streets, with most shops and boutiques around the meeting of Voulgaréous and Y. Theotóki and the streets radiating off Platía Saróko. The alleys between Theotóki and Platía Athinágora, in particular, are full of jewellery and craft shops. Tucked behind the corner of Platía Saróko and Odhós Theotóki is the old **morning market**, specializing in farm produce, fish and other comestibles. This is a lively place, full of exciting smells, and just the place to come if you're self-catering. **Mandoúki**, beyond the Old Port, is a commercial and dormitory area for the port, and well worth exploring, not least for its small bars and restaurants. The smarter areas of **San Rocco**, around the square of the same name, and **Garítsa**, to the west and south respectively, give a good idea of the town's nineteenth-century heyday, especially in the mansions of Odhós Alexándhras and the Garítsa seafront.

The Paleó Froúrio and the Néo Froúrio

Jutting up above its rooftops like two miniature volcanoes, Corfu Town's most obvious sights are the forts, the **Paleó Froúrio** (Mon–Fri 8am–7pm, Sat & Sun 8.30am–3pm; €4) and the **Néo Froúrio** (daily 9am–10pm; closes earlier off-season; €2). Their designations (*paleó* – "old", *néo* – "new") are a little misleading, since most of the visible exterior of both forts is the work of the Venetians over a period of less than two hundred years, and both were modified in tandem by subsequent occupiers. The Paleó Froúrio, however, had its origins in the sixth century after the ancient city was destroyed by the Goths, and was gradually fortified by the Byzantines, particularly in the eleventh century. Up to the thirteenth century it contained the town within its walls and was topped by two castellated towers until the Venetians replaced the old fortifications early in the fifteenth century. The Néo Froúrio was constructed by the Venetians on the hill of St Mark between 1572 and 1645, although the buildings within all date from the British occupation. They have both been damaged down the years by various besiegers and careless overlords.

The Paleó Froúrio is regarded as a masterpiece of military engineering, especially for the casemates inside the main western **bastions**, the largest in the Ionians, which face the municipal gardens across the moat. The small Venetian harbour, the artificial canal joining the northern harbour to the bay of Garítsa, the iron bridge across it (replacing two earlier ones), and the inner dry moat are all still there. Inside the passageway between the moats the **Corfu Byzantine collection** (Mon–Fri 8.30am–3pm) houses an interesting array of marble masonry, early mosaics, some delightful murals and a fine decorated parchment gospel.

The most noteworthy building in the fort is the Neoclassical **shrine of St George**, built by the British in the 1840s and consecrated as Orthodox after their departure; the six unfluted Doric columns reflect the prevailing taste for Classicism. The British barracks also survive. The latest contribution to the fort was an extensive if rather sterile 1990s renovation. Before you leave it's worth ascending the fort's highest point, the Land Tower, to admire sweeping views in all directions.

Looming above the old port, the **Néo Froúrio** is in some respects the more interesting of the two forts for the lay visitor to amble around. The entrance, tucked away at the back of the fort, up steps beyond the *Poco Loco* restaurant on

△ The Listón, Corfu Town

Odhós Solomoú, gives onto a complex of cellars, dungeons, tunnels and battlements, with excellent views over the old town and bay, and a small gallery and café at the summit. Among the British additions are the stone defensive building that crowns the fort and the brick one, overlooking the harbour and now used by the Corfu Naval Station. The **dry moat** that runs along the western side of the fort, starting by the market, is still in excellent condition and a fine example of its kind. Look out for the two lions of St Mark and Venetian inscriptions on the bastion walls above.

The Listón and the Spianádha

The **Listón**, an arcaded street designed during the French occupation, and the green **Spianádha** (Esplanade) it overlooks, are the focus of town life, even if the *kafenía* here charge exorbitant prices. People still play cricket on the Spianádha some afternoons, a tradition (like the local *tsitsibíra*, ginger beer) left over from the British administration, and it's possible to linger for hours over one drink. This is the venue for Corfu Town's evening *vólta*, a relaxed parade of strolling friends, couples and overdressed teenage posers. At the south end of the Spianádha, the **Maitland Rotunda**, now covered in graffiti, was constructed in 1821 to honour the first British High Commissioner of Corfu and the Ionian islands. Built in the form of a circular Ionic temple, it covers an earlier underground cistern. The neighbouring **statue of Ioannis Kapodhistrias** celebrates the local hero and consummate statesman (1776–1831), who led the diplomatic efforts for Greek independence and was made its first president in 1827.

The Palace of Saints Michael and George

Renovated for the 1994 EU summit – hence the incongruously space-aged glass structure to the rear – the interior of the **Palace of Saints Michael and George**, at the northern end of the Spianádha, is the grandest edifice left by the British in the region. It was built between 1819 and 1823 to honour British civil servants in the Ionians and Malta; the imposing statue on a moated pedestal in the gardens is of the British High Commissioner of the time, Sir Frederic Adam. The palace is currently barred to the public, apart from the section that houses the Asiatic Museum and the Municipal Art Gallery. The grounds of the palace are open, however, allowing you to admire the main facade, with a portico supported by twenty Doric columns running its whole length and bending round to the side wings. You can also pass through the two elaborate gates that you'll see, one for the road down to Faliráki Jetty, the other into the palace's magnificent gardens, to which you can gain limited (and free) access; they are a quiet haven containing a leafy café-bar.

Said to be the only one of its kind in Greece, the **Asiatic Museum** (Tues–Sun 8am–3pm; €3) is a must for aficionadoes of Far Eastern culture, and offers enough to detain the casual visitor. Amassed by Corfiot diplomat Grigorios Manos (1850–1929), the collection of over 10,000 pieces was given to the Greek government in 1926, and is displayed in elegant state rooms on the first floor of the palace. It includes Noh theatre masks, exquisite woodcuts, erotic wood and brass statuettes, samurai weapons and decorated screens and fans, as well as art works from Thailand, Korea and Tibet. A recently opened room on the ground floor houses Japanese artefacts from the seventeenth- to nineteenth-century Edu period, among them some exquisite costumes, paintings and tiny Buddhist statues. At the time of writing, plans were being discussed to extend the museum still further in order to display the remainder of the collection, as well as treasures privately amassed by other connoisseurs.

Opened in 1996, the **Municipal Art Gallery** (Tues–Sun 9am–5pm; €1.50) holds a small but growing permanent collection of contemporary art, much of it local. It also houses regular special exhibitions (Tues–Sun 9am–1pm & 6–9pm) – the ticket includes entry to both parts if you go when they are both open. It's well worth the visit to see what Greek artists are currently producing.

Opposite the west front of the palace, another elegant nineteenth-century building houses the **Literary Society of Corfu**, which is the oldest cultural institution in modern Greece and contains a vast collection of works on Corfu and the neighboring islands in Greek, English, French and other languages. There is also a growing collection of maps, engravings, photographs, periodicals and newspapers. The library is open to the public, but timing vary.

The Solomos and Byzantine museums

In a nearby back street off Arseníou, five minutes' walk from the palace, a former private house, restored in 1979, houses a museum dedicated to modern Greece's most famous poet, **Dhionysios Solomos** (Mon–Sat 9.30am–2pm; €1). Born on Zákynthos, Solomos was author of the poem *ýmnos is tin Eleftherían* ("Hymn to Liberty"), which was to become the Greek national anthem. He studied at Corfu's Ionian Academy, and lived in a house on this site for much of his life (it was destroyed in the war and rebuilt). The museum contains a small collection

---

The Ionian School of painting

The Ionian islands have a strong tradition of excellence in the fine arts, particularly iconography. They were in a unique position to bring Greece more in touch with mainstream developments in western European ideas and art, having spent centuries occupied by the Venetians and later the British, rather than by the Turks.

The founder of the **Ionian School of painting** is considered to be **Panayiotis Dhoxaras**, who was born in the Peloponnese in 1662 but, after studying in Venice and Rome, moved to Zákynthos and later lived and worked in Lefkádha and Corfu until his death in 1729. Until the late seventeenth century, religious art in the Ionians, as elsewhere, was dominated by the Cretan School; Crete was another Venetian possession, and there was a great deal of contact between the two islands. Exponents of this school were intent on maintaining the stylistic purity and dignified austerity of the Byzantine tradition. Dhoxaras, however, having absorbed the spirit of Italian Renaissance art, brought a greater degree of naturalism into iconography by showing his subjects, usually saints, in more human poses amid everyday surroundings. He is also credited with introducing the technique of **oil painting** into Greece in place of the older method of mixing pigments with egg yolk. He translated da Vinci's *Treatise on Painting* into Greek and published his own *Manual of Painting*. His most lauded work was the ceiling of Áyios Spyrídhon church in Corfu Town, which succumbed to damp in the mid-nineteenth century and had to be redone by Nikolaos Aspiotis. Originals of his do survive in the Panayía church of Áno Garoúna in Corfu and Áyios Dhimítrios in Lefkádha Town, among other places.

Dhoxaras' work was carried on by his son, Nikolaos, whose best work is the ceiling of Áyios Minás in Lefkádha Town, and over the next two centuries the tradition flourished through the skilled brushwork of a host of talented artists. Among these, **Yioryios Khrysoloras**, another eighteenth-century Corfiot, painted a number of the works on display at Corfu's Byzantine Museum; the Zakynthian **Nikolaos Kandounis** (1768–1834), creator of *The Last Supper* and *Washing of the Feet* at the Panayía Platytéra, was another prolific exponent; and three generations of the Proselandis family, starting with **Pavlos Proselandis** (1784–1837), have left work in various locations. Other artists of the school are mentioned in appropriate sections of the text.

of Solomos manuscripts and effects but, frustratingly, is labelled solely in Greek. If you're also travelling to Zákynthos, visit the far more enlightening museum dedicated to the native poet there (see p.238).

Up a short flight of steps from Arseníou, the splendid **Byzantine Museum** (Tues–Sun 8.30am–3pm; €2) is housed in the restored church of the Panayía Andivouniótissa (it is also known by this name), which dates from the mid-sixteenth century. It houses Christian and pre-Christian artefacts, religious and secular, including sculptures and sections of mosaic floors from Paleópo-lis, Byzantine church **frescoes**, a collection of ninety **icons** dating from the fifteenth to nineteenth centuries, and other religious artefacts from around the island. The collection of Byzantine art is one of the finest in the country, rivalling that of the Byzantine Museum in Athens. Some of the more striking images are the dark, gruesome depictions of a beheaded John the Baptist, triumphant scenes of St George slaying the dragon and a moving portrayal of Christ trampling down the gates of Hell to rescue the holy dead. The anticlockwise direction from the entrance follows a generally chronological order, and culminates in the centre with the atmospherically recreated inner shrine.

Áyios Spyrídhon Church

A block behind the Listón, down Ay. Spyrídhonos, stands the most famous structure on the whole island: the **church of Áyios Spyrídhon** (daily 8am–9pm), whose maroon-domed campanile, the highest on the island, dominates the town and serves as a handy navigation mark. It is dedicated to **St Spyridon**, a bishop of Cyprus and prominent father of Orthodoxy, who was born in the late third century and whose relics were kept in Constantinople until the fall of the Byzantine empire, when refugees managed to salvage them. Having finally arrived on Corfu in 1489, the relics were credited with saving the islanders from a famine in 1553: a sea captain carrying grain claimed that the saint appeared to him in a dream and told him to take it to Corfu. Since then Spyridhon is said to have saved the island from various plagues, invasions and other disasters. His position as **patron saint** is reflected in the popularity of the name Spyros; it can seem that just about every other male here answers to it.

The saint's mysteriously preserved body is kept in a silver and ebony **sarcophagus** near the altar, and on Palm Sunday, Easter Saturday, August 11 and the first Sunday in November, he is paraded through the city. For days leading up to these festivals the casket is opened for the faithful, who queue up to view its contents. Corfiots visiting the shrine on his name day (December 12) kiss his robe to petition for good luck. St Spyridhon is believed by some to be a peripatetic saint, given to the odd *vólta* around town by himself, and each year he's given a new pair of slippers; apocryphal lore holds that the old slippers have been found scuffed from use.

This "new" church was built in 1590 after the original, founded in the fifteenth century in the suburb of San Rocco, had to be destroyed because of structural faults. The ceiling features ornate gilt-framed scenes from the saint's life, nineteenth-century copies of earlier originals by the painter Panayiotis Dhoxaras, leader and instigator of the Ionian School (see box on p.81), which were destroyed by damp. One of the most interesting scenes depicts St Spyridhon breaking a tile into its constituent elements of earth, water and fire, thus demonstrating the tripartite nature of God to support the doctrine of the Trinity. The exquisite iconostasis of white Parian marble has a finely balanced picture of the *Last Supper* in its central upper panel. On the wall to its right is a splendid icon of the saint, dressed in a brown robe patterned with repeated crosses, by eighteenth-century local artist Konstandinos Kondarinis and considered to be the finest on the island.

Orthodox architecture in Corfu

Almost without exception, **Corfu's churches** contain delightfully rich interiors within extremely plain, even drab exteriors. Many are tiny, single-nave basilicas, most with the standard narthex or vestibule on the west side. The sanctuary traditionally lies at the east end of the nave but, given the tight margins of a town like Corfu, the alignment is sometimes not compass-perfect.

The sanctuary itself usually has two, sometimes three, niches: one is for vessels and the preparation of communion, the other acts as a vestry. The altar, invariably with an exquisite crucifix as its centrepiece, always lies on the church's central axis. The sanctuary is divided from the nave by the iconostasis, which gradually replaced the lower barrier of Byzantine times, and is accessed through three doors. This division symbolizes the separation of the divine and the mundane, the triple entrance the trinity.

A common element of all Orthodox churches, and undoubtedly the feature most people would associate with the Eastern Church in general, is the predominance of **icons**. These are not mere decorations, but objects of worship in their own right and an intrinsic part of the ceremony. In Corfu, with its strong artistic traditions, these are often lavish, colourful and highly stylized. The icons on the iconostasis are arranged according to a strict order. The four in the first tier display Christ, the Virgin Mary, John the Baptist and, on the right, in a tradition unique to Corfu, a "guest" saint not connected to that particular church. The second tier usually portrays the twelve apostles, while at the top are icons of the Virgin Mary and John the Evangelist mourning Christ. Other devotional icons are often placed on stands around the nave; devotional icons (ie, icons that are themselves objects of veneration) are often covered in *oklad*, a technical Russian term for the silver cladding which covers all but the face and sometimes hands of the holy figure.

The Mitrópolis

The other unmissable church in Corfu Town is the **Mitrópolis** (Orthodox Cathedral), which stands above a square of the same name near the Old Port. Originally built in 1577 as Panayía Spiliótissa (The Virgin of the Grotto) because of a nearby cave, it is still sometimes referred to by that name. The exterior is typically plain, although the front was modernized in Baroque style in the early twentieth century. Within, the Mitrópolis boasts a wealth of Orthodox art. Apart from another splendid iconostasis, some fragments of seventeenth-century frescoes and the expected array of beautiful icons from different epochs, there are three remarkable paintings of scenes from the Old Testament on the side walls, by unknown artists. There is also some excellent wrought-ironwork on the grilles to either side of the main door and on the railing that separates the raised area before the iconostasis from the rest of the nave.

The Mitrópolis has its resident saint too: in a casket beside the altar lies the body of **St Theodora**, which was rescued from Constantinople at the same time as that of St Spyridhon. Theodora was born in Asia Minor in 815 and later married to Emperor Theophilos, taking over the reins of empire on his death until her son attained majority. She was renowned for her beauty and accomplishments, but her greatest achievement was to re-establish the cult of icons at a brilliant ceremony in Ayía Sofia, Constantinople, on March 11, 843, thus ending the bitter controversy over their veneration that had riven the Orthodox world for a century. She was canonized for this act, which is still celebrated on the first Sunday of Lent; since 1985, her body has been solemnly paraded around the streets on that day.

The Archeological Museum

Corfu Town's **Archeological Museum** (Tues–Sun 8.30am–3pm; €3; full wheelchair access), a few blocks south from the Maitland Rotunda, just off the seafront, is the biggest and best in the archipelago, and the ideal place to catch a glimpse of ancient Corfu, at least in the form of architectural details and artefacts from the era. It contains fragments of Neolithic weapons and cookware, coins, pots and sculpture from the Corinthian era, and Roman architectural features. Most of the collection is upstairs, though the lobby area does contain a few noteworthy exhibits, including bronze statues from different periods, some fourth-century BC armour and a fine stone relief showing the abduction of Persephone from the first century AD.

On reaching the upper level, admire the grave stelae and funerary objects in the vestibule, before entering the central door to the **Lion of Menekrates Room**. The centrepiece is a magnificent crouching lion believed to be the work of a seventh-century BC Corinthian craftsman – it's an extremely rare example of early stone sculpture and was probably placed on a tomb as a guardian of the dead. Straight ahead, in the **Gorgon Room**, is the museum's most impressive exhibit: the massive west pediment excavated from the Archaic temple of Artemis at Paleópolis, just south of Corfu Town: at around 17m long, this dominates the entire room, its mesmerizing central Gorgon figure flanked by panthers and battle scenes between the gods. The room also contains a huge pediment, from an unidentified Classical building discovered near Kanóni in 1973, and a fine sixth-century BC *kouros* head. In the adjoining **Mon Repos Room** there's a variety of finds from the estate of that name (see below), including tools, jewellery and figurines, as well as an impressive temple pediment dating from 500 BC, depicting a Dionysiac symposium. Next door, the **Apollo Parnopios Room** includes an anonymous copy of the famous Athenian statue by Pheidias after which the room is named. Rounding off the collection is the **Numismatic Room**, which predictably showcases a wide selection of ancient coins, but also displays ceramics and household objects from the cemetery at Garítsa.

The British Cemetery

South of Platía Saróko and signposted on the corner of Methodhíou and Kolokotróni, just beyond the psychiatric hospital, the **British Cemetery** – which is still used for civilian burials – features some elaborate civic and military memorials. Most notable is a memorial to the 44 seamen killed in a naval incident in 1946, when an Albanian vessel sank two British warships, leading to the severing of diplomatic ties between the countries. Despite its grim history, the cemetery is a quiet green space away from the madness of Platía Saróko at any time of the year, and in spring and early summer it blooms with dozens of species of orchids and other exotic flowers.

Around Corfu Town

On the outskirts of the city are a number of interesting places that you can easily visit in a morning or afternoon. The nearest to town are the lush **Mon Repos** estate and the scattered remains of the neighbouring ancient city of **Paleópolis**. More popular are the picturesque pairing of **Vlahérna** convent and **Pondikoníssi** islet, further south, and the grandiose **Achílleion Palace** in Gastoúri. Two other day-trips worth considering are the relatively unknown **Vídhos** islet and the ever-popular **Aqualand**.

Mon Repos and Paleópolis

Around the bay from the Rotunda and Archeological Museum, and tucked behind popular Mon Repos beach, the estate around **Mon Repos** villa contains some of the most accessible archeological remains on the island. The **villa** itself, a Neoclassical structure built by British High Commissioner Frederic Adam in 1824, became the property of the Greek royal family when Britain ceded the island to Greece in 1864. The Corfu authorities stirred up a minor international spat in 1996 – at least in right-wing British tabloids – when they unilaterally took over the property – where Prince Philip was born – and began to redevelop it for public visits. The Regency-period villa (daily in summer 8.30am–3pm; €3) has now been tastefully renovated and converted into the **Paleópolis Museum** (daily 8.30am–7pm; closes 3pm in winter; €3), containing a range of ancient pottery and other remains from the area, as well as period furnishings and contemporary art exhibitions. The octagonal atrium, which opens above you on the first-floor landing, is attractively decorated with azure and white plaster reliefs and two rows of semi-circular windows.

The estate's **grounds** (daily 8am–7pm; closes 5pm in winter; €2) make a pleasant shady walk, the thick woodlands concealing the remains of two **Doric temples** dedicated to Hera and Poseidon respectively. The first has some recognizable features such as an altar and fragments of columns, while the second, near the low cliffs overlooking the coast, is better preserved, with walls, foundations, columns and other details partly excavated in a pit. The gardens are home to a number of rare flowers and orchids and are particularly splendid in spring and early summer. It takes about half an hour to reach the estate and surrounding suburbs on foot from the centre of town; otherwise you can get there on blue bus #2.

The suburbs inland from Mon Repos are dotted with remains of different periods, collectively known as **Paleópolis**, from the site of ancient Corcyra (Corfu). Most impressive is the **Early Christian Basilica** (Tues–Sun 8.30am–3pm; free), which stands opposite the entrance to the estate on Náfsikas. The earliest remnants date from the fifth century and recent excavations have revealed parts of the south side, the atrium, the narthex and the sanctuary apse. The church was built by Bishop Jovian on the site of the Roman agora, fragments of which lie beside the wooden walkway that allows easy access to the site. The partial remains of the **Roman baths** on the opposite side of the road to the entrance are closed, but can be glimpsed through the fence. There are also a few fallen columns left of the **Temple of Artemis**, where the Gorgon pediment (see opposite) was found, strewn in a field several hundred metres to the west, towards the Halikiopoúlou lagoon.

Back down Náfsikas, towards town, a couple of blocks from the Garítsa seafront, the other most notable site of Paleópolis is the eleventh-century **Áyii Iáson and Sosípater**. This two-columned church, capped by a single dome, is considered to be the most important Middle Byzantine building on the island. Parts of the exterior walls and the chunky marble columns inside were taken from the ancient city. Sadly only a few of the original frescoes, painted between the eleventh and fourteenth centuries, remain, though the splendid chancel screen from the fifteenth century still survives. Entry times to the church are a little erratic, but it seems to open most days.

Vlahérna and Pondikoníssi

The best-known excursion from Corfu Town is to the islets of Vlahérna and Pondikoníssi, nearly 3km south of town – you can either walk there, along the road past Mon Repos beach or over the causeway that crosses the lagoon from

△ Vlahérna monastery

Pérama to the south, or take blue bus #2 from Platía Saróko to the suburb of Kanóni (20min). Alternatively, the excursion boat *Captain Andreas* (hourly; €7 return) makes the trip from the Old Port during the summer months. Joined to the mainland by a short causeway, the tiny white convent of **Vlahérna** is surrounded by tall cypresses, and must be one of the most photographed images in Greece. The crowds, however, as well as the roar from planes at the nearby airport, significantly detract from what can look like an idyllic setting through a camera lens. Just out in the bay, the small wooded island of **Pondikoníssi** (aka Mouse Island) can be reached by a short boat trip from the dock (€2.50 return). According to legend, it's the petrified remains of one of Odysseus's ships, an act of revenge by Poseidon after the blinding of Polyphemus in the cave – although it's only one of a number of rocks in the region that are said to be this vessel. Barely a hundred metres across, Pondikoníssi contains a deserted twelfth-century Byzantine chapel and a seasonal café. The islet suffers from brief but intense overpopulation by day-trippers, so it's best to go early or late in the day.

Vídhos

A far quieter destination than Vlahérna and Pondikoníssi is **Vídhos**, the larger wooded island visible from the port in Corfu Town. Vídhos has been a strategic point in defending, and attacking, Corfu over the centuries, and over the years has been the site of a prison, a cemetery and an execution ground. Regardless of its history, it's a pleasant place for a picnic and is uninhabited apart from a seasonal scout camp. A shuttle *kaïki* (€1 return) plies between the Old Port and Vídhos hourly, the last one returning at 1.30am to encourage people to dine at the municipally owned restaurant and bar. With a fine range of dishes at reasonable prices, pleasant but not overbearing live music and unparalleled views of the illuminated forts and old town, this makes for a great evening out.

Hard by the Vídhos *kaïki* moors the *Calypso Star*, a large, glass-bottomed, semi-submersible boat, which, for €15 a head (children half-price), takes parties out to explore the waters around Vídhos and to see divers at work.

Achilleion Palace

Built in 1890–91 as a summer residence for the lonely and neurotic Empress Elizabeth of Austria, the Neoclassical folly of the **Achilleion Palace** (daily summer 8am–7pm, winter 9am–3pm; €6) attracts a huge number of coach tours, despite an alarming mishmash of styles that led Henry Miller to describe it (in *The Colossus of Maroussi*) as a "madhouse" and "the worst piece of gimcrackery I have ever laid eyes on". It's certainly a curiosity in its setting, but no more interesting than an average minor country house in England – those on a tight schedule could avoid it with few qualms. If you're tempted, it's located on the edge of Gastoúri, over 5km southwest through the badlands of suburban Corfu, and therefore best reached on the dedicated blue bus #10 from Platía Saróko.

The **house** itself is not particularly large, and only half a dozen ground-floor rooms are open. Pause to take in the colourful, if rather overdone, ceiling painting in the entrance hall. On display inside you'll find furniture, portraits, statuary, jewellery and bas-reliefs, as well as personal effects of the empress and of Kaiser Wilhelm II, who bought the Achilleion after her assassination by an Italian anarchist in 1898. It's difficult to really appreciate the displays as, like much of the building, they're roped off and festooned with "Do not touch" signs.

The terraced **gardens**, planted mainly with indigenous flora, are more worthwhile than the interior. The different tiers afford a range of vantage points with fine views over town and coast. The surrounding flowerbeds are magnificent, and a beautiful double pergola leads to Herter's monumental statue of **The Dying Achilles**, from whom the building takes its name ("I want a palace… worthy of Achilles," the empress is reported to have said). A closed path leads down to the remains of **Kaiser's Bridge**, destroyed by the Nazis, ironically, so they could roll their panzers underneath it. The structure used to span the coast road and led to an elegant Neoclassical stone jetty, which still survives.

You may well find yourself being invited into the tasting room of *Vassilakis* distillery, right opposite the Achilleion entrance, for a nip of liqueurs made with kumquats and other fruit. This is a harmless diversion, especially if you haven't tried the sticky concoction, and there is no compulsion to buy a bottle.

Aqualand

If you are on holiday with children or are a child at heart, then you will probably want or be coerced to visit **Aqualand** (daily: May–Oct 10am–6pm; July & Aug till 7pm; €19, 5–12yrs €13, under 5yrs free; after 3pm €14, under-12s €10), Corfu's well-advertised "water paradise" at Áyios Ioánnis, 5km west of Corfu Town. Reckoned to be one of the biggest water parks in Europe, it features multiple opportunities to get wet on attractions with names like Black Hole, Kamikaze, Hydro-tube and Twister, as well as the usual assortment of pools with slides and diving boards. Plenty of overpriced junk food and drinks are available in time-honoured theme-park tradition. The dedicated blue bus #8 leaves regularly from Platía Saróko, but be warned that Aqualand gets very crowded in high season with bus tours from all over the island.

Eating

It is a pity that so many visitors to Corfu Town return to the resort where they're based for their evening meal, as the island's capital offers the variety of eating possibilities that you would expect of a cultured town. Most **restaurants** are in or around the old town, with some hard-to-find places favoured by locals concealed in the maze of the Campiello. Restaurants on the main thorough-fares – the Listón, Arseníou, around Platía Saróko – tend to be fast, snacky and indifferent. The Garítsa seafront has a number of excellent fish restaurants with outdoor seating and views of the bay, although you need to be careful what you order to avoid an exorbitant bill. All the places listed below are open year round unless stated otherwise.

Adherfi Theotoki M. Athanassíou, Garítsa. By far the best of the several establishments tucked behind the seafront park, this simple taverna offers fresh fish, seafood and tasty *mezédhes* at decent prices and has occasional live music.

Alekos Beach Faliráki jetty. Sharing the tiny harbour below the palace with stunning views of the Paleó Froúrio, this place offers simple meat and fish dishes at good prices. Summer only.

Del Sole Guildford 17. The town's most authentic Italian food is available at little more than taverna prices. A range of *antipasti* such as smoked salmon, mussels or cheese and mushroom croquettes can be followed by tagliatelle or spaghetti dishes, or main courses like marinated beef or fish and clams in wine sauce.

🏃 **Mourayia** Arseníou 15–17. One of the best seafront establishments, this unassuming and good-value *ouzerí*, near the Byzantine Museum, serves a range of tasty *mezédhes*, including sausage and seafood such as mussels and shrimp.

To Paradosiakon Solomoú 20. A family *estiatório*, one block back from Platía Athinágora, this is one of the more genuine places in the vicinity of the Old Port. Although prices reflect the tourist location, the service is welcoming and the oven-baked food is fresh and filling. Particularly recommended is the *kokkinistó*, beef in red sauce.

Poco Loco 1st Párodhos Solomoú 1, Spiliá. At the foot of the steps to the Néo Froúrio, this newly converted Tex-Mex restaurant serves a range of reasonably priced Mexican favourites and slightly pricier items like ostrich and kangaroo.

Rex Kapodhistríou, behind the Listón. Pricey, but some of the best oven-baked food in the centre, mixing Greek with north European. Outdoor seating on the busy pedestrianized street.

Iy Stina Xenofóndos Stratigoú 78, Mandoúki. Quaint traditional taverna one block back from the seafront, serving a fine range of *mezédhes* and main courses, including good meat dishes from the oven.

Sze Chuan Ethnikis Andístasis 61. If you need a break from Greek food, this Chinese restaurant in the New Port provides all the old favourites, but at a price. Closed Mon.

🏃 **Venetian Well Bistro** Platía Kremastí. One of the best-kept secrets in Corfu, mainly because it's so difficult to find, tucked away in a tiny square a few alleys to the northeast of the Mitrópolis. It offers an unusually exotic Greek menu, expensive but with large portions of special-ities such as Iraqi lamb and Albanian calves' livers done in *ouzo*. One warning: beyond the barrelled variety, the wine-list prices climb alarmingly. Some-times closes Mon.

Cafés and Nightlife

Kérkyra Town has a plethora of **cafés**, most noticeably lining Listón, the main pedestrianized cruising street. None of these popular establishments is cheap, but among the more reasonable are the *Aegli, Europa* or *Olympia*, all guaranteed to be packed from morning till late at night. *En Plo* on Faliráki jetty, however, has an unbeatably brilliant and breezy setting and is much quieter, as is the leafy *Art Café*, behind the Palace of SS Michael and George.

The hippest youth **bars** in town are the trio on Kapodhistríou adjacent to the *Cavalieri* hotel, of which *Hook* is the rockiest and *Base* offers a mixture of pop, rock and dance sounds. The rooftop bar at the *Cavalieri* itself is more middle-of-the-road musically but can be heaven at night, given the views and the breeze.

Club action takes place at Corfu's self-proclaimed **disco** strip, a couple of kilometres north of town, past the New Port. This only revs up after midnight, when it becomes classic *kamáki* territory, although in summer many of its macho regulars forsake it for the resorts in order to hunt foreign females. The currently "in" joints are *Privilege*, a standard disco, *Au Bar*, a large indoor club which mixes in some Latin, *Elxis*, which boasts an impressive lightshow for its Euro/Greek sounds, and *Cristal*, whose DJs favour trance and ethnic.

Listings

American Express Kapodhistríou 20a (Mon–Fri 8am–2pm; ⑦ 26610/30 883).

Banks and exchange The town's banks are almost all based on Y. Theotóki, and around Platía Saróko; most have cash dispensers that accept international credit and debit cards. There are also many other 24hr ATMs around Platía Saróko, near the Listón and at the ports.

Beaches and lidos There are no beaches in town, but two lidos offer deep-water swimming off jetties and platforms. The main lido is at Faliráki, below the palace, reached by the sunken road leading down from the corner of Arseníou and Kapodhistríou (daily 8am–7pm; €1.20); it has loungers, changing facilities and a café. The second is the free public swimming area to the south of the Old Fort near the *Corfu Palace Hotel*. Mon Repos Beach, a small private beach of imported sand at Garítsa, a 15-minute walk south of the Spianádha (daily 9am–7pm; €1.20), is very popular with townspeople. There's a bar and taverna, changing rooms, showers, toilets, sunbeds and a diving jetty, plus the ancient ruins behind.

Bookshops Surprisingly for a town with such British connections, there is no real specialist English bookshop. Lykoudis, on Platía Yiorgáki (⑦ 26610/39 845) and Xenoglosso, Y. Markorá 45 (⑦ 26610/23 923), have a limited selection of fact and fiction and stock English magazines, as well as attractive local art cards and photos; bog-standard bestsellers are available at kiosks and tourist shops all over the island.

Bowling Close to the major junction beyond disco strip, Starbowl offers multiple bowling lanes as well as pool tables.

Bus departures Corfu Town's suburbs, and outlying resorts as far south as Benítses and north to Dhassiá, are served by the blue bus system, which is based in Platía Saróko. Some services, notably to Benítses, depart from a stop 100m down Methodhíou, the road leaving the square by the bus stand. For conductorless buses you'll have to buy tickets either at the square's bus stand or the *kafenío* by the Methodhíou bus stop. Island-wide and mainland services leave the KTEL green bus station on Avramíou near the New Port. You'll need to buy tickets for Athens and Thessaloníki in the terminal office; all other tickets can be bought on board.

Car rental Avis, Ethnikís Andístasis 42 ⑦ 26610/24 404, at the airport ⑦ 26610/42 007, ⓦ www.avis.com; Budget, Venizélou 32 ⑦ 26610/28 590, at the airport ⑦ 26610/28 208, ⓦ www.budget.com; Hertz, Ethnikí Lefkímis ⑦ 26610/38 388, at the airport ⑦ 26610/35 547, ⓦ www.hertz.com. Among local companies, try Sunrise, Ethnikís Andístasis 14 ⑦ 26610/44 325, or Ocean, Venizélou 22 ⑦ 26610/32 351, both in the New Port.

Cinemas Corfu Town's two cinemas – the winter Orfeus on the corner of Akadhimías and Aspióti and the open-air summer Phoenix down the side street opposite – both show mostly English-language films. Tickets cost €8.

Consulates Eire, Kapodhistríou 20A ⑦ 26610/32 469; UK, Menekrátous 1 ⑦ 26610/30 055. Citizens of Australia, Canada, New Zealand and the US will need to contact their embassy in Athens; there are some consulates of other countries in Corfu; the tourist office will have contact numbers in either case.

Emergencies Ambulance ⑦ 166; Police ⑦ 100; urban fire ⑦ 199; forest fire ⑦ 191.

Ferry offices There are ticket agencies inside the New Port buildings, and franchises of the major ferry companies bunched together along the seafront road opposite: Agoudimos ⑦ 26610/80 030, ⓦ www.agoudimos-lines.com; Anek ⑦ 26610/24 503, ⓦ www.anek.gr; Fragline ⑦ 26610/38 089, ⓦ www.fragline.gr; Minoan ⑦ 26610/25 000, ⓦ www.minoan.gr; SNAV ⑦ 26610/36 439, ⓦ www.snav.it; Superfast ⑦ 26610/32 467, ⓦ www.superfast.com and Ventouris ⑦ 26610/21 212, ⓦ www.ventouris.gr. High-season ferries to Italy fill quickly, especially car spaces, so phoning ahead is advised. Tickets for other ferries are usually available prior to departure at booths or agencies near the quay.

Hospital On the corner of I. Andhreádhi and Polykhroníou Konstánda, off Platía Saróko ⑦ 26610/45 811–7 or 25 400.

Internet Full Internet facilities are available at X-plore, N. Lefterióti 4, near Platía Saróko; the rate of €4 per hour is much less expensive than the places near the Listón.

Laundry There are at least three ancient *plyndíria* hidden in the alleys of Corfu Town. Most central is the Kyknos on Néa Paleológou, behind the Pisteos Bank on Voulgaréos. Also handy is the Perioteri, in the first block of I. Theotóki off Platía Saróko, and the Christos, tucked in an alleyway to the left of the Orthodox cathedral's front entrance. A reasonable load will cost around €10 and come back freshly ironed.

Motorbike rental Most bike rental firms are based in or around the New Port: try Atlantis, Xen. Stratigoú 48 ☎ 26610/23 665, or Easy Rider, 3rd Párodhos E. Venizélou 4 ☎ 26610/43 026. Both have competitive rates and are open to a little bargaining.

Police Alexándhras 19 ☎ 26610/38 661 or 39 509.

Port Authority in the New Port for up-to-date sailings: domestic ☎ 26610/32 655, international ☎ 26610/30 481.

Post office Corner of Alexándhras and Zafirópoulou (Mon–Fri 7.30am–8pm).

Taxis There are taxi ranks at the airport; by the New and Old Ports (☎ 26610/37 993); at the Spianádha end of the Listón (☎ 26610/39 926); and on Platía Saróko (☎ 26610/30 383). Alternatively, call Radio Taxi (☎ 26610/33 811–2).

Tourist police Samartzí 4, Platía Saróko ☎ 26610/30 265.

Travel Agents Corfu Town is crawling with travel agents, especially around the New Port and Platía Saróko. Two, which are recommended for a variety of services, including cheap flights to Britain and northern Europe, are: Corfu Infotravel, Ethnikís Andístasis 14, New Port (☎ 26610/41 550, ⓦ www.corfuinfotravel.gr), and Eurocorfu Travel, Alexándhras 40, Platía Saróko (☎ 26610/46 886, ⓔ eurocorfu@oneway.gr).

The northeast and the north coast

The northeast is the most stereotypically Greek part of Corfu: mountainous, with a rocky coastline chopped into pebbly bays and coves, above a sea that's often as clear as a swimming pool. A green **bus** route between Corfu Town and Kassiópi serves the resorts on the single coastal road, along with some blue suburban bus services as far as Dhassiá. Another bus runs along the north coast between Kassiópi and Sidhári, but otherwise the north coast resorts – as far west as brash Sidhári and the nearby hill town of Avliótes – are served by direct buses from Corfu Town that travel via often spectacular inland routes.

Kondókali and Gouviá

The landscape immediately to the north of Corfu Town, as far as Kondókali, is little more than motorway and industrial sites, and has about as much rural charm as Brooklyn or Lewisham. Things don't improve much at **KONDÓKALI** itself, a small village once overrun by tourists, which serves the nearby marina at Gouviá. The old town consists of a gently curving street with a number of bars, such as *Beer Busket* and *Arches*, which regularly features live blues. Eating options on the main street include a couple of traditional *psistariés* such as *Gerekos* and several smarter restaurants, such as *Flags*, with an imaginative menu (fish and steaks in exotic sauces) aimed at the yachting fraternity, who comprise much of Kondókali's passing trade; *Lithari*, a pricey music taverna popular with well-heeled Greeks; and the chic new *George Boileau* bistro at the north end, which serves French-style dishes, such as chicken fillets with walnuts and dried figs, for €10 or above. There's very little independent accommodation here and no reason for the uncommitted traveller to stay, although it's fine for an evening: many holiday lets reverted to domestic tenancies during the tourism slump in the 1990s and these days, mercifully, not even many package tourists find themselves billeted here.

Kondókali's neighbouring resort, **GOUVIÁ**, the site of Corfu's largest yachting **marina**, and the launching point of most flotilla and bareboat holidays, is a marked improvement, with a mini buzz about the place. The spacious marina is also the launching point of the much-fanfared **seaplane** service to Paxí (see p.129). Besides the marina facilities and several unappealing luxury hotels on the main highway, the village boasts a few small **hotels**, notably the *Hotel Aspa* (☎ 26610/91 165; ❸) and the *Hotel Popi Star* (☎ 26610/91 500,

E popistar@otenet.gr; **④**), both on the main road. The best source of **rooms** is Karoukas Travel (T 26610/91 596, W www.karoukas-travel.com; **②** and up) on the main street. Catering to a mixture of yachties and package tourists are a number of decent **restaurants**, including *Vergina* and *Gorgona*, both of which specialize in fish and have a good range of *mezédhes*; *La Bonita*, a decent pizzeria; the excellent cheap grill-house *Steki*; and *Gandhi*, an over-decorated but reasonable Indian restaurant. For a **drink** and bop, among the slew of nightspots are the Brit-oriented *Irish Knights* bar and the nearby *Kingsize* club, which draws youngsters from Corfu Town. Hackers Internet Café allows you to surf the Net for €5 per hour. The very narrow shingle **beach**, barely 5m wide in parts, shelves into sand, but given the amount of yacht traffic in the area, water quality must be at best uncertain. Behind the fenced-in marina are the skeletal remains of a **Venetian armoury**, an almost surreal collection of stone buttresses standing in a meadow.

Dhafníla, Dhassiá and Káto Korakiána

Two kilometres beyond Gouviá lies **DHAFNÍLA**, whose small, wooded, pebbly bay is much quieter than the commercial strip of **DHASSIÁ**, just beyond. The former strand is bordered by an appealing river outlet and has just the *Corfiotis* taverna for sustenance – there is nowhere to stay at the beach. The latter, though busy, does offer paragliding and other **watersports**, run by three outfits: Corfu Ski Club, Club 2001 and Dassia Ski Club. Two large A-class **hotels**, the *Dasia Chandris* and *Corfu Chandris* (both T 26610/97 100–3, W www.chandris.gr **⑦**), dominate Dhassiá. The hotels are next to each other on the main road but set in their own extensive grounds, with pools and sports facilities, shops, restaurants, bars and beach frontages. Both take block bookings from north European package companies, but have rooms available for most of the season. A notch or two below these, the *Livadi Nafsika* (T 26610/93 276 or 93 174, W www.eleabeach .com; **⑥**) is a good upper mid-range option with pleasant en-suite rooms and its own pools and gardens, set back from the main road opposite the *Chandris* hotels. There are numerous other places to stay near the main road or down by the beach; the best beachside hotels are the large jointly run *Dassia Beach/Dassia Margarita* (T 26610/93 224, F 93 864; **④**) and more modest *Spiros Beach* (T 26610/93 666; **③**). Private **rooms** are scarce in the resort and are best found through Emka Travel (T 26610/93 738, W www.emkatravel.com; from **②**), or try *Hermes Apartments* (T 26610/93 314, E hermesdasia@in.gr; **③**), studios are located on the main road.

The area has the best **campsite** on the island and the closest to Corfu Town, *Dionysus Camping Village* (T 26610/91 417 or 93 785, W www.dionysuscamping .gr) back in Dhafníla. As well as camping space under terraced olive trees, *Dionysus* has simple bungalow huts (**①**), a pool, shop, bar and restaurant. The camp attracts an international crowd, and the friendly, multilingual owners offer a ten-percent discount to Rough Guide readers. Another more family-oriented campsite, *Karda Beach Camping* (T & F 26610/93 595), is situated off the main road on the north side of Dhassiá.

Eating in the Dhassiá area is mostly a functional affair. Many of the seaside hotels have adequate restaurants with staple dishes on offer, and competition keeps prices reasonable – try *Andreas* for tasty fish, meat and salads. The *Karydia* on Dhassiá's main drag is a popular weekend escape for townsfolk and a cut above most, with an extensive menu of meat and fish served in delicious sauces. On the main road through Dhafníla, the *Greco* taverna is famed for excellent home cooking, such as freshly baked Ioánnina-style pies with a variety of fillings, and good Macedonian barrelled wine. The hottest **nightspots** are trendy *Malibu*, which churns out ethnic and dance music in the centre of Dhassiá beach, and the nearby *Pagoda*, with a spacious patio.

Dhassiá is also the location of the most respected British **general prac-titioner** on the island, Dr John Yannopapas. The surgery (T 26610/97 811, emergencies (mobile T 6932/456 328) is on the opposite side of the main road to the *Corfu Chandris* and displays a prominent Union Jack.

Dhassiá's tourist development has started spreading up towards the once tradi-tional inland village of **KÁTO KORAKIÁNA**, known to locals as Katoméri. Package-tour accommodation is sprouting up along the leafy lanes and there is an increasing number of **bars** and **restaurants**, yet the village, with its bougainvillea-splashed houses, still retains some of its character, and can come as a welcome relief from the buzzing environs of the seaside below. For a good spread of tasty *mezédhes* try *Rosie's Restaurant* or enjoy a refreshing drink at the *Escape* cocktail bar or the oddly named *60 Needles* café. If you want to stay here, try the simple but great-value *Villa Athina* (T 26610/97 252; ❶). The village also harbours an unexpected cultural attraction: the **National Gallery Alexandros Soutsos Museum Annexe** (summer Wed–Mon 10am–2pm, Mon, Wed & Fri 6–9pm; €2), a branch of Athens' principal art gallery, consisting of a modest but fine selection of local artists' works, plus frequent visiting exhibits from other galleries around Greece. It's tucked away inside the hairpin junction where the two roads up from Dhassiá enter the village proper.

Ípsos

ÍPSOS, 2km and one bay north of Dhassiá, can't really be recommended to anyone but hardened bar-hoppers. There isn't room to swing a cat on the long, thin pebble beach, which lies right beside the busy coast road, and the atmos-phere suggests the resort has been twinned with Southend or Coney Island. The seafront comprises a kilometre-long row of snack joints, vehicle rental firms, and most importantly, bars and clubs, which cater to crowds of rowdy youngsters.

Most **accommodation** has been taken over by British package companies, although Pelais Travel (T 26610/97 564, W www.pelaistravel.com; from ❸) can offer rooms, as well as car rental and other services, and the *Hotel Mega* (T 26610/93 208 or 93 216, W www.megahotel.gr; ❹), complete with pool, bars and restaurants, often has vacant rooms. *Camping Ipsos Beach* (T 26610/93 246, F 93 741), in the centre of the strip, has a motel-style reception with bar and restaurant and offers standing tents to those without their own equipment. Ípsos is also the base for a major **diving centre**, Waterhoppers (T 26610/93 867, E diverclub@hotmail.com), which is registered with the British Sub-Aqua Club and run on their guidelines. Claiming to be the only dive outfit in Greece with a 54-inch decompression chamber, the club caters for beginners and advanced divers, as well as offering a number of BSAC and CMAS courses. The daily trips on its own *kaïki* also welcome snorkellers and those who prefer to remain dry.

Eating on Ípsos's main drag is a hit-and-miss affair, with an emphasis on fast food, although it does have a large and stylish Chinese, the *Peking House*, and reasonable curries at the *Viceroy*, both in the centre of the strip. A more traditional meal and a quieter setting can be found in the *Akrogiali Psistaria* and *Asteria Taverna*, by the small marina at the southern end. **Drinking** in Ípsos is mandatory and there is no shortage of places ready to fuel revellers. All of the big clubs like *Monte Christo*, *B52* and *Shooters*, which relentlessly thump out disco beats till the wee hours, are clustered at the northern end of the seafront, while the smaller and quieter joints, such as *Passoa* and *CJs*, are further south.

Pyryí

Ípsos has now all but engulfed the neighbouring hamlet of **Pyryí**, at the northern end of the strip, but it is still much quieter and a jumping off point for the island's largest mountain, Mount Pandokrátor (see below). There aren't many places to stay but the *Taverna Symposion* serves up a fine range of Greek standards and a good place for a drink is the *Temple Bar* – which plays decent rock music.

Mount Pandokrátor

Corfu's largest mountain, **MOUNT PANDOKRÁTOR**, dominates the north of the island and is clearly visible from Corfu Town and from elevated points well to the south of the capital. Unless you take one of the occasional **tours** advertised at travel agents around the island, however, getting to the summit of the mountain requires your own transport or a sturdy pair of legs. The only public transport that goes anywhere near the summit heads for a couple of villages quite high up on the western slopes: two separate **bus** services run every day except Sunday to Epískepsi and to **Láfki** via **Strinýlas**. Most visitors with their **own vehicle** approach Mount Pandokrátor from the north coast via the dull, modern village of Néa Períthia – the starting point for two basic routes. The more easterly one is via Loútses to the charming ghost village of **Áno Períthia**, from where you are a steep 5km from the summit and can only climb any higher on foot or in a four-wheel drive. The main westerly route ascends via Láfki to **Petália** and Strinýlas, before descending south through Spartýlas to Pyryí. A paved road just south of Petália leads all the way to the summit, 5km east. You may wish, however, to take a detour further west to admire the three-storey manor in the Venetian village of Epískepsi, 5km northwest of Strinýlas and linked to it by a direct footpath. Alternative walking or 4WD routes onto the eastern side of the mountain from the northeast coast are via Vinglatoúri, 2km north of Nissáki or via Víngla and Pórta, just west of the coast road north of Kalámi.

In spring and early summer, the route up to the summit blossoms with dwarf cyclamen, irises and orchids, and birds of prey – including the rarely seen golden eagle – patrol thermals above the slopes. If you're interested in hiking the paths it's worth getting a **map** of the mountain by island-based cartographer Stephan Jaskulowski and the useful *Second Book of Corfu Walks* by Hilary Whitton Paipeti (see p.288), both available in Corfu Town's bookshops.

Pandokrátor is a magnet for **bad weather**, so take local advice if it looks at all changeable. Storms and low cloud are not uncommon in all but the driest of high seasons. Whatever the weather, it's advisable to follow the basic **hill walking rules** – make sure you take liquids, cover and sensible clothing, and leave a note of your destination with someone.

Áno Períthia

It is little exaggeration to call the alluring village of **ÁNO PERÍTHIA**, just over 7km south of the coastal road at Néa Períthia, a ghost town, considering that the once thriving community is now home to only six permanent inhabitants. The village is also known as Paliá Períthia and marked on most maps simply as Períthia. There is clear evidence of the former glory days in the crumbling stone walls of the six **churches** – sadly all locked – and once grand houses that are dotted around the dusty barren slopes.

Unsurprisingly, there is no accommodation here, but the village does attract visitors in some numbers throughout the summer because of its two excellent traditional **tavernas**. Of these, the ⚓ *Old Perithia* is particularly renowned for succulent goat and home-produced feta cheese; it also has wonderful views from its shady courtyard. The nearby *O Faros* offers simpler grills but is equally friendly and authentic.

Láfki, Petália and Strinýlas

As you start climbing the northern spurs of Mount Pandokrátor from Néa Períthia, follow the signs to **LÁFKI**, about 5km southwest, through several tiny settlements. There is not much at Láfki itself, but the *Symposium* café on the main road is not a bad spot for a drink or snack. You can also join the main road across the mountain at Láfki from Aharávi (see p.99), to the northwest.

Passing through the tiny hamlets of Tripódhi and Eríva, the road gains several hundred metres in altitude over the 8km up to **PETÁLIA**. The village, surrounded by terraced olive groves, commands fine views back west and has one **taverna** serving standard Greek fare – *The Fog* – whose name hints at the inclement weather that sometimes hits the area in winter.

The most popular base for walkers is the village of **STRINÝLAS**, barely more than 1km further south. **Accommodation** is basic but easy to come by: much of it is in private houses, most easily arranged on spec through one of the three **tavernas** that cluster around the shady village square. The most popular of these is the *Elm Tree*, which has the widest selection of *mezédhes* and main courses, while the adjacent *Oasis*, shaded by the same giant elm, also has a fair range of grilled and baked meat and vegetable dishes. On the opposite side of the road *To Steki* is a simpler *psistariá*.

The summit and Pandokrátoras monastery

The paved road that bears east from the southern edge of Petália snakes up for 5km through pine forest and then an increasingly barren landscape to the 911m **summit** of Mount Pandokrátor. The building of a communications station on the top of the mountain, complete with two large radio masts, led to the road being surfaced and has opened the way to cars and tour coaches which now line the asphalt just below the installations and the monastery on fine summer days. Needless to say, there are some splendid panoramic **views** from the summit. The *Arhondariki* snack bar, just outside the monastery gates, provides light **refreshments** in high season.

Entering the grounds of the **Pandokrátoras monastery** is made slightly surreal by the fact that you have to pass through the giant steel feet of the taller 106m antenna, which is planted firmly in the monastery's courtyard. Nothing remains of the original fourteenth-century monastery buildings and only the main **sanctuary**, built in the late seventeenth century, is open to the public. Simple monastic **cells**, still partly inhabited, line the walls of the courtyard beside the main sanctuary, which has recently been renovated with a triangular tiled roof and stone cladding. Inside the church, the semi-cylindrical ceiling is painted with a grand Pandokrátor and emotive scenes from Christ's life in dark reds and rusts. The marble iconostasis with its gilt panels of icons is also splendid.

Barbáti, Nissáki and Agní

The coast road beyond Ípsos mounts the lower slopes of Pandokrátor towards **BARBÁTI**, some 4km on. Here you'll find the best beach on this stretch of coast: long and wide, away from traffic, with a gently shelving shore of pebbles and sand. There's not much apart from boat hire and a water ski school at the beach itself though, as most of the facilities are spread along the main coast road above it. Barbáti is a favourite with families, though there is now a wider range than the eastern Europeans who used to monopolize the **accommodation** a few years ago. Some rooms are available on the main road – *Paradise* (☎26630/91 320, ☎91 479; ❷) and *Roula Yeranou* (☎20663/92 397; ❷) – and a friendly travel agency, named Helga after its Dutch owner, has a range of accommodation (☎26630/91 547, ✉helga@otenet.gr; from ❸) as well as other services. The local **tavernas** lining the main road vie to give value for money and often advertise specials – the *Lord Byron* has a wide range of starters and main courses, while *Dimitris* serves cheap grills on its terrace overlooking the beach and *Karyatides* rustles up fresh fish and meat dishes. Of the handful of tavernas down on the beach, *Akti Barbati* is the best bet. Back up on the road, the *Free Styler* **bar** is a laid-back place for a cocktail, which occasionally livens up with a little dancing. Barbáti gets the morning sun, but the steep mountain bluffs behind it lose light early, and when bad weather is snagged by Mount Pandokrátor, the coast here tends to get dumped on.

The mountainside becomes steeper and the road higher above the sea beyond Barbáti, as the population of the coastline thins drastically. **NISSÁKI** is more of a sprawl than a village, extending for about 2km and embracing three excellent pebble beaches: the northermost one is dominated by the gigantic and rather soulless *Nissaki Beach Hotel* (☎26630/91 232–3, ⓦwww.nissakibeach .gr; half-board ❺), a couple of shops, a bakery and a few travel and **accommodation agencies**. The British-owned Falcon Travel (☎26630/91 318, ✉falcontr@otenet.gr) rents out apartments above the southernmost of the three beaches, a tiny, white-pebble affair with deep-blue water. Also worth contacting for rooms, apartments and villas is the Nissaki Holiday Center (☎26630/91 116 or 91 448, ⓦwww.nissaki-holidays.gr), by the junction of the main road and first beach road. Far more chic, however, are the beautifully decorated apartments of the *Corfu Residence* (☎26630/91 711, ⓦwww .corfuresidence.com; ❻), further south. A trio of fine, reasonably priced **tavernas** are clustered around the first beach: *Mitsos* has the nicest setting right on the jetty and serves specialities like swordfish, *kleftikó* and even the odd curry; the *Olive Press* just above the harbour offers a fair range of meat, fish and starters; while nearby *Anthi* has a variety of *mezédhes* and pizza. One restaurant on the main road that deserves a mention is *Taverna Anthi*, which specializes in Italian and German dishes.

A real gourmet's paradise, however, is the tiny, picturesque bay of **AGNÍ**, a little further along. Apart from the *Nikolas Apartments* (☎26630/91 243, ✉pkatsaros@aias.gr; ❹), the only buildings backing onto the white pebble beach are *Korina's* snack-bar and a trio of fine tavernas. ⚐ *Nikolas* assures the friendliest welcome and does specialities like lamb in lemon sauce and liver in wine; *Agni* is rather pricey but offers unusual items such as Spanish-style chicken and stuffed sardines; while *Toula's* is also very strong on seafood, with delights such as *mýdhia saganáki* (mussels fried in cheese sauce) and prawns pilaff. As the restaurants are well known to locals, they often remain open at winter weekends.

Kalámi and Kouloúra

The two places no one visiting the northeast coast should miss are neighbouring Kalámi and Kouloúra: the first for its Durrell connection, the latter for its exquisite bay and sole taverna, though neither has a particularly great beach. Sadly, **KALÁMI** is on the way to being spoiled – already, the hillside above the bay is scarred by ugly purple apartment blocks – but the village itself is still small and, if you squint, you can imagine how it would have been in the year Lawrence Durrell spent there on the eve of World War II, when, according to Henry Miller, "days in Kalámi passed like a song". The beach is stony, and pebbly in the water, but many who holiday here rent boats to explore nearby coves. The ⚔ **White House**, where Durrell wrote *Prospero's Cell*, is now split in two: the ground floor is an excellent taverna; the upper floor, housing up to eight people, is let by the week through CV Travel (see p.23) or locally through Tassos boats (☎26630/91 040, ⓦ www.white-house-corfu.gr; ❸), although it tends to be pre-booked months in advance.

Apart from the Durrell pad, most of the **accommodation** in Kalámi – like much of the arc between Nissáki and Kassiópi – has been sewn up by blue-chip villa companies such as CV, Simply Ionian and Corfu à la Carte (see Basics); anything left over for independent travellers probably needs to be booked in advance. *Villa Rita* (☎26630/91 030; ❸) is a small block of well-appointed **rooms**, set just back from the road through the village, while Sunshine Travel (☎26630/91 170, ⓦ www.sunshineclub.gr) and Kalami Tourist Services (☎26630/91 062, ⓦ www.kalamits.com) can also find

The Durrells and Corfu

Between them, brothers **Gerald and Lawrence Durrell** unwittingly persuaded untold hundreds of thousands of Britons to visit Corfu – a fact the former would live to rue. Gerald (1925–95) described the island's arrival on the island in the early 1930s in *My Family and Other Animals;* the "strawberry-pink" villa the family moved into was in Pérama, a suburb of Corfu Town, although they would later move to two other residences. Lawrence (1912–90) was in his twenties and had already published a first novel (*Panic Spring*) pseudonymously when he arrived in 1937 to spend a year-and-a-half living in "an old fisherman's house in the extreme north of the island – Kalamai". The book he produced describing this idyll, *Prospero's Cell* – the title taken from the theory that Corfu was the setting for Prospero's and Miranda's exile in Shakespeare's *The Tempest* – remains in print over half a century on and portrays an island that can still be glimpsed in the more remote corners of the northeast coast.

Lawrence left the island at the outbreak of World War II – Henry Miller's *Colossus of Maroussi* describes a holiday with Durrell on the eve of war – but returned later, and shorter pieces on the island can be found in his collected prose works, *Spirit of Place. Prospero's Cell* was to form part of an island trilogy – joined later by *Reflections on a Marine Venus*, based on his postwar visit to Rhodes, and *Bitter Lemons*, on a later visit to Cyprus.

While Lawrence travelled widely, eventually settling in France, Gerald retained his contact with Corfu up until his death. The environmentalist and author was particularly outspoken about the dangers of chemical pesticide sprays on the olive trees, particularly when an alfresco lunch party of his was "accidentally" sprayed with noxious chemicals. His green successors have managed to get chemical spraying banned in inhabited areas and are fighting for total prohibition. For an interesting and detailed account of the Durrell brothers in Corfu, look for Hilary Whitton Paipeti's little book *In the Footsteps of Lawrence Durrell and Gerald Durrell in Corfu (1935–39)*.

you accommodation, as well as offering car, bike and boat rental, and exchange facilities.

The taverna at the *White House* is recommended for its mussels and swordfish with garlic specials. Down on the beach, *Kalami Beach Taverna* has a lengthy list of vegetarian alternatives to Greek staples, while *Thomas' Place* offers a mix of pizzas and local dishes, and holds traditional Greek music nights. There's not much late-night action, but two pleasant **bars**, *Kalami Cocktail Bar* and *Cocktail and Dreams*, draw a laid-back clientele.

The tiny harbour of **KOULOÚRA** has managed to retain its charm, set at the edge of a (so far) totally undeveloped bay with nothing in it but pine trees, *kaïkia* and the single ⚓ *Kouloura* **taverna**. This fine, authentic restaurant, serving simple but excellent fish, meat and starters, has to be one of the most idyllic settings for a meal in the whole of Corfu, which accounts for its great popularity: if you're coming for lunch, arrive early, as it fills up quickly even during winter weekends, when it remains open. The diminuitive **Houhoulió beach** provides the chance of a dip.

Kerasiá, Áyios Stéfanos and Avláki

Less than two pleasant kilometres by rocky footpath beyond Kouloúra, the large, shady cove of **KERASIÁ** shelters the friendly, family-run *Kerasia Taverna* and a strip of villas along the shore, handled by CV Travel and others. The only road access is from Áyios Stéfanos (see below), 2km to the north, along a lane through olive groves owned by the Rothschild clan. The beach has a jetty, and with reason: it tends to attract day-trip boats most summer afternoons. For most of the year and substantial parts of the day in high season, however, it makes a lovely spot to unwind, away from any distractions.

Without doubt the most attractive resort on this stretch of coast, some 3km down a winding lane from the village of Siniés on the main coast road, is **ÁYIOS STÉFANOS**, not to be confused with the resort of the same name on the west coast above Paleokastrítsa. Buses marked "Áyios Stéfanos" from Corfu Town go to the latter; this Áyios Stéfanos is only ever served by the Kassiópi bus, which will drop you at Siniés. From there, it's a beautiful walk down to the resort, through olive groves and then open country with views across to nearby Albania – though quite a slog on the way back up. Áyios Stéfanos is also probably the remotest resort on Corfu, and the bare countryside around it and across in Albania increases this pleasant – and, for coastal Corfu, rare – sense of isolation.

Most **accommodation** here consists of upmarket villas and apartments run by British travel companies, and the village has yet to succumb to any serious development, which means that available space is thin on the ground; so far, only the *Kochili* taverna, at the southern end of the bay, handles rooms and apartments for independent travellers (☎26630/81 522; ❷); it also happens to be the best place for simple, well-priced food and fine local wine. The handful of other **tavernas** are more upmarket: the *Eucalyptus*, by the village's small and rather gravelly beach in the corner of the bay, is the priciest and serves quality dishes like pork with artichokes and bon filet. Of the two that dominate the centre of the seafront, *Galini* is the better option, with lots of salads and dips to complement the main courses, while *Kaparelli*, although it has some cheaper standards, tries to justify charging extra for meat dishes by fancy presentation and is not particularly friendly. For a shady garden **drink**, the otherwise uninspiring *Damianos* cocktail bar completes facilities apart from a couple of boat rental enterprises.

About an hour's walk from the coastguard station above Áyios Stéfanos, along a newly paved road, is the beach of **Avláki**. In season, it's favoured by those fleeing the crowds on the more accessible beaches to the south and at Kassiópi, just to the west. The pebble bay faces north–northwest, and its cliffs scoop up the prevailing winds, providing lively conditions for the windsurfers who visit the beach's small windsurf club (board hire starts at around €12). Equine activities are available too at Dimitris horse-riding (☎26630/91 172). There is no independent accommodation, but there are two tavernas: the *Avlaki*, located at the point where the access road meets the beach, serving simple meat and fish dishes, accompanied by salads; and, further along the beach, the *Cavo-Barbaro*, which is slightly flashier and also does local favourites like *sofríto*.

Kassiópi and around

About 2km around the coast from Avláki is **KASSIÓPI**, a small fishing village with a long history, now transformed into a major party resort. Emperor Tiberius had a villa here, and the village's sixteenth-century church, locked and a little careworn these days, stands on what is believed to have been the site of a temple of Zeus once visited by Nero. Very little evidence of Kassiópi's longevity survives, however, apart from a sadly derelict thirteenth-century Angevin *kástro* on its headland. This is where the Angevins made their last stand against the Venetian invaders, who later dismantled it, so that it would not fall into the hands of the Genoese. These days the only invaders are northern Europeans with their sights fixed on the nightlife – clubs, video bars, restaurants – and some small pebbly beaches around the headland. Although package tourism dominates, Kassiópi has a more cosmopolitan air owing to an even mixture of nationalities, and the original architecture of some of the streets around the harbour adds to the resort's attraction.

Kassiópi's **beaches** are hidden below its ruined castle and reached by the newly paved narrow road that encircles the headland. They are small but well protected and, because of their geographical distribution, at least two of them should be sheltered, regardless of which way the wind is blowing. Only a couple of minutes' walk from the town centre, Kalamíones is the largest, Pipítos the smallest and Kanóni and Bataría the quietest, although even these two fill up very easily. Kassiópi is also home to one of Corfu's best scuba diving operations, the partly British-run Corfu Divers (☎26630/81 218, ⓦwww.corfudivers.com), with reliable equipment and experienced instructors.

Inland from Kassiópi, the tiny village of **Loútses** has no facilities apart from the quaint *Hansos* taverna (though buses run there from Corfu Town), but the open countryside around is excellent walking terrain, mainly grazing land or wild maquis, free of trees and with fine views over Albania. The walk from Kassiópi, a simple stroll along the coast road to the signed turning for Loútses, can be done in under an hour. For more serious walkers, the Loútses route continues to Ano Períthia, where a path leads onto the summit of Mount Pandokrátor (see p.93).

Practicalities

Most **accommodation** in Kassiópi is through village agencies who, because they're in the marketplace with cut-price package operators, tend to be cheaper than in the classier resorts to the south. The largest, Travel Corner (☎26630/81 220 or 81 213, ⓦwww.kassiopi.com; from ❷), with two branches, is a good place to start if you're planning to stay a while in Kassiópi and want a choice of accommodation. Kassiopi Travel Service

(☎26630/81 388–9, ⓦwww.corfukassiopitravel.com), and Cosmic Tourist Centre (☎26630/81 624 or 81 686, ⓦwww.cosmic-kassiopi.com) also have a range of rooms, apartments and villas. An independent alternative, the excellent-value *Kastro* restaurant-pension (☎26630/81 045, ⓔkyrosai@hol .gr; ❷), is set away from the hubbub of town, overlooking the beach behind the castle, while on the east side of the harbour the friendly *Manessis Apartments* (☎26630/81 320, ⓔdiana@otenet.gr; ❷) have great views across to the *kástro*. If they aren't overrun by package bookings, *Theofilos* (☎26630/81 261, ⓦwww.theofiloskassiopi.com; ❷) offers good rooms on Kalamíones beach at a bargain price, and *Panayiota Apartments* (☎26630/81 063; ❷) has decent accommodation a block back from the beach.

There are a number of reasonable choices for **eating** in Kassiópi. On the harbourfront, the *Three Brothers* taverna has a vast menu, including dishes like stroganoff, and is slightly cheaper than the adjacent *Porto*, which specializes in Corfiot dishes such as *sofríto* and *bourdhéto*. By the road end of Kalamíones beach, the enormous *Janis* taverna offers everything from English breakfast to good-value set menus, while back in the village the *Sze Chuan* has a range of reasonably priced Chinese favourites featuring pork, duck, chicken and prawns. At night, Kassiópi rocks to the cacophony of its music and video **bars**. Flashiest has to be the gleaming, hi-tech *Eclipse*, closely followed by the *Visions* and *Jasmine*, all within falling-over distance of the small town square. Down by the harbour, the *Passion Club* is the liveliest night spot. For **Web access**, head for Photonet (€4.50 per hour) or the gaily-painted Out of the Blue café, which also shows films – both lie between the square and Kalamíonas beach.

Almyrós and Aharávi

The coastline from Kassiópi is slightly overgrown and marshy, until you reach the little-used **Almyrós beach**. Almyrós is in fact the eastern extension of the same beach as at Aharávi and Ródha, and as such is one of the longest on the island. So far, it remains the most undeveloped stretch, with only a few apartment buildings, one package-tour complex, some rooms and a handful of shops, cafés and restaurants backing onto it. The beach is wild and near deserted, although it gets busier as it approaches Aharávi, with sporadic accommodation; a pleasant place to stay along this stretch is *Akti Anastassia Apartment Hotel* (☎26630/63 360, ⓔbakarozou@in.gr; ❸), a purpose-built block with a range of comfortable studio rooms set in spacious grounds, or you could try the peaceful *Villa Maria* (☎26630/63 359; ❷). The best place **to eat** is the *Avra* taverna, a couple of hundred metres east of *Villa Maria*, which turns out tasty grilled fish and meat in a grassy garden. The far eastern end, towards Cape Ayías Ekaterínis, is backed by the **Andinióti lagoon**, smaller than Korissíon in the south of the island, but still a haven for waterfowl, waders, marsh species and any number of other birds lured by the fish farms in the lagoon.

With its wide main road, **AHARÁVI** at first sight resembles a rather unappealing American Midwest truck stop, but the village proper is in fact tucked away on the inland side of this new highway, in a small, quiet crescent of old tavernas, bars and shops, starting at the somewhat redundant roundabout in the centre of the main strip. On the other side of the main road, at about 0.5km distance, is a sand and pebble beach, popular with both family holidaymakers on cheap packages and a more upmarket clientele.

On the whole, Aharávi makes a decent, quieter alternative to the beaches in the southwest, and should also be considered by walkers looking for alternative routes up onto **Mount Pandokrátor**. Signposted roads leaving the Aharávi main road for small mountain hamlets such as Áyios Martínos and Láfki connect with well-signed routes up onto the mountain, and even a walk up from the back streets of Aharávi will find you well up the mountain's lower slopes in under an hour. The hilly ground around Aharávi also offers excellent walking possibilities among the bewildering maze of paths through the olive groves. As elsewhere in the region, though, the olive-grove paths are there for a specific purpose, and will invariably bring you out to another road or village, although not always the one you might expect. The views from the open roads around Láfki, down over Aharávi and Cape Ayías Ekaterínis, are stunning.

Aharávi's other attraction, a little over 1km to the east, is **Hydropolis** (May–Sept daily 10.30am–6.30pm; €15, children €10; after 4.30pm €10, children €6), northern Corfu's humbler rival to Aqualand. This large pool complex includes numerous water slides with names like Toboggan, Free Fall and Kamikazi, as well as landlubber activities such as tennis, volleyball and billiards. Look out for regular discounts through resort agents, especially out of high season.

Aharávi practicalities

Independent **accommodation** isn't always too easy to find in Aharávi, but a good place to start is Castaway Travel (☎26630/63 541 or 63 843, ⓦwww .corfucastaway.com), which handles a wide range of rooms and apartments, and offers other services such as vehicle rental, currency exchange and excursions. Sakar Travel (☎ & Ⓕ26630/63 929) is also friendly and offers a similar range of accommodation and other services. The best independent **hotel** is *Dandolo* (☎26630/63 557, ⒺOdandolo@otenet.gr; ❹), with comfortable rooms, set in lush gardens off the road towards the old village, although it may be block booked to Italians in high season. A couple of the large hotels down by the beach may have space left over from their tour-group commitments; the *Seven Islands* (☎26630/63 129; ❹) is more moderate in both size and price than the gargantuan *Aharavi Beach Hotel* (☎26630/63 102 or 63 124, ⒺOachbht@otenet .gr; ❻), a vast complex with a pool and landscaped gardens, which occupies the lower half of the eastern beach road.

There are a number of reasonable **restaurants** on Aharávi's main drag, among them the *Pump House*, by the roundabout, a steak and pasta joint which also offers a wide range of Italian, German and Greek dishes, and *Tó Ellinikon*, towards the west end, a shady taverna-cum-*psistariá*. A couple of quieter and more traditional places to eat can be found in the old village, most notably *Theritas*, which serves oven dishes like *sofríto* and grills in its leafy courtyard. Of the few restaurants dotted along the beach, the simple meat and fish meals at *Apnoea* constitute the best value, although the *Neraida* has a more imaginative menu with items such as trout salad. Of the many bars along the main drag, the light and airy *Captain Aris* is a friendly place, while the sunken courtyard of *Lemon Garden* makes a fine spot for a cocktail. The liveliest and noisiest place, ironically, is *Whispers*, at the start of the road towards the old village from the roundabout. For a more authentic tipple or strong Greek coffee, head for the anonymous *kafenío* in the old village. To get **online**, facilities are available for €5 per hour at the Internet Cafeteria, behind the western end of the beach.

Ródha

Where Aharávi pulls up short of over-development, **RÓDHA** has tipped over into it. Its central crossroads has all the charm of a motorway service station, and the beach, though an extension of Aharávi's, is rocky in parts and swampy to the west. "Old Ródha", as the signposts call it, is a small triangular warren of alleys between the beach link road and the seafront, where you'll find the best **restaurants**: the *Taverna Avra*, oldest in Ródha and overlooking the beach, is the best for fish, while both *Opa* and the longer established *New Port*, a little further along the seafront, also offer hearty taverna fare at low prices. For **nightlife**, the *Skouna*, just down an alley halfway along the seafront, is the resort's trendiest club, playing the latest sounds at night. On the seafront itself, **bars** like *Big Ben* pull in the punters with pool, sports on TV or videos by day and karaoke with free shots by night. Of the bars that line the lane that cuts diagonally between the seafront and the link road, *Maggie's Bar* is an English-style pub with a decent line in draught ales and cider. *Mouses*, just inland from the main crossroads, is a summer-only *bouzouki* joint.

Although much of the **accommodation** is block-booked, you shouldn't have much trouble finding a place, except perhaps in mid-August. Try HN Travel (☏26630/62 249, ⓦwww.hntravel.gr; from ❷), halfway down the link road, which offers a wide range of rooms, villas and apartments, and rents cars. Corfu Nostos Travel on the seafront (☏26630/64 601, Ⓔekostaki@otenet. gr; ❷) also rents basic rooms and handles car rental. Still on the front, the English-run *Roda Inn* (☏26630/63 358, UK ☏01708/345 053; ❸) is pretty good value, with simple but comfortable sea-facing rooms. Halfway up the link road, on the right as you face the sea, *Irene Rooms* (☏26630/63 577; ❷) are more basic and even cheaper. If you're after something a tad smarter, try the *Pegasus Hotel* (☏26630/63 400, ⓦwww.pegasus-hotel.com; ❸), which is back on the main highway, 200m west of the crossroads, and has a swimming pool and air-conditioned rooms with fridges and TV. The one **campsite**, *Rodha Beach Camping* (☏26630/63 120 or 63 209, Ⓕ63 081), has one disadvantage to its otherwise ideal shady setting to the east of Ródha, in that it is almost 1km uphill from the beach.

If you fancy a canter, Costas **horse-riding** (mobile ☏6944/160 011) is very reasonable at €15 per person for a two-hour session, including transfer from the village – you can also ask at the Enigma gift shop on the link road.

Karousádhes and around

Some 5km west of Ródha, the sizeable village of **KAROUSÁDHES** is well worth a visit if you want to escape the tourist hustle and bustle and see something of everyday Greek life. The main street through the village peels off the highway and gradually ascends between the attractive, eighteenth- and nineteenth-century stone buildings. The street – so narrow in parts that vehicles can barely squeeze through – contains a number of old-fashioned shops, as well as a couple of fine **kafenía**, such as *Iy Pouliá*, towards the lower end. Halfway up the street, the excellent *Thomas* **grill** serves succulent cuts of meat straight from the adjacent butcher's shop and can be washed down with excellent local wine. There is no **accommodation** in the village, but *Karoussades Camping* (☏ & Ⓕ26630/31 415), on the outskirts, has ample shade and some bungalows (❷) and makes a quieter alternative to camping at Ródha or Sidhári.

Within a couple of kilometres to the north of Karousádhes lie the attractive sandy beaches of **Ágnos**, which is usually quiet apart from a few German package holidaymakers, **Astrakerí** and **Áyios Andhréas**, both blissfully devoid of crowds and loungers with umbrellas. All three are contiguous on foot but reached by separate approach roads. At Ágnos you can **eat** tasty grills at the simple *Agnos* taverna, while fairly priced fish can be enjoyed at friendly *O Mourmouras* (*Three Brothers*), further west at Astrakerí. Smaller and more westerly Áyios Andhréas has an eponymous peaceful clifftop taverna, also known as

Yiorgos, and, in the olive groves back from the beach, a co-managed group of apartments – ask about these at *Elli*, which is one of the three (☎26630/31 847, ℱ31 488; ❷). In the opposite direction, a few kilometres south of Karousádhes and just east of **Ágrafi**, is one of the loveliest places to eat on the whole island, the ✻ *Angonari mezedhopolío* (summer evenings only; winter open weekend evenings only). Here you can enjoy a wide range of tasty appetizers, such as cheese croquettes and *kolokythokeftédhes*, to the accompaniment of subtle, live guitar music, played in the leafy garden.

Sidhári and Avliótes

The next notable resort, **SIDHÁRI**, is one of the few on the island constantly expanding under the influence of travel companies such as Thomson and First Choice. It has a small but pretty town square, with a bandstand set in a small garden, though this is lost in a welter of bars, snack joints and some very well-stocked shops. It's extremely popular with British package visitors, whose presence makes it a busy and fairly noisy party resort most nights.

The main beach is sandy but not terribly clean, and many people tend to head west to an area of coves walled by wind-carved sandstone cliffs, which give the coastline a curious, almost science-fiction appearance. Sidhári's star attraction is here, the **Canal d'Amour**, which takes its dire name from a local legend, to the effect that if a woman swam its length she would win the man of her dreams. Erosion continues to reshape the channel, but the name sticks, and many local tour operators offer "romantic" evening cruises here. A more functional, and probably more enjoyable, watery experience is provided by Sidhári's much-advertised **water slide**, away from the beach off the main road. Entrance to the pool is free, but there are varying charges for use of the slide.

There is little about Sidhári that will captivate the first-time visitor, although it gets its fair share of returnees. The main reason you'd probably want to visit or stay is if you are en route to the **Dhiapóndia islands** to the northwest. Day-trips to Mathráki, Othoní and Eríkoussa (see p.125) tend to leave on certain weekday mornings at around 9am, so unless you're able to catch the 5.30am Sidhári bus from Corfu Town, your only option is to stay in the area. The boats are run by Nearchos Seacruises (☎26630/95 248) and cost around €12–15 return per person.

Practicalities

As you might expect for such a package-oriented destination, casual accommodation can become rather a scarce commodity in high season. Independent rooms and apartments are most easily found through any of the agencies that cluster the town centre: try Vlasseros Travel (☎26630/95 695, ℱ95 969), which also handles car rental and a mind-boggling range of cut-price excursions, including horse-riding; Adia Travel (☎26630/95 590, ℱ95 141); and Alkinoos Travel (☎26630/95 012 or 95 550) – all from ❷. Another source for **rooms** is the *Scorpion* café-bar towards the west end of the main road (☎26630/95 046 or 95 369; ❷). Sidhári's **campsite**, *Dolphin Camping* (☎26630/31 522), is quite a walk inland from the T-junction at the western end of the main drag. The site is small and pleasant, with cleaning facilities and a shop, and is positioned to avoid the worst of Sidhári's night-time noise.

Eating in Sidhári is often an event for which people dress up, but more to flash their tanned bodies than to look smart: most restaurants are pitched at those looking for a great night out rather than a quiet meal in a taverna. The best seaside tavernas are to be found beyond the tiny bridge on the quieter eastern stretch of beach – try the cheap and tasty chops, chicken or fish at *Kavadias* or the mixed international and Greek cuisine on offer in the eucalyptus-shaded courtyard of *Bournis*. The *Sea Breeze*, wedged between the western section of the main road and beach, has a huge array of standard starters and main courses. If you want a break from Greek food, head for the road into the village from the south where you'll find the classy *Kohenoor* Indian restaurant and the cheapish Chinese *Hong Kong Palace*. The British influence means that full cooked breakfasts are dirt cheap in many snack bars. It also means that English ale, though too chilled and questionably kept, is easy to come by, although Sidhári is certainly not the place to go for a quiet drink. If you have the urge to join in raucous choruses of "Three Lions" though, it's just the ticket. Among the **bars** that vie for your custom, *Mojo* and *IQ*, both right by the central crossroads, do a lively trade, as do *Falcon* and the *Red Lion*, further along the main strip. *Caesar's*, out of the village towards the Canal d'Amour, has been given a hi-tech makeover and remains the busiest **nightclub**.

Avliótes

The Sidhári bus from Corfu Town usually continues to **AVLIÓTES**, a handsome hill town with a couple of imposing churches and a taverna, *Ilias*, serving delicious meaty grills. Avliótes is barely 1km from sleepy **Perouládhes**, which conceals a real gem in red-cliffed **Longás beach**, just to the west. The one option for eating or drinking at the beach is high above, at the clifftop ⅄ *Panorama* bar-restaurant, which offers both tasty fare and stunning sunset views, and you can even stay at the modern, pinkish *Logas Beach Studios* (☎26630/95 412; ❸). Note that Áyios Stéfanos (see p.97) on the west coast is under an hour's walk from Avliótes, downhill through lovely olive groves.

Paleokastrítsa and the west coast

The northwest of Corfu conceals some of the island's most dramatic coastal scenery and, in the interior, violent mountainscapes jutting out of verdant countryside. Its resorts are fairly developed, though not on the same scale as the north and east coasts, probably because the craggy northwestern landscape just doesn't have much accessible terrain. Further down the west coast, the landscape opens out to reveal long, sandy beaches such as delightful Myrtiótissa and the backpackers' haven of Áyios Górdhis. Given the structure of the bus system, travel along the west coast is at best haphazard: virtually all buses ply dedicated routes from Corfu Town, only rarely linking resorts.

Paleokastrítsa

PALEOKASTRÍTSA's undoubted beauty makes it the honeypot of the west coast, with hotels spreading so far up into the surrounding area that some are a taxi ride from town. As you gradually wind down through the three kilometres of increasingly touristed approach road, it is easy to wonder where the centre of all the action lies, as you catch glimpses of sea off to the left. Eventually the road levels out and reaches the main village, which is small, occupying the neck of a headland surrounded by small beaches and, beyond, dramatic hills and cliffs – an idyllic setting which led British High Commissioner Sir Frederic Adam to popularize Paleokastrítsa in the nineteenth century. It has been suggested as a possible site of the Homeric city of Scheria, where Odysseus was washed ashore, discovered by Nausicaa and her handmaidens and welcomed by her father

△ View of Paleokastrítsa

King Alcinous, although this is a claim shared by a number of other sites in the islands. The thirteenth-century **Paleokastrítsa monastery** overlooks the town from the headland, and a circuitous 6km or so north is the **Angelókastro** castle, one of the most impressive ruins on the island. Although none of the resort's **beaches** are impressive by west-coast standards, there are enough coves to keep most swimmers content.

Accommodation

Accommodation is not usually a problem except in the very peak season in Paleokastrítsa and the area also caters more to the independent traveller than many other resorts. There are excellent-value and cosy **rooms** for rent through the friendly ♣ *Dolphin Snackbar* (☎26630/41 035 or 49 275; ❷) and the *Green House* (☎26630/41 311 or 41 328; ❶), both above Platákia beach, and at *Villa Korina* (☎26630/41 793; ❷), 150m up the first turning north off the road that leads out of the village, just past well-signposted Jimmy's supermarket. In addition, a wide range of places to stay can be found through Michalas Tourist Bureau (☎26630/41 113, ✉michalastravel@ker.forthnet.gr; from ❷), nearly 2km back from the village. Nearby, just off the main road, the **campsite**, *Paleokastrítsa Camping* (☎26630/41 204, ⓕ41 104), has a restaurant, shop and bike rental.

    Hotels in Paleokastrítsa tend to be in the upper grades, and to cater for package tourism. A reasonable independent exception, little more than 500m from the village along the main approach road, is the small, family-run *Odysseus* (☎26630/41 209 or 41 379, ⓦwww.odysseushotel.gr; half-board ❹), a smart hotel with pool, restaurant and sea views. More upmarket is the four-star *Akrotiri Beach Hotel* (☎26630/41 237 or 41 275, ⓦwww.akrotiri-beach.com; ❼), which has rooms aside from its block bookings, is friendly and unpretentious for such a large, modern hotel and is accessible on foot in fifteen minutes.

The beaches and boat trips

Paleokastrítsa has a series of fair-to-middling **beaches** scattered around its elongated coastline. Of the three surrounding the village, the sandy semi-circle of **Áyios Spyrídhon**, on the south side, is the longest and busiest, backed by the majority of the village's restaurants and cafés. It is also home to a plethora of sea taxis and *kaïkia*, which tout for custom from the jetties at each end. The most popular **boat trip** (€8 for 30min) takes you to scenic caves with names like the Blue Grottoes and The Eye, or you can ask to be dropped off at more far-flung beaches and be picked up later. The second village beach, pebbly **Áyios Pétros**, beyond the car park just to the north of the headland's neck, is preferable. The best of the three, however, is **Ambelákia** a narrower, relatively secluded strand reached via a short path beyond the very prominent *Astakos Taverna*. Protected by surrounding cliffs, it's undeveloped apart from the professional, German-run Korfu Diving **scuba-diving** centre (closed Sat; ☏26630/41 604) at the end of the cove. The centre runs trips every day, except Saturday, for beginners and advanced divers to more than twenty sites, taking in reefs, arches and canyons. They can also offer night dives, cave diving and advanced training.

Other beaches a little further back from the village, but easily walkable, are **Alípa** and **Platákia**. The former, barely a flat half kilometre to the southeast, is a fairly long, pebbly bay beside a small, little-used harbour. The latter, one bay further east, is not a lot further, but involves going 500m back from the village up the main road and then down some steps through the pines by the *Dolphin Snackbar*. The beach is narrower and the pebbles a bit larger, but the water is crystal clear.

Paleokastrítsa monastery

On the rocky bluff above the beaches, the beautiful, whitewashed **Paleokastrítsa monastery** (daily 7am–1pm & 3–8pm; free, donations welcome), also known as the Theotókos monastery, is believed to have been established in the thirteenth century, though the current buildings date from the eighteenth. It's a favourite with coach parties and, despite being within walking distance of the town's main car park below, has had to have traffic lights installed to ease the flow of vehicles up and down the bluff.

The small monastery church, set amidst an attractive complex of courtyards, archways, monks' cells, oil presses and store rooms, has a number of impressive **icons**, including depictions of St George and the dragon and an atmospheric *Last Judgement*, while the ceiling features a woodcarving of the *Tree of Life*. There's also a museum, resplendent with further icons, most notably a beautiful *Dormition of the Virgin Mary*, jewel-encrusted, silver-bound Bibles and other paraphenalia of Greek Orthodox ritual, as well as a curious "sea monster", with very large vertebrae and tusks, said to have been killed by fishermen in the nineteenth century. The real highlight, however, are the beautiful paved **gardens**, which afford spectacular views over the coastline.

The Angelókastro

Paleokastrítsa's castle, the **Angelókastro**, perched dramatically on an impossibly abrupt, if diminutive peak, is in fact around 6km from town, up the coast. There are short-cut paths through vertiginous open country from Paleokastrítsa, but the main approach, and certainly the only one by car, involves doubling back to the turning for Lákones and Makrádhes, a route with some of the finest views in the region. These can be enjoyed from the excellent *O Boulis* taverna in the pleasant village of **Lákones** itself or from café-restaurants such as the *Bella Vista* or *Golden Fox* further up the mountain. **Makrádhes** itself is an even more attractive village, built in the Venetian style and including the friendly *Sunset* taverna and a curious tradition of roadside stalls, whose owners will try very hard to sell you local produce. The route to the *kástro* then passes through the smaller hamlet of Kríni before terminating at a car park below the ruins, where the *Castelo St Angelo* snack bar serves refreshments.

The castle itself is only approachable by a steep path, but the fifteen minutes of uphill puffing is rewarded by stunning, almost circular, views of the surrounding sea and land – on a clear day, it's possible to make out Corfu Town some 20km away, as the crow flies. It's easy to see why the castle's Byzantine builders and later Venetian developers chose the site. Indeed, the Angevins of Naples held out here for the best part of a year when the Venetians took over the rest of the island in 1386, and the fortress remained unbreached during the brief but destructive Turkish invasions of 1537, 1571 and 1716. Little remains of the fort, however, except for parts of the main walls; the only structures left within are a vaulted underground cistern, the small church of the Archangels Michael and Gabriel and the tiny cave chapel of Ayía Kyriakí, which still has some original frescoes.

Eating and nightlife

There isn't a huge choice of **restaurants** in the centre of Paleokastrítsa, considering the number of visitors the town entertains. One of the best is the *Astakos Taverna*, on the road to Ambelakia, 50m north of the main road – this serves fresh seafood and a choice of starters, but has the rather unusual habit of closing early in the siesta (soon after 2pm). Beachside restaurants tend to suffer from the same problem of wind-borne sand as the beach itself, but the largest, the curiously named *Smurfs*, right behind the main beach, has awnings to beat the winds and an excellent, if expensive, fish menu, featuring trout and salmon, which you choose from tanks. Also recommended are the very smart *Vrahos*, at the neck of the headland, serving standard mains for €10 or above, and *Alipas*, at Alípa beach, which dishes up the juiciest steaks around.

Nightlife hangouts include the bar-restaurants in the centre, and those straggling up the hill towards the Lákones junction, such as the relaxing *Petrino* cocktail bar. Right by the turning is Paleokastrítsa's one nightclub, *The Paleo Club*, a small disco-bar with a garden, which opens and closes late. **Internet** facilities (€5 per hour) are available next to the bakery near the main beach.

Skriperó, Troumbétas and Dhoukádhes

The most direct route to the coastal resorts north of Paleokastrítsa is via the hill town of **SKRIPERÓ**, the administrative centre for much of central northern Corfu, though you wouldn't think so from the run-down couple of shops and *kafenía* and lazy pace of life. The busiest person in the area must be the enterprising owner of the *períptero* just outside town, who opens well past midnight in high summer to catch the passing night-owl trade. Three kilometres further on lies the village of **TROUMBÉTAS**, where you can wash down inexpensive grills with fine, barrelled red wine at the *Troumpeta* taverna.

A handy inland shortcut between Paleokastrítsa and Skriperó passes through the pleasant little village of **DHOUKÁDHES**. Surrounded by verdant hilly countryside and boasting some impressive neoclassical mansions, the village is little-visited, so you can be assured of a warm welcome at the *Elizabeth* bar-taverna or *Tò Steki* grill, if you decide to stop here for refreshment.

Áyios Yeóryios, Afiónas and Aríllas

ÁYIOS YEÓRYIOS – often referred to as Áyios Yeóryios Pagón in order to avoid confusion with the Áyios Yeóryios near the island's southern tip – can also be reached by the circuitous but stunning route from Paleokastrítsa via Makrádhes and **Prinýlas**. A couple of bends along the mountainous way afford views across the whole northwest of Corfu and to the Dhiapóndia islands beyond.

Like many of the west coast resorts, Áyios Yeóryios isn't actually based around a village, but has developed in response to the popularity of its three-kilometre sandy bay, which cuts deep into the land between Cape Aríllas to the north and Cape Falákron to the south. The coast road weaves back and forth to the beach a couple of times during its length. It's a major **windsurfing** centre, with schools and rental companies at each end of the beach, and tends to be quite busy even in low season. Unlike many resorts, tour operators seem to be increasingly monopolizing the few hotels, but various **rooms** are to be had – ask at the Arista supermarket (☎26630/96 350; ❶) or try the smarter apartments of *Studio Eleana* (☎ & ⓕ26630/96 366; ❸), both by the middle of the beach. Further north, a row of very quaint and inexpensive rooms, tucked away in a walled garden, are available from Kostas Bardhis (☎26630/96 219; ❶). *San George* campsite (☎ & ⓕ26630/51 759) is set in thick woods 1km inland and to the north.

Most of the **restaurants** in Áyios Yeóryios specialize in fish at competitive rates, three of the best being *Dixtia*, on the central section of the beach, *To Vrahos*, right at the northern end, and ⚓ *Ostrako*, a colourfully painted taverna with a huge range of fresh marine produce at the extreme south. *Marina* is a good all-round place for meat, fish or *mezédhes* at the southern end, while *Panorama*, back behind the middle of the strand, serves fine chops and *souvláki* at little cost. **Nightlife** is fairly low-key on the whole, with placid garden bars such as *Butterfly* and *Mythos*, as well as the busier *Noa Noa*. The liveliest place is the *Café Asteri*, an unmistakeable purple D-shaped building above the southern approach road, which plays eclectic dance music, hosts the occasional live punk act and has a signpost advertising "Internet connection and cultural kicks".

The village of **AFIÓNAS** at the north end of the bay has been suggested as the likely site of **King Alcinous' castle** – there are vestigial Neolithic remains outside the village – and the walk up to the lighthouse on Cape Aríllas affords excellent views over Áyios Yeóryios and Aríllas bay to the north. The village itself is very small, but does boast one fine **taverna**, ⚓ *To Panorama,* which serves tasty meals made from organic produce and has great views from its terrace; it has also some good-value rooms (☎26630/51 846, ⓔpanorama_afionas@hotmail.com; ❷).

ARÍLLAS, a small settlement in the neighbouring bay, has a long beach of pebble and firm sand, inferior to the great sweep of sand at Áyios Stéfanos in the next bay, but less crowded. It is an up-and-coming resort that currently strikes a good balance between a choice of facilities and lack of development. The barren rocky **islets** of Kraviá, Yinéka and Sykiá out to sea are yet more on the list of places claiming to be the petrified remains of **Odysseus's ship**.

Of the **accommodation** options, the *Akti Arilla* (☎26630/51 201 or 51 206, ⓔaktiaril@otenet.gr; half-board ❸) is a smart, modern hotel whose rooms have sea-facing balconies, the *Villa Mitsis* (☎26630/51 943; ❷) is a more modest pension, while Arillas Travel (☎26630/51 280 or 51 380, ⓔarillast@otenet.gr) has a fair range of rooms, apartments and even a couple of flashy hotels on its books. *Kostas on the Beach*, with unusual dishes like Hawaian chicken, and the more standard *Arilla Inn* or *Sea Breeze* all provide tasty waterside **dining** possibilities, while inland, the *Brouklis psistariá* is great value and *Wok House* serves up decent Chinese meals. Laid-back cocktail-sipping is encouraged by the presence of several **bars** off the front, such as *Coconut* and *Whispers*, which also show sporting events on a big screen.

Áyios Stéfanos

The northernmost of the west coast's resorts, and the furthest from Corfu Town, **ÁYIOS STÉFANOS** has been attracting a steady flow of crowds, especially families, for some decades, but never seems to get too busy, even in high season. The place takes its name from the beautiful eighteenth-century **chapel** of Áyios Stéfanos at the southerly end of the village. Gentle hills give onto a large beach – sandy for the most part, except for a small marshy area in the middle, with a stream running into the sea. The bay's situation, tucked into an amphitheatrical hillside, means that even if it wanted to, the resort couldn't expand much more. There is not much to do here, which is probably one of its strengths, and it would make a quiet base from which to explore the northwest and the Dhiapóndia islands, visible on the sea horizon. Day-trips to Mathráki, Othoní and Eríkoussa (see p.125) run regularly in season, and cost around €12–15 per person, or, if you prefer to travel independently, you can get there for only €6–8 return on Aspiotis Lines' high-speed *kaïki*.

Its distance from any major settlements – and hence from any major traffic flow – makes Áyios Stéfanos a particularly good base for **walking**. As well as Avliótes and Perouládhes to the north, Magouládhes – which boasts one of the area's finest village tavernas – 3km to the east and other small villages in the gently rolling hinterland are well within hiking distance of Áyios Stéfanos.

Practicalities

Áyios Stéfanos's longest-standing **hotel**, the ✈ *Nafsika* (☎26630/51 051, ⓦwww.nafsikahotel.com; ❷), is a pleasant, purpose-built structure with en-suite rooms and balconies overlooking the southern end of the beach, and has a pool and bar-restaurants. A little further south, the *Hotel San Stefano* (☎26630/51 053, ⓕ51 202; ❷) is a newer venture with smart, good-value rooms. On the north side of the village, the *Sunset Taverna* (☎26630/51 185, ⓦwww.corfusunset.com; ❷) and the *Restaurant Evinos* (☎ & ⓕ26630/51 766; ❸), a little further up the hill, both have smart new **studios**, some with air-conditioning. For those on a tighter budget, the gift shop of Peli and Maria, on the northern edge of the village, offers bargain purpose-built **rooms** (☎26630/51 424, ⓕ52 077; from ❶). Finally, a number of travel agencies handle accommodation, among them San Stefanos Travel (☎26630/51 771, ⓦwww.san-stefano.gr), on the main strip, which has a comprehensive range on its books and can also arrange boat trips, horse-riding and scuba-diving.

Good **eating** options on the seafront include the *Golden Beach Taverna*, with large, varied menus, and the *Waves Taverna*, which is ideal for lunches on the beach. The *Taverna O Manthos*, with a garden above the beach, serves Corfiot specialities such as *sofríto* and *pastitsáda*, and has a barbecue. In the heart of the village *Amigos* serves Tex-Mex cuisine as well as Greek at fair prices. For **nightlife**, there's a pair of lively music bars, the *Condor* and the *Athens*, in the centre of the village, plus trendier places like *Sundowner* and the *Magnet Club*, behind the beach.

Érmones

ÉRMONES, the first major settlement south of Paleokastrítsa, is one of the busiest resorts on the island. Its lush green bay is backed by the mountains above the Ropa river, which empties into the sea here. The beach is a mix of gravel and sand, often hectic with watersports activities, and the seabed shelves quite steeply, making it ideal for good swimmers but not for children or less confident swimmers. A kilometre or so back from the village, in the flatter part of the Ropa valley, the Corfu Golf and Country Club (Tues–Sun; ☎ & ⓕ26610/94 220) is the only **golf club** in the archipelago, and is said to have one of the finest courses in the Mediterranean.

The resort is dominated by the extensive grounds of the upmarket *Calimera Ermones Beach* **hotel** (☎26610/94 241, ⓦsunmarotelermones.gr; full-board ❽), which was the first place in the archipelago to provide its guests with a small funicular railway down the cliff to the beach. A couple of hundred metres back from the beach, on consecutive sharp bends in the road, the *Philoxenia Hotel* (☎26610/94 660, ⓦwww.hotelphiloxenia.com; ❹) and *Athena Ermones Golf* (☎26610/94 226 or 94 236, ⓦwww.corfu-hotels-ermonesgolf.gr; ❺), are both smart, comfortable hotels with swimming pools. More modest **studios** can be found a further 200m inland at the adjacent *Pension Katerina* (☎26610/94 615; ❶) and *George's Villa* (☎26610/94 950; ❷). Head for the *Maria* **taverna** above the beach for some of the resort's best Greek food: the *mezédhes* are often enough for a meal in themselves. The friendly *Nafsica*, just above it, makes a reasonable alternative for well-prepared meat and fish. There are just a couple of mundane cafés behind the beach. The Achilleon Diving center (☎26610/94 615) is attached to the lower reaches of the *Calimera* hotel but is open to all.

Myrtiótissa and Vátos

Far preferable to Érmones are the sandy beaches to the south, especially the one at Myrtiótissa. More than half a century ago, in *Prospero's Cell*, Lawrence Durrell described **Myrtiótissa** as "perhaps the loveliest beach in the world" – though he went on to qualify this by adding that the sand has the consistency of tapioca. Now easier to reach by the road from Vátos (see overleaf), which is paved for all but the last 500m, it was for years a well-guarded secret among aficionados; a shallow, safe strand with rollers, spotted with vast boulders and overlooked by tall, tree-covered cliffs. Nowadays, however, the secret is out and it tends to get very crowded on a summer's day. Nudists and freelance campers now have to share the sand with the increasing numbers who plod down the widened but dusty access track, or invade from the sea on day-trip boats from nearby resorts such as Glyfádha. Although there are now three refreshment stalls and sunshade concessions, the charm of the place hasn't been entirely swamped, but it's best visited at either end of the day or out of high season entirely. Above the north end of the beach is the tiny, whitewashed **Myrtiótissa monastery**, dedicated to Our Lady of the Myrtles, which is open in the daytime and has a curious little gift shop attached. Just off the road down from Vátos, a few hundred metres above the beach, the ✴ *Myrtia* taverna (☎26610/94 113, ⓔsks_mirtia@hotmail.com; ❷) serves tasty home cooking and has the only **rooms** close to the beach. Newly opened and resplendent in pinewood, the *Elia* taverna offers a range of tasty main courses and *mezédhes*.

The small village of **VÁTOS**, 2km inland from Érmones, makes an alternative base if Érmones and Glyfádha are full or if you want to stay close to Myrtiótissa. The lower part of the village is conveniently on the Glyfádha bus route from Corfu Town. There is very little to see up in the old village, though the rickety whitewashed buildings are quaint and the thirteenth-century **church** of Áyios Nikólaos is worth a peep inside if you are lucky enough to find it open. Apart from that, there is just one shop-cum-café in the tiny square, as all the other facilities are 1km down on the main road. Just towards Érmones from the turning up to the old village, the *Olympic Restaurant and Grill* (☎26610/94 318; ❷) has **rooms** and **apartments** as well as the only **food** in the vicinity, while *Villa Frederiki* (☎26610/94 658 or 94 003; ❸), on the opposite side of the main road, has two double apartments that can easily accommodate four people each. About 500m further inland from the turning is the basic but shaded *Vatos Camping* (☎26610/94 393). You can indulge yourself in a tipple at the *19th Hole* **bar**.

Glyfádha and Pélekas

GLYFÁDHA boasts a splendid beach, which is well worth a visit out of high season. The resort is thoroughly dominated by the *Louis Grand* (☎26610/94 140–5, ⓦwww.louishotels.com; half-board ❸), a large luxury **hotel** in its own spacious grounds, with a residents-only pool and a bar and restaurant open to nonresidents. The hotel, which takes up a good quarter of the available beach-front, is used by the major package-tour operators, but has rooms for independent travellers throughout the season. There's a more modest and quieter hotel at the far north end of the bay, the *Glyfada Beach* (☎26610/94 258, ⒻＳ94 257; ❸), with en-suite rooms and balconies overlooking the beach, while much of the space behind the centre of the strand is occupied by the sprawling new *Menigos* complex (☎26610/95 074, Ⓕ94 933; ❺), which has a myriad of self-contained **studios** with room for four people. Some of the cheapest rooms on the whole island, though they're perfectly adequate, belong to the *Glyfada* taverna (☎26610/94 224; ❶), next to the *Glyfada Beach*.

Glyfádha is not blessed with the greatest choice of **restaurants**, but the *Glyfada* taverna (see above) serves tasty fish and meat dishes at prices to match the cheap rooms, while the adjacent taverna, belonging to the *Glyfada Beach*, has slightly higher prices for its decent home-style cooking. The best bet for a wide range of standard taverna fare at the south end of the beach is the *Golden Beach*, which has a snack-bar right on the sand. Average meals are also served at the *Gorgona* pool-bar, towards the centre of the beach, which is better just for a drink. The centre of **nightlife** (and day-life) is the *Aloha* bar, which pumps out sounds from its powerful speakers from mid-morning until the small hours.

The attractive hilltop village of **PÉLEKAS**, 3km inland from Glyfádha, has long been popular for its views – particularly at sunset – and for its welcome summer breezes. In the 1970s it gained something of a reputation as a hippy hangout and traces of its psychedelic past still linger on in a couple of the alternative bars and shops. These days Pélekas attracts independent visitors who come for the friendly atmosphere and mountain air. It is also the only inland resort with any real development and choice of facilities on the whole island. Although there is not much traditional architecture beyond a couple of picturesque churches, it is worth considering as an alternative base to the beaches, at least for a couple of days, especially as a handy **free minibus** shuttles back and forth to the beach at Glyfádha four or five times a day in season. A thirty-minute walk above the village is the **Kaiser's Throne**, a small viewing tower with sweeping views of the coast in both directions, and so called because it was Wilhelm II's favourite spot on the entire island.

There are some good **places to stay**, including the budget-oriented *Nikos* hotel (☎26610/94 486; ❷), as well as the comfortable central *Alexandros Pansion* (☎26610/94 215, ⓦwww.alexandrospelekas.com; ❷) and the very friendly *Pension Paradise* (☎26610/94 530; ❶), on the road in from Vátos. Up near the Kaiser's Throne, the ⚑ *Levant Hotel* (☎26610/94 230 or 94 335, www.levanthotel.com; ❼) is a top-class establishment, with views out over the sea and coastline which are unlikely to be bettered anywhere else on the island. Among **tavernas**, *Alexandros* has a wide selection of well-prepared grilled and baked dishes plus tasty *mezédhes*, while the oddly named *Pink Panther*, on the Vátos road, serves huge portions of tasty items, many with a welcome peppery tang, which you can wash down with their lovely *imíglykos* wine. ⅄ *Roula's Grill House*, on the road to Corfu Town from the tiny square, is highly recommended for succulent cuts of meat, and another good *psistariá* is *Antonis*, right in the centre. Just below the square, the cosy and brightly painted *Zanzibar*, run by a witty Brummie lady, is by far the most conducive spot for a **drink** to an eclectic rock and ethnic soundtrack.

Pélekas's long, sandy **beach**, marked on most maps as Kondoyialós, can be reached by two distinctly hair-raising roads which issue at opposite ends of the bay; the one on the north side off the Vátos road is marginally easier to drive down than the one signposted off the road to Corfu Town. Sadly, the scenic nature of the beach has been rather marred by the monstrous new *Pelekas Beach* package hotel that now looms over it and has brought previously unheard of crowds in its wake. Still, it's not a bad spot for a dip as part of a west coast tour.

At the southern end of the beach, **rooms** are available at *Maria's Place* (☎26610/94 601; ❷), an excellent family run **taverna** with a high reputation for the fish caught daily by the owner's husband. *Spiros* taverna (☎26610/94 641, ⓕ94 971; ❷), towards the northern end, also has decent rooms and a limited menu of old favourites. Fifty metres back along the northern approach road, the smart new *Parnassus* studios (☎26610/95 038; ❶) offers cheap rooms facing the mountain and much pricier ones with a sea view. Perched on a rocky outcrop at the same end of the beach, that rarest of birds, an old-style seaside **kafenío**, with the name of the owner, Yiannis Grammenos, scrawled in Greek above the door, is a superb spot for an ultra-cheap *oúzo* or beer.

Sinarádhes and around

The mountainous interior behind this central stretch of the west coast conceals some picturesque villages, well worth touring if you have your own wheels or a passion for walking. Places such as **Kouromádhes** and **Varypatádhes** are full of character, with archetypal country churches, stone houses crowded into narrow streets, the odd old-time *kafenío* and a sense of Corfiot life long lost at the coastal resorts. This atmosphere of days gone by is best reflected in **SINARÁDHES**, which has the **Folk Museum of Central Corfu** (Tues–Sun 9.30am–2.30pm; €1.50). The museum comprises an authentic village house, complete with original furniture, fittings and decoration and full of articles and utensils that formed an intrinsic part of daily rural life. The town's meagre facilities are clustered around the central square, which occupies an elevated open area beside the main street and thus has excellent views inland. You can enjoy a coffee or something stronger at the **café-bar** *Sinarades*, or grab a tasty and inexpensive meal at the friendly *Igoumenos* **psistariá**, where you are likely to find a lamb or piglet being roasted on the pavement outside. South of Sinarádhes, at a high point in the road that winds south to Áyios Górdhis, the bright *Aerostato* café is a great spot at which to enjoy a drink or snack while admiring the sweeping coastal views its name (Air Balloon) promises.

Áï Górdhis and Mount Áyii Dhéka

Around 7km south of Pélekas, **Áï GÓRDHIS** is one of the key play beaches on the island, largely because of the activities organized by the startling **Pink**

Palace complex (☎26610/53 103–4, ⓦwww.thepinkpalace.com; ❶), which fairly dominates the resort. The beach itself is one of the finest on the island, a long, sandy strand backed by pine-clad hills. The *Pink Palace*, covering much of the hillside and a prime chunk of beachside, has swimming pools, games courts, restaurants, a shop and disco, Internet facilities (€3 per hour) and nearly a hundred staff to run beach sports and other activities. It's open all year and hugely popular with backpackers, who cram into communal rooms for up to ten (smaller rooms are also available) for a bargain €18–26 a night, including breakfast and a buffet dinner. Other accommodation is available on the beach, notably at *Michali's Place* taverna (☎26610/53 041; ❷), at the end of the beach approach road, or further south along the front at ✴ *Calypso* (☎26610/53 101 or 53 369, ⓦwww.divingcorfu.com; ❷), which is primarily a **diving centre** and offers excellent diving packages with accommodation. Rooms can also be found here and elsewhere on the island through the large and efficient Karoukas Travel (☎26610/53 909 or 53 961, ⓦwww.karoukas-travel.com), which in addition handles excursions and vehicle rental. Apart from the standard *Michali's Place*, the nearby *Alex-in-the-Garden* **restaurant** is popular for its baked dishes, while a little further inland, *Sebastian* serves crispy potato skins and gourmet veggie items at a little above regular taverna prices. Best value on the beach is the inexpensive fish and wide range of *mezédhes* at *Sea Breeze*. If you aren't up to bopping at the *Pink Palace's* disco, quieter **drinks** can be had at *Aloha* or the *Mythos* cocktail bar.

Roughly 5km east of Áï Górdhis, right in the centre of the narrowing body of the island, is the south's largest prominence, the humpback of **Mount Áyii Dhéka**, at 576m just tall enough to be designated a mountain. Reached by path from the hamlet of **Áno Garoúna**, which is clearly signposted from Káto Garoúna on the inland route between Górdhis and Paramónas, the mountain is the island's second largest after Pandokrátor. Its **peak** affords panoramic views over the south, as far north as Pandokrátor and over to the mainland. From the wooded lower slopes you can glimpse buzzards wheeling on thermals high above on the upper reaches. The mountain summit also harbours something of a surprise: a shallow depression, the crater of an extinct volcano supposedly, containing an orchard full of fruit and nut trees. These are tended by the monks from the diminutive **Moní Ayíon Dhéka**, a crumbling whitewashed monastery also huddled in the depression. The walk from Áno Garoúna to the top and back can be done comfortably in an hour and a half. Those with more stamina – and a good map or compass – might consider following the path that leads from the summit down into the village of **Áyii Dhéka** and on to Benítses (see p.114). A couple of old **kafenía** in Áno Garoúna and Áyii Dhéka provide the only refreshments along the way.

Pendáti, Paramónas and Áyios Mathéos

Around 2km south of Áï Górdhis as the crow flies, but reached by a country lane skirting around the hills for 5km, the fishing hamlet of **PENDÁTI** sits on a narrow coastal plateau 200m above sea level. Small, winding tracks north and south of the hamlet lead down to tiny inlets from where the local fishermen ply their trade. There is no accommodation in the village, but *Angela's* café and minimarket and the *Strofi* grill cater to villagers and the few tourists who stray here.

Walkers and careful drivers are recommended the four-kilometre coastal road between here and **PARAMÓNAS**, which is still only partially surfaced, but affords excellent views over the coastline. Paramónas itself is slightly larger than

Architecture
in Corfu

Corfu possesses a wealth of architectural diversity that possibly exceeds that of any other Greek island. Whilst not endowed with many remains from the country's Classical period, its strategically desirable position at the head of the Ionian archipelago has meant that successive waves of occupiers, from the Byzantines to the Venetians, the French and the Brtish, have all left their stamp on the look of the island. Moreover, Corfu's northerly location meant that it avoided the catastrophic 1953 earthquake that, to varying degrees, left so many buildings on the islands to the south in ruins.

Classical temples, Roman ruins

Despite the various Homeric myths associated with the island, no Mycenean remains have been discovered on Corfu and precious little has been found from **Classical** times: apart from the minimal ruined temples of Hera and Apollo on the Mon Repos estate south of Corfu Town, the most substantial structure is the nearby Temple of Artemis, dated around 590–580 BC, comprising an extensive collection of foundations and toppled columns. The size of the site alone gives an indication of the temple's original grandeur; it was from here that the terrifying Gorgon pediment, showing the mythical monster gruesomely decapitating a victim, was removed for display in the Archeological Museum. The only significant **Roman** ruins, meanwhile, are the baths at Paleópolis and Benítses, both displaying modest systems of foundations and water cisterns.

Early Christian basilica

Byzantine churches

The other islands

Corfu may have the lion's share of the architectural wealth of the Ionians but there are several gems on the rest of the archipelago. The following is a selection of the best.

Áyios Yióryios fortress, Kefalloniá The most dramatic fort location in the Ionians after Corfu's Angelókastro, with sweeping views of Mount Énos, the central plains, and the sea towards Zákynthos.

Lefkádha Town's churches Of the old churches that survived the 1953 earthquake, Áyios Dhimítrios, Áyios Minás and Pandokrátor stand out for their fine decorative features and Ionian School paintings.

Byzantine Museum, Zakynthos Town Housing a fascinating collection, the museum is also an imposing neoclassical edifice in its own right, reflecting the grandeur of the town's central square.

Áyios Yerásimos monastery, Kefalloniá This vast complex houses a variety of buildings from different ages, as well as beautiful decoration.

The Kástro, Bóhali, Zákynthos The remains of this Venetian fortress are most noteworthy for their commanding position, which provides a fantastic lookout across the capital and its harbour.

Englouví, Lefkádha The tiny, picturesque square in this mountain village is one of the finest spots in the Ionians for traditional island architecture.

From the long-lasting **Byzantine** era, many more tangible remains have survived, the oldest being the huge, early Christian basilica opposite Mon Repos, dating from the fifth century. Although the surviving structure is fairly skeletal, a stroll around the wooden walkway allows you to see the imposing triple entrance to the nave and sizeable parts of the walls. The oldest complete **church**, dedicated to Áyii Iáson and Sosípater in the eleventh century, is not far from here, near the Garítsa seafront; it's a typical example of a Byzantine church, patterned on the shape of the cross with a neat round dome. Although quite austere on the inside and out, it is easy to see how it was built of banded sandstone and brick on top of more solid blocks taken from older buildings. Another surviving Byzantine relic is the lovely twelfth-century chapel of Pandokrátor on the offshore islet of Pondikoníssi.

Paleó Froúrio, Corfu Town

Early strongholds

The Byzantine period saw the first flurry of **fortress**-building, such as the squat thirteenth-century **Gardhíki Pýrgos** in the south and, most notably, the earliest version of the Paleó Froúrio in Corfu Town, which was commenced in the sixth century. Towards the end of Byzantine rule, invaders from the north gradually took control of the island, and the odd-castle-out, in subsequent history, is the ruined fortress at **Kassiópi**, which dates from the short period of **Angevin** ascendancy. This makes for a fun scramble among destroyed battlements on the promontary overlooking the harbour.

Venetian influences

Most of the later work on the Paleó Froúrio was actually done by the **Venetians**, who replaced the earlier structure with their own crenellated bastions, casemates, towers and a moat. These are universally admired by military architects, and the views of – and from – the ramparts are stunning. Shortly afterwards, they also constructed the Néo Froúrio for even greater security and its gargantuan walls remain as imposing as when first built. Another of their creations, on the west side of the island near Paleokastrítsa, was the **Angelókastro**, the lofty location of which, above the coast, ranks among the finest in Greece.

Architects from Venice also left two of the Old Town's most important churches; the one dedicated to patron saint **Áyios Spyrídhon** in 1589 has a single nave and a tower housing two huge bells, the highest structure in town. These free-standing campaniles, sometimes elaborately decorated, are a Venetian tradition and accompany many of the older churches on Corfu and the other Ionian islands.

In contrast with the often plain exteriors of the churches, the interiors are usually a riot of icons and paintings. This is certainly true of the other Venetian ecclesiastical masterpiece, the 1577 grand **Mitropólis cathedral**, down towards the Old Port. Its exterior – an attractive baroque facade with a dramatic sun motif above the entrance – is in fact the product

Angelókastro, near Paleokastrítsa

Colonnaded arcades of the Listón

of a makeover around one hundred years ago. Apart from churches, the Venetians also left many beautiful public buildings, including the baroque-style seventeenth-century **City Hall**. Meanwhile, their surviving private residences, often with elaborately carved doorways, set the the tone for the classy houses that followed under subsequent colonists from further north.

The Colonial era and Independence

The most noteworthy legacy of the short period of **French** dominion is the graceful colonnaded arcade that runs the length of the **Listón** (now the town's prime coffee-sipping spot), as well as many attractive iron-balconied houses like those that crowd the old town. On the heels of the French, came the **British**, with their own grand vision of public building, which in the nineteenth century left the island capital with the huge neoclassical edifice of the **Palace of Saints Michael and George**. Now housing both a museum and art gallery, as well as boasting lovely grounds, it is a delightful place for strolling, whether to peruse the exhibits or to admire the view from the garden café. The British legacy includes several other impressive structures such as the Ionian Bank, the Ionian Parliament building and the Maitland Rotunda. They also exercised their military engineers by adding considerably to both the Paleó and Néo Froúrio.

The post-colonial period has not been without its highlights: **local architects** such as Ioannis Khronis played a role during the early years of Greek Independence, contributing the outstanding Kapodhistrias mansion for Greece's first prime minister.

Old Corfu Town

Pendáti, but still has only a few businesses geared to tourism. Situated on sandy Makroúla Bay, the hamlet is, however, beginning to develop an infrastructure: the ⚓ *Paramonas* (☎26610/76 595–6, ⓦwww.paramonas-hotel.com; ❹) is a smart modern **hotel** a little way back from the beach, while the *Sunset* taverna (☎26610/75 149, ⓕ75 686; ❶) in front of it has some good-value **rooms**; alternatively, well-appointed **apartments** can be found at the quiet *Areti Studios* (☎26610/75 838; ❸), just below the lane in from Pendáti. For **eats**, both the aforementioned *Sunset*, which specializes in inexpensive fish, and *Paramonas Bridge*, a good place for cheap oven food 500m inland, are recommended, while the beachside *Plori* taverna-bar serves up decent food as well as cocktails.

The town of **ÁYIOS MATTHÉOS**, 3km inland and shadowed by Mount Prasoúdhi, is chiefly an agricultural centre, and has little truck with tourism. Its narrow main road is often thronged with local traffic – so much so that visiting motorists have had their vehicles manhandled aside to allow the Corfu Town bus to pass. There is still no noticeable accommodation in the town, although a number of **tavernas** are happy to welcome the trickle of passers-by: head for the *Mouria*, or *To Kadouni*, which are both around the eucalyptus-shaded square and serve up delicious cuts of grilled meat. Hidden among the stone houses that crowd the alleys above the main road, *The Golden Heart* serves authentic home cooking. Most scenic of the several **kafenía** is *O Platanos* by the square, with seating under the huge plane it is named after.

On the other side of Mount Prasoúdhi, 2km by road, is the **Gardhíki Pýrgos** (8am–sunset; free), the ruins of a thirteenth-century castle built in this unlikely lowland setting by the Despots of Epirus. Little remains of the castle apart from its outer walls and traces of frescoes in the southernmost of the eight towers that constituted the whole, but sufficient renovations have been completed for it now to be open to the public. Note the huge gnarled and twisted trunk of the ancient olive tree that guards the entrance. Just off the road south of the castle, a large cave, now empty, was the site of some of the oldest archeological finds on the island, dated back to the Paleolithic age. The road continues on to the northernmost tip of the beach on the sea edge of the Korissíon lagoon (see p.117).

Benítses and the south

Corfu's southeast coast was the first to develop tourism on the island back in the 1960s, and became synonymous with some of the worst excesses of the package holiday culture, in terms of both tacky development and the behaviour of some visitors. In the 1980s, the idea of casting even a sympathetic eye at **Benítses** would have been unthinkable, but the early-1990s slump in tourism wrought many changes. The second half of the 1990s saw the resort spruce itself up and regain popularity as a family destination, while the crowds of drunks and revellers vanished or moved to the island's southern tip at **Kávos** (see p.121). In between the two lie a mixed bag of smaller resorts, along with **Lefkími**, Corfu's second largest town and capital of the south, a functional but not unappealing place that is sadly often overlooked.

Rooms are plentiful throughout the lower half of the island, although there are no longer any campsites south of Corfu Town. **Beaches** along this stretch of coast tend to be narrow strips of pebble or shingle until you reach the two-kilometre stretch of sand at Kávos. Beyond **Messongí**, however, the main road south turns inland, and is more or less equidistant from the coasts, putting the spectacular beaches on the southwest-facing shore, such as the one that stretches from the **Korissíon Lagoon** through **Áyios Yeóryios** all the way to **Ayía Varvára**, within easy reach. The lagoon itself provides the south's natural highlight.

Benítses

Immediately south of Corfu Town, there's little point in recommending anything much before **BENÍTSES**: accommodation in the suburb of Pérama and on the edge of the swamps around the Halikópoulou lagoon is just too close to the airport and its approach paths. Once you reach Benítses, you'll see signs of its grim heyday – the southern end still boasts some tacky bars – but the old centre at the north end has reverted to a quiet, whitewashed, bougainvillea-splashed Greek village with a long landscaped square cushioning much of it from the busy thoroughfare. A few minutes' walk through the alleys behind it and you're in thick woodland with streams. Benítses' beach, however, is at best serviceable; most people congregate on the small spit of land below the *Hotel Corfu Maris* at the southern end of town.

Unlike most resorts, Benítses does have a couple of modest tourist attractions. At the back of the old village there are some small, though rather disappointing, **Roman remains**, the small corner of a bathhouse buried in weeds behind fences. More worthy of a visit is the curious **Shell Museum** (March–Oct daily 9am–7pm, closes later in high season; €4), on the main road north of the village. It contains more than two thousand shells from all over the world, including some splendid conches, as well as some incongruous and rather disturbing freaks of nature like seven-legged lambs preserved in jars.

Practicalities

Rooms are plentiful in Benítses, but often rented through agencies; both the friendly Achilles Tourist Centre (T 26610/72 198 or 72 228, E kapsoandre@ker .otenet.gr), behind the park, and Best Travel (T 26610/72 037, F 71 036), on the south side of the resort, have decently priced options in and around the village. With visitor numbers still not back to the levels of yore, however, some **hotels** are just as cheap. In consecutive side streets towards the southern end, the jointly run *Hotel Benitsa/Agis* (T 26610/39 269 or 92 248; ❷) and more modern *Benitses Arches* (T 26610/72 113 or 72 116; ❸) both offer quiet en-suite rooms. Seemingly conceived as an ironic tilt at the nearby Achilleion (see p.87), the gargantuan *Hotel Potamaki* (T 26610/71 140 or 72201, W www .potamakibeachhotel.gr; ❹) revels in eye-popping Neoclassical detail in its large courtyard bar-restaurant and interior halls, although the en-suite rooms, most with views, are more demure.

Above the coast road 2km north of Benítses is one of the smartest hotels on the island, the *San Stefano* (T 26610/71 117 or 71 123, W www.ellada .net/sanstef; ❻), a vast, international ziggurat-style hotel with pools, restaurants and its own kilometre-long access road, as well as a patch of private beach ten minutes' walk below. Also worthy of note, on the road to the Achilleion just north of the *San Stefano* – though a steep 2km from the sea – is the quiet *Hotel Montagnola* (T 26610/56 205 or 56 789, W www.hotelmontagnola.gr; ❺), with pool, tennis court, restaurant and spacious rooms with sea views.

Benítses always catered to a free-spending crowd, and it has its fair share of moderately chic **restaurants**, as well as cheap snack joints. There's a curiously popular hybrid of Chinese and Greek in the extravagantly decorated *Flower Garden*, in the old village, or you can get well-prepared Corfiot cuisine at *O Paxinos*, just down the lane. On the southern stretch of the main road, ⚓ *Avra* is a genuine Italian restaurant, which serves fine risottos and spaghetti on its vine-covered seaside patio, while colourful *Feng Shui* nearby is the place for gourmet snacks involving such rarities as gorgonzola.

The **bars** at the southern end of town are still fairly lively, despite new rules controlling the all-night excesses; stalwarts such as the *Stadium* **nightclub** opens most nights, as does adjacent but smaller *Casanovas 2000*. Substantially more mellow, unless there's a late-night mob partying, are *Lacey's* or *Sunshine* in the old village.

Moraïtika and Messongí

The coast road south of Benítses is speckled with rooms and small hotels above scraps of beach, although negotiating this road on foot can be a nightmare owing to the traffic. The next two resorts of any note, Moraítika and Messongí, have now more or less merged into one. **MORAÏTIKA'S** main street is an ugly strip of bars, restaurants and shops you could find anywhere in the islands, but the beach running parallel to it is the best between Corfu Town and Kávos, a mixture of shingle and sand, and very busy in high season. The usual range of wind sports is on offer through a couple of enterprises on the beach.

Much accommodation is block-booked for families on package tours, especially from Germany and Scandinavia, so the best source of **rooms** is through one of the agencies or the Municipality of Melitía information bureau (May–Oct 9.30am–2pm and 5.30–11pm; ☎26610/75 475, ✉epadim1@ker.forthnet .gr), halfway along the main road. Of the private agents, the G & S Moraïtika Tourist Centre (☎26610/75 723 or 76 682, ✉gstravelcfu@aias.gr) and Budget Ways Travel (☎26610/75 664 or 76 768, ℱ75 664), both at the southern end of the main road, offer a range of accommodation (from ❷). Reasonable beachside **hotels** likely to have space for the independent traveller include the *Margarita Beach* (☎26610/76 267, ⓦwww.corfu-hotel-margarita.com; ❹) and the *Three Stars* (☎26610/75 263, ⓦwww.corfu3starshotel.com; ❹), both of which have comfortable en-suite rooms with balconies, some with sea views. Confusingly, the luxury-class ⚓ *Messonghi Beach* (☎26610/75 830–3, ⓦwww.messonghibeach.gr; ❼), which offers a vast range of facilities and activities including tennis and scuba diving, occupies the southernmost chunk of Moraítika's beachfront, rather than Messongí's, and extends well inland.

Much of the main drag is dominated by souvenir shops and minimarkets, as well as a range of **bars**: flash joints like *Cadillac*, with the front end of a classic American model suspended over the bar, and *Very Coco*, of which the odd name is a play on the Greek for apricot. The latter concentrates on dance music, while the oldest surviving bar, *Charlie's*, which opened in 1939, is more of a rock aficionado's haunt. The *Premier Internet Café* allows you to surf the Net for €4 per hour, while sipping a cocktail or beer. The resort's largest **dance venue** is *Scorpion*, several hundred metres inland.

The Islands **restaurant** on the main drag is recommended for its huge menu of good vegetarian, Greek and international food, as is the *Rose Garden*, just down an alley on the west side. Of the beachside restaurants, *Kavouria*, as its name ("crabs") suggests, does excellent seafood, as does the *Scorpios* fish taverna.

Áno Moraïtika

The garish main drag is by no means all there is to Moraïtika: the older village on the hill above it, **ÁNO MORAÏTIKA**, is virtually unspoilt. The tiny houses and alleys, overgrown with bougainvillea, are a far cry from the busy modern strip below. It's a few minutes' hike up the steep lanes inland, a climb which takes you past the attractive **church** of Theotókou Kimíseos with its quaint belfry. In the heart of the village, the better of the two **tavernas** is the *Village Taverna*, serving a catholic range of island specialities. Further up the hill on the south side of the village, the *Bella Vista* offers a more limited menu, but justifies its name with a great view over the coast from the lovely garden – on hot days, it's a fine place to park yourself in the breeze. There's little independent **accommodation** in the village, apart from the smart *Corifo Apartments* (T26610/32 891; ❸) on its southern edge.

Messongí

Barely a hundred metres on from the Moraïtika seafront, on the south side of the River Messongís, **MESSONGÍ** is much quieter than its northern neighbour and is frequented by smattering of British to augment the Germanic family contingent. One remarkably good-value **place to stay**, with a pool, gardens, and en-suite rooms with balconies, is *Pantheon Hall* (T26610/76 906 or 75 268, Wwww.corfu-summer.com; ❶), run by Brits; it is liable to be full with groups in high season though. *Hotel Gemini* (T26610/75 211–2, Wwww .geminihotel.gr; ❺), opposite, and *Christina's* (T26610/75 294, F76 515; ❹), round the corner, are substantially more expensive but they do offer cut-price deals on weekly and fortnightly rates. An alternative source of accommodation is the village travel agency, Pandora Travel (T26610/75 329, F75 097), which has a range of apartments and villas.

Messongí has a number of good **restaurants**, notably *Bakhos* and *Memories*, which are both on the beach and specialize in Corfiot dishes, *mezédhes* and their own barrel wine, and the upmarket *Castello*, which mixes local dishes like *sofríto*, with seafood (including mussels) and – a rarity on Corfu – asparagus. The best part of a kilometre towards Boúkari, the *Fisherman's Haunt* is a cheap, traditional *psarotavérna*. Two **bars** bookend Messongí: the cute little *Olive Tree Pub*, a block back from the southern end of beach, which plays an eclectic mix of rock, pop and occasional ethnic sounds, and the more standard *Oasis*.

Boúkari and around

The road from Messongí to **BOÚKARI** is very quiet even in high season, and follows the seashore for about 3km, often only several metres above it. The few available plots of land here have been snapped up by wealthy Greeks, whose discreet villas testify to the appeal of the area. It is out of the way, but an idyllic little strip of unspoilt coast for anyone fleeing the crowds elsewhere. Inland from here is the wooded farming region around Aryirádhes, rarely visited by tourists and a perfect place for undisturbed walks. The hamlet of Boúkari itself comprises little more than a handful of **tavernas** and **hotels**, clustered round a small harbour. The best of these for both food and rooms is the *Hotel Golden Sunset* (T26620/51 853, Wwww.corfu-goldensunset.com; ❸), while a short way up the hill where the main road turns abruptly inland is the cheaper *Helios Hotel* (T26620/51 824, Ealdebara@otenet.gr; ❷). Around 1km north of the harbour, the ⚓ *Boukari Beach* (T26620/51 791–2, Wwww.boukaribeach.com; ❷) is one of the best restaurant-cum-accommodation enterprises in southern Corfu, run by the friendly Vlahopoulos family. The **taverna** is renowned for its delicious home cooking and fresh fish and lobsters, which you can choose from a tank, while their several small, smart **apartment** complexes, *Villa Alexandra*, *Villa Lucia*, and *Hotel Penelope* are all great value.

Petrití and Nótos beach

A short way round the coastline from Boúkari but accessed via 5km of steep and narrow lanes across the intervening headland, the seemingly prosperous village of **PETRITÍ** fronts a small dirt-track harbour, but in general is mercifully free of noise and commerce. It was only created in the 1970s when geologists discovered the hill village of **Korakádhes** was subsiding and had to be evacuated – a warning twelve people have resolutely refused to heed. In its setting among low, olive-covered hills, with tree-covered rocks in the bay, Petrití would be perfect for a quiet getaway if it weren't for the limited swimming potential. Maps claim that it has a beach, but this is a cartographic fancy: the littoral is variously bulldozed rock, thick mud and a small stretch of sand above more mud – though local children do swim here.

The *Pension Egrypos* (℡26620/51 949, www.egrypos.gr; ❸) has simple rooms and a pleasant garden **taverna**, set back among trees near a beautiful white church, a couple of hundred metres from the harbour. At the harbour itself, which is the departure point for yacht flotilla holidays, several tavernas serve the trickle of sea and land traffic: the smart waterfront *Limnopoula*, offering a wide range of locally caught fish and seafood, is best, followed by the simpler *Stamatis*. Also by the harbour, the newer *Pension Christina* (℡26620/52 272, christina@lmsc .com; ❸) has comfortable **rooms** with fridges and complimentary breakfast.

Some way back from the village, tucked away in the middle of woodlands near the hamlet of Vassilátika, is the elegant *Regina* **hotel**, with gardens and pool (℡26620/52 132, www.reginahotel.de; ❹), which specializes in full-board holidays for German tourists, but often has room-only availability.

Barely 2km south of Petrití, the rocky coves of **NÓTOS** beach are little visited and secrete a wonderful and friendly place to stay in the shape of *Panorama Apartments* (℡26620/51 707, www.panoramacorfu.gr; ❷), which has its own swimming pontoons and a fine shady restaurant. Alternatively, you can enjoy a good traditional meal at the adjacent *Elektra Garden*.

The Korissíon lagoon

Over 5km long and 1km wide at its centre, **KORISSÍON LAGOON** is in fact man-made, excavated, with a channel to the sea, by the Venetians. Now a **nature reserve**, Korissíon is home to turtles, tortoises, lizards and numerous indigenous and migrating birds, including ducks, waders, herons and other species that feed on wetlands. Migratory birds are more often observed towards the end of the season (even though rifle-hunting of birds is allowed in the autumn), but they can also be seen in early season as well. You can walk all around the lagoon in about two and a half hours by way of a new footbridge that crosses the channel linking it to the sea. The inland edge of the lagoon is rich in flora (see p.281), varying according to the time of year you visit.

The lagoon is most easily reached by walking from the village of **Línia** (on the Kávos bus route) via Íssos beach. An alternative route is from the north, via **Khlomatianá**, which brings you to an isolated inland shore at the lagoon's widest point. The best approach, however, especially if you have transport, is to the northernmost end: follow the Áyios Mathéos signs from Áno Messongí, then two left turns bring you via the Gardhíki Pýrgos (see p.113) to **Halikoúna** beach, a glorious thick wedge of sand backed by wind-blown dunes, which is even more deserted and beautiful than the southern edge of Korissíon towards Íssos. Just to the northwest, accessed by a dirt track (1.5km) from near the northwest inland corner of the lagoon, is tiny **Alonáki** beach, set below some low reddish cliffs, with plenty of shade and pebble-strewn sand.

Comfortable and isolated **accommodation** is available around 500m inland from Halikoúna at *Marin Christel Apartments* (T & F 26610/75 947; ❹), a smart place with landscaped gardens and mostly German guests, or at *Logara Apartments* (T 26610/76 477; ❸), an equally appealing retreat. At Alonáki, the *Taverna Alonaki* (T 26610/75 872, F 76 118; ❷) has simple rooms and serves tasty grills in its leafy courtyard. Some **rough camping** does take place on Halikoúna beach, but potential campers should make sure they stay at the very northern end of the lagoon, away from the turtle-nesting grounds. The only refreshments available at Halikoúna beach are from a canteen-cum-shack behind the dunes, but a couple of **tavernas** on the access road behind the lagoon provide staple meals at very fair prices; *Spiros*, 400m inland, offers a slightly better selection than the nearby *Nikolas*.

Áyios Yeóryios and around

With its beach spreading as far south as Méga Hóro point, and north to encircle the edge of the Koríssion lagoon, **ÁYIOS YEÓRYIOS** (not to be confused with the Áyios Yeóryios just north of Paleokastrítsa) lies at the centre of 12km of uninterrupted and fairly unspoilt sand, and is the hub of watersport and other tourist facilities. It is not so much a village, however, is an unprepossessing 2km sprawl that's in danger of becoming a real mess. British package-tour operators dominate the scene, with bars and tavernas competing to present bingo, quizzes and video nights. It is also the resort where many of the locals display the most noticeably mercenary attitude of anywhere in Corfu.

As most of the resort's **accommodation** is block-booked, often even in those places that advertise rooms on street signs, the best chance of finding somewhere, should you decide to stay here, is through one of the travel agencies. Each of the following has a range of rooms, apartments and villas, as well as excursions, vehicle rental and currency exchange facilities: Lord Travel (T 26620/91 890, E lord-travel@otenet.gr), Stork Tours (T & F 26620/51 168) or Star Travel (T 26620/52 800 or 52 940, W www.startravel.com). A couple of the seafront **hotels** keep rooms aside: the *Golden Sands* (T 26620/51 225, W www.corfugoldensands.com; ❸) has a pool, open-air restaurant and gardens, but the best bargain has to be the smaller *Blue Sea* (T 26620/51 624, W www.bluesea-hotel.com; ❸), which offers the same facilities for less.

Áyios Yeóryios is hardly the place for haute cuisine but has a sprinkling of adequate **restaurants** on the seafront: *Stamatis* and *Splendid* turn out safe grills and other standards at fair prices, while *Iron Dragon* provides palatable Chinese food for those wanting a change. **Nightlife** centres round music and pool bars like the *Gold Hart* and *Bluebell*, although laid-back *Amazona* cocktail bar and lively *Mad Mike's*, one of the few places off the seafront, have a better atmosphere.

Íssos beach

A few minutes' walk north of Áyios Yióryios, **Íssos** is at the start of the brilliant stretch of sand and dunes that continue past the channel into the Korissíon lagoon. Unfortunately, the beach is not nearly as deserted as it used to be, with boardwalks, canteens, umbrellas and watersports to draw increasing numbers. Parts of Íssos and the Korissíon beach are turtle-nesting grounds, so should be treated with due care. Avoid nests, stay off the beach at night, don't dig or use spiked beach furniture in the day and never approach a turtle, young or old, if you see one.

Apart from the aforementioned canteens, facilities around Íssos are still drastically limited: one **taverna**, the *Rousellis Grill*, lies a few hundred metres from the beach on the lane leading to Línia on the main road, and there is the *Friends* snack bar in Línia itself. On a hillock of olive trees and prickly pear cacti above the lane, the unmistakeable maroon and yellow *Vicky's Apartments* (☎26620/53 161; ❹) offer comfortable new **studios**. An English-run **windsurfing school** (🌐www.mermanwindsurf.com), operating from a caravan on the beach, has a wide range of boards of different sizes for rent (starting around €15 per hour), as well as a beach simulator and rescue craft, and offers tuition for beginners and upwards – prevailing cross-beach winds make it a safe place to learn. Kayaks and jet skis are also available.

Marathiá and Ayía Varvára

Far pleasanter than Áyios Yeóryios are the two burgeoning developments of **MARATHIÁ** and **AYÍA VARVÁRA**, both further southeast along the continuous strand, but reached by separate and convoluted inland routes. The most direct route to Marathiá beach is signposted from the tiny village of **Marathiás**, on the main road to Lefkími, a couple of kilometres southeast of Aryirádhes. Around 2km out of Marathiás, the road forks; the right branch leads after 400m to a low cliff with a couple of **tavernas** above the end of a triangular wedge of beach, while the left branch ends up beside another duo of beach restaurants. These are divided by only 300m of sand and the estuary of a small stream, bridged by wooden planks, from the beachfront of Ayía Varvára (see below).

Of the two adjacent tavernas on the cliff the extremely inexpensive and friendly ☆*Akroama* (☎26620/52 736; ❷) serves up treats like grilled swordfish or village sausage and has a few **rooms** to rent, while *Nikos* also offers solid Greek staples – both places have seating right on the cliff edge, overlooking the beach. A couple of hundred metres southeast along the strand, some distance from the sea, at the back of the thick wedge of sand, are two more cheap eateries, the better of which is *Golden Beach*, which specializes in fresh fish.

Although it is less than 1km along the sand from Marathiá, Ayía Varvára is at least a seven-kilometre drive away. It is signposted from the village of Perivóli, 2km southeast of Marathiás on the main north-south thoroughfare. The village of Ayía Varvára, clustered on the hill just above the beach, is still home to a few fishermen, and there has been minimal development here, but the locals' attention has begun to turn more to tourism. On the beach, the *Santa Barbara Miaris* (☎26620/22 200, 📧biros@pathfinder.gr; ❷) has good-value **rooms**, including breakfast. Its restaurant also serves full meals and snacks such as jacket potatoes; at night, it transforms itself into the village's prime watering hole, with an eclectic taste in music (you can't sniff at T.Rex). The raised balcony of the *Sunset* taverna, just above the beach, is another good place to eat, offering the usual range of fish, meats and salads.

Lefkími

Most guides either ignore or dismiss **LEFKÍMI**, but anyone interested in how a Greek town works away from the bustle of tourism should not miss it. The charm of the place, where donkeys are still occasionally used as transport and some women retain traditional costume, lies in its stubborn resistance to tourism, which seems almost perverse considering its proximity to Kávos.

Maps distinguish between Áno Lefkími and Lefkími proper, but in fact the two flow into each other and also incorporate the eastern suburbs of Potámi and Melíkia. There are several roads into town from the startling new stretch of sodium-lit dual carriageway, which means traffic for the port and Kávos

△ Church of Áyios Arsénios, Lefkími

can bypass the town entirely. The second largest town after Corfu, Lefkími is the administrative centre of the south of the island with a population of about 5000. The facades of the main street and surrounding alleys are attractive and it makes a welcome change to see real shops selling functional everyday items instead of tourist paraphernalia. There's some fine architecture, including several particularly imposing (but usually locked) churches: **Áyii Anáryiri**, with a striking double belfry, and **Áyios Arsénios**, whose vast orange dome can be seen for miles around, pose proudly on raised platforms at the upper end of town, while **Áyios Theodóros** and its beautiful campanile sit on a mound above a small village square, halfway down the hill towards the canal. It's hardly Amsterdam, but the canal that carries the **River Himáros** through the lower suburb of Potámi has some pleasant spots for a drink or meal by the pretty bridge.

Lefkími also hosts the south's major commercial **port**, although it is separated from the rest of town by at least a kilometre of cultivated fields on the east side. Despite the harbour's great size, however, you'll find no facilities apart from a cafeteria that opens to serve lorry drivers awaiting boats. It can seem an eerily lonely and desolate place in between the bouts of activity that accompany the arrival and departure of boats, and it is hard to imagine that the expansive quay-side ever approaches even a quarter of its capacity. The half-dozen or so daily **ferries** to mainland Igoumenítsa only take forty minutes to make the crossing, making it a good alternative to Corfu Town for anyone staying in the south. It is also possible to take a day-trip to Paxí and Andípaxi from here with Brittania Cruises (Mon–Wed, Fri & Sun 9.30am; €19).

Practicalities

Scarcely any foreigners stay in Lefkími but there are some basic **rooms** at the *Cheeky Face* taverna (℡26620/22 627; ❷), by the canal, and the good-value *Maria Madalena* **apartments** (℡26620/22 386; ❷), in a shady arbour off the main street near Áyios Arsénios. On the diagonally opposite side of the canal from the *Cheeky Face*, the best place to eat is the 🪶 *Maria* **taverna**, which dishes up huge portions of excellent oven food such as casseroled fish and *briam* at a snip. Another good spot for a meal is *To Pikandiko*, further up towards the centre of town, although the food is not as spicy as the name suggests. Dotted around town are a few good local **bars** where tourists are rare enough to guarantee you a friendly welcome. Try the low-key *Mersedes*, the rockier *Enigma*, both within spitting distance of Áyios Arsénios, or the relaxed *Esperos* garden café-bar, just below Áyii Anáryiri.

Kávos and around

The very name **KÁVOS** can make most regular island visitors – and not a few islanders – cross themselves in dread. There are no ambiguities here: either you like 24-hour drinking, clubbing, bungee-jumping, go-karts, video bars named after British sitcoms and chips with almost everything, or you should avoid the place altogether. The resort is sizeable, stretching over 2km of decent, if not particularly clean, sandy beach, with watersports, pedaloes, ringoes and serried sun beds. Sport at night consists of several goals set up in the streets for penalty shoot-out competitions and less innocent pursuits in the bars. The bulk of tourism here is package, but if you want independent **accommodation**, Pandis Travel (℡26620/61 400, ✉ncpandis@otenet.gr) and Island Holidays (℡26620/61 357, ✉vvera@otenet.gr) have decent, cheap rooms and apartments (both from ❷). One independent operation on the Lefkími side is *Studios Irini* (℡26620/22 703; ❷), which is at least a discreet distance from most of the mayhem.

The nearest to genuine Greek **food** you'll find is at the central *Pefkos* taverna, which has an attractive old courtyard, or the *Two Brothers psistariá*, further south. British eating preferences are also catered to by the presence of ethnic restaurants such as *Gurujee*, which combines Chinese and Indian

Walking the Corfu Trail

In 2001, years of hard work and planning came to fruition with the opening of the **Corfu Trail**. The trail, 200km in length, covers the whole island from top to bottom, from **Cape Apsrókavos** in the south to Áyios Spyrídhon beach, next to **Cape Ayías Ekaterínis** in the far north. The route avoids roads as much as possible and takes walkers across a variety of terrain – from beaches to the highest peaks. The principal places passed en route are Lefkími, Korissíon lagoon, Paramónas, Áyii Dhéka, Pélekas, Paleokastrítsa, Áyios Yeóryios Pagón, Agrós and Mount Pandokrátor.

Paths along the entire route are **waymarked** with yellow aluminium signs. As usual, ramblers are advised to wear headgear and stout footwear and carry ample water and provisions, as well as all-weather kit in all but the high summer months. It is reckoned that strong walkers can cover the route in **ten days** and you're advised to follow the trail from south to north for two reasons: firstly the southern sections are gentler and allow you to build up fitness and, secondly, the sun is not in your eyes so much as it would be in the other direction.

Those interested in attempting all or part of the trail should pick up a copy of Hilary Whitton Paipeti's excellent *Companion Guide to the Corfu Trail* (Pedestrian Publications, Corfu; €7.50), which contains detailed **maps** and descriptions of the route, divided into ten daily sectors. A proportion of the profits goes towards maintenance of the trail and anyone using the trail is asked to contribute €3 for the same reason. You can also log on to ⓦwww.travelling.gr/corfutrail for information on organized walking packages, including accommodation.

cuisine. The emphasis here, however, is on shoving down a quick hamburger or portion of fish'n'chips and hitting the bar trail. Well before midnight and for hours after it, even walking along the main drag is something of an obstacle course, so legion are the drunken bodies cavorting outside the unbroken chain of noisy rival bars. *Buzz* is one of the biggest **clubs**, with imported north European DJs mixing techno, drum'n'bass and house, followed by the likes of *42nd Street*, *Limelight* and *The Barn*, all rowdy dance spots, while *Sex* is the biggest club on the beach (one of the few by the sea). *The Face*, a huge video bar showing British soaps and Big Brother, is among the more enduring **bars**, while *Black Duck* provides a rockier soundtrack, and the *Jazz Club*, on the quieter southern road, is more laid back but tends to play soul or R'n'B, rather than jazz.

Beyond the limits of Kávos, where few visitors stray, a path leaving the road south to the hamlet of Sparterá heads on through unspoilt countryside; after around thirty minutes it reaches the cliffs of **Cape Asprókavos** and the crumbling monastery of Panayiás Arkoudhílas, which retains its bell tower and supporting walls. This is also the starting point of the newly opened Corfu Trail (see box above). The cape looks out over the straits to Paxí, 19km away, and down over deserted **Arkoudhílas beach**. The beach, however, is inaccessible from here, though it can be reached from **Sparterá**, just over 3km from Kávos. The home cooking on offer at the *Fantasia* and *Paradise* tavernas in Sparterá is superior to any you can find in the nearby resort. Even more deserted than Arkoudhílas is the beach of **Áyios Górdhis Paleohoríou** (as it is called, to avoid confusion with the resort of Áyios Górdhis further north), 2km southwest of Sparterá and reached by a lane from Dhragotiná. It is one of the least visited beaches on the island, with just one municipal snack bar above it, and even in August you may get a great swathe of the sandy arc, backed by rolling dunes, to yourself.

Corfu's satellite islands

Corfu's three sparsely inhabited satellite islands, **Eríkoussa**, **Othoní** and **Mathráki**, togethr forming the **Dhiapóndia islands**, are situated in a triangle 8–15km off the far northwest coast. Each is distinct in character from the others: Eríkoussa is flat and sandy, Othoní rocky with a hilly interior, Mathráki, the most attractive for island collectors, a green hill surrounded by almost volcanic sandy beaches. On each of the trio the roster of permanent inhabitants has dwindled to barely three figures, less in the case of Mathráki, though the numbers are bolstered by returning diaspora in summer. The islands all saw major emigration to the United States, particularly New York, in the latter half of the twentieth century. Consequently you are not likely to encounter any language problems despite the islands remaining largely off the beaten track.

Most foreigners only pay a brief visit to the islands on **day-trips**. Some travel agencies, for example in Aharávi or Ródha, offer excursions to Eríkoussa only, often with a barbecue thrown in – fine if you want to spend the day on the beach. A trip taking in all three from Sidhári or Áyios Stéfanos is excellent value (around €15–20), if a little hurried: the islands are over thirty minutes apart by boat, and most trips allow you an hour on each, usually longer on sandy Eríkoussa. It's now possible to **stay** on all three islands, although connections between them are limited. The most reliable route is from Áyios Stéfanos with the speed **kaïki** *Pigasos*, which runs to one or more of the islands on most days of the week in summer, less frequently in winter; check with Aspiotis Lines (☎26630/72 655, ℉71 263) for up-to-date schedules. There is also a **ferry** from Corfu Town, the *Alexandros II*, which brings cars and goods to the islands, but given that it has to sail halfway round Corfu first, it's the slowest option for reaching them. You should check with the Port Authority at the New Port (☎26610/32 655) for current sailings, but it usually departs from Corfu Town, travelling round the islands in the order Eríkoussa–Othoní–Mathráki, at 7.30am on Tuesday and Thursday, and 4pm on Friday (overnighting at Mathráki, which it leaves at 9am on Saturday). Islanders themselves sometimes use day-trip boats from the resorts, so it's possible to negotiate a lift if the craft is going your way.

Mathráki

Hilly, densely forested and with a particularly splendid, deserted beach, beautiful **MATHRÁKI** is the least inhabited of the three islands, with only about seventy permanent residents. It lies about 8km due west of Áyios Stéfanos with the abrupt uninhabited islet of Dhiáplo halfway in between. Mathráki's tiny harbour of **Plákes** is near the top of the east coast, facing Corfu, and at present sports little more than a taverna. **Portélo beach** begins at the edge of the harbour, and extends south for 3km of fine, reddish sand. This is another nesting site for the loggerhead turtle so care should be taken not to poke or dig into the sand during the summer breeding season. A single road rises from the harbour into the interior and the scattered village of **Káto Mathráki**. On most day-trips there is time to walk the ten minutes up to the village and have a stop for refreshments looking out over the beach and Corfu. The pungent smell of virgin forest and the views are magnificent, as is the sense of isolation, as very few day visitors make it even this far. If you stay on Mathráki, you can savour a stroll along the partly paved road that follows the cypress–rich spine of the island to the small settlement of **Áno Mathráki**, 3km south. Houses were originally built on the wooded crest, rather than by the sea, to avoid the piracy that was rampant in the early nineteenth century. There are a couple of smaller coves with beaches and the abandoned stone port of Fýki Bay on the wilder west coast, but these are only accessible by boat or very tricky paths through the forest.

At present there are only two **places to stay** on the island, though signs of further construction suggest the unwritten law banning commercialization might be a thing of the past. Both existing operations are at the top of the main beach, within 200m of the port: *Tassos Kassimis* (☎26630/71 700; ❶) offers simple **rooms** and *Christos Aryiros* (☎26630/71 652; ❷) has self-catering **studios**. Apart from *Yeïs*, the village *kafenío*-cum-taverna, which also sells basic provisions, there are no shops on Mathráki, so if you plan to stay be prepared for limited taverna menus. The other two **restaurants**, which unsurprisingly specialize in fresh fish, are *The Port Centre*, right behind the jetty at Plákes, and *Taka Taka*, at the southern end of Portélo beach, also reachable by a bumpy road from Áno Mathráki.

Othoní

Eight kilometres northwest of Mathráki, **OTHONÍ** is the largest of the Dhiapóndia islands and constitutes the westernmost point of Greece. It is paradoxically the most rugged yet most populous of the trio but still only has 120 inhabitants who brave the elements year round. In summer this number is swollen by returning emigrants and other visitors, in particular Italian yachties, who moor at the harbour village of **Ámmos**, in the centre of the southern coast. This is where all the island's facilities are to be found and, contrary to what you might expect from the name Ámmos (Greek for "sand"), the strips of beach on either side of the jetty are pebbly rather than sandy, with crystal-clear water for swimming. A little east of the jetty, the whitewashed exterior walls of **Ayía Triádha church**, built in 1892, give no hint at the subtle art within. Inside there are some vivid icons of Christ Pandokrátor and the apostles on the wood-panelled ceiling and some delicate Italianate paintings on the upper sections of the fine iconostasis.

Othoní's **interior** is dramatic, but you will only be able to explore it if you stay a night or more on the island. A footpath up out of Ámmos leads in around an hour through rocky, tree-covered hills to the dwindling main village, **Horió**, in the northwest. If you make it here, look out for the old bells of Áyios Yeóryios church, nestling in the trees. Horió can also be reached by the island's one paved road, which snakes via several hamlets in the northeast before doubling back close to the north coast, covering a distance of 8.5km in all. A path from the northern hamlet of Dhamaskátika leads down to **Fýki Bay** in the middle of the north coast, which boasts the longest and sandiest beach on the island. Another path runs from the helipad for visiting dignitaries to the main lighthouse at the northeast end of the island, an isolated spot with magnificent views towards both sister islands and Corfu. Othoní is one of the many Ionian locations to claim a stake in Homeric mythology. Islanders believe that the cave in **Calypsó Bay**, tucked beneath the smaller lighthouse in the southwest corner of the island, is the place where Calypso bewitched and held Odysseus and his companions captive for many years. There is also a small but exquisite white sand beach in the bay, though it is only accessible by small boat.

In the summer months at least, the seafront of Ámmos is quite a thriving community, with the air of a modest resort. The village **kafenío**, *O Mikros*, doubles as the island's main shop with a reasonable stock of fresh fruit and vegetables, dairy and meat products, and packaged goods. The smartest of the several **restaurants**, ✗ *La Locanda dei Sogni*, has a resident Italian cook who specializes in pasta with locally caught fish and seafood. The other options are *Lakis*, a basic fish taverna, which also serves healthy portions of home-style oven food, or *New York*, which offers a standard selection of tasty fish, grilled meats and salads. **Accommodation** options have increased dramatically of late with the completion of the smart *Hotel Calypso* (☎26630/72 162, ⓕ71 578; ❹), just off the start of the road inland; most of its comfortable, air-conditioned rooms have sea views. *La Locanda dei Sogni* also has pleasant **rooms** (☎26630/71 640; ❸), though these tend to be pre-booked by Italian visitors. Slightly cheaper but cosy rooms are available behind the west end of the beach from Tassos Katehis (☎26630/72 419; ❷). If you don't have any luck with these, the friendly owners of *O Mikros* may be able to help.

Eríkoussa

Roughly 10km east of Othoní, **ERÍKOUSSA** is the busiest of the Dhiapóndia islands, and the most frequent destination of day-trips from the northwestern resorts. It's invariably hyped as a "desert island" trip, although this is a desert island with a medium-sized hotel, rooms, tavernas, a year-round village community, a paved road and an ugly aggregates plant overlooking its small harbour. In high season, it's far from deserted: Eríkoussa has a large diaspora living in America and elsewhere, who return to family homes in their droves in summer, so you may find your *yiásou* or *kaliméra* returned in a Brooklyn accent.

Eríkoussa, almost circular and only 2km in diameter, has an excellent golden, sandy beach right by the harbour village of **Pórto**, with great swimming off it, while quieter, **Bragíni beach** is reached by a path across the wooded island interior. Even when the day-trip craft arrive in high season, the main beach is rarely busy and, when they depart in mid-afternoon, Eríkoussa reverts to something approaching the "desert island" promised by the tour companies. All the island's facilities are at Pórto. The only **hotel**, the ✗ *Erikoussa* (☎26630/71 110 or 71 555, ⓦwww.hotelerikousa.gr; ❹), remains fairly busy through the season; its comfortable rooms are en suite with balconies and views. Simpler rooms are sometimes available from Theodhora Katehi next door (☎26630/71 821; ❶). If you're hoping to stay, phoning ahead is essential, as is taking anything you might not be able to buy on an island where there are no conventional shops, only a snack-bar selling basic groceries. The *Erikoussa* also boasts the only bona fide **taverna**, serving great fish, meat and starters, although a couple of smaller snack-bars, such as the *Oasis*, can rustle up breakfast or simpler meals.

Travel details

Buses

Green **KTEL** buses run from about 6am to between 5 and 10pm, depending on the route. Note that routes have the same duration and frequency in the opposite direction. The following summer timetable will be reduced on most routes during the winter:

Corfu Town to: Aharávi (5 Mon–Sat, 1 Sun; 1hr 15min); Aríllas (2 Mon–Sat; 1hr); Aï Górdhis (6 Mon–Fri, 5 Sat, 3 Sun; 45min); Áyios Mathéos (4 Mon–Sat, 1 Sun; 1hr); Áyios Stéfanos Pagón (in the northwest; 6 Mon–Sat, 1 Sun; 1hr 30min); Áyios Yeóryios (in the south; 2 daily; 1hr 15min); Áyios Yeóryios Pagón (in the northwest; 2 Mon–Sat; 1hr); Áno Korakiána (6 Mon–Sat; 40min); Barbáti 6 Mon–Sat, 1 Sun; 40min); Benítses (15 Mon–Fri, 13 Sat, 6 Sun; 20min); Érmones (3 Mon–Sat, 1 Sun; 55min); Glyfádha (8 Mon–Sat, 5 Sun; 40min); Ípsos (10 Mon–Fri, 7 Sat, 1 Sun; 30min); Kassiópi (6 Mon–Sat, 1 Sun; 1hr); Kávos (11 Mon–Fri, 8 Sat, 4 Sun; 1hr 30min); Lefkími (11 daily, 8 Sat, 4 Sun;

1hr 15min); Messongí (5 Mon–Sat, 4 Sun; 40min); Moraḯtika (15 Mon–Fri, 13 Sat, 6 Sun; 35min); Nissáki (6 Mon–Sat, 1 Sun; 45min); Paleokastrítsa (7 Mon–Sat, 5 Sun; 30min); Pyryí (10 Mon–Fri, 7 Sat, 1 Sun; 35min); Ródha (5 Mon–Sat, 1 Sun; 1hr); Sidhári (8 Mon–Sat, 1 Sun; 1hr 15min); Vátos (3 Mon–Sat, 2 Sun; 45min).

Kassiópi to: Aharávi (4 Mon–Sat; 15min); Ródha (4 Mon–Sat; 20min); Sidhári (4 Mon–Sat; 30min).

Blue town buses run from about 6am to 10pm. All destinations are reached within 20–30min. The following summer timetable will be reduced on most routes during the winter. The most important routes are:

#2 Mandoúki–central Corfu Town–Kanóni (every 30min Mon–Sat, hourly Sun).
#6 Platía Saróko–Benítses (13 daily).
#7 Platía Saróko–Kondókali–Gouviá–Dhassiá (every 20–30min Mon–Sat, every 30min Sun).
#8 Platía Saróko–Áyios Ioánnis/Aqualand (12–13 Mon–Sat, 6 Sun).
#10 Platía Saróko–Achilleion (6 Mon–Sat, 4 Sun).
#11 Platía Saróko–Pélekas (6–7 Mon–Sat, 4 Sun).

Ferries

Corfu Town to: Eríkoussa/Mathráki/Othoní (3 weekly; 2–4hr); Igoumenítsa (every 10–45min; 1hr 15min); Pátra (6–10 daily; 7–9hr); Sámi (Kefalloniá; 2 weekly; 5hr). Also in season regular departures to the following ports in Italy: Ancona (1–2 daily; 14hr); Bari (2–3 daily; 11hr); Brindisi (3–5 daily; 4–9hr); Trieste (2–3 weekly; 21hr) and Venice (2–3 weekly; 25hr). Most services are reduced off season (for further information, see p.27 and p.36).

Lefkími to: Igoumenítsa (6 daily; 40min). Less frequent off season.

Hydrofoil

From May to October three companies now operate hydrofoil services between Corfu Town and Paxí.

Corfu Town to: Gáïos (3–7 daily; 50min).

Flights

All flights are with Olympic or Aegean and operate year round except for the seasonal seaplane service from Corfu to Paxí and Yiánnina.

Corfu Town to: Athens (4–8 daily; 1hr); Kefalloniá (1 weekly; 1hr 10min); Paxí (2–3 daily; 20min); Préveza (1 weekly; 25min); Yiánnina (10 weekly; 40min); Zákynthos (1 weekly; 1 hr 55min).

2

Paxí

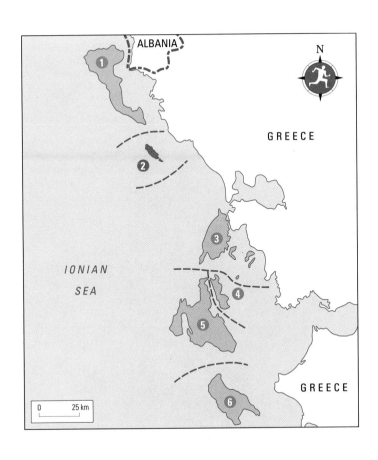

CHAPTER 2   # Highlights

* **Gáïos** The island capital, huddled round a picturesque harbour, contains the only museum and most of Paxí's facilities. **See p.133**

* **Longós** The most scenic of the three main settlements makes a good base from which to explore the rest of the island. **See p.137**

* **Lákka** This is Paxí's liveliest resort and has two of the island's few beaches. **See p.138**

* **Olive groves** Walk among the gnarled and twisted trunks of the island's myriad olive trees. **See p.140**

* **Andípaxi** A day-trip to Paxí's smaller sister is a must for superior swimming and snorkelling opportunities. **See p.142**

△ Gáïos Harbour

2

Paxí

S mall, unusually green and still surprisingly underdeveloped, **Paxí (Paxos)** has established a firm niche in Greece's tourist hierarchy. It has the least to offer of all the major Ionian islands – no sandy beaches, no historical sites, only three hotels and a serious water shortage – yet it has an undeniable air of mystique that makes it one of the most sought-after destinations in the archipelago. It's particularly popular with yachting flotillas and, in high season, young Italian visitors, whose shopping, eating and drinking habits have brought a certain sophistication to the island, but have also led to it becoming the most expensive place in the Ionians. Its three harbour villages can also sometimes feel rather cliquey.

In fact Paxí is so popular in high season that casual visitors are warned to book ahead before boarding a ferry to the island. Most accommodation is block-booked by upmarket north European travel companies (though

there are local tour operators whose holidays might cost half the price) and the few independent rooms that exist tend to get snapped up quickly. To make matters worse, there is no official campsite and freelance camping is not easy.

Although it gets only a fraction of the wet weather that is regularly visited on neighbouring Corfu, Paxí is remarkably verdant. Its abundant **flora** and **bird life** make it a favourite haunt of ornithologists, botanists, walkers and watercolourists. Drenching winter rains produce carpets of dwarf cyclamen in spring; daffodils and antirrhinums flower in February, and by Easter the island's woods and olive groves are full of wild lilies, irises and orchids. Despite the unwanted attentions of hunters, the island is home to numerous native and migratory species of birds. Barn owls and the tiny Scops owl are heard at night, and peregrine falcons nest on remote hilltops. **Walking routes** on Paxí are detailed on the comprehensive map produced by cartographers Elizabeth and Ian Bleasdale and sold by most tourist concerns on the island (€10). *Exploring Paxos and Andipaxos* by Susan Valeria Omar is also informative.

Barely 12km long by 4km wide, Paxí has only three villages of any size, all of them ports: its capital, **Gáïos**, towards the southern end, **Lákka**, at the northern tip, and tiny **Longós**, 2km south of Lákka. Gáïos is where most visitors will arrive, although many immediately head off to the quieter northerly duo. The island's best bathing is around Longós and Lákka, or further afield in the desert island coves and beaches of **Andípaxi**, Paxí's sibling 2km south. Many of Paxí's beaches are not accessible by road or foot, which is where a boat with outboard motor comes in handy. Most village travel agencies and some of the larger international companies offer boat rental by week or day.

Some history

There are two overlapping myths about Paxí's origins. In one, Poseidon needed a place to hide his lover, Amphitrite, and struck the sea with his trident – now Paxí's emblem – to create an island. In the other, the sea god simply wanted somewhere to rest while travelling between islands – odd, given that Homer credits the gods with the power to traverse the Med in a flash – and so created this hideaway between Corfu and Itháki.

Ancient history seems to have passed the island by, apart from a walk-on role in a few key moments. In the third century BC, Paxí was the site of a sea battle between Corcyreans, as Corfiots were then known, and the Illyrian fleet, which resulted in Corcyra becoming the first Greek state to surrender to Roman rule. Antony and Cleopatra are believed to have dined on Paxí on the eve of the ill-fated Battle of Actium in 31 BC, when they were decisively defeated by Octavian's fleet. Paxí is also associated with a piece of Christian mythology, retold by Plutarch in his *Moralia* and interpreted by Spenser and Milton, which cites the island as the place where the death of paganism and the birth of Christ were announced. According to the story, an Egyptian captain taking his craft north through the Ionian found himself becalmed off Paxí, when a mysterious voice called him by name from the island and told him to shout out to the inhabitants of a mainland port as he passed that "the great god Pan is dead". The captain reluctantly obeyed, and reported an unearthly wailing from the mainland at this news.

Paxí is believed to have first been settled by shepherds from the mainland in the sixth century AD; a ruined chapel near the hamlet of Oziás in the south of the island has been dated back this far. Shortly afterwards, it was subsumed into the Byzantine empire along with Epirus and the rest of the northern Ionian. The Venetians, after their invasion of the region from 1386 onwards, proved to be more forward-thinking rulers. They planted olive trees throughout the archipelago, including an estimated quarter million on Paxí alone, and as well as producing a bumper crop, the trees helped to bind the topsoil, allowing the cultivation of fruit, vegetables and vines. Islanders were paid the equivalent of a drachma for each tree planted, and under Venetian auspices produced the extraordinary terracing and intricate dry-stone walling that covers much of the island. The invaders also initiated the construction of basic civic amenities: a harbour at Gáïos, various official buildings, and several small water reservoirs still seen (and some still in use) around the island. The distinctive Venetian architectural style can be observed on the seafront at Gáïos, and as ruins in a few isolated parts of the island's interior.

There were occasional setbacks during the long Venetian era: Paxí suffered a particularly brutal maritime raid in 1537 when the Turkish admiral **Barbarossa** enslaved most of the islanders in a revenge attack, after failing in a siege on Corfu. But it took more than four hundred years before Venetian rule finally came to an end, with the arrival of the French. When the **British** took over in 1809, they improved on the Venetians' building schemes, as well as instituting the basis of a government infrastructure and education system. Britain ceded the Ionian islands to the Greek government in 1864, at which point Paxí slipped into the mainstream of Greek history. During **World War II**, garrisons of German troops were stationed in Gáïos and Lákka, and, it's claimed, the Luftwaffe used Paxí for practice bombing runs from Corfu. Along with the rest of Greece, the island was liberated in 1944 – a popular local story has German troops in Lákka attempting to arrest arriving British troops, only to be told it was they who were being arrested.

Arrival and getting around

Most **boats**, including the larger vessels and hydrofoils from Corfu Town and Igoumenítsa on the mainland, arrive at Gáïos, docking at the new port, 1km to the north of town. There's no bus connection from here, so people either walk into Gáïos (15min) or take an overpriced taxi (€3–5). Some smaller boats, such as the *kaïki* from Párga, moor a hundred metres or so along the quayside from Gáïos's tiny town square.

Buses shuttle between Gáïos and Lákka four or five times a day (30min), with all but one service travelling via Longós. Timetables are posted in each village and available in most travel agencies. Gáïos's bus stop is at the back of the village, 200m from the *platía*, where the village alleys meet the island's one main road. In Lákka buses stop by the *Petrou kafenío* at the back of the village; in Longós they stop on the quay. There are **taxi** stands in Gáïos (by the church in the main square) and Lákka (by the *Petrou kafenío*); an average one-way fare between Lákka and Gáïos is €8. Both buses and taxis, which are often shared, can be flagged down anywhere.

There are at least two **motorcycle** rental outlets in all three villages: by the dock in Gáïos; 50m back from the ferry ramp behind the *Dionysus* taverna in Lákka; and on the northern end of the quay at Longós. Rental starts at around €15 a day in summer. However, riders should beware Paxí's treacherous gravelly roads, which are often slicked with oil from the olive trees – accidents are a daily occurrence in season. Paxí's size hardly warrants the expense of renting a **car**, but if you want to, try one of the established agencies such as Planos Travel or Gaios Travel, in Gáïos and Lákka. It's fiendishly expensive though, costing over €200 a week for a saloon, and in excess of €300 for a 4WD. British-based

Spread over three wooded, hilly coves, **PÁRGA** is the most attractive coastal resort in mainland Epirus (Ípiros in modern Greek). Historically, it was the Venetians' main foothold on the mainland and was also ruled over by the Napoleonic French, as well as being settled by the Turks, each group leaving its architectural mark. Párga's jumble of low, red-tiled buildings faces out towards Paxí, over vegetation-tufted rocks and islets a short swim off some of the best beaches in the region. Unfortunately, it is also Epirus's most popular resort: even in low season it can be hectically busy, and in high summer it heaves. All the same, it can be a welcome change of scene on one of the **day-trips** that leave Gáïos most days of the week in summer (from around €20 per person). You can also use the twice-daily excursion **kaḯki** (9.30am & 5.30pm) to reach Gáïos from Párga, as it is happy to take one-way passengers. There is no proper ferry, however, so out of season the only way to Paxí from the mainland is from Igoumenítsa, 70km north (see p.71). **Buses** to Igoumenítsa (4 Mon–Fri, 2 Sat & Sun; 1hr 30min) and Préveza (4 Mon–Fri, 3 Sat & Sun; 1hr 30min) leave from the KTEL, up on the bypass road, a five-minute walk from the harbour. The crossroads of Spýrou Livadhá and Alexándhrou Bánga, halfway between the port and bus station is the commercial heart of the town, with post office, banks, ATMs, shops and travel agencies.

Of Párga's **beaches**, the pebble strand immediately below the quay is probably the poorest; the smaller **Kryonéri** and **Píso Kryonéri** beaches just to the north are cleaner and quieter; another long strand is **Lýkhnos**, 3km southeast of town. Best, however, is the long, sandy **Váltos beach**, beyond the massive *kástro* that towers above the town. Sea taxis (€1.50) connect Váltos and Párga every fifteen minutes from 9am onwards for those reluctant to face the twenty-minute slog over the headland. The **kástro** that you pass (open all day; free) is the ruined skeleton of a major Venetian fort, built when Párga was Venice's sole mainland settlement during its rule of the Ionians from the fourteenth to eighteenth centuries. It has excellent views, as well as some rather dangerous unguarded precipices, and makes a good stroll or picnic destination.

Reasonably priced **accommodation** in Párga is notoriously difficult to find. Phoning ahead is virtually obligatory, but anyone who finds themselves here without accommodation should first try the Municipal Tourist Office opposite the jetty (☎26840/32 107, ⓦwww.parga.net), which keeps track of what's available. Or you can try one of the friendly rooming houses on the whitewashed lane leading past the *kástro*, such as Kostas and Martha Christou (☎26840/31 942; ❸). More upmarket are the purpose-built *Magda Apartments* (☎26840/31 728, ⓦwww.magdas-apartments.parga.com; ❺) out near the Váltos turning. Among the handful of **hotels** not block-booked are the mostly German-patronized *Galini* (☎26840/31 581, ☏32 221; ❸), set in an orchard below the Váltos road; and the *Achilleas* (☎26840/31 600, ☏31 879; ❹) at Kryonéri. **Campers** should head for either *Parga Camping* (☎26840/31 161), just behind Kryonéri beach, or the newer unobtrusive *Valtos* (May–Sep; ☎26840/31 171), at the far end of Váltos beach by the new yacht harbour.

Párga's **restaurants** are for the most part rather touristy. One notable exception is the simple and friendly *To Kyma*, which provides good oven food right by the boat jetty. The best place on the busier east quay is *To Souli*, which offers non-greasy *mayireftá* and some grills; or you can get decent Italian fare at *Oskar*, at the north end of the waterfront. *Apangio*, up a stepped lane behind the mid-seafront, is the only real *ouzerí*, whose *mezédhes* approach main course proportions. The seafront **bars** such as *Factory* tend to fill quickly at night and play mostly old foreign pop songs for the largely middle-aged clientele; Párga is no youth mecca, although there are a couple of trendier places up towards the *kástro*, including *Blue Bar*.

travel companies such as CV Villas and Greek Islands can rent cars ahead for clients; an alternative for independent travellers is to rent a car on Corfu or the mainland and bring it to Paxí by ferry.

For further information, check ⓦ **www.paxos-greece.com**, a well-organized site with lots of practical information about the island.

Gáïos and around

Named after St Gaius, who is said to have brought Christianity to the island, and whose tomb is to be found in the plain church of Áyii Apóstoli next to the post office, **GÁÏOS** is one of the most attractive villages in the Ionian. Known to locals simply as Gáï, it's extremely compact, consisting of little more than a crescent-shaped quay, a small Venetian town square – the hub of village life – and a few narrow alleys leading away from it. Apart from being Paxí's major port of arrival, it's the island's administrative centre (three banks, one magistrates' court, the sole police station) and shopping centre, including several minimarkets, two delis and a pharmacy.

The town is protected from the open sea by two islands, **Áyios Nikólaos** and **Panayía**. The former is little more than 50m across from the harbourfront and crowned by a magnificent stand of pines. Beyond the pines stands a ruined Venetian fortress built in 1423 and renovated by the French in the eighteenth century. Panayía is named after a white-walled church dedicated to the Virgin Mary (*Panayía*), the site of a major festival every August 15. Both islands are well worth exploring: a sea taxi (there's a desk on the seafront) will take you to either for around €4. Smoking is discouraged on Áyios Nikólaos to prevent fires on its tinder-dry pine forest floor.

The island's only museum is the **Folk Museum** (May–Oct daily 10am–2pm & 7–11pm; €2), housed in an old school building on the seafront about 200m south of the square. One room is set up as an eighteenth-century bedroom with some period furniture and costumes. Other items on display from different epochs include kitchen implements, musical instruments, china, stationery and guns.

If you are here in August, it's worth checking out whether the **Neroladhiá festival** is taking place, during which the islanders recall hard times from the past, when they were forced to share out stale bread dunked in water and smeared with olive oil and whatever leftovers remained. It used to be an annual affair but has been less reliable of late. If it is on, there is live music on the quay and free food (yes, bread dunked in water with a few titbits and covered in oil) and a glass of wine is handed out to anyone who gets in the queue. During the first two weeks of September, the Paxos Festival Trust (a registered UK charity) has for the last twenty years been putting on the **Paxos Chamber Music Festival** (ⓦ www.paxosfestival.org.uk) with classical concerts for a small fee in Gáïos and elsewhere.

Accommodation

Much **accommodation** in Gáïos – and elsewhere on Paxí – is block-booked by British and other northern European travel companies, and the range of freelance accommodation dwindles near high season, when a call ahead is essential. However, villagers offering rooms occasionally meet ferries arriving at the quay in season, and on the harbour front in the centre is one of the biggest Paxiot-run tourism and accommodation companies, Gaios

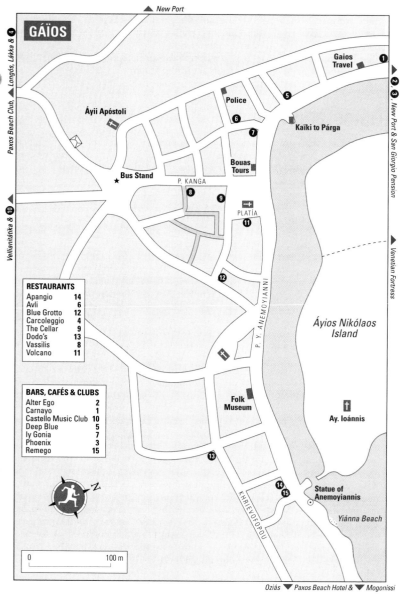

GÁÏOS

New Port

Paxos Beach Club, Longós, Lákka & ❹

Vellianitátika & ❿

Gaios Travel ❶

❷ ❸ New Port & San Giorgio Pension

Venetian Fortress

Police

Áyii Apóstoli

Kaïki to Párga ❺

❻

❼

Bouas Tours

Bus Stand ★

P. KANGA

❽

❾

PLATÍA

❶❶

P. Y. ANEMOYIANNI

❶❷

Áyios Nikólaos Island

RESTAURANTS
Apangio	14
Avli	6
Blue Grotto	12
Carcoleggio	4
The Cellar	9
Dodo's	13
Vassilis	8
Volcano	11

BARS, CAFÉS & CLUBS
Alter Ego	2
Carnayo	1
Castello Music Club	10
Deep Blue	5
Iy Gonia	7
Phoenix	3
Remego	15

Folk Museum

Ay. Ioánnis

❶❸

❶❹
❶❺

Statue of Anemoyiannis

Yiánna Beach

KHRIEVOFOPOU

0   100 m

N

Oziás ▼ Paxos Beach Hotel & ▼ Mogonissi

Travel (☎26620/32 033, ⓦwww.gaiostravel.com). The company shares an office with CV Villas and can also help with money exchange, trips and other business. Another travel agency worth contacting for accommodation is Bouas Tours (☎26620/32 401, ⓦwww.bouastours.gr), also situated on the seafront. The ⚜ *San Giorgio* pension (☎26620/32 223; ❹), just above the coastal road to the new port, is modern, comfortable and welcoming, or at a pinch you could try one of the recently renovated rooms in an old house rented out by Maria-Yiorgia at the Spiros Makris motorbike rental shop in the corner of the harbour (☎26620/32 031 or 31 932; ❺).

Paxí's two most established seasonal **hotels** are both near Gáios. They are heavily used by package companies in high season, but sometimes have rooms available to independent travellers. The secluded *Paxos Beach Hotel* (☎26620/32 211 or 32 333, ⓦ www.paxosbeachhotel.gr; ❻) is sited on a hillside above a small pebbly beach 2km south of Gáios. Accommodation is in bungalows, spread out through the trees, though the place has a rather stilted and regimented air. The hotel has its own irregular minibus service into Gáios; otherwise access is by taxi or on foot. The newer *Paxos Club* (☎26620/32 450, ⓦ www.paxosclub .gr; ❼), 2km outside of Gáios on the main road towards Bogdhanátika, is fairly luxurious. On an island with a severe water shortage, it boasts a large fancy-shaped pool, which, along with its bar and restaurant, welcomes non-residents. Rooms are en suite with balconies, and some large, suite-style apartments are also available. However, the hotel has a fairly short season, and has been known to close in early September.

Eating and drinking

Although there are many establishments to choose from, and although it has been improving, eating out is not one of Paxí's strong points. For a long time many **tavernas** operated on the basis that on a small island customers were a captive audience, and most islanders would have been embarrassed to serve in their own kitchens the sort of food that got served in the village restaurants. More recently, however, increased competition has forced most restaurateurs into seeing the wisdom of upping the quality and variety of their fare. As is often the case, however, the establishments on the seafront itself remain largely uninspiring and overpriced.

Restaurants

Apangio South along the seafront. With an attractively decorated interior and good range of main courses, salads and *mezédhes*, this is the best place on the front.

Avli A block north of the main square. The shady outdoor seating makes this a good spot for tasty grilled meat, washed down with fine barrelled wine.

Blue Grotto Tucked away down an alley on the opposite side of the square, this long-standing taverna is a good choice for its pastas and oven-cooked meat and fish dishes.

Carcoleggio's 1.5km out of town on the main road to Bogdhanátika. Perhaps the most popular place of all, the menu is limited but it fills up with islanders who flock here for its *souvláki* and succulent grills.

The Cellar Right at the top of the square, at the furthest end from the sea, this cheap *psistariá* serves up *souvláki*, tasty chops and chicken, plus a limited range of salads.

Dodo's A couple of blocks inland from the Anemoyiannis statue. A welcoming taverna with a pleasant garden, serving pizza, pasta and Greek standards at reasonable prices.

Vassilis Taverna Halfway towards the bus stop from the main square. This pleasant place does *mayireftá* like rabbit casserole with butter beans, as well as grills. The best of the trio clustered together here.

Volcano Best of the bunch lining the south side of the square. Family run for decades, with vegetarian-friendly alternatives, as well as conventional taverna dishes.

Snacks and self-catering

For self-caterers, the picture is rosy. Thanks to the demands of picky yacht crews, Gáios now offers as sophisticated a range of foodstuffs as you're likely to encounter in the Ionian islands. The **deli** in the southeast corner of the town square offers the widest range of cured meats, dairy products, wines and other delicacies, while the supermarket on the road inland from the square also stocks a wide range of alcohol and deli/dairy foodstuffs. The spread of high-class **zaharoplastía** has now reached Gáïos, with a mouthwatering cake shop on the seafront, and a larger, even fancier store in the arcade to the right at the top of the town square. The **bakery** a few doors inland on the main road out of the square is the only one on the island to stock a daily supply of brown as well as white bread. Finally, the best place for a coffee is *Iy Gonia*, the last surviving traditional **kafenío**, tucked in the corner of the quay opposite the Párga *kaïki*.

Nightlife

As is the case with many small Greek islands, evening entertainment on Paxí is limited to a few tried and tested **bars**. The *Carnayo* on Gáïos's seafront, round the bay to the north of the main square, a source of much amusement and scandal over the years, has toned itself down but is still going strong with a standard mix of Greek and foreign sounds. On the seafront almost opposite the Anemoyiannis statue, *Remego* is the favoured gathering point for posing Italian youngsters, while on the way to the new port *Deep Blue* is a laid-back option and *Alter Ego* is a fairly smooth rock-oriented bar.

There is a choice of two **clubs** for dance action: the *Phoenix*, just past the new port, a lively and popular late-night venue with a terrace for sub-lunar fun, dodgy music policy and pricey bar list; and the smaller *Castello Music Club*, just beyond the bus stand.

Listings

Banks and exchange The branches of the National Bank of Greece, the Agricultural Bank and the Commercial Bank in Gáïos, the only banks on the island, are primarily for domestic accounts but handle foreign exchange too; all have cash dispensers. Most travel companies will change travellers' cheques checked daily with banks, although with a commission.
Doctors and medical emergencies The island's surgery (℡ 26620/31 466), in the village of Bogdhanátika, 3km west of Gáïos, opens weekday mornings – attendance avoids the doctor's call-out fee of around €50. The two doctors both speak English. Serious injuries are taken to Corfu by sea taxi or helicopter. There are no dental services on Paxí.
Ferry agent A tiny caravan at the new port is the only dedicated ferry office on Paxí, although any travel agency (see p.134 or p.140 for examples) will be able to make reservations.
Police station Two blocks inland about 100m north of the square (℡ 26620/31 222).
Port Authority At the new port (℡ 26620/32 259).
Post office The only proper post office and OTE on the island is by the bus stand at the back of the village (Mon–Fri 8am–1.30pm).

Beaches around Gáïos

When it comes to beaches, Gáïos is the least well-endowed of the island's villages. Apart from a tiny pebble strand dynamited a few years back just south of the town, the only true beach is at **Mogoníssi**, 3km south of Gáïos. Mogoníssi is in fact an island, attached to Paxí by a short causeway, and has the dullest landscape on the entire island – flat, part scrubby and part rocky. Wrangling over land ownership means the island's only official campsite closed several years back and doesn't seem likely to open in the near future, although the *Mogonissi* **taverna**, with a fair spread of fish, meat and starters, is up and running again. There is no bus service south of Gáïos, so it's either a foot or taxi job. En route, look out for the circular turrets of the island retreat originally built by Fiat and Juventus supremo Agnelli.

There are, however, numerous **rocky coves** between Gáïos and Mogoníssi, popular with those staying in the capital; the large slabs of rock sloping into the sea make them ideal for swimming and sunbathing. One bay south of Gáïos, the taverna *Klis* overlooks a bay with safe swimming and sometimes, in season, a floating bathing platform with its own bar. Further bays are accessible from the road north beyond the new port, but they're a good few kilometres' walk through a landscape akin to a building site. They're also uncomfortably close to the island's eco-unfriendly municipal dump, a hill of smouldering garbage that glows orange at night while slipping slowly into the sea.

Southwest Paxí

The comparative flatness of the landscape around Gáïos makes the surrounding countryside easy walking terrain. A circular two- to three-hour route leaving the southern end of Gáïos takes in some of the oldest hamlets on the island: through Oziás, Vellianitátika, neighbouring Zenebissátika and on to **Bogdhanátika** on the main road. The chief interest in these hamlets is the architecture, much of it dating from Venetian times and before, but there are hardly any facilities along the way – only Bogdhanátika has a *kafenío* and bar.

The walk can be augmented by taking a path leading from near the church in Vellianitátika. This cuts across fairly rough country to the cliffs above Mousmoúli bay and on to the dramatic Trypitós arch, a hundred-metre limestone sea-stack, attached to the island by a manmade walkway. It's a strenuous and even dangerous trip, with vertiginous drops, and should only be attempted by the sure-footed and never in bad weather.

Longós and around

The smallest of the island's three ports, **LONGÓS** is also the most picturesque and, for its size, blessed with a reasonable range of amenities. Its pocket-sized, east-facing harbour is perfectly sited to catch the morning sun, making alfresco breakfasts idyllic, the handful of tavernas are among the best on the island, and nightlife is laid-back but enjoyable. The one drawback to staying here, which should be taken seriously in high and shoulder seasons, is the lack of space and the high level of noise at night, with bars, restaurants and other tourists right on your doorstep. Indeed, the extent of Longós's facilities can be taken in simply by looking around its harbour: with the exception of one minimarket, a bakery, a bike rental shop and a restaurant tucked into an alleyway, the village's few amenities, including another well-stocked minimarket and all the other bars and restaurants, are here on the quay. There is no bank or post office – exchange transactions are dealt with by the travel agencies.

Longós's seclusion has made it a favourite with upmarket villa companies such as CV and Simply Ionian, whose properties are located in the hills above the port. The village has a small and scruffy beach, but most people swim from pebbly **Levréhio beach**, little over five minutes' walk away in the next bay south. The cove also has some excellent, gently sloping slabs of smooth rock with good access to the water, to sun yourself on and swim from. Above the village to the north, reached by steps rising above the disused factory on the beach, is the small Venetian hamlet of **Dhendhiátika**. While there are no tavernas or *kafenía* here, it has excellent views over the port. If coming from Lákka, the trek up there makes a pleasant diversion: follow the Dhendhiátika road, signposted off the Lákka–Longós road, and then carry on down into Longós.

Accommodation

Like Paxí's other two ports, Longós has little accommodation for independent travellers, and in the high-season months of July and August the supply all but dries up. The bulk of villas and apartments here are controlled by companies such as Greek Islands and CV Villas, through partly British-run Planos Holidays, the island's largest accommodation agency, whose main office is in Lákka and which has an increasingly large stake. Planos's office in Longós (☎26620/31 530, ⓦ www.planos.co.uk; from ❸) is probably the best place to start looking for accommodation, which can range from village **rooms** to country **villas**. Paxos Sun Holidays (☎ & ⓕ 26620/31 341; from ❸) also have an office in the resort. It's possible to rent rooms from the Dendias minimarket (☎26620/31 597 or 31 158; ❸) or from the proprietor's relative Andhreas Dendias (☎26620/ 31 610 or 32 580; ❹). Julia's bike and boat rental, 100m back from the harbour, also has a few rooms (☎26620/31 330; ❸). A certain amount of unofficial **camping** takes place on Levréhio beach, but it's nowhere near as hidden as at Lákka – it's best to ask for advice locally.

Eating and drinking

Two **restaurants** vie for the title of best in Longós: the *Nassos* has the widest variety of fish and seafood dishes, including things like prawns with a side order of mayonnaise (unusually for Greece, they'll bring hot water and lemon finger-bowls, if you ask); the seafront ⚓ *Vassilis*, which has an imaginative menu, full of delightful *mezédhes* and main courses, is immortalized in thousands of holiday tales as the restaurant where those sitting at outside tables have to squeeze in off the street to make way for the island bus when it rumbles by. Both establishments are a little pricey, however, making *O Gios* a less expensive standby for standard grilled and baked items. The cheap and cheerful *Iy Gonia tou Stamou* grill in the corner of the harbour is the best value in the village, with a small selection of starters and vegetable dishes as well as excellent meat.

Nightlife is very low-key and largely limited to the few bars facing the seafront, of which the most pleasant for an early evening drink is the relaxed *To Taxidhi*, with seating on both sides of the quay. The most popular late bars, both featuring the standard mish-mash of Greek and English hits, are *Roxi Bar*, with a cosy roof garden overlooking the quay, and *Ores*, which has a cheap happy hour early on. For more energetic entertainment you'll have to head for Lákka or Gáïos.

Lákka and around

LÁKKA is the hippest and friendliest of the island's ports, attracting a large crowd of loyal return visitors, as well as a fair share of roustabouts, although locals affirm that it is quieter now than in the past, and it doesn't begin to compare with the rowdiness to be encountered on some of the larger Ionian islands. The sea approach into the horseshoe bay has to be one of the most magnificent views in Greece, though arriving from elsewhere on Paxí is disappointing: you're greeted by a jumble of half-built apartment blocks at the back of the village. Beyond these, however, a compact grid of narrow alleys around the village's small **main square**, lined with two-storey houses in the Venetian style, comprises the village's charming centre. It's full of surprising details and strange corners and turns – not least Platía

△ Lákka Harbour

Edward Kennedy, commemorating, probably with tongue in cheek, a visit by members of the Kennedy clan (including, rumour insists, Jackie O) in the 1960s. The *platía* is in fact only a tiny, triangular alley, signalled by a blink-and-you'll-miss-it wall sign.

Lákka is so compact that you'll trip over most of what there is in the first five minutes. Shops are based around the back of the village, bars along the seafront and restaurants along the front and around the village square. Taxis and buses stop metres from each other near the *Petrou kafenío* (officially *Ariston*) at the back of the village. There's no bank or post office, but the two main travel agents, Planos and Routsis, both on the quayside, **change money**, sell stamps and operate quiet payphones, as well as renting watersports equipment; Planos

Paxí olive oil

Paxí's prize-winning **olive oil** is regarded by some as being on a par with, or even superior to, Italian brands. The olive trees originally planted by the Venetians still dominate the island's economy and landscape; olive oil remains the largest business after tourism, and the trees cover around eighty percent of the island.

Unlike crops elsewhere, Paxí's **olives** are allowed to fall before being collected, and until nets were introduced a few decades ago, this was done by hand. The biennial crop would be hand-picked, winnowed, bagged and carried to olive presses in each village. The traditional stone mills were driven by donkeys and sometimes by women and children: a generation of islanders still remembers this backbreaking work. Mechanization of the mills and the introduction of nets has transformed the industry, and most of the stone presses have fallen into disuse, their overgrown masonry and machinery visible at points throughout the island.

Mechanized presses operate in Gáïos, Fountána and, most visibly, Lákka. The olive oil sells at around €9 a litre, but it is rarely seen in shops, less still in restaurants. However, it's a staple in the kitchens of the islanders, most of whom have a stake, if only a few trees, in the crop. The oil is sold chiefly in the presses themselves, which only open when deliveries from the olive groves require processing. If you're planning to take some home, buy early to avoid finding the press closed on your day of departure.

also offers car rental. Nick the Greek rents scooters and there are daily glass-bottom **boat trips** to Andípaxi in season (€15 per person) from the harbour.

Lákka and its bay offer the best swimming and watersports on Paxí – not that that's saying much – with its two public beaches on the western side of the bay: Kanóni is smaller but nicer, while Harámi has a snack bar-taverna of the same name, a brand-new hotel and Jerry's watersports; and another small beach by the schoolhouse opposite. As elsewhere on the island, the beaches are pebble, with occasional tar deposits, but shelve into sand at the edge of the clear, shallow water.

Accommodation

Accommodation is marginally easier to come by in Lákka than either Gáïos or Longós, although even here rooms are scarce at the height of the season. The village has a large number of return visitors, many of whom book the same accommodation year after year. Rooms in the village itself are generally noisy, especially as some bars stay open until dawn.

The growth of the two main village travel companies has resulted in a healthy choice of accommodation that directly benefits the islanders rather than anonymous multinational corporations. Planos (℡26620/31 744 or 31 821, ⓦwww .planos.co.uk; from ❷) is the larger of the two, and can offer anything from a village room the size of a cupboard to a villa with pool up in the hills. It also offers complete holiday packages from its British office (see p.23), inclusive of flights and transfer. The more local Routsis agency (℡26620/31 807 or 31 162, ⓦwww.routsis-holidays.com; from ❷) is fast catching up, and also has a wide range of rooms, apartments and villas in the village and outlying areas. It now also offers bonded flight and holiday deals through its British agents (see p.23). Of the two, Routsis is friendlier, and more likely to have some basic options for the independent traveller, whereas Planos pre-sells much of its accommodation.

Some self-contained apartments above Kanóni are rented out at Marigo's food store (℡26620/30 087 or 31 458; ❹) at the landward end of the main square, and the manager of the small block-booked *Bastas Hotel* (☎26620/31 675; ❹) also has some rooms to let in the hills behind the village. Lákka's newest addition and the island's third bona fide hotel is the huge and undoubtedly comfortable *Amfitriti Hotel* (☎26620/30 011–2, ❽www.amfitriti-hotel.gr; ❼). Sadly, it's grossly overpriced and not especially friendly. Despite the raised tourist profile of the resort, **freelance camping**, which has been tacitly accepted in the olive groves behind Kanóni beach for many years still goes on undisturbed, though it's best to check with locals first, especially if you don't see any other tents pitched here.

Eating and drinking

In recent years, **tavernas** have proliferated in Lákka to a capacity beyond the number of tourists arriving: bad news for the restaurant owners, good news for customers. Restaurants are sited in and around the central square and along the harbour front. There is also a fair range of late-night **bars**, some well-established, others opening and closing according to the vagaries of their clientele's preferences.

Restaurants

Alexandros Tucked in a quiet alley behind the square, this is one of the finest family tavernas on the island. Delights include fresh fish, *gourounópoulo*, and imaginative oven dishes like mussels in a cream sauce with tarragon.

La Bocca On the far eastern side of the bay. The most genuine Italian cuisine in the area, with the odd curry thrown in, but a little pricey. Try the Venetian style liver and onions.

Diogenis This specializes in grills – chicken, chops, *souvláki*, even whole baby lamb – for the flotilla crowd; tell-tale signs of when the fleet's in (tables lined up for twenty or more) should warn you to eat elsewhere.

Nautilus Under a blue-striped awning on the east side of the bay, this has the most breathtaking view of any taverna on Paxí. It

specializes in expensive seafood such as garlic or cream prawns, plus salads and conventional fare prepared with effort and imagination, not least a classic bean soup.

Nionios Right on the square, this is another great place for genuine home-style cooking. Try the pork in lemon sauce, mussels and shrimps in red sauce or spinach and cream pot.

Pouentes On the square, Lákka's newest eatery specializes in *gourounópoulo*, a range of *mezédhes* and pizzas at standard prices. Live music on Tues and Fri.

La Rosa di Paxos The most stylish restaurant on the island, with prices to match (which is why they're left off the menu outside). Good choice of designer Greek and international cuisine, especially strong on lasagna and risotto dishes.

Bars

Spyros Petrou's **kafenío**, by the bus stop at the back of the village, has been the hub of Lákka society since anyone can remember. It's perhaps the friendliest *kafenío* in the whole archipelago, with none of the usual macho atmosphere. Among the new generation of **bars**, *Akis* is a smart cocktail bar overlooking the harbour with exorbitant Web access at €7.50 per hour; it's noisy but popular with younger islanders and visitors. Not far along is *Harbour Lights*, the liveliest bar in town, which opens late and provides a decent soundtrack that hovers between pop and rock. The village's premier cocktail joint, the *Romantica*, is also on the seafront, and offers the biggest nightcap list in town, as well as cool jazz music. *Serano's*, in the square, serves homemade sweets and cakes to induce sugar shock, and is a favourite among long-term visitors, who park their tape collections behind the bar.

Around Lákka

Lákka is perfectly sited for the finest walking on the island. For a simple, short hike, take the track leaving the far end of Harámi beach. This mounts the headland and leads on to the **lighthouse**, where a goat track descends through tough scrub to a sandy open-sea beach with rollers best left to confident swimmers.

Another good walking route heads west into the hills above the village to **Vassilátika**, high on the west coast cliffs, which has stunning views out to sea. From here, the path to the left of the blue-painted stone archway leads on to the most dramatic cliff-edge views (vertigo sufferers beware) and continues to **Magaziá** in the centre of the island, where you can flag down a bus or taxi. There is also the basic *Lilas* **taverna**, if you are in need of a hearty country meal.

The best **walk** on Paxí, however, especially good under a clear early evening sky, is to the church at **Áyii Apóstoli**, almost halfway down the west coast, next to the hamlet of Voïkátika. The rough track is signposted a few hundred metres south of Magaziá, and takes less than half an hour on foot. The church and surrounding vineyards overlook the sheer 150-metre **Erimítis cliffs**, which at sunset are transformed into a seaside version of Ayers Rock, turning from dirty white to pink and gold and brown. If you visit Áyii Apóstoli at sunset, take a torch and, after walking back to the trailhead, prepare to return by bus or – more likely – taxi, either of which can be waved down on the main road. The new *Sunset* **bar**, next to the church, can provide a welcome drink to augment the natural splendour and even hosts full moon parties during the warmer months. Tourism agencies in Lákka and the other ports organize coach trips that trundle down the rough track to the cliffs at Voikátika, taking guests to "Greek night" meals in the sole Voïkátika **taverna** afterwards.

Andípaxi

The neighbouring island of **Andípaxi** is a flawed paradise, with the clearest blue coves in the entire archipelago – and some of the best snorkelling in Greece – but some rather indifferent beaches. And unfortunately, even the quieter low-season afternoons will involve your sharing the two most popular bays with large numbers of day-trippers from Paxí, the mainland and various resorts on Corfu. Even so, this doesn't entirely dent the charms of Andípaxi, and the island still manages to accommodate its invaders. The trick is to head south away from the crowds to find the quieter spots. Sunny Octobers can leave you with a small cove to yourself and a clear sea as warm as a bath.

High-speed sea taxis and more leisurely *kaïkia*, which take in the sea-stacks and blue-water caves of the west coast as well as the east coast bays, leave all three of Paxí's ports for Andípaxi each morning in season. Some craft try to charge substantially more than others and the best deals are to be found in Gáïos, where you should get a round trip for €6, just to be dropped off and picked up later. A glass-bottom boat tour (daily 11am–2pm; €15) takes in the **sea caves** at the back of the island, as well as allowing a swimming stop. These caves are the finest in the Ionians, and large enough to be entered by pleasure craft; according to local legend, one even concealed an Allied submarine during World War II. The sea taxis tend to buzz in and out, while *kaïkia* enter and cut their engines to scare faint hearts.

The first of the two main beaches where the tour boats and shuttle craft deposit their passengers is sandy, family-oriented **Vríka**, which has a taverna at each end – try *Spiros* for a tasty snack such as *imam bealdi* or village sausage in the shade. From the side of *Taverna Vrika*, at the other end of the beach, a path winds up to the sprawling ghost settlement of **Vígla**, which is strung along the northern spine of the island. There are no facilities and, sadly, the wild and deserted west coast is inaccessible owing to the thick rocky scrub, so the sweaty climb should not be undertaken lightly.

The island's ridge can also be reached from the other main beach, the longer but pebbly **Vatoúmi**, which has gorgeous turquoise sea and also two tavernas: the aptly named *Bella Vista* is a stiff climb up the cliff at the southeastern end but rewards your efforts with splendid views beyond the bay to Paxí and the mainland; the newer *Vatoumi* is set back from the beach and serves the less energetic. If you find Vatoúmi too crowded, you can take the wide track on the west side, which hairpins round the valley behind before ascending the other side to join another path. Turn left here towards some villas; a path immediately to their right leads down steps to the first of two coves, collectively known as **Agrapidhiá**. A path on the far side joins the road down to the second, larger bay, which has a concrete jetty for the highly infrequent car ferry to dock at. Both coves have fine rock formations, make for excellent snorkelling and remain near deserted even in high season.

Accommodation is scarce on Andípaxi, and what little there is only caters for those wishing to stay by the week rather than the odd night. The limited number of **villas** can be booked mainly through tourism agencies in Gáïos such as Gaios Travel (see p.133), although *Spiros* taverna (☏26620/31 172, daytime only; Paxí contact ☏26620/32 417, ✉paxoscosmos@hotmail.com), at Vrika beach has a couple of large, well-equipped houses too. Although the level of comfort is high, prospective residents must be prepared to transport provisions with them and cater for themselves. There's little on Andípaxi apart from a smattering of summer houses owned by Paxiots – no shops or bars, and all the beach **tavernas** mentioned above usually only open during the day in season, closing once the day-trip craft depart. The one exception is the *Bella Vista* (☏26620/31 766), which occasionally opens in the evenings if there is demand – call to check.

Travel details

Buses

The reliable island bus service runs 4 or 5 times daily (30min) between Lákka and Gáïos from 9.15am until 9pm. All but one detour via Longós.

Ferries and kaïkia

Ferry services tend to vary from one year to the next but at the time of writing the *Vivi* departs Gáïos once or twice daily for Igoumenítsa (1hr 45min); the early departure is at 7.45am, the second, when running, varies. Check with the Port Authority (☏26620/32 259). There are now no direct ferries to Corfu.

Tourist *kaïkia* provide the only link with Párga on the mainland. They depart from the old port in Gáïos (May–Oct 1–2 daily; 1hr 30min).

Hydrofoils

There are now three hydrofoil companies competing to provide the only direct sea link from Gáïos to Corfu Town; these run May–Oct (3–7 daily; 50min) and occasionally at busy times out of season such as Easter.

Flights

A new seaplane service (see p.75 for details) flies between Gáïos and Gouviá marina in Corfu (2–3 daily; 20min).

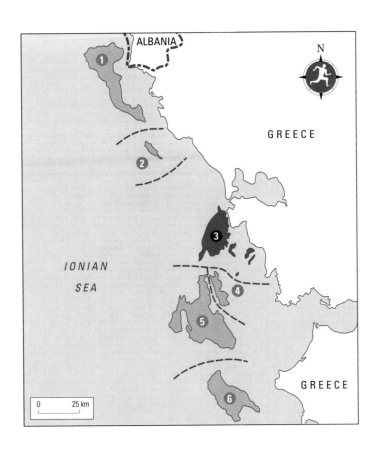

3

Lefkádha

ALBANIA

N

GREECE

IONIAN
SEA

GREECE

0   25 km

CHAPTER 3 **Highlights**

✽ **Pandokrátor church, Lefkádha Town** One of the Ionians' finest examples of ecclesiastical architecture and iconography. See p.154

✽ **Dhessími Bay** Tucked into the green hills on the east side of the Yéni peninsula, this attractive bay is great for campers. See p.162

✽ **Vassilikí** Lefkádha's south-ernmost and busiest resort is a magnet for windsurfers, who make the most of the bay's blustery conditions. See p.164

✽ **Káthisma beach** The most accessible of the splendid west-coast beaches is a deep and long strand of sand and shingle. See p.167

✽ **Karyá** This lovely mountain village of shady plane trees is also home to the island's traditional lace embroidery industry. See p.170

✽ **Meganíssi** The largest of Lefkádha's satellite islands is well connected with Nydhrí and a splendid place to walk, swim or even stay for a couple of nights. See p.173

△ Fishing at Ayía Mávra castle

3

Lefkádha

Although it is home to two very busy resorts, Nydhrí and Vassilikí, **Lefkádha (Lefkas)** is the least developed of the larger Ionian islands. The uninhabited parts are as wild and unspoilt, and the settlements as quintessentially Greek, as you'll find anywhere, making it the favourite island in the archipelago for many purists. Its terrain provides little land on which tourism might develop: almost ninety percent is mountainous or semi-mountainous, and just ten percent lowland. Its typically Ionian geography – cliffs on the west coast and flat land to the east – means the best beaches, though splendid, are difficult to get to, while the more accessible are stony or pebbly, and sometimes rather scruffy.

Much of the island's tourism straggles along the east coast road heading south from Lefkádha Town. **Nydhrí**, overlooking Lefkádha's satellite islands, is a popular package destination, and has been commercialized to meet this demand. **Vassilikí**, set on the vast bay of the same name at the south of the island, is not far behind, and has some of the finest windsurfing in Europe. The mountainous **west coast** is less developed, and shelters some of the most attractive smaller resorts, notably the pretty village of **Aï Nikítas**, and the sandy beaches of **Káthisma**, **Pefkoúlia** and **Yialós**, as well as the phenomenally scenic bay of **Pórto Katsíki**.

Away from the coast, the island conceals breathtaking valleys and hill ranges, offering some of the best **walking** terrain in the entire archipelago. Serious hikers should base themselves in **Karyá**, dead centre of a whole network of easily walkable villages set in an almost alpine landscape. Similarly, the road to Vournikás and Sývros in the south has fine mountain views, and the west coast route beyond Káthisma is also recommended, although probably in sections; the walk from Atháni to Cape Lefkátas is particularly fine, with primeval mountain-scapes and empty arable land.

Lefkádha is also notable for its **satellite islands**. The proximity of the main quartet gives Nydhrí the finest sea views on the island, but only two of these – **Spárti**, and the larger and more interesting **Meganíssi** – are accessible to visitors. Some 20km away are the further satellites of **Kálamos**, **Kástos** and **Átokos**, all nowadays inaccessible from Lefkádha and, in the case of the latter two, reached only by occasional ferries from the Greek mainland. In high season, especially now that the **international cultural festival** (see box on p.155) has been extended throughout the summer, the place can become as packed as anywhere, and rooms can be almost impossible to find in the main resorts.

Outside the main resorts English is not as widely or fluently spoken as on the other Ionian islands, but this should not deter you, as locals are invariably polite and friendly and the undoubted beauty of the island's remoter corners should not be missed. In addition, after Corfu, **Lefkádha Town** is perhaps the most sophisticated of the island capitals, with a cultural centre, a cinema, clubs, bookshops and a main shopping street where you can buy anything from a cowbell to a computer.

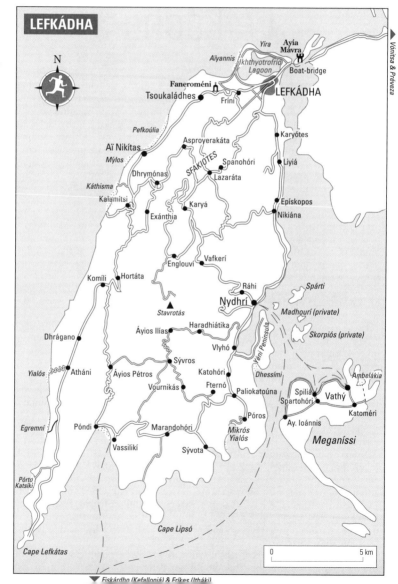

Some history

Lefkádha's **history** largely follows that of the archipelago as a whole. Excavations have produced evidence of settlement on the island dating back to the Neolithic, around 8000 BC. According to local mythology, Lefkádha, known at the time as Leucas, was given by Laertes to Arcadius, on the marriage of their respective children, Odysseus and Penelope. It is this, along with a close geographical reading of Homer's *Odyssey* and the discovery of Mycenaean remains in the hills above Vassilikí, that led archeologist **Wilhelm Dörpfeld** (Heinrich Schliemann's assistant at the excavations of Troy and Mycenae) to spend many years in the late nineteenth century vainly attempting to identify Lefkádha as the home of Odysseus. Some of Dörpfeld's excavations are still visible on the roads just south and north of Nydhrí, but amount to little more than rather forlorn collections of stones fenced into small gardens which are locked to the public.

The island's **name** derives from the ancient Greek for "white", referring to the colour of its cliffs and barren mountain ranges. There has been much pedantic debate over whether it is a real island at all. Lefkádha appears to have been originally joined to the mainland by a narrow isthmus, through which the Corinthians excavated a channel in the sixth century BC – although those who argue in favour of its island status suggest that the Corinthians may simply have been clearing a pre-existing channel that had silted up.

Under the Corinthians, Lefkádha became a major seat of power, and played an important part in the Peloponnesian War in the fifth century BC; however, much of the archeological detail from this period has disappeared beneath farmland and more recent settlements. During the Byzantine period, the island fell into the same Byzantine "theme", or regional administration, as Kefalloniá and Zákynthos. Venetian rule on Lefkádha was shorter than elsewhere in the Ionian, lasting just over a hundred years from 1684 to 1797, and was interrupted, briefly, when the Turks captured the island – not for the first time – in 1715.

Like other Ionian islands, Lefkádha developed an extensive olive industry under the Venetians, but it also built its wealth on currants and wine grapes. The island's other **specialities** include honey (often produced by bees fed on thyme), *mandoláto* nougat, almonds and strong island wines and retsina. Lefkádha also has its own tradition of **kandádhes** and other folk-song forms, which can only be heard in village festivals and in certain tavernas in Lefkádha Town.

Arrival and getting around

Most non-Greek visitors arrive via **Préveza (Áktio) airport**, 25km to the north on the mainland and only 2km west of Préveza town across the narrow entrance to the Amvrakikós Gulf (see box p.150). There are no dedicated buses from the airport to the town of Préveza or to Lefkádha, although the Préveza–Lefkádha Town bus passes the end of the airport slip road half a dozen times daily. The bus can be flagged down at the end of this road, barely 300m from Arrivals. Taxis to Lefkádha Town from the airport are negotiable, but expect to pay €18–20.

It's worth pointing out that Préveza airport is still largely a military base, home to SEAC early-warning planes and hi-tech jets that streak above the islands on training runs. Greek authorities are particularly sensitive about security – evident from the much-publicized detention of a large group of British plane spotters in the Peloponnese in 2001 – and the armed guards will even prevent those queuing for outbound flights from chatting to friends through the fences that bound the tiny airport building. Photography is banned, as at other Greek airports. Beyond a small bar, two car rental booths and an exchange kiosk, there are no other services at the airport.

Préveza

Though the majority of foreign tourists visiting Lefkádha use its airport, few ever see the town of **PRÉVEZA**, 2km to the east. The airport actually stands on, and takes its name from, the sandy peninsula of Áktio, off which the Battle of Actium was fought in 31 BC, when the fleet of Octavian decisively defeated that of Antony and Cleopatra. Anyone wishing to stay in Préveza itself is advised to take the Olympic minibus (at Olympic flight times) or a taxi from the airport terminal (around €5 including tunnel toll) or flag down the Lefkádha–Préveza bus at the stop on the main road only a few minutes' walk away.

Préveza can boast a pleasant seafront and a newly rejuvenated centre, and is very popular with Greek holidaymakers, even though there are no beaches beyond a thin strip of imported sand. It's also a useful base for visiting either **Nikópolis**, the ancient city whose scattered walls and foundations can be seen 7km north of town (site access unrestricted; museum Tues–Sun 8.30am–2.30pm; €3), or the Amvrakikós **wetlands** skirting the Amvrakikós Gulf which extends 20km inland from the town. The wetlands are one of the biggest wildlife sanctuaries in Greece, but are only really accessible with your own vehicle.

The town is built on a grid system, with most facilities a few minutes' walking distance from the quay. The old central area is a very attractive warren of alleys, which secrete most of the town's shops and restaurants. It's bookended by two large medieval **forts**, the castles of St George and St Andrew, but both are in use by the armed forces, who have quite a presence in Préveza, and are off-limits to the public.

All **buses** arrive at the KTEL station on Leofóros Irínis, one kilometre back from the dock behind the old town. Services are basic: three daily from Athens (6hr); two daily from Igoumenítsa (2hr 30min); ten daily (8 Sun) from Ioánnina (2hr 30min); five daily (3 on Sat & Sun) from Párga (1hr 30min); one daily from Thessaloníki (not Sat or Sun; 7hr); and six daily (4 on Sun) from Lefkádha Town (30min). Those heading south travel via the new tunnel (car toll €3). The municipal tourist office (Mon–Fri 8am–2.30pm) is in the government building at the west end of the seafront, next to the post office. There are various banks on Ethnikís Andístasis, the pedestrian precinct two alleys back from the seafront, most with 24-hour cash dispensers.

Because Préveza is very popular with Greek tourists, there is no really cheap **accommodation** in the centre. Of the four central hotels, the smart *Hotel Avra* (☎26820/21 230, ℗26 454; ③), in the middle of the action across the road from the ferry quay, provides the best value, followed by the *Dioni* (☎26820/27 381–2, ℗27 384; ④), a small, comfortable hotel on pedestrianized Platía Papayeoryíou in the centre of town. The seafront Kiss Travel (☎26820/23 753 or 23 157, ℗28 846) offers a wide variety of accommodation, including cheaper rooms 3km northeast in the suburb of Pantokrátoras, and other services. The nearest **campsite** is *Kalamitsi* (☎26820/22 368), around 4km north of town on the main road which skims along a few hundred metres back from the coast.

There are at least a dozen **tavernas** scattered around the inland market lanes in central Préveza, with cafés and bars on the pedestrianized portion of the waterfront boulevard Venizélou. Good eating choices inland include *Psatha*, Dhardhanellíou 4–6 (west of the main shopping strip), for standard oven food; and the long-standing favourite *Amvrosios*, on Grigoríou E, the lane leading seaward from the Venetian clocktower, a budget spot specializing in grilled sardines and good local wine. By night, the bazaar alleys around the clocktower come alive with an assortment of bars, *ouzerís*, cafés (including *Netcafe Ascot* at Vasilíou Bálkou 6–8) and shops. Two of the best *ouzerís* for atmosphere and a great selection of inexpensive *mezédhes* are *Kaíxis* at Parthenogoyíou 7 and *To Rembetiko Steki* on Adhrianoupóleos. If you're here in July and August it's worth checking out the programme of concerts and plays put on as part of the **Nikopolía Festival** in Nikópolis.

Lefkádha Town's **bus station**, on Odhós Dhimítri Golémi opposite the small yacht marina, has connections from Athens and Thessaloníki, and is the hub of island transport. The station's new computerized system issues tickets with numbered seats, which you should use to avoid potential confusion, although outside the town it's normal to pay on board and sit anywhere. The bus station is the most efficient and friendly in the islands: only the remoter services sometimes vary wildly from the handy printed timetable (summer only). It's worth remembering that services to remote destinations such as Atháni stop early, and last buses frequently turn round immediately, with no later return service. There's also a smaller ticket office and bus stop where Golémi turns into 8th Merarhías, but this is favoured by locals using longer-distance island buses to get to the suburbs, and often resembles a small-scale riot.

Taxis are easy to find outside the siesta, and even the smaller villages in the interior have at least one resident taxi driver; they don't come cheap, however, and a cab from Lefkádha to Vassilikí, a distance of some 38km, may cost up to €30, unless your bargaining skills and Greek are well versed. In emergencies, bars, shops and travel agencies will usually telephone a cab for you. Cars and motorbikes can be rented in Lefkádha Town and the main resorts.

For further information, take a peek at ⓦ **www.lefkasgreece.com**, the most comprehensive site for facts, figures and links on Lefkádha (and the place to turn to for the whole Onassis story).

Lefkádha Town and around

LEFKÁDHA TOWN is compact, squeezed between a seawater lagoon – the *Ikhthyotrofrío*, literally "fishery" – and the foothills on the north side of Mount Stavrotás. Sitting on a stunted peninsula, the town comprises one central thoroughfare, named **Dörpfeld** at the northern end by the causeway and **Ioánnou Méla** south of the main square, a trio of seafront roads (Golémi, Panágou and Sikelianoú), and a warren of minor streets and mainly pedestrian alleys that weave in between these parameters. Like neighbouring Kefalloniá and Itháki, Lefkádha was devastated by the 1953 earthquakes, and little remains of the original town beyond a number of small private chapels. As a precaution against further earthquake damage, few buildings are above three storeys high. The dormitory area of the town, west of Dörpfeld, took even greater precautions: most houses are built of stone only on the ground floor, and wood on the second, often with wooden balconies. This district's closely built houses with their small, elaborately planted gardens are reminiscent of Romney Marsh or perhaps even the flatter parts of old San Francisco. You can walk the length of the whole town in fifteen minutes, and traverse it in around ten, but despite its size, Lefkádha Town is surprisingly cosmopolitan, with a spanking-new cultural centre, a cinema, some excellent tavernas, cocktail bars, clubs and a small but hectic souvenir bazaar. In addition, an extension to the **marina** on Golémi, with a reception area and supply facilities, was completed in 2003 and is already making the town an even more attractive draw for yachters.

Accommodation

The few **rooms** that are available in Lefkádha Town tend to be in the dormitory area on the west side, between Dörpfeld and the lagoon, so a short stroll there is likely to prove fruitful. If your Greek isn't up to negotiating a room, householders are usually happy to find an English-speaking neighbour to

LEFKÁDHA TOWN

ACCOMMODATION

Ionian Star	E
Lefkas	B
Nirikos	A
Patras	F
Pension Pirofani	C
Santa Maura	D

RESTAURANTS

Alkyona	13
Bakolas	10
Eftyhia	5
Lighthouse	9
Regantos	4
Romantika	12
Seven Islands	6
Sto Molo	11

CAFÉS, BARS & CLUBS

Atmosfera	1
Café Karfakis	14
Casbah	7
Coconut Groove	3
Cosmos	2
Excess	3
Pendofanaro	8
Totem	7

Préveza & Ayía Mávra

Cultural Centre/
Archeological Museum

OTE

Cathedral

Hospital

Ayios Minas

Library

Sikelianos
Garden Theatre

Pandokrátor

Theotokou

Police
Station

Car Park

Ayios Nikólaos

Ayios
Spyridhonos

Phonograph
Museum

Ayios
Dhimitrios

Bus
Station

Marina

Marina

N

0   100 m

Cinema
Eleni

Yíra, **1** & **2**

Tsoukaládhes & Faneroméni Monastery

Nydhrí & Vassilikí

translate. Rooms still tend to be cheap and very basic, with wooden floors and walls, spare furnishing and shared bathrooms, although some have been given a facelift. To book ahead, try the Lefkádha Room-owners Association (☎26450/21 266; ❶–❸) or either of these individual locations: *Pinelopis Rooms* (☎26450/24 175; ❶), Pinelópis 20, a small alley off the seafront two blocks from the pontoon bridge at the beginning of the causeway, or the nearby *Filion* (☎26450/25 326; ❷), Odhysséos 6, a new set of apartments further back from the coast road. The nearest campsite to town is 4km south at Karyótes (see p.158).

Over the years the number of **hotels** in town has actually shrunk and, sadly, the best old cheapie *Byzantio* is currently closed. The half-dozen that do still exist are all at the northern tip of town, from Platía Ayíou Spyridhónos upwards, and all mid to upper range.

Ionian Star Panágou 2 ☎26450/24 762–3, ⓦwww.ionianstar.gr. Completely unrecognizable from its days as an EOT *Xenia*, this fully refurbished hotel is now the smartest and most efficient in town, with tastefully furnished, air-conditioned rooms and public areas, a pool and plush bar-restaurant. ❻

Lefkas Panágou 2 ☎26450/23 916, ⓦwww .e-lefkas.gr/hotellefkas. In a prime location overlooking the lagoon, with excellent rooms and facilities, all tastefully decorated though rather overpriced. ❻

Nirikos Ayías Mávras ☎26450/24 132–3, ⓦwww .nirikos.gr. Very comfortable modern hotel, with its own restaurant and bar, and air-conditioned en-suite rooms, all with TV, overlooking the causeway. ❺

Patras Platía Ayíou Spyridhónos ☎26450/22 359. A total renovation of this oldie was nearing completion at the time of writing, due to have all rooms newly furnished with cooking facilities and TV. Noise from the square will still be an issue. ❹

Pension Pirofani Kendrikí Agorá ☎26450/25 844, ⓕ24 084. Smartly renovated place above a separately owned taverna of the same name. All rooms have air conditioning and TV. ❹

Santa Maura Spyridhónos Viánda 2 ☎26450/21 308–9, ⓕ26 253. Tucked away in an alley off the top of Dörpfeld, the *Santa Maura* has smart en-suite rooms, with air-conditioning and double-glazing to fight the town's heat and noise. ❹

The Town

Lefkádha Town is the most walkable of all the larger island capitals. Indeed, given the difficulty of actually getting a vehicle into the centre, walking is almost obligatory. Most of the churches, just about all the shops and banks and many of the bars and tavernas are clustered around Dörpfeld and Ioánnou Méla the two streets that converge on the Italianate **Platía Ayíou Spyridhónos**, regarded as the heart of town.

The Archeological Museum and cultural centre

The **Archeological Museum** (daily 8.30am–3pm; €2), which was relocated in 1999 to the new **cultural centre**, ten minutes' walk west along the seafront towards the lagoon, is now second only to Corfu's, in the Ionians, for its collection of antiquities. It is well laid out in four air-conditioned rooms, with interesting background explanations and clear labeling of all exhibits in English.

The largest gallery, **room A**, immediately in front as you enter, contains displays on weaving, fishing, the monetary system, trade and the techniques of wine, oil and bread-making in ancient times. There is a range of original artefacts on each subject, backed up by tasteful modelling. The loom is particularly impressive.

To the left, **room B** has a theme of cults and the worship of deities in ancient Leucas and contains various figurines of gods and goddesses, as well as votive objects. The bronze mirror on a caryatid stand, and terracotta of a female sitting on a swan, which represents the myth of Zeus ravishing Leda, are the most noteworthy. The adjacent **room C** comprises a display of cemeteries and funerary procedures. There are a number of grave stelae, some inscribed, others sculpted, a casket complete with skeleton and numerous objects found at burial sites, including some delicate gold wreaths.

Room D, to the right of the entrance, is dedicated to the prehistoric collection of Wilhelm Dörpfeld, the famous German archeologist. It comprises a concise history of the Paleolithic, Neolithic and Bronze Ages, with an array of mostly broken pottery plus tools, jewellery and photographs of various digs.

Within the same complex the airy **Nautical Museum** (daily summer only 10am–1pm & 7.30–10.30pm; free) warrants a quick peep for its collection of model seafaring vessels, including an ancient trireme and the *Titanic*, and changing art exhibits, largely on marine themes. Since 2004, the **Municipal Art Gallery** (daily 10am–1pm & 7–10pm; free), which is dedicated to respected local painter Theodoros Stamos and features the work of local artists, who are granted regularly revolving exhibitions in the small gallery, has also been relocated here.

The Phonograph Museum

Given the seemingly permanent closure of the old Folklore Museum, the best glimpse into traditional island life is to be had at the **Phonograph Museum** (summer daily 10am–2pm & 7pm–midnight; free) at Konstandínou Kalkáni 14, one block east of Ioánnou Méla. More of a junk shop than a museum and comprising a single room, it contains a dazzling, occasionally bizarre battery of bric-a-brac and paraphernalia such as electrical equipment, household utensils, ornaments, toys, photos, paintings, clothes and some books from the house of poet and politician Aristotelis Valaoritis (1824–79), who vies with the Zakynthian poet Solomos for the title of "father of modern Greek literature" (the books come from his family's private island, Madhourí; see p.172). They also sell cassette recordings of the old 78rpm records in the collection, featuring various *kandádhes*, *rebétika* and other folk music.

Churches

A number of small **churches** dotted around the town, mostly dating from the eighteenth century, have so far survived the earthquakes. Modest in size, their architecture is atypical of the region in abandoning Byzantine design for simple, single-aisled rectangular buildings that can withstand earthquakes, with freestanding bell towers built of iron as an additional precaution. Most of Lefkádha Town's pre-quake churches are privately owned by island families, and open and close erratically; before and after morning and evening services are the best times to visit.

The interiors of these churches are opulently decorated with screens and icons by painters of the **Ionian School** (see box on p.81), including its founder, **Panayiotis Dhoxaras**, renowned for the original ceilings of Áyios Spyrídhon in Corfu which were destroyed by damp. Dhoxaras was responsible for the paintings in the church of **Áyios Dhimítrios** on Zabelíon, his son Nikolaos for the ceiling paintings of **Áyios Minás**, at the crossroads of Méla and Merarhías. The latter church has a striking metal clocktower and some of the best examples of the Ionian School, including work by Nikolaos Koutouzis and Lefkádha's most famous pupil of the school, Spyridhon Ventouris.

The church of the **Pandokrátor**, on Ioánnou Méla, is owned by the family of Aristotelis Valaoritis, who is entombed behind the altar of the church. Further down Ioánnou Méla is the church of the **Theotókou** (or Presentation of the Virgin), which has ceiling paintings copied from the work of Raphael by Lefkadhan painter Spyridon Gazis, and the only remaining stone bell-tower in Lefkádha.

Eating and drinking

Most of Lefkádha's **restaurants** and **bars** are centred on Dörpfeld and the seafront. The small elegant square of Áyiou Spyrídhon, in particular, comes alive on summer evenings, with intermittent performances by busking musicians, jugglers and even fire-eaters. However, establishments in the square itself, such as the pleasant *ouzerí Pendofanaro*, are the priciest in town. The north end of Dörpfeld is as hectic as London's West End in high season, with garish souvenir shops and tourists spilling out of cafés and bars onto the streets. There is no shortage of places to grab a toasted sandwich or *souvláki*; for a pastry or breakfast, try the *Gustoso zaharoplastío* on the seafront at the corner of Dörpfeld and Sikelianoú.

Restaurants

Alkyona Golémi 22. Restaurant opposite the marina with cheap meat and reasonably priced fish and seafood – try the *soupiés*. It's cosy, but traffic noise can detract from its appeal.

Bakolas Skiadharési 10. Small *estiatório* that dishes up authentic island cuisine. Mostly indoor seating with just 2–3 tables on the pavement outside.

Eftyhia In an alley off Dörpfeld, a few blocks behind the *Santa Maura* hotel. Friendly and inexpensive *estiatório* serving great home cooking like baked swordfish and fresh oven vegetables.

Lighthouse Filarmonikís 14. Taverna with a small garden and a standard range of starters, meat and fish dishes, somewhat tourist-oriented and a tad overpriced. Evenings only.

 Regantos Dhimárhou Verióti 17. Island cuisine at its best, from the generous

mezédhes to the main courses. Simple, friendly setting that's always full of locals. Evenings only.

Romantika Mitropóleos 11. Large restaurant with eyebrow-raising, almost postmodern decor, a sizeable courtyard at the rear, and a vast menu of grills, seafood, salads and oven-baked staples at reasonable prices. In season it hosts nightly performances of Lefkadhan *kandádhes*.

Seven Islands In an alley off Dörpfeld. Decent place serving some unusual baked dishes like pork with mushrooms and a fair range of salads and starters.

Sto Molo Golémi 12. One of the best choices for delights such as garlic bread (still rare in these parts), stuffed onions and mussels *saganáki* at very fair prices. Just that traffic noise issue again.

Cafés and bars

Less expensive places are to be found away from the centre, particularly at the southerly end of Ioánnou Méla. One of the best is *Cafe Karfakis*, an old-style **kafenío** with straw-upholstered wooden seats, and ancient phonographs and 78s decorating the interior, where you can order inexpensive *mezédhes*. Most of the town's trendiest **bars** are to be found either on the Áyiou Spyrídhon square, where

---

The Lefkádha Festival of Music, Arts, Literature and Dance

Each summer for around fifty years, Lefkádha has hosted a wide-ranging **cultural festival**, which these days attracts performers and visitors from around the world. Originally only three weeks in August, it now extends from June to September. It still peaks in August, however, adding to the usual high-season demand for accommodation. Troupes come from eastern and western Europe, South America and elsewhere, performing mainly in Lefkádha Town, but also in villages around the island. The island and mainland Greece respond with troupes of their own musicians and dancers: the 2005 festival, for example, featured performances of ancient tragedy and comedy by Greek companies, as well as productions of Shakespeare and modern plays, alongside a host of classical concerts, plus some African, Latin American and jazz. There were also art exhibitions and special cinema showings. For details, contact ☏26450/26 635 or ✉elefkasf@otenet.gr.

adjacent *Cäsbäh* and *Totem* are favourites, or on the seafront road Sikelianoú, which is closed to traffic in the evenings; *Excess* and *Coconut Groove* seem to draw the most revellers. Further out towards Ayiánnis, the *Atmosfera* club is a big disco with foreign sounds, while *Cosmos* is the place to shake your stuff to Greek hits.

Listings

Banks Both the Ionian Bank and the National Bank of Greece have branches on Ioánnou Méla, the former at the southern end, the latter midway down. The Agricultural Bank of Greece is situated in the corner of Platía Ayíou Spyridhónos. All have 24-hr cash dispensers. Banks only open mornings (Mon–Thurs 8am–2pm, Fri 8am–1.30pm); outside these hours the larger hotels and travel agencies will change travellers' cheques, but with heavier commission.

Bookshops There are no dedicated English-language bookshops on the island, although some Greek bookshops stock foreign-language guides and paperback fiction in English, German and Dutch. Most accessible are the Katopodis, Konidaris, Mataragas and Tsiribasis stores, all of them on Ioánnou Méla.

Car/motorbike rental Europcar (☎26450/23 581, ⓦwww.europcar.gr) and Budget (☎26450/24 643, ⓦwww.budget.gr), next to each other at Panágou 16, offer similar rates for car rental. The oddly named I Love Santas (☎26450/25 250), next to the *Ionian Star* hotel, is reliable for two-wheelers.

Cinema The Cinema Eleni, Faneroménis 51, is an outdoor cinema set in a small, overgrown garden with a large screen attached to a handy block of flats. Its fare is mostly subtitled English-language films, with programmes changed daily; as well as the usual parade of American blockbusters, it can also startle with the occasional art-house movie. The first showing is always at 9pm, the second depends on the length of the film. Be sure to wear long clothes and/or mosquito repellent.

Hospital Corner of Mitropóleos and Zambelíou ☎26450/22 336.

Internet Surprisingly, one of the cheapest places for Internet access on any of the islands is at the *Ionian Star* hotel, which only charges €2 per hour.

Laundries There are two laundries/drycleaners on Ioánnou Méla, but laundry doesn't come cheap; you can expect to pay €0.70 and upwards per item, more if you want it ironed.

Library Ioánnou Marínou (Tues–Sat 8.30am–1.30pm, plus Tues & Thurs 6–8.15pm).

Olympic Airlines The town office is at Dörpfeld 1 ☎26450/22 881.

Police Golémi 1 ☎26450/22 100. Tourist Police ☎26450/26 450.

Post office Ioánnou Méla (Mon–Fri 7am–2.30pm).

Around Lefkádha Town

Around Lefkádha Town a couple of places might merit your time, for relaxation or sightseeing. The latter option is provided by **Ayía Mávra castle**, actually on the mainland opposite the town, and the peaceful environs of **Faneroméni monastery**. Meanwhile, swimming, eating and even dancing can be enjoyed at **Yíra** and **Aïyannis** beaches.

Ayía Mávra castle

The main point of interest in the immediate vicinity of Lefkádha Town is the impressive semi-ruined **castle of Ayía Mávra** (Santa Maura) squatting on the far side of the causeway, a ten-minute walk from the north end of Dörpfeld. The fort (daily 9am–3pm; free), which now comprises three structures – Ayía Mávra itself, and the George and Alexander forts built during the Russian occupation – was started in the fourteenth century by the Orsini family, and was extensively rebuilt by the Venetians in the eighteenth century. However, much of the interior was destroyed when an explosives magazine accidentally blew up in 1888, and bombing during World War II further damaged the structure. Not many people bother to visit the castle, so you are likely to have the place to yourself. You can explore the extensive ramparts, which are used as a spectacular backdrop to performances during the arts festival (see box, p.155), although there's not much else inside.

Yíra and Aïyannis beach

There is a distinctive boomerang-shaped strip of land, **Yíra**, which along with the causeway to the east, completely encloses the lagoon north of Lefkádha Town. The entire seaward edge of Yíra consists of shingly sand, the western side of which is known as **Aïyannis beach**. You can catch a bus direct to the beach during high season from the bus station (hourly 10am–2pm), or it's a pleasant thirty- to forty-minute walk from town, heading out westwards along Sikelianoú; alternatively, you can walk to the northeastern end of Yíra across the causeway, perhaps combining it with a visit to Ayía Mávra castle.

Roughly 4km long in total, the quietest section of Yíra is the northern side, which is often virtually deserted even in high season, save for the occasional cuddling couple or nudist bather hiding in its most secluded spots. The monotony is broken by the average *Yira* taverna halfway along. Things liven up a little the further you go west into Aïyannis, which is popular with people in camper vans, who park at the back of the beach. Development has been moving apace and there are now several cafés and **tavernas**, including the *Lioyerma*, which serves fresh fish and meat dishes, and *Tilegrafos*, a busy place with excellent *mezédhes* and some **rooms** (ⓣ26450/24 881, ⓦwww.tilegraphos.gr; ❷). Next door the *Ionian Sunset* (ⓣ26450/23 271, ⓕ25 977; ❹) offers comfortable apartments in a quiet garden. Another fine place to stay is 🏕*Villagio* (ⓣ26450/25 568, ⓕ25 577; ❹), a beautifully landscaped bungalow complex with a pool, which lies just back towards town from the southwest corner of the lagoon. Aïyannis also boasts a couple of **nightspots**: *Club Milos*, housed in the first of four renovated windmills spaced around Yíra, serves as a restaurant by day and a full-on dance club by night, while *Generation X* is another popular club on the western beach road. The presence of the windmills attests to the power of the prevailing winds here, which can produce small, choppy surf, although few windsurfers seem to have caught on to the area, opting for the flatter bay of Vassilikí instead.

Faneroméni monastery

Easily accessible from Lefkádha Town is the picture-postcard **Faneroméni monastery** (open daily 8am–2pm & 4–8pm; free), the major ecclestiastical attraction on the island. To get there on foot, walk to the far end of Faneroménis and up through the hamlet of Fríni. From the outside, the monastery is reminiscent of a large Swiss ski chalet, but this effect disappears once you're inside the spacious courtyard, which houses a chapel with beautiful stained-glass windows and bright murals of biblical scenes, a museum crammed full of ecclesiastical accessories, small and austere monks' cells, a bookshop and (unusually for religious establishments in Greece) public toilets. The monastery was originally built in the seventeenth century, but was destroyed by fire and rebuilt in the nineteenth century. During the German occupation of the island in World War II, the monks were forbidden to sound bells lest this be used as a code; they resorted to sounding a large wooden log, which hangs in the main entrance. Nowadays, a solitary monk tends the building. Skimpy clothing is frowned on, though women can borrow capes (hanging on hooks by the entrance) to cover their shoulders. Near the main entrance to the monastery are some excellent shady walks, along signed paths, through the pine woods.

The east coast to Vassilikí

Lefkádha's **east coast** is the most accessible part of the island, and in stretches is beginning to resemble Corfu's east coast, as the small resorts expand and merge into one another. Largely owing to the bridge link to the mainland, the coast road resembles a noisy motorway during the summer months. Most people head for, or find themselves deposited in, the major settlements of **Nydhrí** or **Vassilikí**, but there are also the constantly expanding resorts of **Liyiá** and **Nikiána** nearer to Lefkádha Town and a number of remoter spots, such as **Sývota** and **Mikrós Yialós**, as well as some fine walking routes around **Mount Stavrotás**.

Karyótes and Liyiá

Travelling south out of Lefkádha Town, the first village you'll arrive at, barely 4km from town, is **KARYÓTES**, now more of a satellite suburb and with no seafront beyond the *alykés* (salt pans) outside the village – which, like those in Zákynthos, are about as fascinating as, well, watching salt dry. Karyótes does, however, have the island's best **campsite**: *Kariotes Beach*, a small site hard by the coast road north of the village, but set back beneath olive trees, with washing facilities, a shop, bar, restaurant and a small pool (☎26450/71 103, Ⓔcampkar@otenet.gr); the island buses stop outside. Just 100m up the lane beside the campsite, *Pension Artemis* (☎26450/71 916, Ⓕ71 917; ❸) is a new three-storey block of smart rooms with its own volley-ball court. Less than ten minutes' walk further south is the village's small square with a supermarket, a couple of cafés and the excellent and friendly *To Syntrivani* taverna, situated, as the name suggests, beside a refreshing fountain.

The first stop of note on the route south is **LIYIÁ**, a working fishing harbour, with views across to the ruined castle of Áyios Yeóryios on the mainland, and a couple of narrow but clean shingle beaches on its outskirts – the best bet is **Tembéli**, just south of the port, with a beach bar and shady pines. There's little here to detain the independent traveller, though the choice of **accommodation** is reasonable, including the pricey *Konaki* (☎26450/71 127 or 71 397, Ⓦwww.hotelkonaki.gr; ❻), a smart B-class hotel on the northern edge of the village with pool and gardens. Down a sideroad opposite, towards the scraggier northern beach, is the *Lefkada Beach* (☎26450/72 215, Ⓦwww.lefkadabeach.gr; ❺), where the air-conditioned rooms all have TV. If you prefer an apartment try *Mavra* (☎26450/24 587, Ⓔpanayiotis19782001@yahoo.gr; ❸) or *Verde Apartments* (☎26450/22 536; ❷), both around the village centre. The fishing trade supplies a number of excellent **tavernas**, such as the extremely popular *Green Stop* on the beach and *O Xouras* on the quay, which also has a good range of meat dishes. The best place, however, is ⌖ *Iy Limni*, a friendly taverna with unbeatable prices, set in a quiet, leafy location back from the road south; among the delights on offer is their stuffed sausage, special lamb and unique *spartiátiko*, made with pork, peppers, mushrooms, cheese, wine and cognac. A couple of **bars**, *Polyxenis* and *Art Club*, which features live football as well as loud music, provide the only nightlife.

Epískopos and Nikiána

Two kilometres to the south is the shallow pebbly bay of **EPÍSKOPOS**, which shelters *Episcopos Beach* (☎26450/71 388), a basic but shady **campsite** with a shop, restaurant, grill and bar, and wash facilities. It shares the beach with the good-value *Dukato* (☎26450/71 122, Ⓦwww.heliosagora.com; ❹), a stylish **hotel** with gardens overlooking the bay, and the *Villa Thomaïs* (☎26450/71 985, Ⓕ72 220; ❻), a posh new place that has the disadvantage of being on the opposite side of the road to the sea.

Less than 1km further south, **NIKIÁNA**, which is smaller but prettier than Liyiá, also has a working harbour, with a beach just beyond. The beach is another narrow strand of shingle, with rocky outcrops; far better is the strand on the other side of the bay, accessible from the main road but with no facilities. Nikiána has several **hotels**, among them the family run *Pegasos* (☎26450/71 766, ⓦwww.hotelpegasos.gr; ➌), with gardens and en-suite rooms that have sea views, and the similar *Alexandros* (☎26450/71 376, ⓕ71 131; ➌). There are also a number of apartment developments such as the *Christina* pension (☎26450/25 194; ➌), nicely set back from the main road. There are three **tavernas** overlooking the small harbour, of which the best is the *Pantazis Psist-aria*, which also has studios to let (☎26450/71 211; ➌). South of here, the *Lefko Akroyiali* taverna is good for fish. The *Litrouvio* café is a laid-back spot for a drink on the harbour. Nikiána is also home to the Lefkas Diving Center (☎26450/72 105, ⓦwww.lefkasdivingcenter.gr).

Nydhrí

Beyond Nikiána, there is sporadic development along the coast road pretty much all the way south to Nydhrí. The road climbs a fair way above sea level at some points, with the result that most of these places leave you with an awkward walk down to the nearest beach and some distance from any restaurants. Some of the new hotels are rather plush, however, most notably the *Sunrise* (☎26450/71 400, ⓦwww.sunrise-lefkada.com; ➏), set on a bluff affording sweeping coastal views. From here a series of small coves leads on to the hamlet of Periyiáli, where the sprawling resort of **NYDHRÍ** begins.

Nydhrí is where most package holidaymakers to Lefkádha will find themselves, and it offers boat excursions and passenger routes to the satellite islands and further afield. Although it has some fine pebble beaches and a lovely setting, at the mouth of a three-kilometre-long inlet, facing out towards the Yéni peninsula and the islands of Madhourí, Spárti and Skorpiós, the resort has been ruined by untrammelled development. Sadly, just as breathtaking as the sea views in Nydhrí are the car fumes. Some high-season mornings and evenings, when whistle-wielding traffic cops are fielded to massage traffic flow, the town actually develops its own mini smog problem.

Nydhrí's core is the dozen or so tavernas and bars that line its wide **quay**, the grandly named *Aktí Aristotéli Onási*, with a statue of the famous tycoon, jacket slung casually over his shoulder, halfway along. At night, the quay comes alive: day-trip boats string lights in their rigging and there's usually a street market, with much of the space that used to be given over to car parking now occupied by a series of stalls selling anything from candy floss to Indian trinkets, or offering henna tattoos and tarot readings.

There's a tailor-made natural escape from the hectic resort in the shape of Nydhrí's very own **waterfall**, about a 45-minute walk inland (5min by car) – though even this can get busy in high season. Follow the road to Ráhi, clearly signposted off the main street in Nydhrí; from just beyond here, a signposted track leads beyond the summer canteen and past a small waterfall on the left. Do not mistake this for the main fall; the real thing is a bit further along the path. Depending on the preceding months' precipitation, the waterfall's pool can be big enough for a refreshingly cool swim, and makes a great place for a picnic. The walk from Nydhrí is pleasant and on level ground, through a rocky gorge with overhanging rocks and a floodstream strewn with snowy-white boulders. There's some shade en route, but the walk is best attempted in the cool of early morning or late afternoon.

Accommodation

Those **hotels** not already block-booked tend to fill up fast in Nydhrí and are not generally cheap, but the town does boast one of the better places to stay on the east coast: the ⚔ *Hotel Gorgona* (☎26450/95 634 or 92 197, ⓕ92 268; ❹), set in its own lush, subtropical garden two minutes' walk along the road to Ráhi, offers modern en-suite rooms with balconies, and its owner and staff are unfailingly friendly and helpful. There are also a number of hotels on the beach, notably the *Avra Beach* (☎26450/92 741 or 92 269, ⓦwww.avra-beach.gr; ❺), which offers modern, air-conditioned comfort in en-suite rooms, some with good views of the islands. To the north of town, the smarter *Bel Air* apartment-hotel (☎26450/92 125, ⓦwww.hotel-belair.gr; ❻) is also air-conditioned and double-glazed against the noise, with its own pool, bar and other facilities. Two smaller but not especially cheap apartment operations that often have space at the south end of the main road are *Angelos Studios* (☎26450/92 920, ⓕ29 168; ❹) and *Phillipos Studios* (☎26450/92 783; ❸). The best source of independent **rooms**, which can be very scarce for much of the season, is through Nydhrí's many travel agents (see Listings opposite for details).

Eating and drinking

There are plenty of adequate restaurants in Nydhrí, though no spectacularly good ones. Of the unbroken chain that line the back of the quay, the *Barrel* **taverna** at the north end dishes up an interesting variety of local dishes and north European food, especially fish, with exotica such as bream cooked in a whisky sauce, but is pricey and typically tourist-oriented. *The Old Flame*, further south, also does the same bream special and pepper swordfish at slightly cheaper rates. If you want a quieter waterside meal head for the beachfront ⚔ *O Titanikos* taverna, north of the quay, which serves up tasty grills and starters, including a delicious Russian salad. Of the many places on the main drag, which are usually better value if you can put up with the traffic, two that stand out are *Tò Liotrivi*, which provides a good range of standards in an attractive stone building on the southern stretch, and the more central *Festino*, where you can enjoy Italian classics such as risotto in a quiet garden, although the service is a tad surly.

Among the many **bars** vying for the night-time trade, *Status*, which has a garden down by the sea, and *The Old Saloon Pub*, on the corner of the Ráhi turning, are firm favourites, as is the newer *Bubbles*, a Brit-oriented enterprise featuring Sky Sports. Finally, the *Sail Inn Club*, a music bar-disco on the northern side of the resort, claims to stay open 22 hours a day and projects powerful laser beams all over the night sky and surrounding mountains.

Boat trips

Most people staying in Nydhrí seem to spend a lot of their time trying to leave it, if only on the myriad **boat trips** heading out to the islands of Spárti, Skorpiós and Meganíssi. Some tours go further afield to Itháki and Kefalloniá. The boats line up along the quay each morning, ready for departure between 9 and 10am, returning late afternoon. Tickets are around €10 per person for the local trips, €15 for the longer distances. Most craft to the nearby islets are interchangeable: small fibreglass *kaïkia*, with bars and toilets, and open seating areas on the top deck or aft. Where they do differ, however, is in their itinerary – some will take in the sea caves of Meganíssi, others not, so it's advisable to check. The islands are all close to each other, so the journeys between them are short and sheltered. One of the best alternatives to these fibreglass buckets is the large wooden *Motor Sailer Panagiota*, a handsome old-fashioned *kaïki* run by and moored behind the *Barrel* taverna; the *Barrel* also offers day-trips on yachts that can take up to sixteen people. Another vessel with character is the wooden *Odysseas*, modelled on an ancient trireme, whose captain/guide is an enthusiastic old salt to boot; at €35 a head it's not a cheap day out but the experience is sure to be far more memorable.

Listings

Bus tour A bus tour of the island is available from Borsalino Travel (see below) for €30, including museum entry.

Car/motorbike rental As well as from the travel agencies mentioned below, car rental is available from branches of Eurohire (℡ 26450/26 776), Avis (℡ 26450/92 136), Budget (℡ 26450/92 008) and Hertz (℡ 26450/92 289), all in the centre of Nydhrí. Of the numerous bike outlets, I Love Santas (℡ 26450/92 668) is one of the most reliable.

Doctor Surgeries by the town hall (Mon–Fri mornings only) and next to the *Lefko* hotel.

Exchange The only proper banks in Nydhrí are small branches of the National Bank of Greece and Alphabank on the main road. There is also a large cash dispenser booth and most travel agencies offer bank rates but charge commission.

Internet Internet facilities are available for €3 per hour at Borsalino Travel on the main road.

Laundry The island's sole self-service laundry,

Sunclean, is situated at the southern end of town, opposite the *Athos Hotel*, and opens till late.

Port Authority For up-to-date information on all sailings ℡ 26450/92 509.

Post office There is now a small permanent post office building in the centre of the village (Mon–Fri 9am–2pm).

Travel agents Nydhrí's travel agencies are all close to each other on the central section of the main road. Biggest is the island-wide Samba Tours (℡ 26450/92 658 or 92 035, ⓦ www.sambatours .gr), which offers rooms as well as the usual range of travel, car rental and exchange services. Similarly, Nidri Travel (℡ 26450/92 514, ⓦ www.nidri .com) offers rooms and apartments, car rental and tickets, and can also arrange sailing-boat charters and jeep safaris to the more inaccessible parts of the island. Borsalino Travel (℡ 26450/92 528 or 92 134, ⓔ borsalin@otenet.gr) offers accommodation, tours and sells KTEL bus tickets.

Vlyhó and the Yéni peninsula

When Nydhrí finally peters out, the country reverts to flat olive groves. Just outside the village limits, near the hamlet of Stenó, are the main set of **excavations** by Dörpfeld, a small circle of Mycenaean burial chambers, which produced some of the finds displayed in the Archeological Museum in Lefkádha Town. A kilometre beyond the Dörpfeld site is the turning for the tiny hamlet of Haradhiátika, which is one of the main routes up onto the island's highest mountain, **Mount Stavrotás**. Haradhiátika is erratically served by the Vassilikí bus and has just one taverna, but is a favourite with walkers, who use the road to the even smaller hamlet of Áyios Ilías to reach the 1167-metre summit.

About 3km from Nydhrí, the main road comes to **VLYHÓ**, which looks out over the marshy flats at the bottom of the inlet – a veritable mosquito incubator in summer. Vlyhó is popular with freelance and bareboat yacht sailors, but has no hotels and little to detain the traveller, apart from a few rooms and a handful of tavernas such as *O Thalassolikos* and *To Limanaki* dotted along the seafront.

From Vlyhó, a minor road leads round to the **Yéni peninsula**, where those who want to enjoy the view of the inlet but escape the madness of Nydhrí can find accommodation: *Villa Maria* (℡ 26450/95 153, ⓦ www.vlihobay.com; ❹) and the bright-yellow *Australis* apartments (℡ & ⓕ 26450/95 521; ❹) are both near the bend at the top of the peninsula, while the *Ilios Club* apartments (℡ 26450/95 277, ⓔ ilioclub@otenet.gr; ❺) and the smart, new *Vliho Bay Hotel* (℡ 95 619, ⓦ www.vlihobay.com; ❺), all of whose rooms are air conditioned with TV, are further along in the village of Yéni itself. Surprisingly for such a backwater, five or six tavernas such as *Oasis* and *Hippocampus* punctuate the peninsula's waterfront but they seem to operate erratically, and, as there's not much to choose between them all, it's a case of seeing who's open. The road ends after 3km at the tiny chapel of **Ayía Kyriakí**, where Dörpfeld is buried under a simple stone memorial, and which has excellent views of Nydhrí and the hills beyond.

Over the saddle of the Yéni peninsula, **Dhessími bay** is a large expanse of blue water cutting deep into high green hills, behind which it loses the sun early. It is flanked by two neighbouring **campsites** which, confusingly, are reached by two different (and steep) lanes, even though they are separated by little more than 100m of beach. *Santa Mavra Camping* (☎26450/95 007, ⓕ26 087), the further and larger of the two, is a well-developed site with washing facilities, shop, bar and a simple taverna-snack bar, set in the shade of numerous olive trees. The beach in front is narrow, pebbly and, in high summer, tangled with the lines from innumerable powered inflatables in the water; that said, the sea is deep and clear for swimming. The similar *Dessimi Beach Camping* (☎26450/95 374 or 95 225), which gives onto a wider and cleaner stretch of beach, has a better taverna, but in high season is packed bumper to bumper with large 4WD vehicles. There are plenty of watersports available and, when you've worked up an appetite, the mid-beach *Pirofani* taverna offers a wide selection of tasty meals, especially fresh fish and vegetable dishes. Panos rent-a-boat has pedalos for €7 per hour.

Póros and Mikrós Yialós

From Vlyhó the main road south winds sharply up into the hills, passing through the quiet hamlets of Katohóri and Paliokatoúna, where a turning leads down to the attractive village of **PÓROS** and on to the small resort of Mikrós Yialós. Don't mistake Póros's presence on the map as a sign of tourism development – it's quiet even at the height of the season, and its sole taverna and bar close during the daytime. A few hundred metres down a rough track north of the village is the sixteenth-century **Analípseos church**, a tiny whitewashed, hut-like structure with visible earthquake damage but some faded original frescoes inside.

MIKRÓS YIALÓS, known locally as Póros beach, is a four-kilometre trek downhill (the twice-daily bus from Lefkádha Town turns back at Póros), and the number of cars using the road is a sign that this isn't the quiet beach you may have hoped for. The small bay boasts an increasing amount of **accommodation** and a few **tavernas**. Most facilities line the main beach to the right as you hit the seafront. The best-value are the smart, new *Eptanisa* apartment-hotel (☎26450/95 762 or 95 125,ⓦwww.eptanisahotel.gr; ❹) and *Oceanis Studios* (☎26450/95 095–6, ⓕ95 095; ❹), set down a quiet lane behind the beach, while the seafront *Rouda Bay* apartments (☎26450/95 634, ⓔmanolitsis@otenet.gr; ❺) are slightly more upmarket. Spreading up the hill in the corner of the bay, the well-kept *Poros Beach Camping* (☎26450/95 452, ⓦwww.porosbeach.com.gr) has self-contained bungalows (❷), shops and a pool. The *Rouda Bay* is the best beachside taverna, offering an array of grilled meat and fish, plus some oven dishes, while the *Café del Mare* is a pleasant grassy spot to escape from the sun for a refreshing drink or snack. The pebble beach is clean, and the lack of any waterborne traffic in the long Rouda Bay that leads out to the open sea keeps the water clear. On the east side of the bay there is a concrete quay and tiny sandy beach in front of several more establishments, including the good-value *Captain Nick* studios (☎26450/95 731; ❸) and fine *Zolithros* taverna, good for fish.

Inland to Sývros

Back on the main route south from Nydhrí to Vasslikí, about 2km on from the Póros turning, a right turn leads further up into the hills, making a pleasant alternative route to Vassilikí. A short way up this road, a side lane leads to the untouched village of **FTERNÓ**. The village *kafenío* and the *psistariá*, *O Filippas*, are good spots to break your journey, though the sight of a tourist is still enough to draw the odd inquisitive look.

Fternó itself is quite literally a dead end, but further on from the Fternó turning, along spectacular and sometimes vertiginous mountain roads, are the neighbouring villages of **VOURNIKÁS** and **SÝVROS**. The former sports a pretty town square and fountain, the excellent *O Yiannis* grill and two traditional but anonymous *kafenía*. Similarly, Sývros, which has stunning views down over the farming plain behind Vassilikí, is a quiet hill town with the pleasant *Watermill* café and two fine *psistariés* near the square, *O Nionios* and *Dilina*. There are some private rooms in both villages, but they're difficult to find: enquire in a restaurant or café, or ask for a local taxi driver, who might be able to help. The two villages offer few other facilities, but either could make an excellent walking base, perhaps after an initial investigative trip, away from the hubbub of Vassilikí. One pleasant stroll is south along the dirt track to the church of **Áyios Ioánnis**, formerly a monastery and before that a temple of Artemis. The English-speaking priest may be willing to show you the disused monastic cells and fragments of the ancient walls. A path that branches right off the road before the church leads through pine forest to the small mountain lake of Písas.

Sývota

The next bay round from Mikrós Yialós – 14km away by road – is **SÝVOTA**, a long, crooked and beautiful inlet where the open sea is not actually visible from the village. Already, however, apartment developments are appearing on the hills around the harbour, and Sývota has become a favourite with yachties, visited by **flotillas** of the British tour operators Sunsail and Sailing Holidays. Nights can be lively, but during the day, even in high season, the place tends to remain fairly quiet, making it a good spot to come for a swim, even though there is not much in the way of a beach – just a thin pebbly strand that can be reached by taking an overgrown path along the north side of the harbour and a recently imported strip of sand in the corner of the harbour itself. Only two **buses** a day thread their way down from Lefkádha Town; beyond that you're stuck here, unless you're prepared to negotiate the two-kilometre hike up to the main road to wave down the Vassilikí bus.

There are **rooms** of varying sizes available above the middle of the harbour at *Sivota Apartments* (℡26450/31 347, Ⓕ31 151; ❷), or you can ask at any of the seafront supermarkets. Sývota's list of facilities also includes bars, bike and car rental, a pizzeria and a number of excellent **tavernas**. The ⚓ *Palia Apothiki*, attractively converted from a 1710 stone and wood warehouse, is the best, serving quality dishes like giant shrimps wrapped in bacon at fair prices. *Spyridoula*, also tackily titled *No Problem*, is the resort's oldest establishment with a fair range of oven items, while *Delfinia* serves simple grilled meat and fish. A couple of pleasant **café-bars** on the quay are aimed at the flotilla crowd, namely the trendy new *Yacht Bar* and the *Liotrivi*, which has an attractive stone terrace. *Trocolo*, however, has the trendiest soundtrack and attracts the local youth.

Vassilikí and around

Visitors tend either to love or loathe **Vassilikí**. Its nightlife and watersports make it very popular with a young crowd, but island-hopping purists shudder at the intensity of commercialization along its narrow streets and quayside. Nevertheless, the crowds and traffic congestion – eased a little by a one-way system around the village – can't entirely obliterate the charm of its waterfront bars and tavernas, or the view out over its huge bay and spectacular mountains. It is certainly an improvement on Nydhrí. Be warned, however, that in high season Vassilikí can simply overload with tourists, to the extent that frustrated visitors sometimes have to take a taxi to another part of the island to find a bed for the night. Here, even more than at Lefkádha Town or Nydhrí, it's crucial to phone ahead to book accommodation.

Accommodation and services

Much of Vassilikí's **accommodation** is on or around the one-way system at the centre of the village, which tends to be both busy and noisy. The two main hotels are the *Vassiliki Bay Hotel* (☎26450/31 077, ⓦwww.hotelvassilikibay .gr; ❹), whose prices are very reasonable for its stylish, modern en-suite rooms with balconies and views, and the simpler *Hotel Lefkatas* (☎26450/31 801–3, ⓕ31 804; ❹), a large, modern building with bar, restaurant and disco, which only opens in high season. Both are in the thick of things though, so a better bet is to go southeast round towards the wooded headland beyond the dock or west along the road that leads along the back of the beach towards Póndi. The most reasonable place to stay in the direction of the headland is the friendly ⌖ *Pension Hollidays* (☎26450/31 011, ⓕ31 426; ❸), which has sea views from its raised position behind the small seafront park. Accommodation options along the beach road to Póndi include *Billy's House* (☎26450/31 418 or 39 363; ❸) and the smart new *Hotel Kalias* (☎26450/31 033, ⓦwww.kalias.net; ❻). Vassilikí's only **campsite**, the large *Camping Vassiliki Beach* (☎26450/31 308 or 31 457, ⓕ31 458), is about 500m along the beach road. It has its own restaurant, bar and shop, but is comparatively expensive.

Rooms in the centre of town tend to disappear into the maw of the package companies and windsurfing schools who bring clients here. As is often the case, the best way to find a room at peak times is through one of the local **travel agencies**, which keep a range of accommodation on their books, as well as offering car rental, exchange facilities and the usual spectrum of **tourist services**: try Hortis Travel on the Póndi road (☎26450/31 414, ⓕ31 127) or Samba Tours, open all year, on the road running down to the quay (☎26450/31 520, ⓦwww.sambatours.gr). Cars can also be rented from GM Rental (☎26450/31 650–1, ⓕ31 651) and Chris and Alex's (☎26450/31 580), both near the Póndi turn. There are no banks but you'll find an ATM near *Alexander* taverna. Vassilikí has its own Health Centre, which can be contacted round the clock on ☎26450/31 065.

The beaches

Vassilikí's **beach** is a disappointment, at least for those hoping to spend time on it, as opposed to windsurfing off it. Much of it is gritty, although it improves towards Póndi. The deep bay, protected by an eight-kilometre promontory leading to Cape Lefkátas and by Cape Lipsó on its eastern side, is ideal for **windsurfing**, and forms the venue for regular top-quality tournaments. The prevailing northwesterly winds and local topography produce a fairly stable pattern of onshore winds in the morning, and increasing cross-shore winds in the afternoon. Four windsurfing centres now ply their trade on the beach, including Club Vassiliki (@www.clubvass.com), which claims to be one of the largest in the world. It offers boards, equipment and tuition from beginner to advanced levels, with simulator boards and video tuition in its clubhouse. Half-day board hire costs €25–30 in the morning (9am–1pm) and around €30–35 in the afternoon (2–6pm), depending on the season. The Nautilus Diving Centre also operates under its aegis. Club Vassiliki and Fanatic Board Centre can offer complete windsurfing packages to Vassilikí through agents in Britain (see p.23).

The number of boards on the water at Vassilikí makes swimming slightly hazardous, so most people join the morning queues for the *kaïkia* that ply between the quayside and the excellent sandy beaches of Egremní and Pórto Katsíki, on the wild, uninhabited west coast of Cape Lefkátas (see p.169).

Eating, drinking and nightlife

Vassilikí's quayside **tavernas** are mostly standard affairs, the best of the bunch being the mid-harbour *Yiannis Psistaria*, which offers fish and seafood as well as succulent cuts of meat; *Alexander*, whose menu includes pizza in addition to Greek staples; and ⚓ *Penguins*, which specializes in lobster, swordfish and steaks served with exotic sauces. If you're looking for somewhere more peaceful, head southeast round the quay to the *Apollo*, which has a lovely leafy setting on the wooded headland, or the *Jasmine Garden* en route to it, which serves decent Chinese favourites.

Vassilikí's **nightlife** matches its popularity with high spending youth, although a cynic might diagnose style outstripping content. Bars along the front have different music policies and each attracts its own faithful following. Surprisingly, one of the cheapest places to drink on the entire island is in the centre of the L-shaped quay: the *Livanakis kafenío* next to the bakery, with tables on the edge of the harbour, which is much favoured by savvy Greeks. The best bar on the road down to the harbour is *Abraxas Tunnel*, a cosy hole-in-the-wall place with imported beer. Meanwhile, on the beach, *Remezzo* gets more than its fair share of poseurs and designer beefcakes.

Póndi

Barely a twenty-minute walk along either the beach or the road, the micro-resort of **PÓNDI** has become a quieter alternative to Vassilikí. It has a better, less crowded section of beach, which even has some patches of sand on the foreshore. The amount of **accommodation** here has been steadily increasing, although there's still only a handful of tavernas. About a five-minute walk up from the beach, the *Ponti Beach Hotel* (☎26450/31 572–5, ⓕ31 576; ❺) is a dated 1960s-era place, but it is very popular with Greek visitors and has en-suite rooms with excellent views of the bay, a tiny pool, and a bar and restaurant that are open to non-residents. Cheaper rooms are available on the beach at the *Surf Hotel* (☎26450/31 740, @surf-h@otenet.gr; ❸) and the comfortable *Nefeli* (☎26450/31 515, @clubnefeli@hotmail.gr; ❹), which has a lively outdoor bar and rents windsurfing boards for the very competitive rate of €35 per day. Its brand new sister hotel next door, the ⚓ *Grand Nefeli* (☎26450/23 435, @www.grandnefeli.com; ❻) is impressively decorated and unusually friendly for its class. The most appealing **restaurant** is *Panorama*, which offers specialities like garlic prawns and steak Diana, but *To Kyma* is also fine for meat and fish staples and *Kammares* is a specialist *psarotavérna*. A horse-riding club, *Hippokambos* (☎26450/31 607), is tucked away in the fields behind the beach.

The west coast

The mountainous and often sheer west coast is the least developed part of Lefkádha, but is blessed with the most attractive resort in picturesque **Aï Nikítas**, the best beaches, such as **Pefkoúlia**, **Káthisma** and **Yialós**, as well as some of the island's most interesting villages clinging to the high mountain roads. It is worth making the effort to travel down the west coast at least once, as it offers some of the most splendid vistas of rugged mountains tumbling into startling blue seas to be found anywhere in Greece. **Buses** from Lefkádha Town travel as far as the small, remote village of Atháni, from where the road continues 14km to Cape Lefkátas, but it is advisable to procure your own wheels to get the most from this exquisite part of the island.

Tsoukaládhes and Pefkoúlia beach

TSOUKALÁDHES, just 4km from Lefkádha, has two small, sandy beaches a couple of kilometres' hike below the hamlet and is beginning to develop a road-side tourism business, with some eateries such as the *Psaropoula* fish restaurant and *Tò Rodhon* garden taverna, and the odd bar and cafeteria. There is also the cosy *Pension Philoxenia* (T26450/97 040 or 97 240; ❸) and small new *Adoni Hotel* (T26450/97 450–1; ❹), complete with pool. The resort is nothing special though, and the only real reason to stay here is if you have transport and want to be close to Lefkádha Town for nightlife and within easy reach of the west coast beaches.

Four kilometres on, the road plunges down to the sand-and-pebble **Pefkoúlia beach**, the longest in the northwest of the island and one of the best spots for swimming. The only access road descends just south of the centre to the small cluster of facilities. There are rooms at the *Pelagos* taverna (T26450/97 070, ✉mypelagos@can.gr; ❹), which serves a healthy range of fish, meat and *mezédhes*, as does the *Jorelos* taverna next to it. Back at the north end, over 1km away, there is unofficial camping reached via a footpath down from the main road. Buses from Lefkádha Town to places further down the west coast stop at this access point and also earlier at the turning to the beach. This part of the island suffered severe structural damage but mercifully no fatalities in the earthquake of summer 2003, which for several months closed the main road, now protected by huge concrete and steel mesh barriers.

Aï Nikítas

Jammed into a gorge between Pefkoúlia and the next beach, splendid Mýlos, is **AÏ NIKÍTAS**, the prettiest resort on Lefkádha, its wood-clad buildings jumbled together claustrophobically. The village's own beach is small and pebbly, and loses the sun before 6pm even in high season, but it's blessed with crystal-clear water and a gentle family atmosphere. Small **boats** ply from here to the difficult-to-reach, kilometre-long sandy beach at Mýlos (€4 return). The back of the village, however, has been left as an ugly, dust-blown car park, which has now completely taken over the terraced olive groves that used to be a campsite. The silver lining is that cars are not allowed into the village proper, making its long pedestrianized lane of shops, bars and tavernas a pleasant place to stroll. Aï Nikítas has three daily **bus** services connecting it to the capital. If you want to rent a vehicle for exploration further down the west coast, try the Europcar rental agency at the top of the village, which shares an office with the general tourist agency Travel Mate (T26450/23 581, ✉trvlmate@otenet.gr).

Accommodation

Most **accommodation** is situated in the alleys that run off the central lane. Tourism here tends to be upmarket but there are a few bargains to be had. If tourism levels outside high season remain as low as in the last couple of years, it's worth bargaining over rates at such times. As well as the places listed below, the *Elena zaharoplastío* (T & F 26450/97 385; ❸), halfway down the village lane, rents some simple **rooms**.

Aphrodite Halfway along the village lane, on the east side T 26450/97 372. Probably the best all-round-deal for its cosy rooms with kitchen facilities, set round a leafy courtyard; friendly welcome and competitive rates. ❸

Fetsis Apartments Behind the beach T 26450/97 487, W www.lefkada-fetsis-apartments.gr. Six two-bedroom apartments, all comfortably furnished and with sea views. ❻

Odyssey Towards the top of the village lane, on the west side T 26450/97 351–2, W www.odyssey-hotel.gr. Plush, new hotel, with air-conditioned rooms and a swimming pool. ❻

Olive Tree Just below the main road in from Lefkádha Town T 26450/97 453, W www.olivetreelefkada.com. Friendly and comfortable Greek-Canadian owned hotel in a quiet location above the village. ❹

Pension Ostria Between the village lane and the main road, on the east side T 26450/97 483, E agnikitasostria@e-lefkas.gr. A beautiful blue-and-white building above the village with a bar overlooking the bay, decorated in a mix of beachcomber and ecclesiastical styles. The cosy en-suite rooms all look out on the garden and sea, and the bar makes a good spot to relax and enjoy the view. ❹

Santa Marina On the hill above the car park T 0645/97 455 or 97 111, W www.santamarina.gr. The resort's biggest and newest hotel with all the luxury amenities imaginable, though let down by its location. ❻

Villa Milia At the junction of the village lane and main road T 0645/97 477. The number one bargain. Friendly, family run place with comfortable en-suite rooms and a small courtyard. Smarter block opposite. ❶

Eating and drinking

Teetering just above the beach, the **taverna** *Sapfo* offers the best views in Aï Nikítas and a choice of seafood, pasta, grills and salads. Tucked up an alley on the west side of the village is the quieter and cheaper *T'Agnantio*, with an extensive menu of fish, meat and starters and views over village and sea. Of the numerous restaurants lining the village's high street, *Taverna Portoni* also juggles a wide range of fish, pasta and traditional Greek dishes; *Klimataria*, halfway down, offers specialities such a *frygadhéli* and *sefteliés*; while *O Lefteris* has an extensive menu of inexpensive standards. A fine selection of sweets and pastries is to be found at the *zaharoplastío Elena* opposite.

Nightlife is fairly low-key, with *Captain's Corner* at the seaward end of the main street being the liveliest, followed by the gentler ambience of *En Plo*, to the left as you hit the beach, and *Barbarossa* to the right, which actually juts out over the water.

Káthisma beach and Kalamítsi

Beyond Mýlos beach is the first of the west coast's magnificent beaches, **Káthisma**, served by three daily buses from Lefkádha Town. Viewed from the cliffs above, the beach is stunning, a perfect line of gold sand and dazzling blue sea with a creamy turquoise wash at the water's edge. Close up, the reality is a little more prosaic, and in high season the main section of beach can be scruffy, and often remains so until the winter storms hoover the Ionian. Few people, however, wander far beyond the craggy rocks that mark the southern end of the busiest strip, and yet there is a huge stretch of much more appealing sand in this direction, right along to the section below Kalamítsi. Clothing is optional along this stretch too.

There are several canteens and two **tavernas** on the main beach, the vast, barn-like *Kathisma Beach* (T 26450/97 335, W www.kathisma.com; ❺) at the north end, which boasts a huge menu and has some first-class, air-conditioned studios with TV, available all year, and the quieter *Akroyiali* towards the rocks, which has reasonable food but rather lackadaisical service. The nearby *Club Copia* is a flashy nightspot that attracts the young and beautiful to its house parties during the hotter months. On the winding road in a pleasant setting above the beach there are two more places to stay, the modern *Hotel Sirios* (☎26450/97 025, ⓦwww.hotelsirios.gr; ❺) and the spacious refurbished studios of the *Sunset* (☎26450/97 488 or 97 474, ⓦwww.sunsetstudios.gr; ❻).

A large sign on the beach insists "Camping strictly forbidden", although there remain pockets of discreet **freelance camping** at the far end of the beach, beyond the rocks. Káthisma has little natural shade, but there are enough sun beds and umbrellas on the main strip to relax an army, and the *Kathisma Beach* offers free showers and a range of watersports and paragliding.

From here the coast road takes a series of spectacular hairpin bends on the way to the mountainside village of **KALAMÍTSI**, the last tourist-oriented settlement on the coast before distant Atháni. Most of the houses here are the barely modernized shells of cramped peasant cottages, although tourist **accommodation** tends to be in purpose-built, two-storey houses. There is the modest but comfortable *Hotel Lenia* (☎26450/99 125; ❷), while great-value rooms and apartments are available at ✴ *Hermes* (☎26450/99 417; ❷), which has a pleasant kitchen garden, the *Blue and White House* (☎26450/99 413, ⓦwww.bluewhitehouse.com; ❸) and the newer *Pansion Nontas* (☎26450/99 197 or 99 451; ❸). In the centre of the village there are a few shops and bars, including the surprisingly hip *Nostos Club*, as well as three **tavernas**: the *Paradisos*, in its own garden with fountain, the more old-fashioned and basic *Ionio* and the small *Steki* grill. Just outside the north end of the village, the aptly titled *Panoramic View* restaurant offers a good selection of decently priced seafood, pasta, grills and taverna staples. Three kilometres down a recently paved road is the village's quiet sandy **beach**, in effect the southern end of Káthisma. The *Avali Beach* taverna sits at the end of the road, while a dirt track beforehand leads to some smaller rocky coves.

South to Atháni and beyond

Beyond Kalamítsi, the road climbs the mountainside then dips into a valley behind the cliffs. The first settlement you reach is the workaday, yet appealing village of **HORTÁTA** with an attractive plane-shaded square and a few shops, restaurants and cafés. On the way in, look out for the excellent ✴ *Lygos* taverna, which cooks fresh home produce and also rents comfortable rooms at low rates (☎26450/33 395, ⓔlola26@ch.gr; ❶). Just before Komíli, a turning skirts the mountains of the interior and leads all the way to Vassilikí bay, via the lively village of **Áyios Pétros** with its charming little square and fine tavernas – try *O Kotselis* or *Ta Badzanakias*.

Komíli itself is more mundane, with just one taverna and a smattering of houses. Beyond it, the landscape becomes eerily empty, although the four-kilometre stretch before Dhrágano, with its magnificent near-deserted wheat-farming landscape, makes for an excellent walk. As the road winds on south through the continually captivating landscape, there are ample opportunities to take home a sweet memento in the form of the pure local honey, made by bees fed on wild thyme and sold at roadside trestle tables.

Some guides speak misleadingly of **ATHÁNI** as a centre for this region of the island. In fact, it's a bit of an outpost – three tavernas, two shops and a public phone – albeit a very pleasant one. Most visitors head for the ✴ *Panorama*

(☎26450/33 291 or 33 476; ❶), which, as well as a **restaurant** with balcony, has an upstairs cocktail bar and very cheap **rooms** with, as the title justifiably claims, panoramic views over the sea as far as Cape Lefkátas and, on clear days, Kefalloniá in the south. You may even find yourself being serenaded by the musical proprietor. *O Alekos* (☎26450/33 484; ❷) is a more traditional taverna, also with rooms, but only opens in July and August. Another good spot for a meal is the family run *Lefkatas* taverna on the northern edge of town, specializing in seafood. Just south of Atháni, the new *Porto Katsiki* studios (☎26450/33 136; ❸) have added another comfortable base to the area.

Directly west of Atháni, a now fully surfaced road winds 4km down to the splendid beach of **Yialós**, which is several kilometres long, rarely at all crowded and has the *Yialos* café-restaurant and a couple of seasonal canteens for refreshment. Meanwhile the main road south – now decently surfaced too – continues for about 2km along the barren Lefkátas peninsula to the *Cavo Dukato psistariá*, where a steep track, still mostly unpaved, snakes down to **Egremní beach**, which has just one canteen above the final steps down to the strand. After a further 7km on the main road, most traffic turns right and winds down a series of hairpin bends to the clifftop above the twin beach at **Pórto Katsíki**. Sandy and shady, Egremní and Pórto Katsíki are two of the most picturesque beaches on the island and are popular with boat day-trippers from Vassilikí. Pórto Katsíki is particularly appealing, with chalky turquoise sea near the shore, deepening to violet, and dramatic overhanging cliffs, upon which perch several well-stocked snack bars.

Cape Lefkátas

Cape Lefkátas is a shadeless 14km from Atháni, and, while the terrain is suitably rugged and majestic, you'll find little to celebrate here beyond a lighthouse and a sense of achievement for actually having made it this far. The cape, which can be quite fearsome in bad weather, rises an almost sheer 60m on its west coast, and is little gentler on the protected east side. It has numerous mythological associations, not to mention a barely recognized role as one of the key sites in early gay history.

The rocks have been identified as the site of human sacrifices as long ago as 1200 BC. By the fourth century BC the ritual victims were criminals, with feathers and even live birds tied to them to help ease their descent, and boats at hand in the sea below; if the victims survived the plunge, their lives were spared. By this time, the promontory was the site of a temple of Apollo, who was believed to take care of seafarers and whose cult promoted the idea of leaping from the cliff to cleanse mind and body – not only from the stain of crimes, but also from the torment of unrequited love. Aphrodite is said to have been the first to go over the edge, in response to the death of her lover, Adonis. Byron describes the cape in *Childe Harold's Pilgrimage* as "the lover's refuge, and the Lesbian's grave" – a reference to **Sappho** of Lésvos, who according to local myth threw herself off Cape Lefkátas out of frustrated love for a man, Phaon. Nineteenth-century engravings of her suicide tend to figure the iconic lesbian in a state of bliss, lyre clasped to her bosom, eyes closed and raised to the heavens, fearless on the western precipice and about to jump. Perhaps the greatest irony, however, is that despite the untold number of tavernas and bars that sport her name, Sappho probably never actually visited Lefkádha at all: the suicide is inferred from literalist readings of the few remaining fragments of her poetry, and the boyfriend was written into the story by historians mortified at the fact that she dated girls.

Karyá and the interior

No one should leave Lefkádha without venturing into its **interior** at least once. Whereas the interiors of some other Ionian islands are either too easily accessible or just plain dull, inland Lefkádha can startle with panoramic hillscapes or hidden valleys which nurture the island's wheat industry. The elephantine humps of **Mount Stavrotás** and its neighbour Mount Eláti block communication across the island, so that communities such as Sývros and Vournikás (see p.163) have to be approached from the south, though the majority of the inland villages can be easily reached from Lefkádha Town itself (buses visit most villages at least once a day) and the road from Karyá via Vafkerí is now paved all of the way to Nydhrí. Cross-island jaunts may soon be made even easier by the projected construction of a direct link from Hortáta to the Sývros–Nydhrí road.

The road to Karyá

The road south from Lefkádha Town forks at the urban limits, the right-hand prong rising into the hills to enter the district of **Sfakiótes**, a conglomerate of some half a dozen tiny villages, a couple of which merit a break in your journey. **Lazaráta**, 8km south of Lefkádha Town, has a handful of cafés and restaurants – try the large *Klimataria* taverna, which serves a mean *kondosoúvli* – huddled around the small square, marred only by its proximity to the main road, upon which stand the comfy *Pension Filoxenia* (☎26450/61 533 or 61 427; ❷) and new *Dionysos Apartments* (☎26450/61 300 or 61 602; ❷). Two kilometres further on, the pretty, vine-growing village of **Asproyerakáta** also offers a couple of small **hotels**, *Iy Zoí* (high season only; ☎26450/61 136; ❷) and *Villa Karidia* (☎26450/61 196; ❷), and a couple of tavernas, such as *Ta Platania*, as well as the traditional *Monte Carlo kafenío*. All these establishments can be found around the small village square, also the site of the cute white and ochre Áyios Athanássios church.

Karyá

About 3km beyond Asproyerakáta lies **KARYÁ**, which boasts an extremely scenic main square, shaded by plane trees, with excellent views out over the Liyiá/Nikiána coast to Etolo-Akarnanía on the mainland. As well as a post office and petrol station, the village is noted for the number of shops selling carpets and other woven goods, and **lace embroidery**. This timeworn tradition is celebrated in the fascinating **folklore museum** on the edge of the village, run by the family of one of Karyá's greatest lacemakers (April–Oct daily 9am–9pm; €2.50). Even if the notion of lacemaking causes your eyes to glaze over, this renovated peasant home is worth a visit for its wealth of social detail, with eating, sleeping and living quarters carefully reconstructed, and clothing, implements and lacework artfully arranged around the house. The museum has recently been expanded into a weaving school, where visitors can see young apprentices being trained in these traditional skills.

Practicalities

The *Karia Village Hotel* (☎26450/41 004–5; ❹), tucked away 200m along the first lane rising above the village, is a surprisingly large **hotel** for its setting but was closed for renovation at the time of writing. **Rooms** are available from Haritini Vlahou (☎26450/41 634; ❶), the Kakiousis family (☎26450/61 136; ❶) or Olga Lazari (☎26450/61 547; ❷).

Karyá's square, where island buses turn round, is an excellent place for lunch or dinner, or just chilling out. As well a couple of *kafenía*, such as *Bio*, it has two popular *psistariés*, *Ta Platania* and *O Rousos*, while just off the corner of the square is the smarter ✗ *Klimataria* taverna, with the widest choice of food and best views. Curiously, the village also boasts a German-style beer cellar, the *Alt Kelerei*, hidden away on the northern edge.

Around Karyá

To the south of Karyá, rising up the slopes of Stavrotás' smaller but nonetheless impressive northern neighbours, are two of the oldest villages on the island, with architecture dating back to the sixteenth century. The one most worth visiting is **ENGLOUVÍ**, the highest village on Lefkádha, with spectacular

△ Central square, Englouví village

views, and the centre of the island's lentil crop. The name means "encaged", which makes perfect sense when you stand looking out from the pretty village square or sit at its one surviving traditional *kafenío*, surrounded by mountains on three sides. Unfortunately, the nearest peak is dominated by ugly military installments, adding an ominous edge to the otherwise pristine natural surroundings. Less than a kilometre outside the village, a small cave, barred to the public, is claimed to have been the cave of the *Odyssey*'s one-eyed giant, Polyphemus. From Englouví, a track, signposted at the south end of the village, leads circuitously up to the 1167-metre summit of Mount Stavrotás – a good half-day's round walk there and back.

The road to Englouví branches off from the much improved road to the other old settlement of **VAFKERÍ**, which is nearly deserted today, but still has some fine island architecture and is worth a halt if you are continuing along the useful road linking it to Nydhrí on the east coast. The only accommodation is a smart new trio of stone villas, each luxuriously furnished and with a pool, named collectively ✈ *Villas Nousias* (☎26450/29 108, ⓦwww .lefkada-villas.com; ❽), ideal for families with their own transport, looking for fresh mountain air. Sustenance is available locally at *O Platanos* taverna/grill during the summer months at least. On the way between Karyá and Vafkerí, the small village of **Platýstomos** is less appealing architecturally, but it also has a grill, affords fine views across the eastern valleys and offers decent local wine for sale at the well-advertised family vintners. Beyond Vafkerí the road winds gradually down towards the east coast, passing close by the waterfalls (see p.159) before reaching Nydhrí.

On the opposite side of Karyá, recently paved roads skirt the lesser peak of Mount Méga to reach the two main west-coast mountain villages, **DHRYMÓNAS** and, 3km further, **EXÁNTHIA**, high above the beaches of Káthisma and Kalamítsi. Clinging to the side of the mountain, both villages have a few shops and cafés, primarily to serve local people, and spectacular views of the sunset out at sea. In Dhrymónas the *psistariá O Memis* is located in a shady spot with views down the valley below, but Exánthia is more picturesque overall. Note the ornate metal framework of the campanile of Áyios Stéfanos, the church that dominates the centre of the village. *Iy Rahi* café/grill is the best spot to stop for refreshment and sweeping coastal vistas.

Lefkádha's satellites

Lefkádha's four main satellite islands lie a short way off its east coast and can be reached – or at least viewed – by day-trip boat from Nydhrí (see p.159). **Meganíssi**, the largest and most interesting, can also be reached by regular ferry. The nearest, tiny **Madhourí**, is owned by the family of nineteenth-century poet and political hero Aristotelis Valaoritis, and is off-limits to visitors. **Spárti** is deserted and covered in scrub. **Skorpiós**, purchased in the 1960s by Aristotle Onassis, is held in trust for Athina Onassis, daughter of the late Christina, and is patrolled by armed guards. Daily tours pass close by – some even stop to let you swim off the boat in a sheltered bay – and you can spot a few buildings through the trees from the Meganíssi ferry, but the island, where Onassis and Jackie Kennedy were married, is virtually a ghost estate. Up to twenty different ent *kaïkia* circle the islands daily, which must make life for the few inhabitants rather like living in a zoo.

Lefkádha's more distant satellites, the near-deserted islands of Kálamos, Kástos and Átokos, are in fact closer to the Greek mainland. Nowadays, none of them can be reached from Lefkádha, and only **Kálamos** has a regular ferry service, from Mýtikas on the mainland (south of Vónitsa on the coast road between Préveza and Astakós). **Kástos** has a small village and harbour, but can only be reached by finding a lift with an independent yacht heading in that direction or by hiring a *kaïki* to take you – enquire in Mýtikas or Kálamos. **Átokos**, to the southwest of Kástos, is now deserted.

Meganíssi

Almost barren **MEGANÍSSI** has remained a well-kept secret for many years, kept quiet by visitors who like their islands nearly deserted. Little has changed over the decades, although there has been gradual development, suggesting that Meganíssi should be visited before it's sucked into the mainstream of Greek tourism. An excellent, year-round (weather permitting) **ferry** service connects Nydhrí with the small port of **Spiliá** and the main port of **Vathý**. The ferry takes under half an hour (single €2) and exists to serve the inhabitants of Meganíssi, which is why the first services leave Meganíssi, and the last Nydhrí (see also p.159).

Spiliá and Spartohóri

The first port, **SPILIÁ**, is little more than a landing stage and a pebble beach, though it does have three **tavernas** and a very basic semi-official **campsite**. The campsite is behind the *Stars Taverna*, the best of the restaurants by the quay, which also has a basic shop and shower facilities, for which there is a nominal charge. Five minutes' walk around the bay is a longer, sandier beach with a couple of snack bars and the excellent *Spilia* taverna.

Ten stiff minutes up the hill from Spiliá is the small, whitewashed village of **SPARTOHÓRI**. Unspoilt for decades, Spartohóri now has a souvenir shop and a couple of more tourist-oriented **restaurants**: a pizza place, the *Tropicana*, which can direct you to **rooms** (✆26450/51 486; ❸), and the *Rooftop Cafe*, which serves up a wide range of Greek and international dishes on a balcony with panoramic views over the satellite islands and Lefkádha. The two more traditional **tavernas**, both in the centre of the village, are *Lakis* and *Gakias* (✆26450/51 050; ❸), the latter also an outlet for rooms. Apart from a few shops (where you could also ask about rooms), that is all there is to this quiet, pretty village – walk too fast and you'll find yourself out in open country in minutes.

The part of the island most likely to be developed is its finest beach at **Áyios Ioánnis** on the west coast, forty-five minutes' walk from Spiliá by the more scenic coastal road. A more direct paved road from Spartohóri also leads to it and, though there is currently just one taverna, *Il Paradiso*, which acts as a semi-official campsite, the addition of apartments would seem to be only a matter of time.

Katoméri and Vathý

The island's oldest road rises over the hills to the east of Spartohóri, giving panoramic views, notably of the wild, narrow peninsula to the south. Traffic is rare, and the silence and sense of isolation at the centre of the island are to be savoured, especially if you've just escaped the craziness of Nydhrí. After about an hour's walk, you'll reach the main village of **KATOMÉRI**, which can lay claim to a couple of bars and *kafenía*, and the island's one **hotel**, the ✠ *Meganisi*, a small and comfortable place with en-suite rooms and balconies, swimming pool, restaurant, bar and terraces (℡26450/51 240, ℻51 639; ④); it is surprisingly open year round.

The port of **VATHÝ** is a ten-minute walk down from Katoméri and can also be reached direct from Spiliá by the new coast road. While unremarkable, and lacking any swimming facilities, it's still a very attractive place, with a deep bay and little development beyond a handful of tavernas and bars, and one or two villas on the surrounding hills. There's now **accommodation** in Vathý at the waterfront *Different Studios* (℡26450/22 170; ③). The *Rose Garden Taverna*, with a surprisingly varied menu of starters and main courses, vies for custom with the basic *Restaurant Greco*, but the favourite among Greek visitors – where Lefkadhans flock for Sunday lunch – is the waterside ⚓ *Porto Vathi*, which serves vast portions of locally caught seafood. The *Twins Bar* by the ferry dock is a friendly spot for a drink. The most popular of Meganíssi's beaches is **Ambelákia**, to the east of Vathý, but still accessible only by the path which heads east and then north out of Katoméri.

Kálamos

KÁLAMOS, lying the best part of the way towards the mainland from Meganíssi, is another drowned mountain, mostly bare but with some evergreen woods reaching down as far as its pebbly beaches. It's mainly seen as a stopping-off point for bareboat sailors, some of whom favour it above any other small island in the region. A **kaïki** leaves mainland Mýtikas – which sports several hotels, among them the *Kymata* (℡06460/81 258 or 81 311; ②), and has rooms at the *O Glaros* taverna (℡06460/81 240; ①) – once a day at noon (sometimes more often in high season) for the voyage to the island.

Kálamos has just one village, **HÓRA**, with some **rooms**, although these are often booked through the summer – try calling the Lezentinos family (℡06460/91 238; ①). Hóra is spread out above the small harbour, and is one of the few villages in the area that survived the 1953 earthquake, the epicentre of which was quite close by. Beside the harbour there's the large taverna *Akroyiali* (℡06460/91 358; ②), which offers an extensive menu and sometimes has rooms, an old-fashioned grocer's shop and a café/snack bar, while up the hill you can find several more shops and a post office, as well as a couple of snack bars and cafés and the village butcher's, which doubles as a basic grill. There are passable beaches within ten to fifteen minutes' walk either side of Hóra and the westerly one has a sporadically opening taverna. Freelance camping is quite acceptable on these or any of the island's other coves, many of which are only really accessible by sea.

With just one road winding around the 920m top of Mount Vouní, Kálamos provides excellent, if limited, walking terrain. The fortified former capital, **Kástro**, now deserted and overgrown, is near the summit, a ninety-minute walk from Hóra, and its five-bastioned castle is surrounded by derelict buildings. The road also goes to the monastery of **Áyios Yeóryios**, which is open to visitors. The island's most attractive beaches are to be found on the north coast, between Hóra and Episkopí, although almost all involve a hair-raising scramble down through the woods. The longest walk on the island, to the deserted village of **Pórto Leóni** (abandoned owing to water shortages, hence the expansion of Hóra) is a two-hour hike across the mountainside with fantastic views over Kástos. If you had a vessel for easier access or were prepared to cart provisions along the path, the eerie uninhabited buildings and adjacent patch of beach would make a fine spot for the hardy to live out post-apocalyptic fantasies.

Travel details

Buses

The details given here apply year-round; there may be extra services to the beaches in July and August.

Lefkádha Town to: Aï Nikítas (3 daily, 1 on Sun; 45min); Atháni (2 Mon–Sat; 1hr 30min); Athens (4 daily; 6hr); Englouví (3 daily, ex Sun; 1hr 15min); Kalamítsi (2 Mon–Sat; 1hr 15min); Karyá (7 daily, 1 on Sun; 1hr); Káthisma (3 daily; 50min); Katohóri (2 daily, ex Sun; 1hr); Nydhrí (15 daily, 6 on Sun; 30min); Póros (2 daily, ex Sun; 55min); Préveza (6 daily; 30min); Sývota (2 daily; 1hr); Sývros (2 daily, 1 on Sun; 1hr 30min); Thessaloníki (3 weekly; 12hr); Vassilikí (5 daily, 3 on Sun; 1hr 20min); Vlyhó (21 daily, 17 on Sun; 40min); Yíra (4 daily; 10min).

There is also an express service from Nydhrí to Aï Nikítas and Káthisma in summer only (2 daily; 1hr 20min).

Ferries

During the summer months (July–Sept), the services listed below connect Lefkádha to Kefalloniá and Itháki. These are gradually scaled up and down on either side of high season, but at least one triangular route of Nydhrí–Fiskárdho–Fríkes–Vassilikí runs all year:

Nydhrí to: Fiskárdho, Kefalloniá (1 daily; 2hr 30min); Fríkes, Itháki (1 daily; 1hr 30min); Meganíssi (7 daily; 30min).
Vassilikí to: Fiskárdho, Kefalloniá (2 daily; 1hr); Fríkes, Itháki (1 daily; 2hr).

Flights

The flights listed below are all from Préveza on the mainland.

Préveza to: Athens (1 daily; 55min); Corfu (1 weekly; 25min); Kefalloniá (1 weekly; 25min); Zákynthos (1 weekly; 1hr 15min).

Itháki

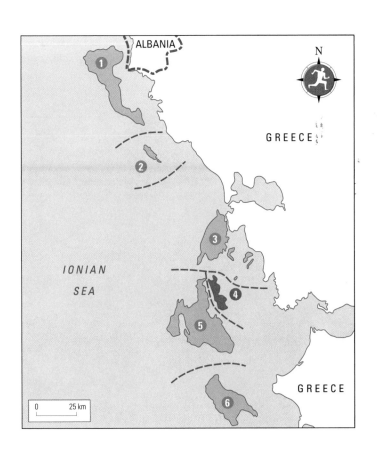

CHAPTER 4 # Highlights

* **Vathý** Itháki's capital is set inside a beautiful bay within a bay. See p.182

* **The Arethoúsa Spring** The walk along the isolated coastal path from the capital to this place of Homeric myth affords splendid views. See p.186

* **Afáles bay** This stunning sweep of stone and sand in the north is the best beach accessible by road. See p.190

* **Fríkes** The most pleasant place to stay outside of the capital, with a decent selection of tavernas and some nearby coves for swimming. See p.190

* **School of Homer** An atmospheric, and perhaps genuine, Homeric site, just outside the appealing village of Stavrós. See p.190

△ Vathý town harbour

Itháki

O dysseus's legendary homeland, **Itháki (Ithaca)**, is described thus in Homer: "There are no tracks, nor grasslands… it is a rocky, severe island, unsuited for horses but not so wretched, despite its small size. It is good for goats." In some ways not much has changed; the island's landscape, much of it almost vertical, precludes any significant development. Like its larger neighbour, Kefalloniá, Itháki is essentially a series of drowned mountains – three of them, joined by a tall, narrow isthmus, with human settlements on a number of plateaus around the peaks. In C.P. Cavafy's splendid poem *Ithaca*, the effort to reach the island symbolizes man's journey through life:

Always keep Ithaca in mind.
Arriving there is your destiny.
But do not hurry the journey in any way.
Better that it lasts for years,
so you are old when you reach the island,
enriched by all you have gained along the way,
not expecting Ithaca to make you wealthy.

Itháki is, however, well worth visiting for its own sake, not just on a classical whim, or under the influence of ancient myths, and once you've decided to go, you should certainly be able to get there a lot more quickly and easily than Odysseus. It is the **least spoilt** of all the major Ionian islands, but precisely because of that it is also the most difficult for visitors to get settled into during the busy summer months. Accommodation is scarce (there are only two small hotels on the entire island outside Vathý) and much of it is pre-booked by overseas travel operators, which only increases competition for the remaining beds. There is no official campsite, but, as usual, the discreet pitching of tents is ignored in select spots.

The Homer/Odysseus industry has led to an orgy of theming, but otherwise there are few signs of the commercialism that has blighted other islands. There are no burger joints on Itháki, no pubs or video bars named after British sitcoms, yet it is very Anglophone – much more so than Lefkádha, for example – and it is also welcoming to foreigners. The preponderance of English speakers is due to the statistic that around eighty percent of Ithacans have lived at some time in the diaspora, mostly in Australia and the US – Vathý may be the only place in Greece with a hairdresser's named after the Magellan Straits. Many have returned to take up full-time residence, while others only spend the summers in the land of their fathers.

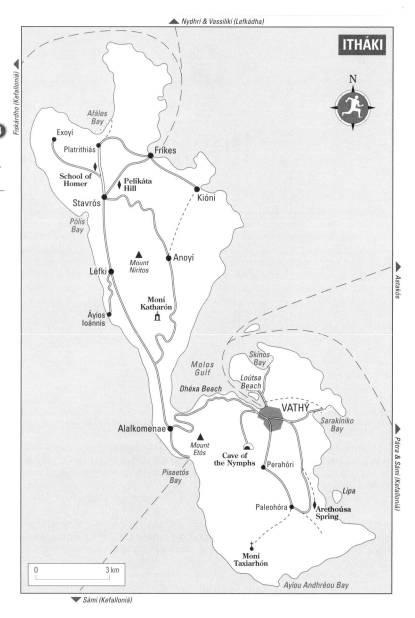

The capital, **Vathý**, is separated from the three outlying villages, **Stavrós**, **Fríkes** and **Kióni**, by a journey of over 20km along the one main road, making getting around surprisingly difficult for such a small island. Ease of movement is not helped by the island's almost non-existent bus service.

Ithaki's **beaches** are almost entirely pebble, with some sand deposits and sandy seabeds. The best are in the south, around Vathý, although there are some decent stretches between Fríkes and Kióni, and others are accessible by boat.

Some history

Itháki is known to have been inhabited since at least 3000 BC from Neolithic finds in the north of the island. One local history suggests more than half a dozen possible origins for the island's **name**; from the ancient mythical figure Ithacus, son of the sea god Poseidon, through a variety of possible Phoenician, Turkish and Venetian roots, although the last two seem fanciful given the clear references in Homer. The first settlers lived in the north, but by 1500 BC the south was also inhabited. During the Mycenaean period, Itháki became the seat of power for the Kefallonian state, which extended over the other Ionian islands and parts of the Akarnanian mainland as well. The peak of this period, prior to 1000 BC, probably coincides with the composition of the much-disputed **Odyssey** (see box on p.187); archeological finds from this period, which have been used to support a reading of the epic as a literal description of historical events, can be seen in Vathý's archeological museum.

In 1000 BC Itháki fell under Dorian rule and slipped from its position of power. Under Corinth (800–180 BC) it became a political backwater, and was similarly undisturbed when power transferred to Rome. During the Byzantine era (395–1185 AD), Itháki was annexed to Kefaloniá, and from then on shared much of its larger neighbour's history. However, the smaller, unprotected island fell prey to repeated attacks by pirates and Turkish invaders, and in the 1470s was sacked by Turkish forces. Most survivors abandoned the island, and the new Venetian rulers were forced to offer land and tax exemptions to lure settlers back. By the 1570s, the island had a new, fortified coastal capital, **Vathý**, set on a generous natural harbour from which it derives its name (meaning "deep" in Greek). Under Venetian rule, the population on the island rose from only sixty families in the 1560s to an estimated 12,000 people in the 1790s.

Ithacans were prominent among the activists who, led by the Friendly Society, fomented the War of Independence against the Turkish rulers on mainland Greece in 1821. In the early part of the nineteenth century, growing emigration saw Ithacans travelling around the world and gaining a widespread reputation for their **seafaring** skills. This in turn transformed Itháki into a wealthy and powerful island. As well as building the Neoclassical mansions that can be seen in Vathý today, Itháki's middle class financed a strong and vibrant social and cultural infrastructure. However, maritime success abroad ultimately led to further emigration, initiating an economic decline that only began to bottom out in recent decades. During World War II, Itháki was overrun by Axis forces, first the Italians (1941–43), and then the Germans (1943–44). Like neighbouring Kefaloniá, Lefkádha and Zákynthos, the island was devastated by the earthquakes of 1953 (see box on p.203).

Arrival and getting around

There isn't a flat piece of ground on Itháki that's long or straight enough to land anything other than a helicopter, so everyone visiting the island arrives by sea. Package tourists will frequently find themselves **flying into Kefaloniá**, whereupon, depending on ferry timetables, they are bused to either Sámi on the east coast or Fiskárdho in the north, for ferries to **Pisaetós** and **Fríkes** respectively; the latter route is far more time consuming but also more visually stunning – sit on the left side of the coach to Fiskárdho for the best views. Sámi also has less frequent sailings, to Itháki's capital, **Vathý**, a sensible place to stop and get your bearings on arrival. This is also the arrival point from Pátra and Astakós (see box above) on the mainland, while ferries from Lefkádha dock at Fríkes.

Only one **bus** runs daily between Vathý, Stavrós, Fríkes and Kióni, timed to take schoolkids to the capital from the north at 7am, returning around 2pm. Out of term time, including high season, it is at the whim of the driver whether it runs at all. A **taxi** from Vathý to Fríkes costs around €20, while to Pisaetós the standard fare is an outrageous €10. Moped or bike **rental** can be arranged in all the major settlements and car rental through the larger agencies, although given the size of the island this is of questionable value: there are relatively few navigable roads – to Perahóra and Pisaetós in the south and Anoyí and Exoyí in the north – and it would probably be cheaper to go by taxi. In any case, apart from the journey between Vathý and Stavrós, most points on the island are within reasonable walking distance of each other. Another option is to bring a rented vehicle from Kefaloniá on the cheap Sámi–Pisaetós ferry and visit Itháki as a one-day or overnight trip.

For further information, check W**www.ithacagreece.com**, one of the best of all Greek island sites, with unusual features like a visitors' photo album and an agony aunt column, as well as comprehensive practical help.

Vathý

Itháki's capital has the most idyllic setting of any port in the archipelago. Ships approaching **VATHÝ** have to turn into a large outer bay, and again into a smaller one, then pass between headlands into an interior bay, where the town sits at the crux. Vathý is entirely hidden from the open sea, in such convoluted folds of terrain that its visitors sometimes fail to realize that the mountains in the distance are in fact the northern half of the island. It was for this reason that islanders chose the bay as the site of their first major seaport in the sixteenth century, when the threat of piracy had been largely eliminated with the help of the Venetians.

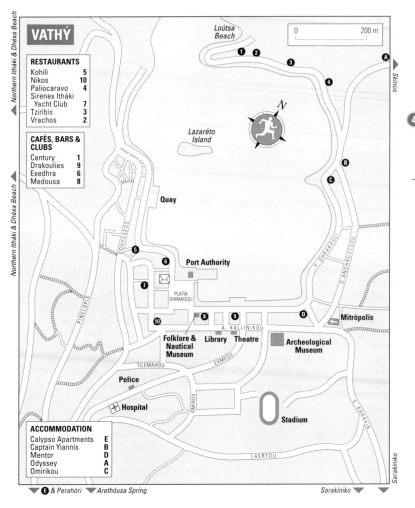

VATHÝ

RESTAURANTS

Kohili	5
Nikos	10
Paliocaravo	4
Sirenes Itháki Yacht Club	7
Tziribis	3
Vrachos	2

CAFÉS, BARS & CLUBS

Century	1
Drakoulies	9
Exedhra	6
Medousa	8

ACCOMMODATION

Calypso Apartments	E
Captain Yiannís	B
Mentor	D
Odyssey	A
Omirikou	C

Loútsa Beach

0   200 m

Lazaréto Island

Quay

Port Authority

PLATÍA DHRAKOÚLI

Folklore & Nautical Museum

Library   Theatre

A. KALLINIKOÚ

Mitrópolis

Archeological Museum

Police

Hospital

Stadium

LAERTOU

& Perahóri   Arethóusa Spring

Sarakíniko

ODYSSEOS

PINELOPIS

Y. DHRAKOÚLI

O. ANDHROUTSOU

TILEMAHOÚ

EVMEOU

OMIROV

E. KARAVIA

Skínos

Sarakíniko

Northern Itháki & Dhéxa Beach

Accommodation

Vathý has four **hotels**, all round the bay towards Loútsa, and all but one fairly expensive. The town's newest and poshest place to stay is the attractively designed ⚲ *Omirikon* (☏ 26740/33 598, Ⓦ www.omirikonhotel.com; ⑥), with large, tastefully furnished rooms, located above the seafront road. Slightly further from town, just off the seafront, is the smart *Captain Yiannis* hotel (☏ 26 740/33 419, Ⓕ 32 849; ③), with large, comfortable rooms, a tennis court and a pool, while the smaller *Odyssey* (☏ 26740/32 268, Ⓕ 32 668; ④), with nice views, is a short way up the new road to Skínos beach. Only one of Vathý's older town hotels has survived: topped by a big neon sign at the Loútsa end of the quay, the *Hotel Mentor* (☏ 26740/32 433, Ⓦ www.hotelmentor.gr; ⑥) has newly furnished en-suite rooms with balconies, some with full-on sea views, but is distinctly overpriced. And although it's open year round, it's a favorite with walking-tour companies, and can sometimes fill up, even out of season. The hotel has its own restaurant and bar, much favoured at night for its illuminated patio.

It is no longer so common to find townspeople meeting ferries to offer **rooms**. So the best area to case out is the quiet warren of back streets rising into the hills above the town, although they can be hard to find. Especially worth seeking out are the rooms owned by Vassilis Vlassopoulos (℡ 26740/32 119; ❸); surrounded by pleasant gardens, they're clearly visible from the bay on the Venetian steps leading from behind the ferry quay towards the church. Vathý's two main travel agencies, Polyctor Tours and Delas Tours (see p.186), offer a range of rooms, apartments and villas in town and across the island. More accommodation is becoming available up in the suburb/village of Perahóri above Vathý, but it's a long way to go to be disappointed. One snazzy place though, with fantastic views, is the *Calypso* apartments (℡ 26740/33 138; ❸), just below Perahóri.

The Town

Much of Vathý was destroyed by the 1953 earthquake, leaving only a few of its magnificent Neoclassical mansions and a number of churches, including the small **cathedral** (Mitrópolis) and the church of the **Taxiárhi**, which contains an icon of the Crucifixion believed to be the work of El Greco. However, the modest size of the town and the comparative wealth of its seafaring population seem to have worked in its favour after the earthquake: it was reconstructed far more sympathetically than either Zákynthos Town or Argostóli. And a preservation order passed in 1978, forbidding unsightly development, has protected the town from excessive commercialization. Its boutiques, souvenir shops, tavernas, *kafenía*, cafés and cocktail bars are all discreetly housed in vernacular architecture.

The focal point of the town is the large **Platía Dhrakoúli**, which occupies the southwest corner of the elongated seafront and has many of the town's facilities on or around it. The alleys behind are an atmospheric jigsaw of swish new shops, small shiny banks and old *kafenía* or packed *pandopolía*, but they soon give way to quiet residential streets. Sections of the seafront on either side of the square have been suitably gentrified, mostly with smart eating and drinking establishments or tourist shops, but long stretches further away are unutilized, a surprising waste of such scenically situated property. This does, however, add to the impression of Vathý being a functioning port, with fishing still a major source of income and only limited pretensions to being anything else.

Vathý Archeological Museum

While many of the best finds have been taken to Athens, or simply looted by unscrupulous north European archeologists, Vathý's **Archeological Museum** (Tues–Sun 8.30am–3pm; free), one block back from the *Hotel Mentor*, maintains a decent collection of exhibits related to the *Odyssey* myth. Mainly domestic wares, they include Mycenaean tripods that support the theory that Odysseus's home was indeed on Itháki. The museum is connected with the **Library** just down the road, which has an extensive collection of editions of Homer, including one in Chinese.

Folklore and Nautical Museum

Worth a brief visit is the newly opened **Folklore and Nautical Museum** (summer Tues–Sat 10am–2.30pm & 5–9pm; €1), in the corner of the inner bay, close to the square. The downstairs room displays a variety of traditional costumes and embroidery, musical instruments and workshop tools, while upstairs is given over to household items and a series of nautical etchings and relics, as well as furniture from the nearby Drakoulis mansion (home to the *Drakoulies* café).

Beaches

If you're staying in Vathý or, perhaps more importantly, visiting from Kefaloniá with only a few hours to spare, it's good to know that there are decent beaches within fifteen minutes' walk in either direction around the bay. The biggest, and busiest, is **Dhéxa** on the western side of the bay, over the hill along the main road rising above the ferry quay. This long pebble strip offers watersports and a snack bar, which does simple meals, and has been claimed as the site of Phorcys (it's actually signposted "Forkinos Bay"), the beach where the Phaeacians deposited the sleeping Odysseus.

The nearest and smallest beach is at **Loútsa**, on the opposite side of the bay to the ferry quay, a sandy cove with a snack bar in season. Loútsa is also the site of one of the few surviving Venetian fortifications, whose cannon emplacements are visible on a low bluff above the beach. A very narrow path leads on from Loútsa past some microscopic coves towards the headland.

The paved road that strikes off to the right and uphill before Loútsa leads over the headlands towards the superior deserted pebble beach in **Skínos Bay**. An even longer track, leaving the centre of town, trails over the hills to **Sarakíniko bay**, which is a good hour's hike but, like Skínos, worth the effort for the swimming. The one drawback to this part of the coastline, though, is the noisy industrial plant overlooking Sarakíniko, which fills the area with an insistent drone that can be heard as far as the Arethoúsa Spring.

Eating and drinking

Vathý's nightlife unfolds around its tightly packed seafront and the few short streets behind it. There is little to differentiate between the **cafés and bars** on the main drag facing the fishing quay – here it's perhaps best to follow the locals to the *Exedhra kafenío* in the middle of the strip. For a yet more traditional atmosphere, seek out the ancient but refurbished *kafenío* behind the seafront near the National Bank – though unaccompanied women may find the predominantly male atmosphere off-putting. An excellent alternative is the magnificent Neoclassical mansion on the seafront that's recently been transformed into the *Drakoulies* café. The grounds, with a curious seawater pond connected to the bay by a tunnel under the road, are spread with tables during the summer, and the large bar inside, though it looks like some sort of swank gentlemen's club, is open to all. On the way you'll pass the *Medousa*, a hip music, booze and snacks hangout that's popular with townies and visitors alike. For louder music and dancing, head for *Century*, a large outdoor club towards Loútsa.

Restaurants

When it comes to dining options, you're surprisingly spoilt for choice in such a small town. Many visitors head off around the bay, where a trio of **tavernas** punctuate the road towards Loútses, and there are a number of good places in town too.

To Kohili The best of the half-dozen places between the quay and the square, offering a range of specialities like lamb *kléftiko* and other meats in original sauces, as well as good local white wine, all at decent prices.

O Nikos In the side street south of the square. An excellent point-at-what-you-want-to-eat *estiatório*; its few tables fill early, though it's not as cheap as it looks.

Paliocaravo 400m before Loútses beach. Also known as *Gregory's* after the friendly owner; very popular for its home-cooked lamb and fish plus excellent *mezédhes*, also the scene

of occasional impromptu sing-alongs. Good local rosé wine.

Sirenes Itháki Yacht Club One block behind the square. Nautical-theme restaurant serving specials like Smyrna meatballs with a red sauce, fish in rosemary and raisins, shrimps in lemon and mustard sauce. Not as expensive as you'd expect.

Tziribis 250m before Loútses beach. Standard range of grilled and oven dishes and ample fresh salads are available in an attractive location.

O Vrachos Just under 200m before Loútses beach. Specializes in fish and grills. The views back across to Vathý are excellent, but bills reflect the setting.

Listings

Banks and exchange The National Bank of Greece is visible from the junction of the two harbourside roads; the Commercial Bank and the Agricultural Bank are just behind it (all Mon–Thurs 8am–2pm; Fri 8am–1.30pm); all have cash dispensers. Hotels and travel agencies will change currency and travellers' cheques, but shop around for the best deal.

Car rental As well as the travel agents listed below, AGS on the seafront is a reliable outlet (☏ 26740/32 702).

Doctor There's a 24-hr clinic in the hospital on Evmeïou, 350m back from the seafront (☏ 26740/32 222); the pharmacy on the quay by the bus stop is also able to give advice on minor ailments.

Internet The *Net* café is tucked in the corner of the quay, near the square (€4/hr).

Police station On Evmeïou, just before the hospital (☏ 26740/322 05).

Port Authority On the seafront corner of the square (☏ 26740/329 09).

Post office On the square (Mon–Fri 8am–2pm).

Shopping Vathý has many well-stocked minimarkets, a bakery, fish and meat stores, as well as other shops, including a couple of excellent local art galleries and craft outlets, one quaintly named *Fish and Ships*.

Travel agencies There is no tourist information office in Vathý or elsewhere on Itháki, but commercial travel agencies and hotels are usually happy to provide information. Polyctor Tours in the town centre (☏ 26740/331 20, ✉ polyctor@ithakiholidays .gr) has a range of rooms and apartments and is the agent for most ferries as well as for Olympic Airways, useful if returning to Athens via Kefalloniá. Polyctor's smaller neighbour, Delas Tours (☏ 26740/32 104, ✉ delas@otenet.gr), offers accommodation as well as other travel services.

Odysseus sites

The **Odysseus sites** at this end of the island – the Arethoúsa Spring, the Cave of the Nymphs and Alalkomenae, suggested location of Odysseus's castle – are all within reach of Vathý, the first two on foot, the third by bus or taxi. Trips to either (but not both) the Cave of the Nymphs and Arethoúsa Spring can be fitted into a day-trip from Kefalloniá; to Alalkomenae only if you take a cab (a return fare should be no more than €15, with waiting time).

The Arethoúsa Spring

The walk to the **Arethoúsa Spring** – allegedly the place where Eumaeus, Odysseus's faithful swineherd, brought his pigs to drink – is a three-hour trip there and back, setting off along a signposted track out of Vathý next to the OTE. The isolation and the sea views along the way are magnificent, but the walk crosses some slippery inclines and might best be avoided if you're nervous of heights. It's also shadeless, particularly where it turns off the rough track onto a narrow path, so take a hat and plenty of liquids in summer. When the weather's fine it's worth taking a picnic, but the route shouldn't be attempted in poor weather and isn't recommended for lone walkers.

On the way out of Vathý, near the top of the lane leading to the spring path, a signpost points up to what is said to have been the **Cave of Eumaeus** – if you're tempted, the tortuous path zigzags up to just below the bluff high above, and the cave is a large single hollow with a tree growing up through a hole in the roof.

Meanwhile, the route to the spring continues along the track for a few hundred metres, and then branches off on to a narrow footpath through the maquis that covers the sloping cliffs. Parts of the final downhill track involve scrambling across rock fields – follow the splashes of green paint and take care. The lie of the land around the spring, which is sited at the head of a small but vertiginous ravine below a crag known as Kórax (the raven), seem to fit with Homer's description of the meeting between Odysseus and Eumaeus, to the delight of literalists. However, the spring itself is distinctly underwhelming – in summer it's just a dribble of water sounding like a kitchen leak in a shallow cave.

Homer, the Odyssey and Itháki

Anyone travelling in the Ionian will soon become either confused or cynical about the sheer number of places – from Paleokastrítsa in northern Corfu to Alalkomenae on Itháki – competing to be accepted as the actual sites of events in the *Odyssey*. Classical authorities still take a dim view of arguments for placing so much of Homer's epic in Greece, preferring the traditional reading, which identifies sites as far afield as Gozo, the Messina straits between Italy and Sicily, Italy's Aeolian islands and Tunisia. Indeed, some interpretations of the story have taken it entirely outside the Mediterranean basin, to such improbable locales as Iceland. The safest interpretation is that Homer – whose single authorship is itself questioned by theories that hold the *Odyssey* to be a group effort put together over the centuries – was mixing myth and legend with actual historical and geographical detail. The most probable answer to the authorship debate is that Homer was the first to commit the formulaic oral tradition to writing, embellishing it and imbuing it with his own muse in the process.

Explorer Tim Severin, however, in his book *The Ulysses Voyage: Sea Search for the Odyssey*, comes down in favour of siting Odysseus' adventures around Itháki, the island the epic names as his home – even if German archeologist Wilhelm Dörpfeld (see p.149) tried unsuccessfully to cart it off to Lefkádha. In 1985, following earlier expeditions to reconstruct Jason's search for the Golden Fleece, Severin and a group of fellow explorers set off in a full-scale model of a Bronze Age galley to retrace Odysseus's journey home from Troy. Using estimated times of journeys described in the *Odyssey*, and matching descriptions of landscape and astronavigational details, Severin pieced together Odysseus's adventures around Itháki and neighbouring islands.

Among Severin's key propositions is that King Alcinous' castle was probably sited at Paleokastrítsa on Corfu, and that Odysseus was washed ashore at Érmones. Severin cites Paxí, in particular Harámi beach in Lákka bay, as the likely position of Circe's home of Aeaea, which concurs with the local nickname of Circe's Grove for a glade at nearby Ipapánti. He speculates that Scylla and Charybdis may have been natural features in the landscape at the northern tip of Lefkádha, and further suggests Dhéxa bay on Itháki as the likely site of the Cave of the Nymphs, Pelikáta as Odysseus's castle and Arethoúsa as the site of the spring where Eumaeus watered his swine. Ultimately, however, even Severin concedes to the many ambiguities surrounding the text, and Homer's tale resists the attempt to moor it definitively to dry land.

It's also worth knowing that the area is a dead end – the only way out is back the way you came. A small pebble beach a short way down from the spring, reached by a steep, narrow path, is good for a swim if time allows.

Even if you feel a little uneasy about the gradients involved in reaching the spring, it's still worth summoning up the courage to continue along the main track that runs above it, a journey up through woodlands that affords some excellent sea views. The track loops round and heads back into the village of **Perahóri** above Vathý, which has views as far as Lefkádha to the north and is actually the island's second largest settlement. There are several places to stop for a bite here, including the *Ovenos* and *Kaliora* grills, both of which have stunning views. On the way, you'll pass **Paleóhora**, the ruined medieval capital abandoned centuries ago, but with vestiges of houses fortified against pirate attacks and some churches still retaining details of Byzantine frescoes of the saints. Around 3km southwest of Paleóhora, through densely forested highlands, is the site of the sixteenth-century **Moní Taxiarhón**. The monastery was destroyed in the 1953 earthquakes, but its small church has since been rebuilt.

The Cave of the Nymphs

The **Cave of the Nymphs** (known locally as *Marmarospíli*) is about 2.5km up a rough track signposted on the brow of the hill above Dhéxa beach. The cave is atmospheric but nothing like as impressive as the caverns of neighbouring Kefalloniá, and these days is illuminated with coloured lights. The claim that this is the *Odyssey*'s Grotto of the Nymphs, where the returning Odysseus concealed the gifts given to him by King Alcinous, is enhanced by the proximity of Dhéxa beach (see box overleaf), although there is some evidence suggesting that a cave above the beach, which was unwittingly demolished during quarrying many years ago, was the "true" Cave of the Nymphs.

Alalkomenae and Pisaetós

Alalkomenae, Schliemann's much-vaunted "Castle of Odysseus", is signposted on the Vathý–Pisaetós road, on the saddle between Dhéxa bay and Pisaetós, with views over both sides of the island. The actual site, however, some 300m uphill, is little more than foundations spread about in the maquis. Schliemann's excavations unearthed a Mycenaean burial chamber and domestic items such as vases, figurines and utensils (to be seen in the archeological museum), but sections of Cyclopean wall and the remains of what has been suggested as a temple to Apollo date from three centuries after Homer. In fact, the most likely contender for the site of Odysseus's castle is above the village of Stavrós in the north, and intriguingly close to the site of the ruined ancient capital of Pólis.

The road continues to the harbour of **Pisaetós**, about 2km below, with a large pebble beach that's good for swimming, though popular with local rod-and-line fishermen. Other than that it's pretty much a non-event, with just a canteen on the quay to serve the ferries from Sámi on Kefalloniá and Astakós on the mainland. Unfortunately, there is no local bus connection with Vathý.

Northern Itháki

The road to the north of the island rides high on the side of **Mount Níritos**, affording breathtaking views of neighbouring Kefalloniá. At the hamlets of Agrós and Áyios Ioánnis, new roads are continually being upgraded to allow access to small remote beaches along this hitherto wild stretch of coastline. The only facilities along this road are a couple of shops in **Léfki**, halfway to Stavrós, which was a notable centre of Resistance organization in the Ionians during World War II. If you fancy a scenic base for a longer stay, you can't do better than contact Ilias Vassilopoulos, whose house, with just two double rooms, commands views across to Kefaloniá (℡26740/31 395; ❺).

Stavrós and around

STAVRÓS is the second largest town on the island, counting Perahóri as part of Vathý, and the administrative centre of the north, although its inland position and distance from any decent beaches – the nearest, a steep 2km below the town, shares Pólis bay with a small fishing harbour – make it a less than ideal place to stay. It's a pleasant enough town nonetheless, with *kafenía* and tavernas edging an elongated *platía* that doubles as the main thoroughfare. The square is crowned by a modern but imposing yellow-and-white church and hosts a rather fierce statue of Odysseus – the only such public monument dedicated to him in the islands. The small **museum** (Tues–Sun 8.30am–3pm; free), displaying local archeological finds, is situated just above the main road to Platrithiás about 500m from the centre. Stavrós's Homeric site is on the side of **Pelikáta Hill**, where remains of roads, walls and other structures have been suggested as the possible site of Odysseus's castle. Items from the site, including part of an ancient mask engraved *EFHIN ODHYSSEI* ("Dedicated to Odysseus"), can be seen at the museum.

Stavrós is probably only useful as a base if both Fríkes and Kióni are full up, and is an obvious stopping-off point for exploring the northern hamlets and the road up to the medieval village of Anoyí on Mount Níritos. Both the Polyctor and Delas agencies (see p.186) handle **accommodation** in Stavrós, and a number of the town's traditional tavernas, including the *Petra* (℡26740/31 596; ❸), offer rooms. The *Tritsarolis* studios (℡26740/31 393; ❸) and *Porto Thiaki* (℡26740/31 245 or 31 363, ✉asobola@otenet.gr; ❷), above the pizzeria, are also options. Of the **tavernas**, *Fatouros* is the oldest and best for grills and *kondosoúvli*, while the friendly *Petra* and *Polyphemus*, with its garden and upstairs bar, are also worth trying. For a drink, the old-style *To Kendro kafenío*, *Sori's Ways* café and the *Margarita zaharoplastío*, which specializes in the local sweet *rovaní*, provide pleasant surroundings. There is an ATM by the pizzeria.

Anoyí

A mountainous and highly scenic road leads some 5km southeast from Stavrós to **ANOYÍ**, whose apt name roughly translates as "upper land". It was once the second most important settlement on the island, but is almost deserted today. The centre of the village is dominated by a free-standing Venetian campanile, built to serve the (usually locked) church of the **Panayía**; enquire at the one *kafenío* about access to the church and its frescoes and striking reredos, originally painted in Byzantine times but mostly replaced after earthquake damage over the intervening centuries. The village only comes alive when it hosts a major Panayía festival on August 14, the eve of the Virgin Mary's big day. On the outskirts of the village are the foundations of a ruined **medieval prison**, and in the surrounding countryside, some extremely strange **rock formations**, the biggest being the eight-metre-high Arakles (Heracles) rock, just east of the village.

The **monastery of Katharón**, 3km further south along the road, has stunning views down over Vathý and the south of the island. The monastery houses an icon of the Panayía discovered by peasants who were clearing scrubland in the area. Local mythology claims that a temple to Artemis stood on the site, and also suggests a link to the medieval Cathar sect. Byron is said to have stayed at the monastery in 1823, during his final voyage to Messolóngi. Every year the monastery celebrates its own festival on September 8, when the icon is displayed and everyone sings and dances.

North of Stavrós

Two roads leave Stavrós heading north towards Fríkes: one, to the right, heads 2km directly down to Fríkes, while the main road, to the left, loops round via Platrithiás. Just over halfway along this route, a road branches left to **Exoyí**, which has a basic *kafenío* and incredible views from the bell-tower of its Ayía Marína church. A short way from the main road on the way to Exóyi, a motorable track to the right leads 1km to the unfenced **School of Homer**, where excavations continue apace. Apart from the usual foundations, a well and a fine set of stone steps have already been unearthed. Mycenaean graves and buildings establish the great antiquity of the site. It is also a fine spot to sit and survey **Afáles bay**. The bay itself, the largest on the entire island, with an unspoilt and little-visited pebble beach, is reachable down a partly paved road from the edge of Platrithiás, where the *Yefiri* taverna is a great place for tasty *mezédhes* or a full meal. Among a group of tiny settlements above Platrithiás are the abandoned hamlet of Kálamos, 3km north, and Koliéri just a kilometre away, with its curious folklore monument – a towering column of millstones, next to a stone mill with wheels and grinding channel intact. The landscape around here, thickly forested in parts and dotted with vineyards, makes excellent walking terrain.

Fríkes

Viewed from the daily ferries that arrive from Lefkádha or Kefanloniá, or passing through by vehicle, **FRÍKES** doesn't appear to have much going for it. You could sprint around its tiny harbourfront in under a minute, and find yourself in open country towards Stavrós in five. Wedged in a valley between two steep hills, Fríkes was only settled in the sixteenth century when the threat from pirate raids had diminished. Waves of emigration in the nineteenth century have further capped its size – as few as 200 people are estimated to live here today – but its maritime prowess and proximity to other islands have made it a natural trading post and year-round port. Consequently, it stays open for tourism far later in the season than its neighbour Kióni, and at present has a better range of tavernas. There are no beaches in the village, but plenty of good, if small, pebble strands a short walk away towards Kióni. When the ferries and their cargoes have departed, Fríkes falls quiet, and this is its real charm: a downbeat but cool place to lie low from the tourist rat race.

Fríkes' one **hotel**, the upmarket *Nostos* (T 26740/31 644, W www.hotelnostos-ithaki.gr; ❺), is a small but smart family run affair, with en-suite rooms, a bar, restaurant, garden and pool; it's about 150m from the quay, along the more easterly turning of the two roads leaving town for Stavros. Just before it, the *Aristotelis Apartments* (T & F 26740/31 079; ❹) has TV in its comfortable rooms, some with sea views, and lower rates. The partly British-run seafront Kiki minimarket (T & F 26740/31 762; from ❷) can help find **rooms**, provide general info and has Internet access (€3/hr). The Gods souvenir shop next door (T 26740/31 021; from ❷) also has contacts for basic rooms and rents out bikes and boats. None of the places listed above is likely to have space on spec during the early to mid-August peak. Arriving without a reservation at that time means you'll probably have to sleep in one of the nearby coves. A more secluded and acceptable freelance **camping** spot is among the olive groves at a lovely little pebble beach fifteen minutes' walk along a footpath that starts just beyond the last seafront houses on the west side of Fríkes.

For such a small place, Fríkes has a wealth of good seafront **tavernas**. The *Rementzo* offers excellent grills, seafood delights such as prawn *saganáki*, and a range of *mezédhes*, while the *Ulysses* specializes mostly in succulent meat dishes, fish and live lobster. *Symposeum* serves a variety of grill and oven dishes, seafood and some unusual vegetarian options, such as baked beetroots and potatoes. The quartet is completed by the *Penelope*, marginally the most upmarket of the cluster, with a varied menu covering north European and Greek. The *Café Bemenis* in the corner of the quay is a quiet spot most of the day but jerks into action after midnight as the prime nightspot venue in northern Itháki, and often develops into quite a raucous affair. It now has a new rival in the shape of the *Porto Fríkes kafenío*, which has a pool table.

Kióni

KIÓNI sits at a dead end in the road, 5km southeast of Fríkes (although a rough footpath ascends towards Anoyí from the back of the village). It too was only established in the sixteenth century, when settlers from Anoyí felt it was safe to move down from the hills. On the same geological base as the northern tip of Kefalloniá, it avoided the very worst of the 1953 earthquakes, and so retains some fine examples of pre-twentieth-century architecture. It's an extremely pretty village, wrapped around a tiny harbour, comparable in prospect and features to Longós on Paxí and Fiskárdho on Kefalloniá. Tourism here is dominated by British blue-chip travel companies, and by flotilla and bareboat sailors, so it can feel rather claustrophobic at times.

△ Angel sculpture at Kióni

Kióni's bay has a **beach** of sorts, 1km along its south side, a small sand-and-pebble strand below a summer-only snack bar. Better pebble beaches can be found within walking distance northwards towards Fríkes, where bizarre rock formations along the roadside are stacked upright in places like matchsticks. You can also rent a boat from the Moraitis boat rental agency (from around €35 per day – see below) to explore quiet nearby bays and coves, and larger *kaïki* trips to further beaches are occasionally organized.

There are two major dates in Kióni's summer calendar: June 24 when the church of **Áyios Ioánnis** celebrates its saint's day, and anyone called Yiannis has his name day; and July 20, the festival of Áyios Ilías, when the village's 200 or so inhabitants set off in boats to attend a service at a small chapel that sits on Kióni bay's southern promontory.

While the best **accommodation** has been snaffled by the Brits, some local businesses have rooms and apartments to let, among them *Maroudas Apartments* (☎26740/31 691, ℗31 753; ❹), near the harbour, and the friendly *Captain's Apartments* (☎26740/31 481, ⓦwww.captains-apartments.gr; ❹), set back from it. A quieter option, just a short walk uphill on the main road in the tiny hamlet of Ráhi, are the rooms and studios run by ⚞ Captain Theofilos Karatzis and his family (☎ & ℗26740/31 679; ❸), with panoramic views over the area.

For all its chic tone, Kióni's **restaurants** do not compare favourably with Fríkes. There are four waterfront tavernas: *Oasis*, which has the best selection and prices, the traditional *Avra*, which concentrates on fish, *Galatis*, which does a range of starters to complement its seafood, and the more expensive *Calypso*, where the menu offers gourmet dishes such as artichoke polita and roquefort pie. There is also a pizzeria and a couple of **bars** that do snacks – *Spavento*, just behind the front, plays the most interesting sounds, especially when pop maestro Dimitris (formerly of the Greek–Australian band, Hard Candy) is behind the bar. Apart from that, **village facilities** stretch to two well-stocked shops, a post office and a couple of cafés, of which *Lygia* offers decent breakfasts.

Travel details

Buses

Vathý to: Kióni via Stavrós and Fríkes (1 daily; 45min).

Ferries

The frequencies of the ferry services given below apply in season, from May to September; out of season, there is usually only one daily service on each route. All the ferries carry vehicles.

Fríkes to: Fiskárdho, Kefalloniá (1 daily; 1hr); Nydhrí, Lefkádha (1 daily; 1hr 30min).

Pisaetós to: Sámi, Kefalloniá (3 daily; 45min); Astakós (1 daily; 2hr 30min).

Vathý to: Sámi, Kefalloniá (2 daily; 1hr); Pátra (2 daily; 3hr 30min).

⑤

Kefalloniá

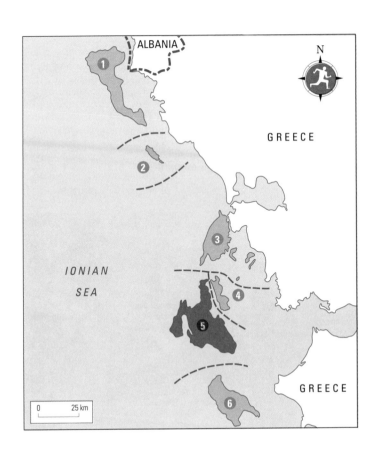

CHAPTER 5 **Highlights**

✳ **Archeological Museum, Argostóli** A collection of antiquities rivalling Corfu's as the best in the archipelago. See p.203

✳ **Áyios Yióryios fortress** A mighty medieval castle commanding spectacular views. See p.208

✳ **Mount Énos** Dominating the south of the island, this huge hogs' back is a national park with wild scenery and its own species of fir tree. See p.208

✳ **Robola winery** A beautiful place in which to sample Kefalloniá's respected local wines. See p.209

✳ **Petaní beach** Simply one of the top Ionian beaches, with rock overhangs for shade. See p.212

✳ **Melissáni and Dhrogaráti caves** These cave systems display a fascinating variety of geological features. See p.218

✳ **Ássos** The most picturesque west-coast resort sports a tiny harbour at the neck of a promontory, capped by a Venetian castle. See p.220

✳ **Fiskárdho** Kefalloniá's most chic resort attracts yachties by the flotilla and its restaurants and cafés exude a refined atmosphere. See p.222

△ Lithóstratou street, Argostóli

5

Kefalloniá

Rugged, mountainous and blessed with some of the most dramatic scenery in the region, **Kefalloniá** is the largest Ionian island, but has resisted the sort of development that has overtaken Corfu and some of its neighbours. The island is variously known as Kefalloniá, **Kefal-línia** and **Cephalonia** – the first is the phonetic transliteration of the present Greek name, the second the modern version of its ancient moniker (which is also used for its airport) and the third the anglicized version. Like its tiny neighbour, Itháki, it's little more than a series of mountain tops piercing the waves – **Mount Énos**, which looms over the south of the island, is one of the highest in western Greece – with towns and villages sheltering in the valleys and on the lower slopes. Despite its area, there are only three towns of any size: the handsome and spacious capital, **Argostóli**; the main ferry port, **Sámi**, a quiet and under-used base on the eastern coast; and **Lixoúri**, which because of the convoluted landscape is 35km away from the capital by road yet barely thirty minutes by ferry.

Until well into the 1980s, the islanders resisted mass tourism and the only foreign visitors were independent travellers who were not too fussed about levels of comfort. Indeed, Kefallonians had quite a reputation amongst other Greeks as being rather eccentric and xenophobic, and it is only recently that Greeks without family connections here have been attracted in any numbers too. This has gone hand in hand with the creation and constant upgrading of the **seaside resorts**, which has continued apace since the locals decided that the money-making potential was too great to be ignored. That is not to say that the attitude is predominantly mercenary; most Kefallonians come across as genuinely welcoming, and the island can boast a noticeable number of eccentric characters. Its other great virtue is its size, so it can comfortably absorb the larger numbers now arriving without seeming overcrowded or unduly compromised.

Kefalloniá's seaside resorts are all based around small villages and ports. The **beaches** in the south tend to be sandy, those in the north, pebbly, including the exquisite white crescent of **Mýrtos**, one of the most famous and most photo-graphed beaches in the entire Ionian. Below the thumbnail of limestone around the popular port and resort of **Fiskárdho**, much of the northern coastline is sheer cliff, with the most terrifying mountain roads in the archipelago and some of the most breathtaking views. Kefalloniá also conceals two unmissable geological quirks, the **Dhrogaráti caves** and the **Melissáni underground lake**, as well as some minor archeological sites and locations said to be associated with the Odysseus myth.

The island sits close to the fault line that has given this area of the Ionians a history of cataclysmic **earthquakes**. The most violent ever recorded, in 1953,

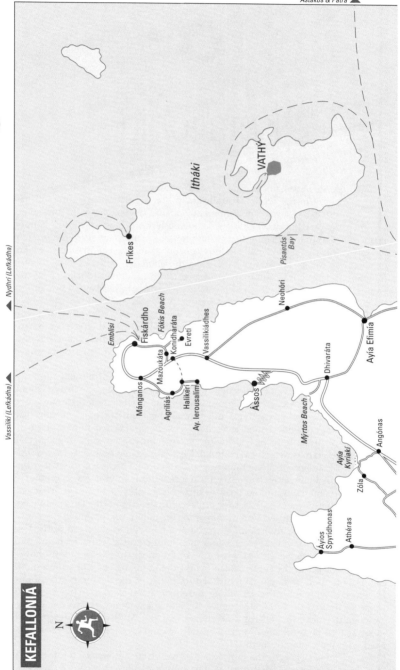

KEFALLONIÁ

Astakós & Pátra ▲

Nydhrí (Lefkádha) ▲

Vassilikí (Lefkádha) ▲

Emblísi

Fiskárdho

Fókis Beach

Mázoukáta

Konidharáta

Eyretí

Vassilikiádhes

Mánganos

Agriliás

Halikéri

Ay. Ierousalím

Ássos

Myrtos Beach

Dhivaráta

Ayía Efímia

Neohóri

Frikes

Itháki

VATHÝ

Pisaetós Bay

Angónas

Ayía Kyriakí

Zóla

Áyios Spyridhonas

Athéras

N

▲ *Kyllini*

Skála

Póros

Tzanáta

Ratzakli

Kaminia

Pá333... Pástra

Káto
Kateliós

Markópoulo

Andisamis

SÁMI

*Ayía
Paraskeri*

Melissáni Cave
Karavómylos

Dhrogaráti Cave

▲
*Mount
Énos
(1628m)*

**Monastery
of Sissiá**

Áyios
Eléfthérios

Áyios
Yerásimos

**Robola
Winery**

Mousáta-
Poriaráta

Vlaháta

Loúrdháta

*Trapezáki
Beach*

► *Áyios Nikólaos (Zákynthos)*

Valsamáta

Pessádha

Sparti... Spartiá

Koriána

**Áyios Yeóryios
Fortress**

Peratáta

Metaxáta

Keramiés

Lakíthra

Kourkomeláta

*Ávythos
Beach*

► *Kyllini*

Fársa

Dhavgáta

▲
*Mount
Evmorfía*

ARGOSTÓLI

*Koútavos
Lagoon*

*Dhrépano
Causeway*

Lássi

*Makrýs
Yialós*

*Platýs
Yialós*

Katavóthres

Lixoúri

*Lépedha
Beach*

*Xi
Beach*

*Mégas Lákkos
Beach*

Mantzavináta

**LIKHOÚRION
PENINSULA**

**Monastery
of Kipouréon**

Áyios Nikólaos

Kounópetra

*Cape
Akrotíri*

Petaní Beach

0 ___ 5 km

The busiest mainland port after Pireás, **PÁTRA** (Patras) is a major stopping-off point for travellers moving between the islands and mainland. There are ferries to Kefalloniá and Itháki and a direct bus service via Kyllíni to Zákynthos. It also has train and bus connections with Athens and services to the rest of the Peloponnese and some northern destinations – though, oddly, no civil airport. It is also a major terminal for ferries to Italy, many of which call at Igoumenítsa and Corfu.

Pátra itself is not particularly attractive and has little to detain the traveller, although if you find yourself in between connections you can easily while away a few hours. Patra's two main sights, visible from most parts of the city, are the Kástro and basilica of Ayíou Andhréou. Reached via some 190 steps from the end of Ayíou Nikoláou street, the **Kástro** ruins are set in a quiet park, commanding stunning views north to Messolóngi, and are sometimes the site of outdoor concerts. The giant jelly-mould **basilica of Ayíou Andhréou**, at the far end of town, opened in 1979 and houses the relics of St Andrew, who is said to have been martyred on this spot. There are no beaches or major historical sites in the immediate vicinity, but Pátra is handy for ancient **Olympia**, two hours away by regular bus or train.

Buses (every 30min; 3hr) and **trains** (9 daily; 3–5hr 30min; OSE ☎2610/221 311) from Athens arrive within a few hundred metres of the ferries on Óthonos & Amalías, in an area that resembles a rail shunting yard. If you're passing through with time to spare, the train station has a handy **left luggage** office. For **tourist information**, the city has opened the helpful, large Info Center Patras in an old raisin-processing factory at Óthonos and Amalías 6 (daily 8am–10pm; ☎2610/461 740, ⓦwww.infocenterpatras.gr), with a good photographic gallery of the province's attractions. They also have a kiosk on Platía Tríon Symáhon (daily 9am–1pm & 5–8pm). The **tourist police** (daily 7am–11pm; ☎2610/452 512) is at the western end of Nórman near the new Italy ferry terminal, where the **EOT** office also is (Mon–Fri 7am–9pm; ☎2610/430 915). **Banks** with exchange facilities and ATMs abound, while the main **post office** is on the corner of Mézonos and Zaïmi. You can surf the **Internet** for about €3/hr at a number of places, including Netrino at Karaïskáki 133. There is also a small **British Consulate** (☎2610/277 079) at Bótsi 2, several hundred metres west of the train station.

Pátra is built on a grid system, much of it one-way. The long cross-streets are very busy, so it's best to try for accommodation off the main roads and away from the seafront. **Hotels** are often booked out, despite standards not being all that high for the rates charged, so expect to have to shop around. Handy mid-range places include the *Atlanta*, Zaïmi 10 (☎2610/220 098, ☎220 019; ❹), the *Mediterranee*, nearby at Ayíou Nikoláou 18 (☎2610/279 602 or 279 624, ✉mediterran@otenet.gr; ❺), and the *Adonis*, Kapsáli 8 (☎2610/224 213, ☎226 971; ❹). There is also a **youth hostel** at Iroón Polytekhníou 68 (☎2610/427 278; €9 per bed) but it's 1.5km from the centre.

Much of the town's **eating** is uninspired, like the cheap *souvláki* joints around Platía Tríon Symáhon, with better places well hidden or in the flashier suburbs. Try the seafront *Apanemo*, opposite the fishing harbour at Óthonos & Amalías 107, a seafood taverna also noted for its *galaktobóreko* dessert, or the *Avli tou Yennéou*, another good place for fish on Paraskhoú, not far from the youth hostel. The overpriced *Majestic* and cheaper self-service *Nikolaras*, both on Ayíou Nikoláou, are old-style *estiatória* with a good range of fare. While the seafront and central Platía Tríon Symáhon have cafés, bars and a few shops, most of Pátra's **nightlife** goes on some blocks back from the port, around the central Platía Yioryíou, youth-oriented Platía Ólgas and the pleasant Psilá Alónia park, some ten blocks from the sea. Yerokostópoulou, north of Yioryíou, also has a number of **music bars** and restaurants, while the most concentrated conglomeration of loud and trendy bars is to be found around the foot of the steps at the top of Ayíou Nikoláou. For a drink away from the obvious places, try the popular *Beer Society*, tucked away in an alley off Ríga Ferréou near Ermoú and Kolokotróni.

levelled its graceful capital, Argostóli, destroyed almost all of its outlying villages, and in some places killed up to eighty percent of the population (see box on p.203). Argostóli was rebuilt with overseas help, not quite to its former elegance, though it remains a pleasant town. Most of the interior villages were rebuilt, often beside earthquake ruins which can still be seen today. Many Kefallonians were forced or chose to live abroad after the earthquake, but a large number have returned, bringing languages and a sophistication absent in some other parts of the Ionians.

Kefalloniá's **bus** system is basic but functional, and with a little legwork it can be used to get you almost anywhere on the island. Key routes connect Argostóli with Sámi, Fiskárdho, **Skála**, a small development with a long sandy beach and pine woods, and **Póros**, a slightly shabby resort built around a fishing port. There's also a useful connection on from Sámi to the tiny resort of **Ayía Efimía**, which attracts many package travellers. The island has a plethora of **ferry** connections, principally from Fiskárdho to Lefkádha and Itháki, and from Sámi to Itháki and the mainland, as well as links to Zákynthos, plus Kyllíni and Pátra in the Peloponnese.

For further information, check ⓦ**www.kefaloniathewaytogo.com** (the site includes history, practical information and visitor feedback) and ⓦ**www .kefalonia-travel-guide.com**, a British-run site with practical information on renting and buying property plus interesting sections on history, wildlife, culture and religion.

Some history

Remains excavated around Kefalloniá, and now on display in Argostóli's Archeological Museum, have established that there were settlements on the island as long ago as 50,000 BC – before the modern Mediterranean began to take shape. Kefalloniá was once covered in its exclusively indigenous fir trees – **abies cephalonica**, named after the island – which formed a large part of its trade in ancient times: *cephalonica* wood has been discovered in the structure of the Minoan palace at Knossós on Crete. The island is believed to have acquired its **name** from legendary king Cephalus, whose escapades were recorded by Hesiod, Ovid, Apollodorus and others. Son of Hermes and Herse, he was known above all as a hunter – an activity keenly pursued by modern Kefallonians, to the chagrin of animal lovers and walkers harassed by hunting dogs.

By the seventh century BC, the island had split into four democratic cities; the most famous of them was Same (modern-day Sámi), named in Thucydides and Homer, who records that Odysseus sailed for the Trojan War with twelve ships from the city. During the Peloponnesian War (431–404 BC), Kefalloniá was overrun by Athens which, although an ally, distrusted the island and seized it to use as a base for attacks on Corinth to the east – to no avail, as the Ionian islands fell to Sparta at the end of the war. In the **Byzantine** period, Kefalloniá became the seat of the *theme*, or administrative district, of the islands. Out of the mainstream of Byzantine politics, however, it – like the rest of the Ionian islands – fell prone to attack by pirates and other opportunists. In 1082, the Ionians were attacked from Italy by the Normans, under Robert Guiscard. When his son failed to take Kefalloniá, Guiscard and his forces sailed from Corfu to back him, but within weeks of reaching the island the Norman leader had succumbed to plague. The port where he died, Fiskárdho, derives its name from his.

The island was handed over to Venice in 1204, and for some time was administered by the powerful Orsini dynasty of Rome, who imported their own aristocrats and introduced a feudal system. Over the following centuries, Kefalloniá ricocheted between the Turks, the Venetians, the French and the Russians, until in 1809 the **British** took over in a bloodless invasion, whereupon Kefalloniá promptly became focus for the widespread resentment of the British in the Ionians. In 1848, this erupted in open rebellion, with violent clashes in Argostóli, followed by heavy jail sentences for activists. Not until 1864 did Britain finally cede Kefalloniá and the other Ionian islands to Greece.

During World War II, Kefalloniá was taken over by the **Germans** in a particularly gruesome fashion. The island had been seized by the Italians, who controlled it briefly prior to the fall of Mussolini and Italy's capitulation in September 1943. At this moment of administrative confusion, with contradictory orders both to surrender and to repel the Germans, the Italians were left helpless and hopelessly outnumbered. Rather than herd them into POW camps, the Germans, according to Ionian historian Arthur Foss, "decided in cold blood to massacre their former allies". In villages on the slopes of Mount Énos, and out near the sea mills of Katovóthres at Argostóli, over 5000 Italian soldiers were shot and their bodies burnt. The massacre is a key event in Louis de Bernières' novel, *Captain Corelli's Mandolin*, a tragicomic epic spanning the start of Greece's involvement in World War II up to the present day (see box p.217).

Argostóli

Despite the 1953 earthquakes, **ARGOSTÓLI** is a very attractive town, with some remaining pre-quake architecture, a large and airy main square and a busy waterfront facing east across the Koútavos lagoon to the wooded slopes of Mount Evmorfiá. The waterfront doubles as a working quayside used by fishermen and freighters, and an illuminated promenade at night. Day- and evening-tour craft line the parts of the quay not used by working boats. The lagoon is traversed by the Dhrépano bridge, a remarkable feat of engineering overseen by the Swiss-born soldier and politician, Charles Philippe de Bosset, British governor of Kefalloniá from 1810 to 1814. Originally built of wood, the bridge caused some controversy among islanders, who feared that it might help potential invaders. It has recently turned into a pleasant promenade as it has been pronounced unfit for traffic and it is uncertain if it will be strengthened to allow vehicles to cross it again. Although most package tourists to Kefalloniá will find themselves based along the Lássi peninsula (a 20min walk from Argostóli) or at outlying resorts such as Skála, Póros, Ayía Efimía or Fiskárdho, there is still a high level of tourism based in town, with restaurants and bars catering to both townspeople and visitors.

Arrival and information

Argostóli's modern **Kefallínia airport**, built in the mid-1990s, lies 11km south of town. There are no airport buses, and suburban bus routes to nearby villages like Sv024onáta are so infrequent there is little point in recommending that you try to connect with them. As with every airport in the Ionians, expensive taxi rides into town (at least €10) have become an unofficial tourism surcharge. Feign disbelief and *always* negotiate a price. Apart from a bar-café, a couple of car rental outlets and an exchange booth which opens to meet international flights, there are no other facilities at the airport.

Those arriving in Argostóli by bus from other parts of the island will wind up at the new KTEL **bus station**, a minute from the Dhrépano causeway, which sports a café-bar and modern toilets. Unless you're booked into a hotel or travelling straight on from Argostóli, it's best to head for the main square, **Platía**

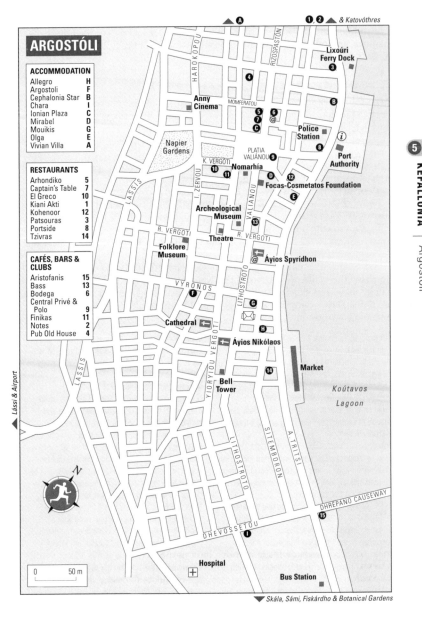

Valiánou (formerly Platía Metaxá), if only to get your bearings, or to dump your bags at a bar and look for a hotel or room. This is easiest done by heading along the seafront, renamed Andoníou Trítsi after the popular leading Pasok politician from here, who died prematurely in the early 1990s.

Argostóli's friendly **EOT office**, one of only two in the Ionians, is right in the middle of the quay, in a one-storey building opposite the police station.

The office has information about rooms, and can advise on transport and facilities around the island (Mon–Fri 7.30am–2.30pm; ☎26710/22 248 or ☎ & ℱ26710/24 466).

Accommodation

Argostóli never seems a particularly crowded town, and **accommodation** is rarely a problem, despite a brisk business clientele. Unfortunately for the budget traveller, all the cheap hotels but one have closed down or gone upmarket, leaving mostly mid to upper range establishments, although recently many of them have had to peg back prices.

In a working town with a large permanent population, **private rooms** aren't too plentiful, but the tourist office has a list of what's available, or you can contact the Room-owners' Association at A. Trítsi 64 (Mon–Fri 8.30am–4.30pm; ☎26710/29 109, ℮oeeddki@otenet.gr). A number of travel agencies also offer rooms, apartments and villas: try Myrtos (☎26710/25 895 or 25 023, ℮myrtostr@hol.gr; from ❸) on A. Trítsi, towards the main quay, or Ainos Travel (☎26710/22 333, ⓦwww.ainostravel.gr; from ❷) on Y. Vergóti, near the Archeological Museum.

The town's one **campsite**, *Argostoli Camping* (☎26710/23 487), lies 2km north of the centre, just beyond the Katovóthres sea mills. The site has only patchy shade and basic amenities so campers are strongly recommended to head for the superior campsite at Sámi (see p.217), unless they particularly want to be close to Argostóli.

Allegro Andréa Hoïdha 2 ☎26710/22 268. A block from the front, in an alley off A. Trítsi just north of the market, recently renovated with classy en-suite rooms, some a/c. Jun–Sep only. ❸

Argostoli Výronos 21 ☎26710/28 358, ℱ23 179. Brightly redecorated, mid-range hotel with functional en-suite rooms. Set further back from the hubbub of seafront and shopping areas, but rather overpriced. ❺

Cephalonia Star A. Trítsi 50 ☎26710/23 181–3, ⓦwww.ioniantravel.gr. Large waterfront hotel, with spacious en-suite rooms whose balconies overlook sea and hills, all with TV and a/c. Restaurant and bar. Closes part of the winter. ❺

🏃 **Chara** corner Dhevossétou and Y. Vergóti ☎26710/22 427. A small and drastically simple rooming house with shared bathrooms very close to the Dhrépano bridge and the bus station, with a friendly manager who offers coffee in the leafy courtyard. The only budget hotel left in town. ❶

🏃 **Ionian Plaza** Platía Valiánou ☎26710/25 581–4, ⓦwww.ionianplaza.gr. One of the ritziest hotels in the archipelago, and surprisingly

cheap for what it is – designer decor down to its swagged curtains and chic bathroom fixtures. If it's in your budget, this is a good place for some pampering. ❺

Mirabel Platía Valiánou ☎26710/25 381–3, ℮mirabel@compulink.gr. Tucked into the southeast corner of the main square, with large and comfortable, air-conditioned, en-suite rooms. Reasonable value for its position. ❹

Mouikis Výronos 3 ☎26710/23 455–6, ⓦwww .mouikis.com. Anonymous decor but very comfortable en-suite rooms with a/c, balcony, phone and TV. Comparable to *Mirabel* but in a quieter setting. Now one of the priciest hotels in town. ❺

Olga A. Trítsi 82 ☎026710/24 981–4, ⓦwww .olgahotel.gr. Imposing, seafront hotel with a/c and TV in all rooms, but the rooms do not match the grandeur of the lobby. Sizeable off-season discounts. ❺

Vivian Villa Dheladhetsima 9 ☎26710/23 396, ⓦwww.kefalonia-vivianvilla.gr. New set of apartments, all fully furnished with TV, fridge and (they claim) British plumbing. Tucked in a quiet spot a few minutes' north of the square. ❹

The Town

The mansions on the palm-lined boulevard of Rizospastón leaving the north side of **Platía Valiánou** give an idea of the elegance and wealth of Argostóli before the 1953 earthquakes. The *platía*, with its restaurants and bars, is the

Earthquakes in the Ionians

Three **tectonic plates** meet in the region of Kefalloniá, Itháki and Zákynthos: the Eurasian Plate, which carries Italy, parts of northern Greece and the Balkans; the Turkish–Hellenic Plate, which carries southern Greece and the Aegean, as well as Turkey and Cyprus; and the African Plate, which supports most of the southern Mediterranean. These plates are in constant, minute motion, part of a process called subduction which is causing Greece to sink slowly into the Aegean. The tension between the plates causes continual, usually minor, **seismic activity**. Major earthquakes occur only a few times each century, and the Twentieth seemed to have its quota, notably in the violent upheavals of 1948 and 1953.

The worst quake on record, in **August 1953**, wreaked destruction across Kefalloniá, Itháki, Lefkádha and Zákynthos, and inspired an international aid campaign by America, Britain and France. No fewer than 113 distinct tremors or aftershocks hit the islands over a period of five days from August 9 to 14. Argostóli and Zákynthos Town were virtually razed to the ground, with roads piled up like waves, and huge vents opened up in the landscape. Over six hundred islanders died and thousands more were injured. The toll would have been higher if the main quake had not struck on a summer afternoon, when many people were outdoors. An estimated seventy percent of buildings throughout the islands were destroyed, and some communities were wiped out altogether. Argostóli's Archeological Museum exhibits some remarkable photographic records of the event.

Tremors are common throughout the Ionians every year, but are normally so minor that they go unnoticed. The most recent one to cause significant damage but mercifully no loss of life hit northwestern Lefkádha in August 2003. Islanders are generally phlegmatic about the threat of another major earthquake; beyond limiting the height of buildings and reinforcing foundations, there is nothing else they can do. Your chances of experiencing a tremor, less still an earthquake, while on holiday here are nonetheless very slim.

focus of town life. The square's southwest corner, next to the small park, makes a useful landmark, as K. Vergóti leads off towards both Lássi and the nearest beaches. Argostóli's main retail and commercial street, pedestrianized **Lithóstroto**, where you'll find shops, banks and the post office, runs south of the Archeological Museum, parallel to the seafront. Amidst the street's busy activity, you'll also find an imposing bell-tower, the grand Catholic church of Áyios Nikólaos, whose plain exterior conceals a colourful riot of wall hangings within, and at the northern end the smaller church of Áyios Spyrídhon, with some exquisite icons and a splendid gilded iconostasis.

The Archeological Museum

Though modest compared to Corfu Town's, the **Archeological Museum** (Tues–Sun 8.30am–3pm; €3) in Argostóli, at the corner of Valiánou and R. Vergóti, has recently been fully refurbished and its collection is well labelled in English. Its three spacious rooms contain a plethora of artefacts excavated on the island, mainly pottery, coins, jewellery, glassware and other domestic items, dating from the fifteenth to second centuries BC, as well as some prehistoric tools and photos of excavations. There are also fragments of architectural details and some statuary, including a ribald Pan figure found at the Melissáni cave-cult shrine, who was once obviously priapic but is now in a state of blunt detumescence. One of the most imposing displays is from the *tholos* tomb at Tzanata, with a variety of funerary relics and grave stelae.

The Folklore Museum

The **Korgialenío History and Folklore Museum** (Tues–Sun 9am–2pm; €3), on Ilía Zervoú behind the Municipal Theatre, is rich in detail of domestic life and island culture over the centuries. Its collection of furniture, clothing and other memorabilia is presented in a series of mock rooms from various eras and social strata: from a peasant kitchen to the drawing room of a wealthy family's mansion. The mock chapel contains some glorious icons, a tomb and several carved marble stelae. Another quaint feature is a pair of flat stand-up oxen labouring under the yoke. Most fascinating is its extensive collection of photographs of the island before and after the 1953 earthquakes, which record both the sophistication of Kefallonian architecture and culture, and the extent of the devastation after the tremors.

The Focas-Cosmetatos Foundation

Housed in a beautiful old mansion on Valiánou, opposite the Nomarhía (County Hall), the **Focas-Cosmetatos Foundation** (May–Oct daily 9.30am–1pm & 7–10pm; €3) was set up as a museum and cultural foundation by the two noble families whose name it shares. It is arranged as a family house of the old ruling classes, with an array of fine furniture and ornaments, as well as a selection of paintings and lithographs, including original works by English nineteenth-century artists Edward Lear and Joseph Cartwright. There is also an interesting display on the history of money and a couple of flowery but confusing family trees. Whilst on the subject of trees, the ticket includes entry to the Botanical Gardens, 2km south near the base of the lagoon, where a variety of plants and flowers are at their best in spring.

Napier Gardens

A short way up the hill, west of Platía Valiánou, there is another pleasant escape from the town's concrete in the shape of the Napier Gardens. Created in honour of Charles Napier, governor of the island from 1822 to 1830, and resident during Byron's brief visit prior to his fateful journey to Messolóngi, its appealing stone paths and pine-shaded picnic tables are well lit at night. There are also detailed information displays and a suitably austere bust of Napier.

The sea mills

The disused **sea mills** at Katovóthres, built over an intriguing geological oddity forty minutes' walk north through pine woods from the centre of Argostóli, have become something of a tourist trap, dominated by a huge space age bar-restaurant to which coachloads of tourists are bussed in shifts starting at 6pm. During the day, though, anyone can walk into the concreted-over complex of pools and disused waterwheel. The view of Lixoúri, the Gulf of Argostóli and the mountains is magnificent, as are the sunsets. The sinkholes at the tip of the peninsula into which seawater drains were first discovered in the 1830s, and before World War II were harnessed to provide electricity. However, it took until the 1960s for scientists to discover where the water went: they dumped green dye into the sinkholes, and two weeks later the traces started to appear in the Melissáni cave and in springs along the Sámi–áyia Efimía coast. Moving at something like 1km a day, the water seeps under the mountains to reappear 20km away on the other side of the island.

Nearby is the **Áyios Theódoros lighthouse**, no more than a small Doric rotunda with a light on its roof. It was built during the 1820s by Charles Napier, although the original was in fact destroyed by an earthquake in 1875 and rebuilt to the same design. It resembles a smaller version of the Maitland rotunda in

Corfu Town, built only a few years before, which might suggest a certain rivalry between the two men. There are a couple of tiny pebble coves nearby on the peninsula, but they aren't especially good for swimming.

Eating and drinking

Argostóli offers a comprehensive range of **restaurants** from basic *souvláki* joints and *estiatória*, through a variety of tavernas and the odd foreign cuisine establishment, to the snazzy hotel dining rooms of Platía Valianoú. **Zaharoplastía** around the square and on the waterfront serve continental breakfasts, but at a price. The best is the *Igloo* on Andréa Hoïdha, a few blocks south of the *Mouikis Hotel* and a block from the waterfront. Alternatively, the waterfront fruit and veg **market** is a great place to assemble your own breakfast or lunch, with provisions from the bakeries and supermarkets opposite. As befits an island capital, it also boasts a commensurate number of **cafés** and **bars** to keep nightowls happy.

Restaurants

Arhondiko Rizospastón 5. Newly renovated, this friendly spot with a small patio, from which you can hear the *kandádhes* from *the Captain's Table* next door without paying silly prices, offers a range of tasty dishes, including some originals like *biftéki* in roquefort sauce.

The Captain's Table Rizospastón 3. The smartest independent taverna in town is recommended for a splurge to anyone keen on experiencing the little-heard Kefallonian style of *kandádhes* singing (nightly from 9pm). The smaller seafront annexe on the seafront a block or two north of the *Olga* Hotel has much more moderate prices.

El Greco K. Vergóti 3. Tucked just southwest of the main square, this family taverna belies its blatantly touristic name by serving some exquisite dishes – try the *poutsin italien* (baked potato and cheese) – in a cosy little garden.

Kiani Akti A. Trítsi, five minutes' walk north of the Lixoúri ferry. Unmissable dining experience on a large wooden deck jutting out above the water. Specialises in seafood such as razor clams in mustard sauce and shrimps in ouzo. Friendly service and reasonable prices.

Kohenoor Lavrága, just southeast of the square. British-run curry house with an Indian chef, one of the most authentic in the Ionians. All the favourites like *balti*, *korma* and *vindaloo* dishes are available.

Patsouras A. Trítsi 32. Popular seafront restaurant, a long-standing favourite with locals, which serves a good range of starters, fish and meat, as well as fine local wine.

Portside A. Trítsi 58. Another friendly place on the front, offering an inexpensive selection of grilled and baked meals and salads, washed down with an excellent, aromatic house wine.

Tzivras V. Vandhórou 1. A classic daytime-only *estiatório* (closes 5pm) with an impressive range of staples from the oven, including a lot of vegetarian options such as *briám* (potato and courgette bake), helpings of which tend to be large and should probably be ordered on their own.

Cafés and bars

Platía Valiánou is the main attraction for a daytime coffee or evening *vólta* and drink in one of the competing **cafés** such as *Polo* and *Central Privé*, which tend to buzz with both conversation and music. The best-sited location in the whole of Argostóli, however, is the modest but welcoming *Aristofanis kafenío* right by the Dhrépano bridge, with a view other bar-owners would kill for.

The oldest and friendliest drinking hole is *Pub Old House*, a few minutes north of Platía Valiánou at Harboúri 13-15, which plays mostly classic rock. More cutting edge rock can be heard at the trendy *Bodega cervezería*, on the corner of Rizospastón and Momferátou. Other **bars** include *Finikas*, which has a fairly lush garden off the southwest corner of the square. The one bona fide indoor **nightclub** is *Bass*, bang opposite the Archeological Museum, while the summer-only *Notes* is a fairly rough and ready *skyládhiko*, out just beyond the campsite.

Listings

Art Exhibition Works by resident English artist Peter Hemming are on show and sale at revolving exhibition locations around town: look out for posters or log onto ⊛ www.thegallerykefalonia.com.

Banks and exchange The Ionian Bank, A. Trítsi 73; the Bank of Greece on Valiánou; the National Bank, corner of Konstandínou and Sitebórou (all Mon–Thurs 8am–2pm, Fri 8am–1.30pm). Numerous ATMs are dotted around town.

Boat Tours A half-day trip to local beauty spots and isolated beaches costs €25 on the glass-bottomed *Pub Old House kaïki*, moored on the seafront down from Platía Valiánou.

Bookshop The only dedicated English language bookshop is The Bookmark, next to *Café Metropolis* on Lithóstroto. A wide range of new and used books are on sale at UK prices. Open 9.30am–2pm & 6.30pm–10 in summer.

Car and bike rental Recommended for both two- and four-wheelers is the island-wide Sunbird agency, whose head office is at A. Trítsi 84 (☎ 26710/23 723, ⊛ www.sunbird.gr). Budget can be found at Lássi 3 (☎ 26710/24 232, ⊛ www.budget.com).

Cinema The pleasant open-air Cine Anny (€8) is on Harokópou, three blocks northwest of Platía Valiánou.

Ferries The Bartholomos agency by the Lixoúri ferry dock (☎ 26710/28 853) is the main agent for Greece–Italy lines. The Vassilatos agency, A. Trítsi 54 (☎ 26710/22 618 or 28 000), also handles international ferry bookings.

Hospital On the corner of Devossétou and Souidhías ☎ 26710/22 434 or 24 641.

Internet Full Internet facilities are available at Excelixis, Minóos 3, just off Lithóstroto by Áyios Spyrídhon church (Mon–Sat 9am–2.30pm & 6–10pm; €4 per hour) and at the café next to Bodega bar.

Laundry The self-service Express laundry is at Lássis 46b, three blocks up from the Napier Gardens (daily 8am–10pm); the minimarket opposite sells tokens for the machines and individual one-wash bags of powder.

Olympic Airlines Y. Vergóti 1 ☎ 26710/28 808; airport ☎ 26710/28 881.

Performing arts The imposing blue-and-white Municipal Theatre at the corner of Y. Vergóti and R. Vergóti opens occasionally for special performances of music and drama. It also has eclectic film showings and art exhibitions.

Police A. Trítsi, by the main ferry jetty ☎ 26710/22 300 or 22 200. Tourist Police ☎ 26710/22 815.

Port Authority On the quay, next to the EOT office ☎ 26710/22 224.

Post office At the corner of Konstandínou and Lithóstroto (Mon–Fri 7.30am–2pm).

Taxi ranks ☎ 26710/28 505 or 22 700.

Around Argostóli

Just over the hill southwest of the island capital lies one of the main package holiday destinations, **Lássi** and its crowded beaches. Further on, beyond the airport, the low-lying **Livathó peninsula** contains a mosaic of small villages and a few less visited beaches. Meanwhile, to the north and east the picturesque **Áyios Yióryios fortress** stands below the imposing peak of **Mount Énos**, whose foothills hold a couple of worthwhile sights.

Lássi

LÁSSI, a twenty-minute walk south from the centre of Argostóli, is an unattractive package resort that sprawls along the busy main road to the airport. The beaches, to be fair, are well maintained, although their modest size and the concentration of tourism in the area means they are very busy even in low season. Lássi's ribbon development has a number of good **restaurants**: the *Il Gabbiano* pizzeria also does spaghetti and Greek items; the *Panorama* offers a full range of standard starters and main courses and the best view; the upmarket *Trata* is a quality fish taverna; the *Sirtaki psistariá* is the place for tasty grills in its huge garden; and the *Chinese Dragon* provides an alternative to Greek cuisine. If you fancy a sunset cocktail, you can't do much better than the *Trentis Bar*.

These and other establishments amply serve those holidaying here, but given that there are far superior beaches around the southeastern tip of Kefalloniá, the independent traveller would be wasting time staying here. Immediately beyond Lássi, **Makrýs Yialós** and **Platýs Yialós** are good sandy beaches for a day out if you're staying in Argostóli, with snack bars, restaurants and hotels overlooking the beach – try the *Makris Gialos psárotaverna* at Makrýs Yialós or the excellent *1900 ouzerí* not far beyond it.

The Livátho peninsula

The **Livátho hills** to the southeast of Argostóli, beyond and inland from the beaches at Makrýs Yialós and Platýs Yialós, are ideal for gentle walking. This lush green range of rolling farmland and tree-shaded country roads slopes down to some fine beaches, most notably at Ávythos. The pretty little villages that dot the hills between Lakíthra and Pessádha are home to many wealthy islanders, which gives places such as Kourkomeláta the air of chintzy suburbs – though there is surprisingly little in the way of facilities. The walking hereabouts is excellent, except in the hunting season (Sept 25–Feb 28), when the possibility of attack by off-leash hunting dogs has to be taken seriously. Take a walking stick and wave it or pick up a rock if threatened. Three **buses** a day run from Argostóli to **Kourkomeláta**, stopping at Lakíthra, Metaxáta and Svoronáta. On the road out of Svoronáta the *Dum Spiro(s) Spero* taverna deserves a refreshment stop for its curiously written name. Meanwhile the sandy beach at **Ámmes**, 1.5 km south, backed by low cliffs and a fish taverna of the same name, is a usually deserted spot; this is no doubt owing to its proximity to the airport runway, although the infrequency of flights means it is worth considering as a getaway.

Ten kilometres southeast of Argostóli, the well-preserved village of **Metaxáta** boasts a number of large, pre-earthquake mansions shaded by ancient palm trees. In the small, deserted town square, a bust of Byron marks the site of a house where the poet stayed. Substantially rebuilt after the 1953 earthquake, **Kourkomeláta**, 1km to the southwest, sits on a bluff overlooking the coast. The *Marina* **café-bar** here, with a garden and excellent views, is virtually the only such establishment between Lakíthra and Spartiá. Kourkomeláta also has a large, impressive church, Áyios Yerásimos (usually locked), and a Neoclassical cultural centre, used occasionally for special events. Just downhill from Kourkomeláta is **Kaligáta**, dominated by a beautiful blue-and-white campanile attached to its Baroque Panayía church. **Ávythos beach**, a gentle two-kilometre walk south of Kaligáta, is in fact two large coves, with a solitary beach taverna, *Tó Enetiko*, and views out to Dhías islet. It's the last sign of sand before the longer beaches of Lourdhá bay to the east and offers good, safe swimming.

East of Metaxáta, the terrain alters from green woodland to flat farmland. Two kilometres further on, **Keramiés** is a working country town, with a large square and fountain. It's an oddly quiescent place: the population still seems to get by with just one *kafenío*. On the coast at Lourdhá bay, **Spartiá** sits above a small harbour with a smattering of holiday bungalows and the fine *Waterway* taverna. **Pessádha**, further round the bay, is uninspiring: apart from a couple of tavernas, it's notable solely for its daily summer ferry connection with Zákynthos. Note that the two daily buses from Argostóli pointedly miss the two ferry crossings and leave you up in the village about 1km from the dock. There is a small canteen near the quay and a decent beach round the corner to while away time. *The View* (☎26710/69 991; ❸) has adequate rooms – useful if you're planning to catch the morning ferry or arrive on the evening one.

Áyios Yióryios fortress

Although an earthquake destroyed much of its interior detail in the seventeenth century, the Venetian fortress at **Áyios Yióryios** (summer Tues–Fri 8.30am–7pm, Sat & Sun 8.30am–3pm; winter Tues–Sun 8.30am–3pm; free) is one of the best-preserved structures of its kind in the archipelago. The *kástro* is reached by a steep one-kilometre walk up the lane signposted at the centre of the town of Peratáta, 7km from Argostóli and on the bus routes to both Skála and Póros. The remaining walls and battlements command spectacular views out over the entire Livátho region, Argostóli itself and Mount Énos to the east.

It's estimated that a defensive structure has existed on the rocky pinnacle since the fourth century AD, and the fortress was established as the island's capital by the Normans in the twelfth century. It was extensively expanded by the Orsinis in the thirteenth, and remained the centre of island life for several centuries, with a population of as many as 15,000, as a bulwark against repeated Ottoman attacks.

The fortress has undergone major restoration in recent years, largely for safety reasons, and although much of the interior is still ruined, a good number of walls, towers and subterranean features such as dungeons remain. Most remarkable is a secret **tunnel**, some 9km long, leading from the *kástro* to a point on the road around the south of the Koutávos lagoon. Now disused, the tunnel was originally dug as an escape route in case the *kástro* were ever over-run. It was last used in 1943, when a group of Italian soldiers, besieged inside the *kástro* by German troops, were spirited out of it by sympathetic islanders. Just outside the gates, the *Astraia* café-bar is a great spot to linger over the view with a drink or snack.

Mount Énos

Mount Énos, the vast hogback mountain that dominates the south of the island, has been declared a national park, more to protect wildlife than to

△ Ayios Yióryios fortress, with Mt Énos behind

attract visitors. Facilities are nonexistent and walking to the summit, 15km from the Argostóli–Sámi road, isn't a very welcoming option, though a road does go all the way for motorists. Minor routes lead up onto the mountain from the south, at Astoupádhes and Áyios Yióryios, and from the north at Dhigaléto, but the most direct approach is to take the signposted turning some 14km from Argostóli on the main Sámi road. From the turn-off, it's 3km to the hamlet of Áyios Elefthérios, and 12km further by rough road to the highest peak. Note that you'll need to take local advice on weather before setting out for Mount Énos, particularly out of season, when conditions can deteriorate very quickly. Take some warm clothing and waterproofs and let someone know you're going.

As well as being one of the highest mountains in western Greece at 1628m, Énos is also unusual for the amount of vegetation, notably the indigenous Abies cephalonica firs. Despite vast fires and animal deforestation over the centuries, the mountain remains one of the largest areas of forest in the archipelago. A herd of a dozen or so wild horses forages in the woodlands, but they tend to avoid humans. Falcons, eagles and other raptors are commonly sighted. The views are the best in the entire Ionians, reaching as far north as the mountains of Corfu, across to the Peloponnese, and to nearby Zákynthos, Lefkádha and Itháki.

The old US army installation at the top is now being put to better use as the location of the only fully robotic **telescope** in Europe outside of the UK; it is hoped that this facility will soon open its doors to the public. With the backing of the local *nomarhía*, a non-profit educational trust (Ⓦ http://eudoxos.snd.edu .gr) is being set up which hopes to see the facility open its doors to the public in the near future.

A worthwhile detour from the Argostóli–Sámi road, 4km before the Mount Énos turn, is to the village of **Frangáta** and on to **Valsamáta**, whose southern fringes conceal two diverse attractions. Nestling in the plain below Mount Énos, the renowned monastery of **Áyios Yerásimos** (daily 8am–1pm & 3–7pm, till 8pm in summer) welcomes visitors, though the usual modest dress should be worn. The main entrance is at the back of the landscaped gardens and gives onto a small courtyard. A side chapel contains some moodily dark paintings and a gilt iconostasis, in front of which stands a casket containing the saint's relics. The most surprising feature is to be found at the back of the chapel, where steep metal steps lead down through the floor into a pair of **caves** where the saint used to spend hours in meditation. Entrance to the small inner cave is possible only by squeezing through a half-metre square hole – not for the claustrophobic. The vast main church in front is modern but vividly painted inside, with a splendid creation scene around the lower part of the dome. The monastery hosts two of the island's most important festivals; on August 15 the saint's death is commemorated, and on October 20 the removal of his relics. On a far more secular note, you can visit the nearby **Robola** winery for free wine tasting (April–Oct daily 7am–8.30pm; Nov–March Mon–Fri 7am–3pm; Ⓦ www.robola.gr) – follow the signs down the lane beside Áyios Yerásimos.

Lixoúri and the Lixoúrion peninsula

The workaday town of **Lixoúri** has little immediate appeal. It has many fans, however, who use it as a base for the quiet sandy beaches that dot the south coast of the **Lixoúrion peninsula** to Cape Akrotíri, and for exploring the more elevated central and northern sections of the peninsula by car or motorbike, especially the glorious beach of **Petaní** and lesser-known strand of **Áyios Spyrídhonas**.

Lixoúri

LIXOÚRI was flattened in the 1953 earthquake, and little of it has risen above two or three storeys since. The waterfront it presents to ferries arriving from Argostóli is uninspiring: a smattering of tavernas and bars on either side of the town square, Platía Petrítsi, but all of it rather dowdy. Like a shrunken mirror image of Argostóli, Lixoúri consists of a long, narrow grid of alleys extending along the seafront, with little beyond apart from the odd hotel in the dormitory area at the back of town. The beach immediately to the south is narrow but sandy, and popular with families. A better beach, however, can be found 2km south, at **Lípedha**, with its rich red sand and unusual sandstone rock formations. While there are rooms within a kilometre of Lépedha (see below), the only facilities at the beach are a sole café-restaurant.

Practicalities

Ferries from Argostóli operate from 7.30am to 1.30am and leave every half hour in summer, hourly in winter (30min; €1.30 per person, €1 per motorbike, €3.60 per car). Lixoúri has a small strip of beachside **accommodation** a few hundred metres south along the coast road from the waterfront. The two best establishments here, the smart *Summery* hotel (☎26710/91 771 or 91 871, ⓦwww.hotelsummery.gr; ❺), which has a pool and tennis courts, and renovated *Poseidon* (☎26710/92 518–9, ⓔposeidonhotel@internet.gr; ❸), should have rooms free for independent travellers during most of the season. The classiest place to stay in Lixoúri, however, is ⌘ *La Cité* (☎26710/92 701, ⓕ92 702; ❹), four blocks back from the front – take the road leaving the right-hand corner at the back of Platía Petrítsi – which has been tastefully refurbished and offers en-suite rooms, pool, restaurant and bar.

Perdikis Travel (☎26710/91 097 or 93 077, ⓕ92 503; from ❷) on the ferry quay is an agent for **rooms** in Lixoúri and outside town, as is the friendly

---

Ancient Palíki as Homer's Ithaca

The Lixoúrion peninsula is also sometimes referred to by its more ancient name of **Palíki**. This area has now become the centre of one of the newest theories about the real location of the **home island of Odysseus**, traditionally considered to be Itháki. In his book *Odysseus Unbound – The Search For Homer's Ithaca*, published in October 2005, amateur archeologist Robert Bittlestone suggests that Palíki was in fact the hero's home, after extensive research based on computer technology and satellite imagery, as well as archeological and literary data. He claims that in the time of Homer the peninsula would have been a separate island and the strait separating it from the rest of Kefalloniá has subsequently silted up, a theory lent credence by John Underhill, a geology expert from Edinburgh University. Bittlestone also matches all twenty-six of the locations describing Ithaca in Homer with spots on the peninsula. In this he is supported by Cambridge Classics professor James Diggle, who says it solves the mystery of certain Homeric passages that refer to Ithaca as "low-lying" and "towards dusk", neither of which apply to more mountainous and easterly Itháki, which Bittlestone identifies with Homer's island of **Doulichion**. Of course, cynics would point out the lack of any major archeological finds on the Lixoúri peninsula but then little of structural substance has been dug up in Itháki either.

A.D. Travel (☎26710/93 142, ⓦwww.adtravel.gr; from ❷), on the main road through town just north of the square. An attractive, if out-of-the-way, alternative is the *Taverna Apolafsi* rooms and studios (☎26710/91 691, ⓦwww.apolafsi .gr; ❹). Blissfully quiet except on music nights, the taverna is a twenty-minute walk south from Lixoúri just before Lépedha beach.

If you're **eating** in Lixoúri, the first place to head for is the ⅄ *Akrogiali* on the seafront: this authentic and friendly taverna has an extensive menu and attracts customers from all over the island; food prices are very reasonable, and the local wine is not only excellent but must be the cheapest in the Ionians. Nearby *Bella Mafia* offers fairly authentic Italian food such as antipasti, pizza and pasta. One block behind the southern seafront, *Iy Avli* is a nice garden restaurant serving items like schnitzel, while *Maria's*, further towards the square, is a cheap and basic *estiatório* that has seen better days, but can still produce tasty home-cooking. Also south of the square but back on the front, the *Archipelagos* restaurant-*ouzerí* has a good range of seafood and pasta, and doubles as a bar in the evenings. At night, youngsters tend to congregate in trendy *Overdose* on the square or at pricey seafront **bars** such as *Sousouro* and *LA Dreams*. There is also a small **Internet café** (€3.50 per hour) called Factory in an alley southwest of the square.

The south coast of the peninsula

The flatter, southern part of the peninsula, known locally as **Kátoï**, still bears some of the most dramatic scars of the 1953 earthquakes. This farming region was one of the worst hit on the island, and in places there remain eerie landscapes of subsided fields and orchards, and small hills shunted up out of the earth. Flocks of bell-laden sheep graze on the weird tumuli left by the quake, sending crazed gamelan music drifting across the countryside. The only bus service on the peninsula connects Lixoúri with Xi beach, 6km away to the south, three times a day. On the way it detours to **Mégas Lákkos**, whose name means "big hole", where the narrow beach is a rich, almost silky, red, set below stunted cliffs and served by a couple of tavernas – the *Oasis*, 300m inland, does a fair range of meat, seafood and salads; the price at the smart *Kefalonia Beach* bungalows (☎26710/92 679 or 92 409; ❺), attached to the second taverna at the back of the beach, includes half-board. From here you can walk along the beach to Xi in a quarter of an hour.

Xi itself, with its serried ranks of sun loungers, has the trendy *Averto* beach bar, a couple of tavernas, the standard *Ocean View* and *Dolphins* fish taverna, which also serves *ouzerí*-style *mezédhes*, and the *Jolly Fisherman* 500m inland, a fun café with delicious cakes and traditional games. Apart from the good-value rooms and apartments of the ⅄ *Village Xi* complex (☎26710/93 733, ⓦwww .xi-village.gr; ❸), the only other **accommodation** is the plush *Cephalonia Palace* hotel (☎26710/93 112 or 93 190, ⓦwww.kefaloniapalacehotel.gr; ❼), where the price includes breakfast and an evening meal. Popular with British tourists, this has all the typical facilities of a large, self-contained resort hotel – vast pool, restaurants, bars, shops and gardens.

To get further west, if you have your own transport, you have to pass through the scantily vegetated moonscape that separates Xi from the nearest village of Mantzavináta. From here a road leads 4km southwest to the quieter bea~′ **Kounópetra**, site of a curious rock formation. Until the 1953 eartho~ rocking stone, as the name signifies in Greek, had a strange rhythm~ that could be measured by placing a knife into a gap betwe~ its base. However, after the quake the rock became motio~

little more than a headland with a tiny harbour and beach; you'll find a better beach at nearby Agrosykiá, backed by chalky white cliffs, and site of the very reasonable *To Meltemi* restaurant. Development is gradually creeping in to the Kounópetra area, though it would still make a peaceful base for those with wheels; try staying at the *Villa Carina* (℡26710/93 604; ❸) or *Kounopetra's Studios* (℡26710/93 252 or 93 772; ❹), both comfortable purpose-built apartment blocks, or the larger *Hotel Ionian Sea* (℡26710/92 280, ℻92 980; ❺), about 500m inland.

Two kilometres further west, in an area known as Vátsa, the last beach of any size on the southern tip of the peninsula is sandy **Áyios Nikólaos**. The strand is very quiet and has no accommodation, but the friendly 𝕏 *Spiaggia* restaurant (℡26710/92 760, ⓦwww.vatsa.gr)can put you in contact with local villas (from ❹). It'll also provide you with pasta, seaweed salad and seafood, as well as the occasional serenade from groups of merry Italians in high season.

The west coast of the peninsula

The peninsula has one of the finest vantage points for sunsets on the entire island: the **monastery of Kipouréon**, hefted up on the cliffs above the wild west coast some 14km from Lixoúri. The views are magnificent, but the monastery itself is minor, most of it having been rebuilt in the 1970s. Like the rest of the west coast of the peninsula, Kipouréon is only really accessible by private vehicle, though that is easy now the roads have been improved.

If you do have your own transport, you could also reach the magnificent beach at **Petaní**, 14km northwest of Lixoúri, a dramatic two-kilometre stretch of smooth pebbles that's possibly the finest, and certainly the remotest, on the island. Even this haven, however, is in the process of being discovered and can get surprisingly busy at the height of summer. Two seasonal tavernas provide refreshments, one of which, the friendly Greek-American owned 𝕏 *Xouras* (℡26710/97 128, ⓦwww.petani.gr; ❸) provides ample quantities of tasty food and has rooms in the pipeline. In the meantime they direct those wishing to stay up the hill to *Niforo* (℡26710/97 350 or 97 471; ❹). As usual, **camping** is officially forbidden but tolerated in practice, if done discreetly at the north end of the beach.

The **Áyios Spyrídhonas** inlet, also known as Pórto Athéras, as it serves the traditional village of Athéras, a short way inland, has a sandy beach with shallow water that's safe for swimming, though unfortunately it seems to catch seaborne garbage. There is an *ouzerí* and the *Yialós* **taverna**, whose garden acts as home for families with camper vans and could be used for camping.

Southeast Kefalloniá

The main coast road to the east of Peratáta yields few places to stay, although there are some pleasant dining and swimming spots to which you could make a detour, while the vast **Kateliós bay** to the west of Skála has the finest sandy beaches on Kefalloniá. The resort of **Skála** is the preferred package destination at this end of the island, as its rival **Póros**, with a narrow pebble beach and crumbling concrete seafront, has begun to look a little careworn recently.

Vlaháta and Lourdháta

Leading east from Peratáta, you might make a detour at tiny Moussáta-Pori-... before Vlaháta). From here a road leads south to the excellent beach of **Trapezáki**, whose only development is the popular taverna of the same name. On the hill about 500m above it the brand new *Trapezaki Bay Hotel* (☏26710/31 502-3, ⊛www.trapezakibayhotel.gr; ❻) offers all mod cons, albeit in a rather stiff atmosphere.

Otherwise, the first stop of any note beyond Peratáta is the village of **VLAHÁTA**, which is slowly blending with the micro-resort of Lourdháta on the coast below. It is still possible to stay in Vlaháta itself, in places such as *Maria Studios* (☏26710/31 055; ❸) or *Madison Studios* (☏26710/31 294; ❹), and you can even get a drink here, at joints such as the *Castra Club* and *Muses* cocktail bar.

But the area's main tourist action lies 2km south, towards the sea. Here the hamlet of **Lourdháta**, perched above a fine shingle beach, a kilometre or so long, is growing into an ever more popular resort. There are several **tavernas** in the area, including the *Diamond*, which has a large range of vegetarian alternatives to its standard Greek fare, on the tiny, plane-shaded village square. Better value though are *Spiros* steak-and-grill house and the *Dionysos* taverna, with a large selection of staples, both on the road from Vlaháta. The modest *Adonis* (☏26710/31 206; ❸) and *Ramona* (☏26710/31 032; ❷) have **rooms** just outside the village, on the one side road that you'll find.

Down on the beach itself, the comfortable and spacious one-bedroom **apartments** at 𝕏*Thomatos* (☏26710/31 656, ✉critithomatos@yahoo.com; ❺) make for a splendid stay. The *Blue Sea* **taverna** offers fish, meat and starters at reasonable prices, but the vine-covered garden of *Klimitis*, 100m along the beach, is pleasanter and particularly good for fish. Up on the hill a short way behind it, *Lorraine's Magic Garden* is a quiet spot to unwind for a snack or drink.

Sissiá and Markópoulo

Beyond Vlaháta, the road passes beneath the peak of Mount Énos, through primeval mountainscapes and boulder fields veined with flood drains to channel the sometimes apocalyptic winter storms. Four kilometres from Vlaháta, a lane leads 1km down towards the sea and the ruins of the thirteenth-century **monastery of Sissiá**, associated in myth with a visit by St Francis of Assisi, who is said to have been forced ashore here in a storm. The original building was abandoned centuries ago, and devastated in the 1953 earthquakes. A new and rather nondescript monastery was built after the quake.

Three kilometres on, the main road forks – left to Póros, right to Skála. The villages in this region are small and mostly resistant to tourism, although **MARKÓPOULO**, 5km along the Póros road, is more interesting. Not only is it claimed by local wags to be the birthplace of a certain Italian traveller, but more importantly – every August 15, on the occasion of the festival of the Dormition of the Virgin Mary – its church of the **Panayía of Langouvárdha** is the site of a bizarre **snake-handling ritual**. The church stands on the site of the monastery of Our Lady of Langouvárdha, destroyed in the earthquake, which in turn had been first established as a nunnery. The story goes that when the nunnery was attacked by pirates, the nuns prayed to be transformed into snakes to avoid being taken prisoner. Their prayers were answered, and each year the "return" of a swarm of small, harmless black snakes is meant to bring the villagers good luck. As Mother Nature is unlikely to keep such a schedule, some discreet snake-breeding on the part of the village priests must be suspected.

Kateliós

Along the Skála fork of the coast road, the mountain landscape opens out into a wide valley around **KATELIÓS** and the neighbouring resort of **KÁTO**

KATELIÓS, which are undergoing continual expansion. Manos Holidays already brings clients here, and a number of other enterprises are now capitalizing on the long and fabulously sandy beaches. Of the new **hotels**, the smart, modern *Odyssia* (☎26710/81 615, ℉81 614; ❺) and sprawling *Galini Resort* (☎26710/81 582, ⓦwww.galini.de; ❹), complete with pool and mini-golf course, are typical of the developments a little way inland. There are also reasonable beachside rooms at the *Faros* taverna (☎26710/81 355; ❸). The seafront has half a dozen **tavernas**, bars and cafés in a row. The best is the 𝕏 *Blue Sea*, so highly rated for quality fish and seafood that visiting dignitaries often dine here – yet the prices remain reasonable. *Ostria* also offers a good selection of marine dishes and *mezédhes*. Meanwhile the *Cozy* **bar**, decked in gay summer colours at the far end of the front, is the choicest spot for a drink.

It is important to bear in mind that the beaches looping around eastwards to Kamínia, before the village of Ratzaklí, are **loggerhead turtle** nesting grounds, so care should be taken to avoid nests and the usual guidelines followed (see box on p.249). Because of the turtle presence, freelance camping isn't advisable; you would, in any case, face a strenuous hike to Ratzaklí to find water, toilets or shops.

Skála

The popular resort of **SKÁLA** attracts a sizeable return clientele, who keep it busy into October when other resorts have all but closed down. Its beaches closely rival those of Kateliós bay, running away for several kilometres in either direction and backed by a sweep of native Kefallonian pines, which give the place an oddly un-Mediterranean feel, more akin to parts of the Scottish or New England coastline. A small **Roman villa** (May–Oct daily 10am–2pm & 5–8pm; free), signposted on a path above the beach just by the *Golden Beach Palace*, was excavated in the 1950s to reveal a pair of well-preserved mosaics, one of a man being attacked by wild cats, the other of a scene around a sacrificial altar. The mosaics are protected in a modern wood-and-glass structure.

Rebuilt after the 1953 earthquake, the compact village spreads out from a small square above the beach, with the main action on the short high street that runs up from it rather than on the strand itself. Much **accommodation** is pre-booked well in advance, and private rooms are scarce, although there are studios at *Dionysus Rooms* (☎26710/83 283; ❸), a block south of the high street. Rooms can also be found at the cosy *Captain's Hotel* (☎26710/83 389, ⓦwww.captainshouse.net; ❷), parallel to the main drag, and the *Golden Beach Palace*, 100m south of the seafront square (☎26710/83 327; ❹). The more upmarket 𝕏 *Tara Beach Hotel* (☎26710/83 250 or 83 341–3, ⓦwww .tarabeach.gr; ❺) can offer comfortable en-suite rooms or individual bungalows in lush gardens on the edge of the beach. If all else fails, try Panem Tours (☎26710/83495, ℮panem@forthnet.com.gr) or Etam Travel Service (☎26710/83101, ℮etam-kef@otenet.gr), two of a number of agencies that offer accommodation and other tourist services in the village; Sunbird car/bike **rental** has an office just off the main drag (☎26710/83 313, ⓦwww.sunbird .gr), while down on the beach the Dolphin Ski Club offers parasailing, banana rides and speedboat-rentals.

Skála falls behind neighbouring Póros in terms of seafood **restaurants**, but it does have a number of good eating options. On the main street try *Ta Pytharia*, with its full range of north European and local dishes, or the nearby *Flamingo*, which offers a mix of seafood, steaks and island dishes such as Kefallonian meat pie. *Noufara* has more of the same in a pleasant garden. The beach also has two conventional tavernas, both good for lunches; the friendly *Paspalis* specializes in fish and home-cooking and the *Sunrise* adds pizzas to its Greek fare. The *Chinese House*, near the turning down to the beach, rustles up all the usual favourites for those wanting a change of diet. For a **drink**, *Pikiona* is a trendy pool-bar on the seafront, while *Marabou*, near the church on the main drag, shows Sky Sports and has Net access (€5/hr). The northern beachside *Stavento* bar-restaurant plays the best sounds and stays open until the small hours.

Skála to Póros

With stamina and three or four hours to spare, it's possible to reach Póros on foot from Skála, along 13km of coastal road through fairly wild, undeveloped countryside; 1km out of Skála, you'll pass the vestigial remains of a Roman temple. Only three buses a day (Mon–Sat) run between the resorts, so the journey is most easily covered by car or motorbike. An alternative route between Skála and Póros is inland over the final hump of Mount Énos, through the hill towns of Áyios Yióryios and **TZANÁTA**. The latter, 4km before Póros, is worth a halt to visit the large Mycenaean burial chamber unearthed outside the village, findings from which are on display in the revamped Archeological Museum in Argostóli (see p.203). The chamber, a lined circular underground vault with entrance-way, was only excavated in 1991, and is believed to be the last resting place of a local Bronze Age chieftain. Archeological investigations are continuing, as this is another site contending for the crown of Homer's "real" Ithaca. Beyond here, the road to Póros plunges down through a small but dramatic gorge which carries a river (usually dry) through the town.

Póros

PÓROS in fact comprises two bays: the larger, northerly one is the centre of tourist activities; the second, a five-minute walk over the small headland to the south, is the port proper, which has ferry connections with Kyllíni on the mainland – the only route to Zákynthos during winter months. After the three main towns, Póros is the largest development on the island, and there's certainly plenty to do and consume. Away from high and mid-season, however, when the bus services dwindle, Póros is geographically isolated, and anyone holidaying here without their own transport may feel they've picked the short straw.

These days, Póros looks distinctly frayed at the edges, with a scruffy concrete seafront in the first bay, which is where most package tourists will find themselves billeted, and a narrow, kilometre-long pebble beach stretching to the north. Paths off the road south to the port lead down to inviting blue-water swimming off rocks. Most of the action takes places in the main street running down to the seafront of the first bay, and along the seafront itself.

Practicalities

Póros has quite a few **hotels**, although many of these places are block-booked by tour operators. The elegant new *Odysseus Palace*, on the crossroads at the back of town (☎26740/72 036, ⓦwww.odysseuspalace.com; ❺), has very stylish en-suite rooms with balconies, and offers bargain discounts of up to sixty percent at any time but August. Nearby, the great-value ⚲ *Santa Irina* (☎26740/72 017, ✉maki@otenet.gr; ❷) throws in breakfast despite the cheap rate but only opens for a short season. Two reasonable options backing onto the northern stretch of beach are the old-fashioned *Riviera Hotel* (☎26740/72 327, ⓕ72 579; ❷) and the drab but functional *Poseidon* (☎26740/72 428; ❸). **Rooms** and **apartments** tend to cluster around the bridge crossing the riverbed: best value is *Pension Elena* (☎26740/72 407; ❷) or you could try the smarter *Blue Bay* apartments (☎26740/72 500, ℱ72 550; ❸). Among **travel agents**, *Poros Travel* by the ferry dock (☎26740/72 476 or 72 284, ℱ72 069) offers a range of accommodation, as well as services such as car rental and ferry bookings. Ford car rental has an office on the main drag (☎26740/72 675) of the first bay.

The main seafront has the majority of the **restaurants**, the best of which for setting and value is *Fotis Family* (aka *Romantza*), tucked into the corner of the headland, while *To Steki* is a cheap *psistariá* towards the northern beach. At night, however, the old port is quieter and has more atmosphere, with tavernas such as *O Tzivas* and *Dionisos* that are strong on locally caught seafood. **Nightlife** centres around *Zanza Bar*, overlooking the sea on the main bay, which also hosts the *BBs Club*, whose clientele seem remarkably well behaved (the initials stand for Bad Boys), and Mythos, an Internet café with comfy seating.

Sámi and around

The former capital, **Sámi**, is where the majority of independent travellers will arrive on Kefalloniá. It's the only surviving settlement of the island's four ancient city-states, although little remains from this time beyond fragments of foundations dotted about the hill above the modern town. The town itself is not particularly attractive, but has a pleasant seafront, a range of facilities and a long sandy beach that becomes more attractive the further you get to Karavómylos. The fact that it has been largely abandoned by the British tour companies means it does not easily get overcrowded, and its brief spell of fame as the location for *Captain Corelli's Mandolin* (see box overleaf) has not really reversed that trend. There is a fine pebble beach 2km east at **Andísamis**, which now has the lively *Andissa Club* for snacks, drinks and watersports facilities. More importantly, Sámi is the natural jumping-off point for the two major tourist attractions on the island, the **Drogharáti** cave system and the underground lake of **Melissáni**. Given the good ferry service between Sámi and Itháki, day-trips to the latter's capital, Vathý, are also easily manageable.

Sámi comprises a long, L-shaped seafront with a small harbour to the east and a compact grid of dormitory roads behind it. Most bars and restaurants are close to the crossroads – rather grandly dubbed Platía Kyproú – at the centre of the seafront. Hotels and rooms tend to be in the streets behind the seafront, and on the roads out of town: the main road to Argostóli, and the coast road north towards Ayía Efímia.

Daily **ferries** arrive in Sámi from Vathý and Pisaetós on Itháki, and Astakós and Pátra on the mainland; there are also connections from Italy and Corfu in high summer. The *Sami Star* (ⓦwww.samistar.com) does full-day cruises daily to Vathý, Kióni and a couple of quieter beaches on Itháki for €25. There are **bus** services (Mon–Sat) between Sámi and Argostóli, although the last leaves Sámi at 5.30pm. In season, there are also two buses a day (Mon–Sat) from Sámi to Fiskárdho via Ayía Efímia. Buses stop on the seafront not far from Platía Kyproú and, for those needing to move on at awkward times or on Sundays, **taxis** meet ferries and congregate on Platía Kyproú. For renting a car the handiest agency is Gerolimatos (☎26740/23 405), while two-wheelers can be procured from Sami Center (☎26740/22 254); both establishments are on the seafront. In medical emergencies, there is a health centre (☎26740/22 222), also on the harbour. If you need to get **online**, head for the Break Internet

> ## Mandolin Wind
>
> Kefalloniá is the setting for most of the action in Louis de Bernière's novel *Captain Corelli's Mandolin* (which for some inexplicable reason loses the word "Captain" in the American edition). The prose is stunning, the vocabulary rich with vivid similes, and the characters lovingly crafted and artfully brought to life. The story chronicles life immediately before and during the Italian and German occupation of the island in World War II, and briefly skims over events in the lives of the surviving characters up to the present day. The detailed evocation of island life in the middle of the twentieth century, and the references to many places you are likely to visit, can certainly enhance your stay. The historical detail, shocking in places, appears to be thoroughly researched.
>
> The book was turned into a big-budget Hollywood production in 2000, which blunted the book's philosophical and political edge, turning it instead into a fairly mundane love story, starring Nicholas Cage, Penelope Cruz and John Hurt. The stunning cinematography, however, couldn't have served as a better advertisement for Kefalloniá, as it was filmed entirely on location. Huge compensation was paid to the proprietors of businesses on one half of the seafront at Sámi, which was requisitioned for several months and covered with a facade to recreate wartime Argostóli. Other scenes were shot in the lush countryside and at the beaches of nearby Andísamis and across the island at Mýrtos, where the beached mine was dramatically exploded. So far the film doesn't seem to have had much impact on the island's tourism – certainly not in the way that *The Big Blue* has had in Amorgós. There has also been a remarkable show of restraint by bar and restaurant owners to avoid the anticipated orgy of theming and renaming – the jointly owned *Captain Corelli's* establishments in Sámi and Ayía Efimía are the only examples so far.

Centre (11am–2pm & 5.30–11pm; €5 per hour), just off the seafront behind the *Kastro Hotel*.

Accommodation

Sámi has a good, though not particularly cheap, range of accommodation. Blue Sea Travel (℡26740/22 813 or 23 007, ⓦwww.samistar.com) can help you find apartments and villas; otherwise you should head for the miniature suburb just north of the town centre, which has walk-up signs for rooms in private homes. It's also worth considering the small, if rather dull, suburb of Karavómylos, around the bay from Sámi itself: try the purpose-built *Calypso Apartments* (℡26740/22 933; ❹) attached to the pottery workshop. Sámi's **campsite**, *Camping Karavomilos Beach* (℡26740/22480, ⓔvalettas@hol.gr), is a short walk along the path behind the beach towards Karavómylos, with an expensive taverna, bar and shop. The site, however, is excellent, with over three hundred pitches on flat, shady ground, and a gate leading directly on to the beach.

Hotels

Given the prices of rooms in Sámi, you might just as well opt for a **hotel**, either one of the small establishments in town or grander places further out.

Athina Beach Karavómylos beach ℡26740/23 067 or 22 779, ⓦwww.athinahotel.gr. The smaller and more intimate of the two resorts in Sámi's northern neighbourhood. ❺

Kastro Hotel On the seafront ℡26740/22 656 or 22 282. Small but plushly decorated air-conditioned rooms, in a convenient central location. ❹

Melissani Just above the harbour ℡ & ℡26740/22 464. A small and friendly establishment with a/c and TV in all rooms, signposted behind the main parade of quayside tavernas. ❹

Pericles Over 1km along the road to Argostóli ℡26740/22 780–5, ℡22 787. Popular with British tourists, boasting extensive grounds, with two pools and sports facilities, restaurant, bar and entertainment. ❹

Sami Beach Karavómylos beach ☏ 26740/22 802 or 22 824, ⓦ www.samibeachhotel.gr. Fairly grand seaside resort with pool, bar, restaurant, and rooms overlooking the hotel gardens and the beach. ❻

🏃 **Thodora Hotel** A block back from the seafront ☏ 26740/22 650, ⓕ 23 109. Cosy rooms and studios open all year, with comfortable fittings and a friendly reception. ❹

Eating and drinking

Sámi doesn't have a great many **tavernas** beyond those on the seafront. The most genuine and reasonably priced is *Gorgona* (*Mermaid*), a classic *estiatório* with a good range of oven-cooked food, including Kefallonian meat pie. Most of the others on the main strip are adequate but somewhat touristy, like the *Dolphins* and *Faros*. The best taverna, however, on the quieter stretch of seafront out towards the campsite, is *To Akroyiali*, which serves delicious grilled meat and fish as well as casserole dishes, washed down with fine barrelled wine.

The *Captain Corelli's* and *Aqua Marina* are among the favourite **bars** in the evenings, pumping out nondescript Euro faves. The former's *zaharoplastío* is also great for after-dinner sweets or **breakfast**. The best place for a snack breakfast, however, is *Captain Jimmy*, which is also recommended to anyone who has to feed an ice-cream habit.

Melissáni and Dhrogaráti caves

These two small but dramatic cave systems are both within walking distance of Sámi. At **Melissáni**, 3km away off the Ayía Efimía road, there's an underground lake, illuminated by sunlight falling through a large hole in the ceiling. **Dhrogaráti** is a conventional cave-tunnel system, but with a large central cavern. If you're stuck for time and have to choose, Melissáni is the more spectacular of the two.

Melissáni

Melissáni cave (daily 8am–sunset; €5) is at least 30,000 years old, with stalactites that have been dated at around 20,000 years. Although it was only opened to visitors in the 1960s, it is known to have been used as a shrine to Pan in prehistoric times; artefacts from the shrine, including a risqué Pan figure, are displayed in Argostóli's Archeological Museum.

From the entry in a small car park off the Sámi–Ayía Efimía road, stairs lead down to a short tunnel, which slopes to a small balcony overlooking the underground lake. The roof of the cave above the lake collapsed during the 1953 earthquakes, admitting a light that turns it brilliant turquoise. The waters that you see here have arrived from sinkholes at Katovóthres on the other side of the island (see p.204); they will then drain from here into the so-called Karavómylos Lake, which is actually a salt-water duckpond at Karavómylos beach, 500m away. On the tour, you are taken by boatmen in groups into the middle of the lake, and through to an interior electrically-lit chamber, where the Pan shrine is believed to have been. The boatmen give a curt and hurried commentary in Greek and English, pointing out features such as the "duck's head" stalactite and "diving dolphin" stalagmite. The lake is best seen around midday in high summer, with the sun overhead filling the cave with light, but it's almost as impressive on a sunny October afternoon. A change of ownership in late 2005 means the caves may no longer be open all year, so check at the tourist office in Argostóli.

Dhrogaráti

The **Dhrogaráti** caves (daily 9am–8pm; €3.50) are a good 2km along the main road to Argostóli and then just under 1km along a signposted road to the right. You can enter on your own, or guides take small groups through a series of illuminated cave sections, leading to the stunning, cathedral-like central chamber. As well as an impressive array of illuminated stalactites and stalagmites, the chamber has extraordinary acoustics, and is still occasionally used for musical performances: past events include a concert by Maria Callas. Care should be taken not to slip on the floor, which is treacherous in some parts, and you might need additional clothing to protect yourself against the cool damp air, especially if you intend to hang out and drink in the subterranean atmosphere.

Ayía Efimía

Built around a small port, 9km northwest of Sámi, **AYÍA EFIMÍA** is an amiable little town in which to lie low, although its beaches are among the worst on the island. The main one – laughably called Paradise – is a pebble cove barely 20m in length; those who find Paradise too tiny to squeeze onto will, however, find quieter coves along the road to Sámi. One of these, Ayía Paraskeví, boasts the excellent ⚵ *Agia Paraskevi* taverna, which serves a marvellous mussel marinade on spaghetti, among other delights. The town itself comprises an L-shaped quay around a tiny harbour, with a handful of back streets and terraced alleys mounting the hillside above; virtually all the action takes place on the quay, or just behind it.

In low season, Ayía Efimía isn't a place to get stuck in without wheels, although it makes a fairly convenient base if you do have your own transport. In summer, however, there are two **buses** every day except Sunday to Sámi and to Fiskárdho, timed to enable you to spend the day in either. It is also a prime base for scuba-diving and is home to Aquatic World (☎26740/62 006, ⓦwww.aquatic.gr), which can issue certification or take you on simple introductory dives.

Practicalities

Of Ayía Efimía's two independent **hotels**, the seafront *Pyllaros Boulevard* (☎26740/61 800, ⓦwww.kefalloniatravel.com; ➏) is completely air-conditioned, with TV in all rooms, but *Moustakis* (☎26740/61 030, ⓦwww.moustakishotel.com; ➍), a couple of blocks back from the quay, has a cosier feel. The newer *Gonatas* hotel (☎26740/61 500–3, ⓕ61 464; ➎), round the headland past Paradise beach, mostly takes groups but may have some space for sole travellers. Both Dionysios Logaras (☎26740/61 202 or 61 349; ➍), on the road inland across the island, and Yerasimos Raftopoulos (☎26740/61 233, ⓕ61 216; ➌), on the way in from Sámi, have comfortable modern rooms and apartments.

The ⚵ *To Steki Tou Kalofaga* **taverna**, above Paradise beach, is the best place to go for authentic island cuisine and barrel wine, though the *Paradise Beach*, further round the headland, offers simpler and cheaper fare. On the harbour front, the long-established *Pergola Restaurant* also has a wide range of island specialities and standard Greek dishes, while its neighbour, the newer *Finikas* taverna, offers a costlier mix of fish, steaks and international cuisine. The largely laid-back **nightlife** centres on *Captain Corelli's* bar-restaurant and the conventional *Asteria* cafeteria; those intent on more active head-banging flock to the *Paranoia Music Club*, 700m along the road inland. The *Strawberry zaharoplastío* is the place for a decadent breakfast, and Gerolimatos Rentacar (☎26740/61 036, ⓕ61 516) can supply a getaway vehicle.

Northern Kefalloniá

Kefalloniá's northern tip is most easily reached along the main road north from Argostóli, which provides some jaw-dropping views on the left as you go. The link road from Ayía Efimía on the east coast to Dhivaráta sees fewer buses, though it's easily manageable if you're making a loop by car or motorbike.

After leaving the island capital, the road climbs above the Gulf of Argostóli into a series of small mountain villages. The first, **Fársa**, where you can enjoy a break at the *Astrolavos* or *Marina* cafés, was rebuilt after the earthquake; the ruins of the original village can be seen just above. A detour before Fársa can be made to **Dhavgáta** to visit the Museum of Natural History (daily 9am–1pm, plus Mon–Sat 6–8pm; €1.50), which chronicles the island's land and marine life and has displays on environmental issues. Between Fársa and Mýrtos beach there is little else of note apart from the hamlet of Agónas, where a steep road twists down to the long, sandy beach of **Ayía Kyriakí** below. This fine strand has a canteen near the approach road and the shack-like *Iy Kalyva tou Psara* fish tavern at the western end; as it already draws a fair few sun-seekers in high summer, further development is to be expected; a new boat hire enterprise has already appeared. A bumpy road leads up from the west end of the beach to the pretty village of **Zóla**, where the *Toucano psarotavérna* has very reasonable prices for seafood and great views. You can also stay in the village at the modest *Anna Studios* (☏26740/85 132; ❷).

Mýrtos

From the near-sheer cliffs above it, **Mýrtos** appears as a dazzling crescent of white pebble next to a turquoise sea, and is one of the most photographed spots in the Ionians – though if you have to make the four-kilometre trip down from Dhivaráta on foot it loses a little of its sparkle. Buses only stop at Dhivaráta, although with your own transport you can drive all the way down to the beach. Mercifully, permanent building is prohibited on the beach so there's just one large seasonal **snack bar**, which, along with a cave in the cliffs, provides the only shade for most of the day unless you hire one of the myriad umbrellas – for the beach is heaving with visitors in summer and not the place for a quiet swim. The west-facing beach is, however, a great place to catch the sunset, although given the bus times this is the preserve of the motorist or biker – or anyone prepared to stay up in **Dhivaráta**, which is developing its own little tourist business on the back of the famous beach below. Comfortable **accommodation** is now available here at *Mina Studios* (☏26740/61 716 or 61 754, Ⓔmarkela1@hol.gr; ❸), by the junction with the road from Ayía Efimía, or in the village itself at *Tzannatos Apartments* (☏26740/61830, Ⓔtzanhl@aias.gr; ❷). If you turn up on spec, you can ask about the latter at the *Klima psistariá*, which turns out good, inexpensive grills. A wider range of food is available at the *Alexandros* taverna, which does special bargain meals for two.

Ássos

Ássos should not be missed, even if you have to visit it on one of the coach trips that swing through nearly every afternoon. The most atmospheric village on the island, it clings to a tiny isthmus leading to a huge fortified rock, which protects the pocket-sized harbour and pebbly beach. Ruined walls of pre-quake mansions surround the plane-shaded village square, dubbed "Paris" by villagers in honour of the French, who financed its reconstruction after the 1953 earthquakes. A path, zigzagging up through woodland and terraces, leads to the

△ ÁSSOS

ruins of the **Venetian fortress**, which itself contains the vestiges of three small churches, including the Catholic church of Áyios Márkos. Until 1815, part of the fortress was Kefalloniá's version of Alcatraz, a virtually inescapable prison whose foundations are visible today.

Unfortunately, Ássos is also one of the most difficult places on the island to get to, as there are no scheduled KTEL services that run right into the village. The buses that run between Argostóli and Fiskárdho do however stop at the Ássos turning if you ask, and the early afternoon bus from Argostóli sometimes will detour down to the village if it has school students to drop off. The 10am bus out of Argostóli and the 4.30pm schedule back from Fiskárdho make it possible to spend a few hours in Ássos if you allow time and energy for the walks down and up (about forty minutes and an hour respectively). Getting there on your own wheels is decidedly less dicey than it used to be now that the road has been resurfaced and widened, but care is still in order on the sharper hairpin bends.

Practicalities

Staying in Ássos is not easy, as much of the **accommodation** is block-booked throughout the season. The best place to start is ⚓ Andreas Rokos (☎26740/51 523; ❶), whose great-value rooms are on the right-hand side as you enter the village, with a telltale NTOG plaque outside – enquiries in the village are often directed to him, anyway. Almost directly opposite, the *Kanakis Apartments* (☎26740/51 631, ℗51 660; ❺) offer far more luxurious surroundings, while further down towards the bridge, the *Linardos Apartments* (☎26740/51 563, ⓦwww.linardosapartments.gr; ❸) are also pretty smart and rather less costly. Any of the harbour tavernas or shops may also be able to help with accommodation.

Ássos is cut off from the rest of Kefalloniá and charges accordingly. It has a small number of good but pricey **restaurants** on the waterfront, including *Nefeli*, famed for its Kefallonian meat pie, and the *Platanos Grill*, whose wide-ranging menu includes oven food, while the *Nirides* restaurant at the end of the quay has a lovely setting and offers mainly grilled meat and fish. The *Assos*, set a little way back from the front, offers an equally good range of tasty fare at much more reasonable prices. Meanwhile, the *Seaside* cafeteria is the spot for light refreshments. Apart from that, there are just a couple of shops for basics; fruit and vegetables can be bought from a small truck that stops in the village most afternoons. It's possible that staying for any length of time here might make you feel that you are living in a goldfish bowl, but Ássos lacks the development of somewhere like Fiskárdho, and in low season it can be truly idyllic.

Fiskárdho

Beyond Ássos, the road heads inland and the terrain begins to change. The northern tip of the island around **FISKÁRDHO** sits on a bed of limestone which buffered it against the worst effects of the 1953 earthquakes, and the coastline here is reminiscent of the tree-lined pebble coves of Paxí. Fiskárdho is the island's premier resort, a small fishing port built around a horseshoe bay lined with handsome old houses – most of them restaurants, bars or boutiques – with *kaïkia* and yachts moored at the quay. Day or night, the scene is picture-postcard pretty, its only drawback the lack of a beach other than one poor patch of shingle. After Sámi, Fiskárdho is Kefalloniá's busiest passenger port, with daily **ferry** connections to Itháki and Lefkádha.

Fiskárdho has an **upmarket** reputation, with prices to match, and its boutiques teeter on the edge of flat-out chi-chi; it even has its own website (Ⓦ www.fiskardo.com). As one restaurateur proudly boasts, "we attract mainly middle- and upper-class English people", which could either hasten your step

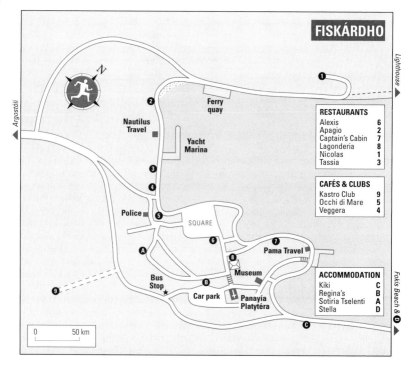

RESTAURANTS

Alexis	6
Apagio	2
Captain's Cabin	7
Lagonderia	8
Nicolas	1
Tassia	3

CAFÉS & CLUBS

Kastro Club	9
Occhi di Mare	5
Veggera	4

ACCOMMODATION

Kiki	C
Regina's	B
Sotiria Tselenti	A
Stella	D

or send you in the opposite direction. At night it's a very vibey place, even in low season, though it tends to be a little cliquey and some visitors find the atmosphere claustrophobic. Although the village remains small and development is fairly contained, it's also the busiest resort, and remains so up until the last days of October.

Accommodation

Much of the prime accommodation was snapped up years ago by blue-chip travel companies such as Greek Islands Club and Simply Ionian. However, the recent nationwide decline in visitor numbers has had an impact here too, pegging prices slightly and resulting in accommodation being available most times of the year. The best bargain for **private rooms** in Fiskárdho is through ⚒ *Sotiria Tselenti* at the bakery (☎26740/41 204, ⓦ www.fiskardo-ellis.gr; ❸), whose simple en-suites are a couple of blocks back from the square. *Regina's* (☎ & ⓕ26740/41 125; ❸), at the back of the village just beside the car park, has some basic rooms with shared baths and a pricier, smart new building. On the north side of the harbour, the large *Nicolas* taverna (☎26740/41 307; ❻) offers good, modern rooms, also away from the front and with the best views of the village, which explains the fact that their prices have escalated in recent years.

Around the bay and towards Fókis beach, there are a number of **apartment** buildings, many for three, four or more people: ⚒ *Kiki* (☎26740/41 208, ⓕ41 278; ❺) can offer studios and apartments with a pool overlooking a small beach; *Stella Apartments* (☎26740/41 211, ⓦ www.stella-apartments.gr; ❺) have kitchens and lounge/dining areas, and balconies with views of Lefkádha.

Pama Travel (☎26740/41 033, ⓦ www.pamatravel.com), on the southern quay opposite the lighthouses, is the main **travel agency**, which handles rooms in Fiskárdho, and also offers accommodation in Mazoukáta, a short walk or drive into the hills above the village. Nautilus Travel (☎26740/41 315, ⓕ41 470), further towards the ferry dock, also has rooms in Fiskárdho, as well as a wide range of services, including yacht charter, car and boat rental, ferry tickets, tours and excursions. Typical of the day-trips on offer are those by large motor cruiser to Itháki, Lefkádha and satellite islands for around €30, while motorboat hire is available on the quay from €65 per day.

The Village

The northern tip of Fiskárdho bay is guarded by the remains of a Venetian **lighthouse**, and above it on the headland are the crumbling ruins of what is believed to have been a Norman **church**. Arthur Foss, in his *The Ionian Islands*, speculates that the structure might be a relic of Norman invader Robert Guiscard's plans for a settlement here in the eleventh century. Guiscard, however, died of the plague a few weeks after arriving, and the settlement was probably abandoned, although the port derives its name from his. Below the church on the north shore of the bay, a Friends of the Ionian **nature trail**, reached through a low gate below the *Nicolas* taverna, runs through the shady woods, where you can bathe from the rocks. The trail can be followed with an FOI self-guide leaflet, available in the village shops or from the Simply Ionian office on the quay. The only church in Fiskárdho itself is the attractive Panayía Platytéra, reached by steps from various points on or behind the harbour. The plain, whitewashed building dates from the seventeenth century and was a monastery from 1676 to 1911. One of the icons inside, *The Birth of Christ*, dates from the monastery's inception.

Fiskárdho's only real tourist attraction is the **Environmental and Nautical Museum** (Mon–Sat in season 10am–2pm & 5–7pm; donations), which occupies one half of a grand Neoclassical mansion on a hill facing the sea, close to the church. Run entirely by volunteers, the museum has an interactive computer, a model of the island and interesting displays, shedding light on Kefallonian history, with an emphasis on shipping, sea life, the environment and pollution issues. **Scuba diving** can also be arranged here (☎26740/41 182, Ⓦ www.fnec.gr).

Beaches

There are two excellent pebble **beaches** within a few minutes' walk on either side of the village. To the north, **Emblísi**, signed down a turning off the main road into Fiskárdho, is a pleasant spot, with flat, white rocks for sunbathing and signs of discreet freelance camping. The Emblísi taverna near the turning above provides a standard range of food and drink. The only drawbacks are the humming electricity sub-station at the back of the beach, where the island's power line comes ashore, and a super-luxury hotel now nearing completion. On the other side, **Fókis** is set in a beautiful fjord-like cove ten minutes' walk south of the village, with plenty of olive-tree and tamarisk shade on the pretty patch of land just behind it. On the opposite side of the road, *To Foki* taverna is open until 7pm throughout the summer and serves a mixture of full meals and lighter snacks.

Eating and drinking

Carousing tends to end late in Fiskárdho, though it revolves more around long sessions outside the quayside restaurants and cafés than in youth-oriented clubs. *Kastro Club*, the sole disco, is mercifully located out of ears' reach 200m off the main road behind the village. Of the seafront **cafés**, *Veggera* and *Occhi di Mare*, both near the square, are the most popular. As usual, **restaurants** on the seafront are pricier and more touristy than those on the back streets.

Alexis Set in the small square behind the seafront, this taverna does chicken and other meats in a variety of sauces, plus pizzas and pastas, at competitive prices. It also has a cheap and quiet bar independent of the restaurant.

Apagio Expensive quayside taverna with a wide range of food, including such dishes as curry, in addition to Greek staples.

The Captain's Cabin Major waterside eating house, with Greek and Kefallonian specialities such as succulent *keftédhes* and a huge range of *mezédhes*. Fills up with British tourists and flotilla folk who stay till late.

Lagonderia Just south of the square. Specializes in grills but also cooks food in trays, home-style. Great *briám* and *spetsofái*.

Nicolas Alone on the north side of the bay, with a stunning night-time view of the village and occasional bouts of Greek dancing. Huge menu of fish, meat and vegetable dishes.

Tassia One of the largest and most expensive harbourfront tavernas. Enormous choice of fish, ranging from lobster and red mullet to fish in Kefallonian garlic sauce, squid and fish soup. Be sure to specify what weight of fish you want to avoid unexpected bill.

Around Fiskárdho

Kefalloniá's slim northern tip offers some interesting diversions away from the focal point of Fiskárdho. There are some **walks**, outlined below, as well as the administrative capital of the north, **Vassilikiádhes**, which can provide useful accommodation overspill. The west coast of the peninsula also hides some coves, which are among the least visited beaches on the island.

Walks from Fiskárdho

Fiskárdho sits at the knot of three pleasant **walks** along the lanes circling the limestone northern peninsula, with excellent sea views on either side of the

The **Ionian coastline**

With over a thousand kilometres of coastline, the Ionian islands are extremely well-endowed with great beaches and dramatic scenery. Indeed, as there are no major archeological sites, it is the idea of stretching out on a sun-soaked strand that draws more people to the archipelago than anything else – even though foreign sun worshippers descend in their hordes during summer, a little legwork can usually find you a secluded spot beside the lapping waves.

Pebble beach, Kefalloniá

From sand to stone

The surprising diversity in types of beach is mainly due to the variety of geological features. From the typical crescent-shaped **pebble coves** that punctuate the eastern coasts from Corfu to Zákynthos, to the grand **sweeps of sand** that can be found on the west coasts of Kefalloniá and Lefkádha, beaches can have a very different appearance. Some, like Longás in northwest Corfu, are backed by stunning **cliffs**, tinted with subtle hues of red in layer-cake formation, while others, like the long stretch around the Korissíon lagoon in southern Corfu, are largely backed by low-lying **dunes** and tufty grasses. **Caves**, menawhile, can be enjoyed as unusual swimming spots, either from boats or diving platforms such as on Andípaxi and Zákynthos.

Blue Flags of Europe

In 2005 the Ionians accounted for 45 of the 383 Greek beaches awarded with the prestigious EU Blue Flag, the lion's share of which went to Corfu with 31. Flags are awarded according to a range of criteria, including cleanliness of the sea and coast, organisation and safety, and the protection of nature and the environment. Samples are taken to check water quality and litter collection is monitored, as is the amount of information available to the public . If a beach passes muster, it gets to wave its flag prominently for a year, whereupon it must be tested again. Obviously, this system bypasses remote and really tiny beaches where few go, but it's encouraging to know that this is a matter the local authorities take seriously and that they are striving to provide a cleaner environment in their attempts to attain official approval.

Vatoúmi Bay, Andípaxi

Petani beach

Natural aspects

Greek beaches are often stark and nearly shadeless as the country is too dry to support much lush vegetation. Despite this, you will find some shelter from the sun under pine cover in the western and northern islands and rows of inviting tamarisk trees. Nature-lovers will find much appeal in Greece's coastal areas: hikers will be rewarded with a refreshing dip as part of a walk along a coastal route – the west coasts of all the larger islands offer dramatic views from the pine- and olive-tree clad clifftops down to the milky turquoise sea. Indeed, sections of the Corfu trail touch pristine beauty spots such as the Korission lagoon, home to migratory wading **birds**. Some Ionian beaches, especially Yerakás on Zákynthos, are also nesting grounds for the endangered loggerhead **turtle**, which should not be disturbed under any circumstances.

Resorts for all

Throughout the islands there are **family resorts** that fill up with Greeks in August, as well as foreign tourists throughout the season. These tend to be calm spots, chosen because the sand shelves gently into the water, making ideal swimming conditions for kids. Such places, like Kefalloniá's Skála, or the long stretch between Ródha and Almyrós on Corfu, have either grown out of tiny fishing villages or nothing at all into self-sufficient communities. They can, however, be a bit short on fun for small kids, aside from the occasional playground or bumper cars outfit. Other beach resorts, most notably notorious Kávos on Corfu and Laganás on Zákynthos, cater exclusively to young party animals, to whom nocturnal entertainment is as important as daytime sunbathing. Somewhere in between lie places like Sidhári on Corfu and Nydhrí on Lefkádha, where there is a mixture of age groups. All the above are largely the preserve of cheap package tourists, unlike the few **chic resorts** that attract yachting flotillas and the top-end villa dwellers. Chief among these is Fiskárdho on Kefalloniá, followed by Kióni on Itháki, Sývota on Lefkádha and pretty much the whole of Paxí.

Nude beaches and naturists

Although nudity is officially illegal almost everywhere in Greece, there are pockets where the practice has become a de facto reality that is tolerated by the locals and ignored, if not actually sanctioned, by the authorities. These spots are, unsurprisingly, usually in fairly isolated locations, such as beautiful Myrtiótissa on Corfu.

Mýrtos beach

The top ten Ionian beaches

Petaní, Kefanloniá A wide, wild, pebble beach with shady rock overhangs.
Longás, Corfu Firm sands tucked under dramatic red cliffs.
Yialós, Lefkádha Coarse-sand lapped by milky waves at this often deserted spot.
Vríka, Andípaxi This small sandy cove is perfect if you can catch it at a quiet time.
Vassilikí, Lefkádha The shallow waters of this sandy bay make for ideal windsurfing conditions.
Límni Kerioú, Zákynthos A pretty bay with just the right level of tourism.
Issos, Corfu One of the finest sandy stretches in the Ionians.
Mýrtos, Kefanloniá A sweeping arc of pebbly sand, carved out of the mountainous coast.
Shipwreck Bay, Zákynthos Stunning, photogenic place, only accessible by boat.
Áyios Nikítas, Lefkádha The fine beach is the icing on the cake at this picturesque fishing village resort.

Watersports

Activities like **inflatable-banana rides**, **water-skiing** and **parasailing** are almost ubiquitous at the busier spots, while Lefkádha's Vassilikí has achieved a worldwide reputation as a **windsurfing** haven. The popularity of **scuba-diving** is also on the rise at spots on most of the islands – Kassiópi on Corfu and Límni Kerioú on Zákynthos rank among the most highly rated locations. Small **motorboats** and **dinghies** can be rented on spec almost everywhere, though **yachting** requires a bit more planning and a certain level of expertise.

Reach your beach

Accessibility can vary enormously. All the resorts mentioned here, as well as the odd town like Sámi on Kefanloniá and some traditional villages, such as Kassiópi on Corfu and Lefkádha's Aï Nikítas, hand you decent beaches on a plate. Others can require a little effort, as they are a drive away or can be reached only on foot or by boat – Mýlos on Lefkádha or Shipwreck Bay on Zákynthos, for example – but these are often the most rewarding. It is also worth noting that contrary to what many hotels would have you believe by their fences and signs, national law clearly stipulates that all Greek land between the winter high tide mark and the water is **public domain** – though whether you want to risk anyone's ire by invoking your right to their self-declared corner of sand is another matter.

Blue caves, Zákynthos

promontory. The easiest, heading beyond Fókis beach, cuts up into the hills overlooking Itháki for 4km to **Mazoukáta**, which has a taverna and *kafenío*, before rejoining the main Argostóli–Fiskárdho road at Mánganos 1km further on. The second follows the same route to begin with, before veering south after 2km at the partly ruined village of **Tselendáta**, where there are some fine old stone buildings and the smart and spacious *Loula* rooms (☎26740/51 808 or 51 857; ❹), for groups of at least four; after another 2km you'll reach the dead-end hamlet of Evretí, which has great views across to both Itháki and Lefkádha, and is claimed to be the place where Penelope's suitors set their ambush for the returning Odysseus. The third heads northwest up the main road from Fiskárdho to **Mánganos** (5km), before veering off southwest to the villages of Agriliás (1km on) and Halikerí (2km on), above small coves on the west coast (see below). You'll reach the main road again at **Konidharáta** (3km on), where if you time it right you can catch a bus back to Fiskárdho; otherwise it's around 8km downhill on foot. Konidharáta also has good-value alternative accommodation in the shape of the *Donados Apartments* (☎26740/51 502; ❸).

Vassilikiádhes

Surprisingly perhaps, the seat of local government for Érisos, the northernmost municipality of Kefalloniá, is not Fiskárdho but the more mundane village of **VASSILIKIÁDHES**, some 10km to the south. The tiny town hall and other facilities straddle the main road and are mostly unappealing modern constructions, although there are some fine, traditional stone buildings dotted around the old village on the hill to the west. What the place does have to offer is a real sense of life in a functional island community, with its mixture of old and new customs, as opposed to the rather forced quaintness and downright commercialism of Fiskárdho.

It is also a viable alternative to Fiskárdho for **accommodation**, when all the rooms there have reached capacity. Of the several options, the brand-new *Nicolas Studios* (☎26740/51 231; ❸) and *St Ferentinos Studios* (☎26740/51 281; ❸) are both on the main road and recommended. For **eating** there are several choices: *Makis* grill, which also has rooms (☎26740/51 556; ❸), stands out with tasty meat dishes like rabbit and a range of salad and veggie options, while *Iy Enosis* offers pizza and pasta dishes and *Café Ektos* serves snacks.

Less than 1km away, the small village of **Mesovoúnia** – the name means "amidst mountains" – certainly has a lazy mountain feel, and a seat at *Iy Synandisi* café-snack bar or the old *kafenío* opposite is a good place to drink in the soporific atmosphere. The diminutive church of Ayía Paraskeví boasts a stylish pre-earthquake campanile.

The west coast

The northern section of Kefalloniá's **west coast** does not offer grand sweeping views like those around Ássos and Mýrtos, largely because the road does not run along the edge of such a precipitous drop, but it does conceal some charming seaside nooks and crannies, which can provide welcome relief from midsummer crowds. The access point is a turning off the main road at the village of Mánganos down through hedgerow-lined fields and past Agriliás, beyond which there are two appealing options.

The first turning, by the tiny settlement of Halikerí, leads down a reasonable track to **Alatiés**, where a tiny beach is tucked in between folds of impressive white volcanic rock. It has the advantage of being sheltered and safe for swimming even in quite rough weather, and you can pick your way across the rock, which turns to black on the seaward side, past drying salt-pools (hence the name), to the exhilarating point where the waves crash in, sending plumes of foam high into the air and misty spray into the faces of onlookers. The *Alaties* café-restaurant offers traditional fare like *soutzoúkia* and pastas.

Alternatively, you can continue south from Halikerí and follow the road as it winds down to the larger bay of **Ayía Ierousalím**. Although less scenic, the gravel and sand beach here is wider, the sea shallower and you may have the place to yourself even in August, although it would seem to be only a matter of time before it becomes more popular. Currently, there are no land phone lines, and the only development is the extremely friendly ⚓ *Odisseas* **taverna** (mobile ☎6937/714 982; ➊), which has inexpensive rooms and allows camping in its spacious grounds, charging only a small fee for the use of facilities. The family cooks exquisite and very unusual olive bread and other baked goodies, and all the meat is free range, another rarity.

Travel details

Buses

Argostóli to: Ayía Efimía (Mon–Sat 1 daily; 1hr); Áyios Yerásimos (Mon–Sat 3 daily, 1 on Sun; 30min); Athens (4 daily; 7hr); Fiskárdho (Mon–Sat 2 daily; 1hr 45min); Kateliós (Mon–Sat 3 daily; 50min); Kourkomeláta (Mon–Sat 3 daily; 25min); Lássi (10 daily; 10min); Pessádha (Mon–Sat 2 daily; 30min); Platýs Yialós (10 daily; 15min); Póros (Mon–Sat 2 daily; 1hr); Sámi (Mon–Sat 4 daily; 45min); Skála (Mon–Sat 2 daily; 1hr).

Lixoúri to: Ayía Efimía (Mon–Sat 1 daily; 50min); Athens (2 daily; 8hr); Sámi (Mon–Sat 1 daily; 1hr); Xi beach (Mon–Sat 2 daily; 15min).

Póros to: Argostóli (Mon–Sat 3–4 daily; 1hr); Athens (1 daily; 6hr); Kateliós (Mon–Sat 3 daily; 45min); Skála (Mon–Sat 4 daily; 30min).

Sámi to: Argostóli (Mon–Sat 3–4 daily; 45min); Athens (2 daily; 6hr); Fiskárdho, via Ayía Efimía (Mon–Sat 2 daily; 1hr).

Note that all these services are for summer and may be reduced during other months. Currently, the only Sunday services are the Argostóli–Lássi route and those coming from the mainland. A summer timetable in English is available at the Argostóli KTEL and with some travel agents.

Ferries

Argostóli to: Kyllíni (1 daily; 1hr 45min); Lixoúri (every 30min, hourly in winter; 30min).

Fiskárdho to: Fríkes, Itháki (1 daily; 1hr); Nydhrí, Lefkádha (1 daily; 2hr 15min); Vassilikí, Lefkádha (3 daily; 1hr).

Pessádha to: Áyios Nikólaos, Zákynthos (2 daily in summer; 1hr 30min).

Póros to: Kyllíni (3–6 daily; 1hr 15min).

Sámi to: Astakós (2 daily; 2–3hr 30min); Corfu Town (2 weekly in summer; 4–5hr); Pátra (1–2 daily; 2hr 30min); Pisaetós, Itháki (3 daily; 40min); Vathý, Itháki (2 daily; 1hr 15min).

The summer services listed are reduced out of season. Connections to the mainland remain much the same off season, while those to other islands should retain at least one daily service, except where stated.

Flights

Kefallínia airport to: Athens (1–3 daily; 1hr).

Zákynthos

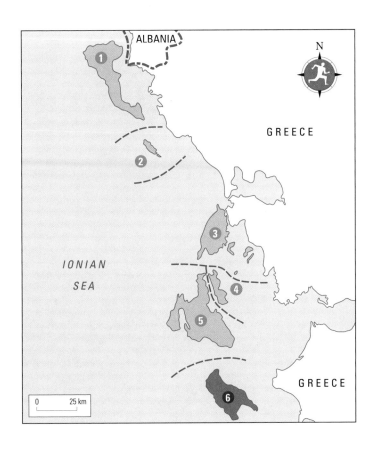

CHAPTER 6 # Highlights

✳ **Platía Solomoú, Zákynthos Town** The capital's huge main square oozes class and contains several important cultural buildings. **See p.237**

✳ **Kandádhes and arékia** Listen to the two forms of traditional Zakynthian music in one of the tavernas in the capital. **See p.238**

✳ **Áyios Dhionýsios church, Zákynthos Town** The vast church dedicated to the island's patron saint is decorated with colourful murals and has a fascinating

museum in its grounds. **See p.240**

✳ **Vassilikós peninsula** The numerous beaches dotted around this peninsula are ideal for exploring on a rented two-wheeler. **See p.245**

✳ **Kambí** The tavernas in this tiny clifftop village are the ideal spot to enjoy a stunning sunset. **See p.255**

✳ **Shipwreck Bay** Whether you take a boat trip or admire it from the cliffs above, this photogenic, isolated beach is not to be missed. **See p.256**

△ Zákynthos Town

Zákynthos

hird largest of the Ionian islands after Kefalloniá and Corfu, **Zákynthos** has three distinct landscapes: the deserted, mountainous north and west coasts, the undulating central plain – where the green, rolling hills and red-roofed hamlets resemble parts of Tuscany – and the extremely busy southern coasts, which approach the worst of Hellenic tourist excess. But even in the south, large areas of the interior are untouched by commerce. Indeed, while **Laganás** is among the most commercialized resorts in the entire archipelago, a few kilometres away there are ancient hill villages as pristine as any to be found on Lefkádha or Kefalloniá.

Two things have shaped modern-day Zákynthos: an **earthquake** and an airport. This area of the Ionian Sea is a site of fairly constant seismic activity (see box on p.203), most of it minor and largely indiscernible. However, on August 9, 1953, an earthquake comparable to that of 1989 in San Francisco hit the region at midday. Two hundred died on Zákynthos, thousands were seriously injured, and in some rural areas whole communities were wiped out. The force was such that an estimated seventy percent of buildings on the island were destroyed. Zákynthos Town, which had won the nickname of "Venice of the South" for its elegant architecture, was further damaged by fires that spread from wood- and gas-burning stoves and raged for ten days; contemporary photographs in the Zákynthos Museum show the town's streets heaped up like waves.

After the earthquake, Zákynthos had to rebuild itself from the ground up, and Zákynthos Town has become a pleasant place in which to stay once again. But many villages had to be abandoned and rebuilt away from the quake ruins. One curious consequence of this relates to the island's **maps**, insofar as few places now stand where they were originally built. Village names are now officially held to refer to "areas" rather than specific places, but the disorientation is only increased by haphazard road signs (anyone planning trips on the island should bear this in mind, as some older maps imply a settlement where the visitor will find only beach or forest).

The earthquake also left Zákynthos clear to rebuild itself for the tourism boom, which in the last twenty years has taken hold of parts of the island with a vengeance. Thanks to the presence of the busiest international **airport** in the Ionian islands outside Corfu, over 300,000 Britons alone are likely to visit the island in any one year – that's ten times the indigenous population of roughly 30,000 (and this is without mentioning the Italian, Dutch, German and Scandinavian tourists). So huge an influx of visitors has given rise to unspoken cultural tensions, but many islanders are still profiting from the building explosion that continues to engulf the southeast and much of the central plain as well, even though the seasonal invasion has shrunk slightly in recent years.

ZÁKYNTHOS

Cape Skinári

Shipwreck Bay

Áyios Yióryios Ton Kremnon

Anafonítria

Volímes

Mount Astéri (583m)

Askós

Blue Caves

Pessádha (Kefaloniá)

Áyios Nikólaos

Pórto Vrómi

Anafonítria

Skinári

Makrýs Yialós

Orthoniés

Xygiá

Stenítis Bay

Mariés

Alykón Bay

N

Alykés

Kambí

Éxo Hóra

Katastári

Mount Vrahiónas (756m)

Alikanás

Loúha

Pigadhákia

Yíri

Ammoúdhi

Yerakári

Yerakári

Dhrosiá

Áyios Léon

Ayía Marína

Tragáki

Kypséli

Pahýs Ámmos

Pórto Limniónas

Mount Athéras

Kilioméno

Tsiliví

Plános

Maherádho

Vanáto

Kástro

Akrotíri

Bóhali

ZÁKYNTHOS

Megálo Vounó

Kyllíni

Laganás

Argási

Kerí

Limní Kerioú

Áyios Sóstis

Kalamáki

Mount Kakavakia (413m)

Marathiá Caves

Marathoníssi

Mount Skopós (492m)

Kamínia

Dháfni

Pórto Zóro

Áno Vassilikós

Peloúzo

VASSILIKÓS PENINSULA

Banana

Áyios Nikólaos

Yérakas

Pórto Róma

0   5 km

The reason why much of Zákynthos remains relatively unspoilt lies in a combination of its geography, infrastructure and the way tourism has developed. The party resort of Laganás and its more subdued neighbour, **Kalamáki**, as well as eastern resorts such as **Tsiliví**, are all fairly self-contained. The local bus system is poor outside the main resorts and – combined with some of the most hair-raising driving in Greece – doesn't encourage mobility among visitors. Some of the beaches aren't served by public transport at all and don't even have a taverna or a beach bar, but **Áyios Nikólaos** on the Vassilikós peninsula has cleverly launched its own free bus service, luring tourists away from other resorts. Thankfully, exquisite **Yérakas** beach is served by buses from the capital but the coves beyond Tsiliví and in the northeast are not.

Independent travellers who take the time to find accommodation away from the busy southern end of the island will be well rewarded by finer scenery as well as more peace and quiet around the less-developed coastal areas and the lush interior. Since the time of the Venetian invasion of the fourteenth century, olive trees have been a conspicuous feature of the island's landscape. The main agricultural produce of Zákynthos, however, has traditionally been **raisins**, to which, at the peak of the industry in the eighteenth century, two-thirds of the island's cultivated land was devoted, creating fortunes for its aristocracy. The central plains are still blanketed in a stunning canopy of vineyards, stretching for miles in all directions, contrasting sharply with the abysmal concrete suburbs of workshops and factories you have to pass on the way to them. Some local **wines**, such as the white Popolaro, Calliniga or Solomos, compare with the best in the archipelago, and Zákynthos produces its own brand of the sticky, white *mandoláto* **nougat**, commonly sweetened with sugar but also available in its superior honey-sweetened variant. The best local **cheese** is the pungent *grapéria*, which may be a little too strong for some northern palates; *ladhotýri* is another favourite.

The island has in effect two springs: early in the year, and again between October and November, when autumn rains revive cyclamen, irises, lilies and wild orchids. The Venetians, for whom the island's name was **Zante**, also dubbed it *fior di Levante*, "flower of the Levant", because of its luxurious vegetation. Even today islanders sometimes use the name "Zante", at least when addressing foreigners.

Some history

Zákynthos was first settled by Achaeans from what is now the northern Peloponnese in the Mesolithic era (12,000–3000 BC), and earned a brief mention in the *Odyssey*: Homer refers to "woody Zákynthos" and includes twenty young men from the island among the small army of doomed suitors who proposed marriage to Penelope. Zakynthians fought alongside the Athenians in the Peloponnesian War (431–404 BC), but the island was subsequently overrun by the victorious Spartans, who were themselves supplanted by successive waves of invading Macedonians and Romans. The Byzantine empire, heir to Rome's eastern provinces, retained its hold on the region until the twelfth century.

Finally, in 1185, Zákynthos and neighbouring Kefalloniá broke away to form a semi-independent palatinate, to be ruled by a succession of regional aristocrats sanctioned by Rome. In a complex game of regional politics, the islands frequently changed hands between Rome, Venice, Naples and Ioánnina, capital of the northern mainland region of Epirus. After years of skirmishes, the Turks took the region in 1479, but were expelled by the Venetians in 1485. One local history describes the Turkish onslaught on Zákynthos as a "holocaust". Few islanders survived, and the Venetians began a campaign of settlement.

A taste of Olympic spirit

If your whole stay in Greece is on Zákynthos or a combination of Ionian islands and you are contemplating one visit to the mainland, then the most obvious and interesting choice from here is a trip to the site of **ancient Olympia** in the Peloponnese. Even the least classically minded person is aware that the Olympic Games were born in Greece, and their original home is up there with Delphi and Mycenae as some of the most moving and atmospheric remnants of the country's ancient heritage. For well over a millennium the **Panhellenic Games** were held at the sanctuary, and it is well known that a truce was called in all conflicts for their duration. Since the modern games were revived and first held in Athens in 1896, it has been the custom to rekindle the Olympic flame here every four years to be carried to each new venue in turn. During the Athens Olympics of 2004 it was brought back into use as the venue for the discus competition.

The setting of the site is remarkably beautiful: a luxuriant valley of wild olive and plane trees, spread beside the twin rivers of Alfiós (Alpheus) and Kládhios, and overlooked by the pine-covered hill of Krónos. The site itself (daily: May to Oct 8am–7pm; Nov to April 8am–5pm, Sat & Sun 8.30am–3pm; €6, or €9 combined with museum) is a little jumbled and leaves a lot to the imagination. The games were originally held in the **Altis**, along whose walls you enter the site. On the right are the remains of the **Gymnasium** and **Palaestra** (Wrestling School), where the competitors were obliged to train for a month before the contests. Other impressive structures are the **Theokoleion** (Priests' House), a colonnaded building whose southeast corner was later converted into a Byzantine church, and the **Leonidaion**, a large hostel for important festival guests, but the most important edifices were the two principal temples: the great Doric **Temple of Zeus**, built between 470 and 456 BC, was almost as large as the Parthenon, while the earlier **Temple of Hera** behind it is the most complete building on the site, with thirty-odd columns surviving to some extent, along with parts of its inner wall. The remains and foundations of numerous lesser structures are dotted around.

Pride of place for most visitors, however, goes to the huge **stadium**, where the competitions were held as the games expanded. You enter through a long arched tunnel at the back of the site to the confines of the 200m track, surrounded by seating ridges, now grassed over, where the 20,000 spectators used to sit. The starting and finishing lines and judges' thrones are still there. Many awed visitors can't resist doing a lap or at least a length in the hope of being rewarded with a makeshift laurel leaf by their travelling companions. Behind the southern slope is the site of the **Hippodrome**, where the chariot races were held.

The **Archeological Museum** (May–Oct Mon noon–7.30pm, Tues–Sun 8am–7.30pm; Nov–April Mon 10.30am–5pm, Tues–Sun 8.30am–5pm; €6 or €9 combined with site), some 200m to the north of the site across the road, is also not to be

---

Under Venetian rule, Zákynthos expanded beyond the port to establish settlements elsewhere on the island. The Venetians imported their own stratified social system, with the names of the nobility inscribed in the *Libro d'Oro* (Golden Book), which became the social register of Zákynthos society and a despised symbol of privilege and power. This caste system created great wealth for Zákynthos's dynasties, but was clearly hated by the impoverished majority, who staged an uprising in 1628 that was bloodily put down by the Venetians. When the latter were finally unseated by the French in 1797, the *Libro d'Oro* was burnt by jubilant crowds in Platía Ayíou Márkou, though just one year later the French themselves were ousted by a Russian–Turkish alliance; and in 1800 these two powers signed a treaty to establish the Eptánissos (Seven Islands) state of the Ionian islands. The new constitution still favoured the island's elite, however, and the Zakynthians once again

missed. It contains some of the finest Classical sculpture in existence, both Greek and Roman, all superbly displayed. The two most famous pieces are the **head of Hera** and the **Hermes of Praxiteles**, both dating from the fourth century BC and found in the Temple of Hera. There are many other fine sculptures and objects in bronze and terracotta, as well as finds from the workshop of **Pheidias**. The centrepiece, however, occupying the grand central hall, is a brilliantly reassembled set of statuary and sculpture from the Temple of Zeus. This includes a frieze of the **Twelve Labours of Hercules**, the east pediment of Zeus presiding over a **chariot race** and the **Battle of Lapiths and Centaurs** from the west pediment. Other rooms display objects connected with the games. For more detailed descriptions of the site and museum, see the *Rough Guide to Greece*.

The modern village of **Olympía** has grown up to service the excavations and has no real character. It does, however, have an abundance of **accommodation** to put up transient visitors, and competition keeps prices low. The *Hercules* (☎26240/22 696; ③), by the church and school off the main street, and *Achilles* (☎26240/22 562; ②) are typical of the small, functional hotels available. There is also an average Youth Hostel (☎26240/22 580, ☎23 125; dorm €9) and three campsites, of which the closest is *Diana* (March–Nov; ☎26240/ 22 314, ☎22 425), one kilometre from the site, with a pool and good facilities. **Food** is equally easy to come by, as most hotels have a restaurant and there is a plethora of independent tavernas, all bashing out the usual Greek staples at mildly inflated prices for the Peloponnese. For a more authentic meal in a lovely, leafy setting, try the *Kladhios* taverna, 2km outside the village on the banks of the Kládhios river. There is a **tourist office** (Mon–Sat: May–Oct 9am–3pm; Nov–April 11am–5pm; ☎26240/23 100), on the right of Praxitéles Kondhýli, as you come into town from Pýrgos. Olympía has three **banks**, all with ATMs, on the main avenue, and a **post office** just uphill.

Reaching Olympía from Zákynthos by public transport is a little convoluted, and an overnight stay is really required. You will first have to catch the ferry from Zákynthos Town to Kyllíni and then take a bus up to the national road, to connect with another one coming down to Pýrgos; from Pýrgos to Olympía there are five trains a day on the refurbished branch line and hourly buses, both taking around forty minutes. Otherwise, you could make the trip in a rented car, but the ferry crossing is not especially cheap and you should first check with your rental agency that the vehicle is allowed off the island. Not surprisingly, most people go for the easy option of an **organized day-trip**. Tours run at least twice a week in summer and can be booked at agencies all over the island from around €25 per head. Check what is included in the way of site/museum entry, guides or lunch. These bus tours usually leave on the first ferry and return on the last, making quite a tiring day of it, but at least you get a reasonable amount of time amid the ancient glories.

rebelled, raising the Union Jack on the Venetian fort as an appeal to the new trading power now beginning to dominate the Mediterranean. In 1807, the island was briefly handed to the French again, but in 1809 the British finally did take Zákynthos. The island remained a British protectorate until the archipelago was ceded to Greece in 1864. Zákynthos was overrun by the Italians and then by the Germans in World War II, though it didn't suffer as badly as neighbouring Kefalloniá.

Arrival and Information

Most visitors arrive at the island **airport**, equidistant from Laganás and Kalamáki in Kólpos Laganá (Laganás Bay) on the southern coast. It has recently been enlarged and improved, so waiting is more comfortable, although there is still a shortage of seating and no facilities beyond a snack bar, gift shop and several car rental outlets. There's no dedicated bus service from here, although the Laganás–Zákynthos Town bus does pass the bottom of the road leading away from the airport at least once an hour. Taxis into Zákynthos Town or to Laganás cost an expensive €6; it is possible to haggle, but the drivers know you're pretty stuck without them. The only alternative is to walk: either to Zákynthos Town, 5km or so to the north, or to Laganás, 4km south.

Ferries from the mainland port of Kyllíni, the main year-round point of access, arrive at **Zákynthos Town**. Oddly, there is no year-round ferry connection between Zákynthos Town itself and the rest of the Ionian islands to the north, except via Kyllíni/Pátra. In summer a twice-daily ferry sails between Pessádha on Kefalloniá and the port of **Áyios Nikólaos** in the north of Zákynthos (not to be confused with the beach complex of the same name in the south), but unfortunately there is no longer any bus connection from there to Zákynthos Town.

For further information, take a look at ⓦ **www.zakynthos.com.gr** (a practical travel directory, full of hotel booking links and news on eating and drinking on the island) and ⓦ **www.zanteweb.gr**, an easily navigable and comprehensive site of both practical and cultural interest.

Local transport

The island's skeletal **bus** system radiates out from Zákynthos Town to serve the larger resorts and some outlying villages, but little else. The KTEL bus station is on Filitá, one block back from the seafront, and buses usually run on time, though the timetable is subject to change without notice. A printed timetable is available for peak season and is reliable.

There are **taxi stands** in Zákynthos Town and some of the larger resorts; taxis also cruise the smaller resorts when they're in the area (but tend to disappear during the siesta). You could try phoning for a taxi (see p.242) but this of course incurs the standard extra charge.

Zákynthos Town and around

Zákynthos Town is a small, busy working port that has made few concessions to tourism. But it is the only sensible place to base yourself in if you want to explore the island by public transport, and it is certainly more authentic than the resorts. Its principal squares are grand, and its back streets quite interesting to meander in. There are sufficient places to stay, eat and drink for visitors, as well as a number of museums and historic buildings – notably the **Kástro** that towers above the town.

The downside to the town is that its seafront restaurants and bars give onto a busy main road, Lombárdhou (also known as the Strada Marina), and are prone to its noise and fumes. A further drawback to this part of Zákynthos Town is its one-way system, which has the novel effect of speeding up the traffic. After school and in the evenings bored teens sometimes race each other on bikes and mopeds around the town centre until late, which can give even the smartest of restaurants the ambience of a racetrack. The best advice for those seeking reasonable accommodation or a decent meal is to head north beyond Platía Solomoú.

There is no tourist office in Zákynthos Town or indeed elsewhere on the island, but the **tourist police** (☎26950/24 482–3), housed within the main police station on the seafront, offer brochures, maps and a limited amount of information, if pressed gently. Hotels and travel businesses can also help with

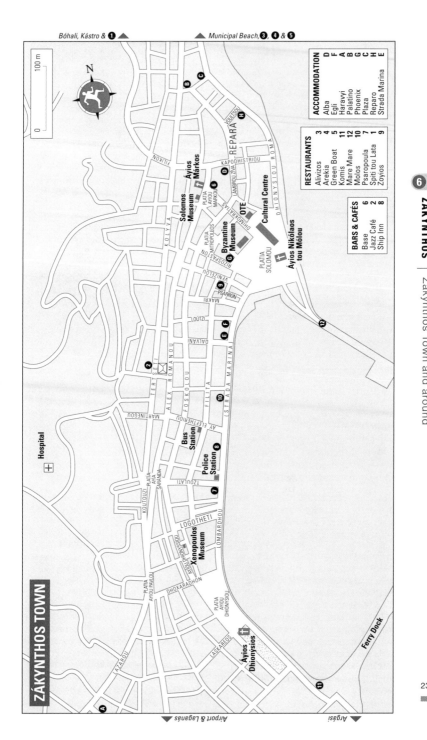

ZÁKYNTHOS TOWN

100 m

0

N

Hospital

Áyios Márkos

Solomos Museum

Byzantine Museum

Cultural Centre

OTE

Áyios Nikólaos tou Mólou

PLATIA SOLOMOU

Bus Station

Police Station

Xenopoulos Museum

Áyios Dhionysios

ACCOMMODATION
Alba	D
Egli	F
Haravyi	A
Palatino	B
Phoenix	G
Plaza	C
Reparo	H
Strada Marina	E

RESTAURANTS
Alivizos	3
Arekia	4
Green Boat	5
Komis	11
Mare Mare	12
Molos	10
Psaropoula	7
Spiti tou Lata	1
Zoyios	9

BARS & CAFÉS
Base	6
Jazz Café	2
Ship Inn	8

Ferry Duck

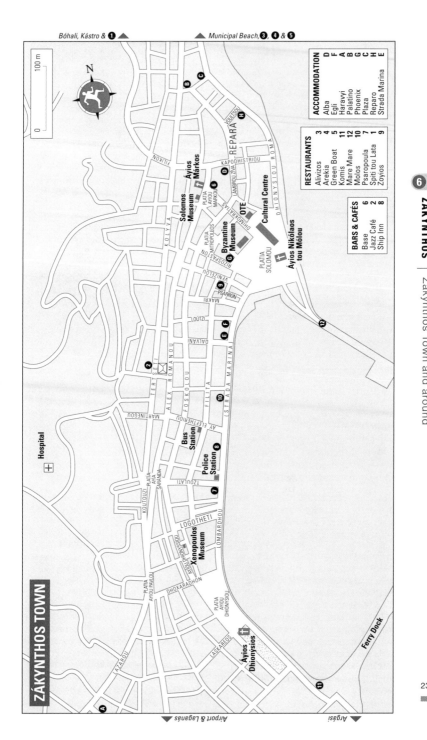

REPARÁ

KOMISSI

KAPODHISTRIOU

DHIONYSIOU ROMA

LAMBROU ZIVA

DHIMITRATAS

PLATIA AYIOU MARKOU

PLATIA MITROPOLEOS

RIZOSPASTON

VENIZELOU

PSARRON

MAKRI

LOÚTZI

DALIVANI

TERSETI

ALEX ROMANOU

FOSKOLOU

FILITA

ISTRADA MARINA

MARTINEGOU

KOLYVA

TILIXON

AY ELEFTHERIOU

TZOULATI

PLATIA AYIA SARANDA

KOUTOUZI

LOGOTHETI

LOMBARDHOU

DHOXARADHON

AYIOU DHIONISSIOU

PLATIA AYIOU PAVLOU

LAZAROU

LASKAREOS

PLATIA AYIOU DHIONYSIOU

Boat and bus tours

At least ten **boats** circumnavigate the island daily in season, visiting spots such as the otherwise inaccessible **Blue Caves** and **Shipwreck Bay**; all depart from Zákynthos Town's quayside in the morning. The going rate is around €15, depending on the season. You can pay on board or in the offices along the quay; tickets are also sold by agencies at outlying resorts, which arrange transport into town to join the cruises. One of the best is the modern MV Pelargos, which visits six coastal sites, though the classiest vessel has to be the wooden Dias, which has the advantage for non-swimmers of being able to edge right into the main Blue Cave. The boat trips make much of the Blue Caves at Cape Skinári on the northernmost tip of the island, but not all trips actually take you into them – and those that do often employ outboard dinghies, involving a precarious transfer from the main vessel. It is wise to check this and the exact number of stops the boat is going to make; also ensure the one you pick is going to complete the full circuit. Cruises to the neighbouring islands of Kefaloniá and Itháki run most days in season and prices start at around €25.

There are also full-day **bus tours** of the island, usually including monasteries, Shipwreck Bay, and the embroidery centre of Volímes, costing around €14. Some tours round off with a sunset dinner at Kambí. Tours across to Olýmbia in the Peloponnese (see p.233) usually depart on Wed & Fri and cost €30–35. You can find out about all tours at any of the Travel Agents listed on p.242.

information, and usually have free advert-packed maps to supplement the superior ones on sale in the shops.

Accommodation

There is a limited range of **hotels** on the seafront road, which are convenient if you arrive late but hardly cheap. Other than that, the only real cheapie left is the *Haravyi*, up in the back end of town. Anyone planning to stay more than a day or so and willing to pay a little more is advised to head for the relatively quiet district of Repára, just beyond Platía Solomoú.

Most of the town's hotels stay open year-round. Rented **rooms** in Zákynthos Town are sparsely dotted about and difficult to find so the best bet is to contact the Roomowners Association (☏26950/49 498).

Alba Lámbrou Zíva 38 ☏26950/26 641, Ⓦwww .albahotel.gr. Buffet breakfast included in this small, new hotel, with smartly decorated and cosy rooms, all a/c with TV. ❺

Egli corner of Loútzi & Lombárdhou ☏26950/28 317. Tucked in at the side of the plush *Strada Marina*, a traditional, family hotel offering the same views as its smarter neighbour. All rooms with en-suite bathrooms, balconies and sea view. ❹

🏃 **Haravyi** Xanthopoúlou 4 ☏26950/23 629 or 42 778. Quaint little pension opposite the *Omonia* with small, comfy, en-suite rooms. ❷

🏃 **Palatino** Kolokotróni 10, at corner with Kolyva ☏26950/27 780, Ⓦwww .palatinohotel.gr. Surprisingly good-value and trendy hotel with startling purple lights outside and modern rooms within. Snazzy bar, TV, a/c. ❹

Phoenix Platía Solomoú ☏26950/42 419, Ⓦwww.zantephoenix.gr. Nicely appointed rooms in a fairly luxurious hotel, tucked in a relatively quiet corner of the main square. ❺

Plaza Kolokotróni 2 ☏26950/45 733, Ⓕ48 909. Small hotel in the Repára area with en-suite bathrooms and balconies, some with sea views. ❺

Reparo corner of Dhionysíou Róma & Voúltsou ☏26950/23 578 Ⓕ45 617. A friendly and modern, purpose-built hotel, which has undergone an upgrade in quality and price. All rooms are en suite, with balconies and some with sea views. ❻

Strada Marina Lombárdhou, at the Platía Solomoú end ☏26950/42 761–3, Ⓦwww.stradamarina.gr. The largest establishment in town, dominating the seafront: a/c and TV in the rooms, 24-hr restaurant, bar, coffee shop and a rooftop pool and restaurant. Wheelchair access. ❻

The Town

The obvious first port of call in Zákynthos Town is **Platía Solomoú**, which was named after the island's most famous son, **Dhionysios Solomos**. This vast marble-flagstoned square is impressive both by virtue of being the largest in the Ionians and due to the imposing nature of the buildings that surround it. Chief among these are the cultural centre, built on the site of the destroyed opera house designed by Ziller, which doubles as a cinema; the Library (daily 8.30am–1.30pm), which features an interesting display of photographs of old Zákynthos; and the huge Byzantine Museum (see below).

Museums

Zákynthos Town's two oldest museums are close to each other in Platía Solomoú and nearby Platía Ayíou Márkou. The gargantuan **Byzantine Museum** (Tues–Sun 8am–2.30pm; €3), sometimes referred to as the Zákynthos Museum, concentrates mostly on works from that period and has a splendid collection of art rescued from churches destroyed in the seismic calamity of 1953. On display here are examples of the Ionian School of painting (see box on p.81), though they are not as good as those in the churches of Lefkádha Town. Chiefly influenced by painters of the Renaissance, the school flourished on Zákynthos in the seventeenth and eighteenth centuries, and was noted for a distinctly realist approach to its religious subject matter. Saints and other figures are represented in workaday settings and in distinctly earthbound form, far removed from the sunbursts and wings beloved of earlier religious imagery. There are also works by earlier and later religious and secular artists. Apart from icons and framed

---

The Ionian School of poetry

The Ionian School of poetry is less of a coherent school than that of painting (see box on p.81), in the sense that it had no distinctly unified style or philosophy. Rather it is a tradition of Heptanesian bards, whose writings are intrinsically linked with the blossoming of Greek thought that accompanied independence.

The first and foremost of these bards was **Dhionysios Solomos** (1798–1857), the so-called Dante of Zante; born in Zákynthos in 1798 and regarded as the father of modern Greek literature, he lived the last thirty years of his life in Corfu. A firm belief in the freedom of man's spirit underpinned all his writings, and his *Hymn to Liberty* was adopted as the words to the Greek national anthem. He was also a great champion of the demotic language, and established it as a literary medium. His fellow Zakynthian, **Andhreas Kalvos** (1792–1869), also leant heavily on the independence struggle for inspiration, but his twenty *Odes* were written in the purist literary Greek known as *katharévoussa* rather than the demotic.

Probably the second most important nineteenth-century Ionian poet was **Aristotelis Valaoritis** (1824–79) from Lefkádha, who was also an active parliamentarian. Many of his patriotic poems are modelled on demotic klephtic songs (named after the *Klephts*, Greece's hill bandits). Lesser lights in the same school were **Yerasimos Markoras** (1826–1911) from Kefalloniá, and two Ithacans, learned classicist **Lorenzo Mavilis** (1860–1912) and, more recently, leftist freedom fighter **Nikolaos Karvounis** (1880–1946). Finally, one of Greece's most highly rated poets of the twentieth century was **Angelos Sikelianos** (1884–1951) from Lefkádha. His lyrical work is firmly grounded in the demotic tradition of the previous century, but contains more contemporary philosophical preoccupations. His mammoth *Prologue to Life* adds a mystical touch to a synthesis of folkloric, naturalistic and religious themes, while his later works display a passionate belief in the beauty and harmony of the world, expressed in clear, incisive language.

paintings, there are some fantastic iconostases (altar screens) on the ground floor, while the first floor contains fragments of carved marble slabs from medieval churches and a complete re-creation of the interior fresco designs from Áyios Andhréas in the town of Volímes. Perhaps the two most moving exhibits, however, back on the ground floor, are the intricate model of Zákynthos Town before the catastrophic earthquake and the accompanying giant photograph of the aftermath.

The **Solomós Museum** (daily 9am–2pm; €3) on Platía Ayíou Márkou is dedicated not only to Dhionysios Solomos, but also to other prominent Zakynthians and has recently been extended to display more exhibits. One upstairs room is devoted solely to Solomos and contains some of the poet's effects and manuscripts (many other items remain in Corfu, where he spent most of his working life). By the museum entrance there is what is said to be part of the tree under which he sat and composed the *Hymn to Liberty*. His bones rest in a casket on the ground floor alongside those of his wife, and those of the island's second most famous poet, Andhreas Kalvos. A long hall on the upper floor contains numerous portraits of noted Zakynthians, among them Kalvos and another acclaimed poet, Ugo Foscolo.

The third museum in the centre of town is the newly created and municipally run **Xenopoulos Museum** (Mon–Fri 9am–2pm; free), on tiny Odhós Gaïta, not far from Áyios Dhionýsios church. It is dedicated to the celebrated novelist and playwright Grigoris Xenopoulos, whose works span the first half of the twentieth century and are renowned for their pointed portrayal of the burgeoning educated middle class lifestyle of independent modern Greece during that period, both in Athens and provincial capitals. Among his most revered novels, the *Red Rock* stands out, while *Countess Valerena's Secret* is one of his most popular plays. The museum constitutes the Xenopoulos family house, which was renovated and opened by the mayor in November 1998. Exhibits include the author's personal effects, manuscripts, documents, rare editions of his books and periodicals to which he contributed, photographs and furniture. There are also articles belonging to his daughter, Efthalia and her sculptor husband, Khristoforos Natsios.

The other museum worth a visit, especially for old salts, is the **Maritime Museum** (daily 9am–2pm & 6–9pm; €2.50), some way out of town on the

---

Kandádhes and arékia

Venetian influence is notable not only in the architecture of Zákynthos Town, but also in two popular song forms unique to the Ionians. The Zákynthos opera house may have disappeared in the 1953 earthquakes, never to be replaced, but a hybrid of Italian *bel canto* and Greek folk styles, imported by a wave of refugees who fled Crete following the Cretan War of 1669, survives to this day. The two dominant forms of this hybrid are **kandádhes** and **arékia**, quite distinct from the traditional, eastern-tinged *syrtáki* or *rebétika* "blues" heard in other parts of Greece. Kandádhes display a more direct lineage from light operatic ballads, sung in trios and quartets, predominantly male (although women do join in), and often romantic or comic. Arékia tend to be quieter, more reflective, sometimes sung by a single voice, and often take the more traditional form of love ballads or a lament for family or home. Both can be heard in more traditional tavernas in Zákynthos Town (*Alivizos* and, best of all, *Arekia*), Bóhali (*Panorama*), Laganás (*Zougras*) and elsewhere. Local variants, songs invented for specific festivals and family events such as weddings, can also be heard during celebrations in hill villages such as Kerí and Katastári. It's a difficult music to find in recorded form, although authentic recordings of traditional songs by Zakynthian composer Dimitris Layios are available in many shops in town.

road up to the Kástro. It contains a fairly comprehensive maritime history of Greece, covering all the main eras from ancient times to the twentieth century. You are confronted by a bewildering hotchpotch of model vessels (from triremes to hydrofoils), shields, flags, knots, medals, costumes, books, paintings, armoury and equipment. Some of the labelling is in Greek only, but there is enough to hold the attention of the most committed landlubber for a while, even if some of the best exhibits have been spirited away to a new rival museum in Tsiliví (see p.242).

Churches

Few of the town's **churches** survived the 1953 earthquake. **Áyios Nikólaos tou Mólou** (St Nicholas of the Quay), a former fishermen's chapel at the edge of Platía Solomoú, is the only one to have been renovated after the quake using

△ Áyios Nikólaos church tower

its original stones (though the interior was restructured using modern materials). Inside are the vestments of the island's saint, Dhionýsios, patron saint of fishermen, who preached here in the sixteenth century.

More spectacular is the church of **Áyios Dhionysios** itself (daily 7am–1pm & 5–10pm), at the other end of the seafront to Platía Solomoú, lit at night like a fairground ride. Built of concrete in 1948, with a bell-tower modelled on St Mark's in Venice, it survived the earthquake more or less intact. Strangely, the church is formally consecrated as a monastery, so weddings, baptisms and funerals are not permitted to be held here. It contains some remarkable icons of the saint's life, as well as a magnificent sculpted silver coffin containing his relics. Recent years have seen the completion of colourful frescoes around the interior – the one depicting Creation on the back wall to the right of the entrance is particularly vivid. The marble mosaic floors are also dazzling. On the upper level of the adjacent building, you can visit the church's small **museum** (daily 9am–1pm & 5–9pm; €2), which houses some fine paintings and icons, as well as Orthodox robes and paraphernalia.

Áyios Márkos, on the square of the same name, near the Solomós Museum, is the only Catholic church on the island. It is relatively plain, both inside and out, though a large and striking painting of St Mark receiving the gospel hangs above the white marble altar. The dark, ominous painting of a very male-looking Ayía Paraskeví is another highlight.

The Kástro

Zákynthos Town's only major historic site is the **Kástro** (daily: summer 8am–7.30pm, winter 8am–2pm; €1.50), a huge, ruined Venetian fortress to the north of town, sited on a bluff which was a defensive enclave from the Byzantine era onwards. Little of the original structure remains beyond a few minor outbuildings (mostly from the seventeenth century), some foundations and ruins of the massive walls, but it is a remarkable piece of stone engineering, with stunning views in almost every direction. The keep, long since overgrown by firs, now has the air of a small, walled forest. It's an ideal spot for a picnic, or a quiet afternoon, in the shade on the scented green carpet of fallen needles.

Less than an hour's walk from the centre of Zákynthos Town (or a short taxi drive), on the edge of the small hamlet of **Bóhali**, the fortress makes for a pleasant excursion. Just be warned that there are no public facilities, beyond one taverna and several cafés in Bóhali; and that the *Kástro* is occasionally inundated with coach parties. If you make it up here, it is also worth visiting the old church of **Zoödhóhou Piyís**, just down the hill in Bóhali, for its vibrant frescoes and icons. The principal icon of Mary as Panayía tis Zoödhóhou Piyís (Holy Mother of the Life-giving Spring) was rescued from Constantinople before its fall in 1453.

Eating and drinking

Zákynthos Town is the best place for **eating** on the island, although that isn't saying much. Travellers on a budget can snack in the cheap *psistariés, estiatória* and takeaways on and around Alex. Románou and Konstandínou. The seafront tavernas offer reasonable fare, but the smartest restaurants are in elegant Platía Ayíou Márkou, along with a couple of seriously hip and ferociously expensive music bars. The best food, however, is to be found at the trio of tavernas along the shady sea road fifteen to twenty minutes' walk north along Dhionysíou Róma beyond Platía Solomoú.

Alívizos Dhionyssíou Róma. The first taverna along the sea road north to Akrotíri offers a wide range of sophisticated staples and is very popular with Zakynthians. Open later in season and, unusually, during the siesta. Live music most evenings.

🏃 **Arekia** Dhionyssíou Róma. If you eat only one meal in Zákynthos Town, eat it here. This small, family run taverna performs miracles with traditional dishes: succulent meat and fish, mouthwatering meatballs and small *tyropittákia* to die for. Patronised almost solely by Zakynthians, who throng here for its nightly free *kandádhes* and *arékia* sessions (from 10pm). Open evenings only; go early at weekends.

Green Boat Dhionyssíou Róma. Past the first two places in this list, this fish taverna offers excellent-value *pikilíes*, plus the usual main courses, and seating right beside the water.

Komis On quay near Áyios Dhionýsios. Expensive and subtly decorated taverna serving an imagina-tive range of quality fish, seafood – try the sea urchins – and salads.

Mare Mare Halfway along the quay nearest to Platía Solomoú, this smart restaurant and bar in a two-storeyed wooden building has a wide selection of Greek and international cuisine. Expensive but popular for its fine harbour view.

Molos Lombárdhou 26. One of the most reasonable seafront tavernas offering full meals and snacks, but the pavement seating suffers from noise.

Psaropoúla Next to the police station on Lombárd-hou. The best of the main seafront eating houses. Excellent meat and fish, including good value *pikilíes*, a range of veggie dishes and fine barrelled wine.

To Spíti tou Lata Bóhali. The sole survivor of the tavernas up by the *kástro* serves specialities like smoked trout and *pantséta* at fair prices, plus all the usual *mezédhes*.

O Zoyíos Psárron 9. Great little *estiatório* serving tasty home-cooking, mostly in trays. Some pave-ment seating.

Nightlife

The hub of **nightlife** in Zákynthos is Platía Ayíou Márkou – the most expensive place to eat or drink in town, though competition and a couple of lean years have kept prices within the bounds of reason. A favourite with local and visiting youth is *Base*, at the corner of the square, a bar which usually has a DJ playing anything from dance imports to Miles Davis or Philip Glass. The *Jazz Café* on Tertséti may have the same name as the famous London jazz venue, but is actually a small and friendly disco-bar with a small cover charge and house/techno DJ. More sedate and appealing to rock fans is the *Ship Inn* on the seafront. Clubbers, however, head for the larger nightspots on the road to Argási (see p.244).

Listings

Banks and exchange Most of the main regional Greek banks are on Konstandínou, and all have ATMs; other machines are dotted elsewhere. Otherwise, travel agencies and larger hotels will exchange travellers' cheques for a commission. The Ergo Bank represents Western Union; there is no American Express representation on Zákynthos.

Beaches The only beach in Zákynthos Town is the municipal pebble strand ten minutes' walk north beyond Platía Solomoú, which has changing rooms, toilets and showers. Entry is free if you don't use the sunbeds or umbrellas. The taverna-bar *Asteria* further along also has bathing facilities for its customers. Otherwise, the nearest beaches are south at Argási and north at Tsiliví.

Bike and car rental Euro Sky at Makrí 6a (☎26950/26 278) and Sakis at Dhimokratías 5 (☎26950/23 928) rent cars and scooters at standard rates. For two-wheelers, you'll probably get the best deal at Spiros on the seafront at Lombárdhou 20 ☎26950/23 963.

Cinema In winter the theatre of the cultural centre often shows films. In summer there is an open-air cinema at the back of the municipal beach.

Hospital Above town on the continuation of Marteláou and Martinégou (☎26950/22 514–5). The outpatients and casualty departments regularly deal with tourists.

Internet Full Internet facilities are available for €4 per hour at Ayíou Dhionyssíou 18, a couple of blocks back from the police station.

Laundry There's a tiny old-fashioned *plindírio* tucked away on Ayíou Tavoulári at the far end from the seafront, between Platía Ayíou Pávlou and Platía Ayíon Saránda.

Olympic Airlines Alex. Románou 16
℡ 26950/28 611; airport ℡ 26950/28 322,
Ⓦ www.olympicairlines.com.
Taxis Taxi ranks on Platía Solomoú and corner of
Lombárdhou and Dalváni; also available by phone
℡ 26950/48 400, 23 623 or 24 036.
Travel Agents A number of travel agents line
Lombárdhou. By far the best of the bunch is Smart

Travel (℡ 26950/24 430–1, Ⓕ 24 365), followed by
Spring Tours (℡ 26950/48 004 or 41 746, Ⓦ www
.springtours.gr); both offer a range of cruises
and day-trips, plus all the other standard tourist
services.
Vice-consulate UK; Vicky Vitsou Kotsoni,
Fóskolou 5 ℡ & Ⓕ 26950/22 906 (Mon–Fri
8am–1pm).

Around Zákynthos Town

As the number of visitors grows, more and more accommodation appears, with new mini-resorts springing up along Zákynthos's **east coast** wherever enterprising businesspeople can bulldoze a path down to something that might pass muster as a beach. Here, as on the other Ionian islands, the east coast is green, fairly flat and protected from the open sea to the west. The beaches here are sometimes prone to oil and tar pollution, but despite this, they are safe and the water's usually fairly clean, although often at the mercy of prevailing north-westerly winds, which increase in strength in the afternoon. To the north of Zákynthos Town, villas and apartments block-booked by British tour operators make up the bulk of accommodation, especially around **Tsiliví** and **Plános**, although the new mini-resorts mentioned above tend to have more room for independent travellers. This area – on an island not noted for good walking – is also a good bet for some relatively quiet walking among small hill hamlets of **Yerakári** and **Tragáki**. The main resort on the coast just south of Zákynthos Town is **Argási**, the most mundane of the island's package destinations.

North via Akrotíri

The coast road that extends north from Zákynthos Town past the municipal beach soon becomes very attractive, once it has emerged from the drab suburbs. As it is not too busy, the 2km or so up to the small hamlet of **Akrotíri** can make for a fine walk, and it is certainly worth driving this way if you have your own transport. The road winds up beside some rocky coast to the hamlet, nestling above Cape Kryonéri with its lighthouse. There is not much here, apart from an excellent garden taverna, *To Akrotiri*, which serves up tasty grills and starters such as cheese balls and courgette pie. On a pine-clad, hairpin bend at the highest point, the *Hotel Balcony* (℡ 26950/26 179, ebalcony@zakynthos-net.gr; ④) commands an amazing view north and east and has an expanding number of rooms; its terrace café does snacks and is a great spot to admire the coastal vista. From here the road snakes down to the more commercialized coastal plain around Tsiliví.

Tsiliví and Plános

Five kilometres north of Zákynthos Town, **TSILIVÍ** is the first real resort on this coastline, with a number of good sandy beaches offering watersports. It has now merged with the inland village of Plános, whose centre is nearly 1km back from the beach, to make a lively resort that is starting to attract more youngsters, though it is still way behind Laganás and even Argási. Still, there seems little reason to stay here, although it might make a short-term base if you want to explore the northern half of the central plain, which starts west of here.

Just north of Plános, a block behind the *Mediterranee* hotel, lies the **Milanio Maritime Museum** (daily 9.30am–2pm & 6–9.30pm; €2.50), opened in 2001. The museum houses many sea-themed paintings by the owner and a host of model ships and other nautical trappings, most of which used to be on display in the older museum at Bóhali (see p.240). Perhaps the most interesting exhibit is equipment from the Greek naval ship *Leon*, formerly the *USS Eldridge*, which reputedly took part in the infamous "time-warping" Philadelphia Experiment of 1944, in which the ship was supposedly made invisible and teleported from Philadelphia to Norfolk Virginia. The ship itself is currently in the hands of a Pireás scrap-metal company.

Accommodation options by the sea in Tsiliví include the smart, compact *Neraida* (☏26950/63 051, ✉neraidas@otenet.gr; ❸), the plusher and more spacious *Christy's Apartments* (☏26950/48 890 or 44 586, ⓦwww .zantechristysbeach.gr; ❻), which are air conditioned, have TV and accommodate at least four people, or the simpler *Dimitra* rooms (☏26950/49 238; ❷). Among the handful of restaurants, *Moby Dick* does curries as well as Greek food, and *Iakinthos* is a huge beachside taverna serving snacks or full meals, while the *Mango Club* provides light refreshments, and you can catch up on your football at the outer bar of the *Millenium Club* disco.

Most places to stay are in **PLÁNOS**, ranging from good, purpose-built **rooms** – try *Gregory's* (☏26950/61 853; ❸) or *Dolphin* (☏26950/27 425; ❸) – to smarter **hotels** such as the huge *Mediterranee* (☏26950/26 100–4, ⓕ45 464; ❹), on the road north, which has a range of en-suite rooms, a restaurant, a pool and a fifty-room luxury wing. Beds can also be found through Tsilivi Travel (☏26950/44 194, ✉akis-125@otenet.gr) on the main road into Plános, and there's a good basic **campsite**, *Zante Camping* (☏26950/61 710, ⓕ63 030), 1km further on from Plános, beyond the tiny Boúka harbour, above the beach and away from any other settlements. An indication of the increasing tourist presence is the fact that there are now no fewer than three Chinese restaurants; *Passage to India* also serves reasonable Indian food. Otherwise it's the usual pot-pourri of plastic Greek tavernas, such as the *Majestic*, with a vast, partially covered courtyard. *The Olive Tree* is the oldest taverna and one of the most upmarket, serving dishes like mussels à la chef and pork in a coriander-and-red-wine marinade. There are plenty of **bars**: *Escape to Paradise* is a popular joint in the centre with features like karaoke, while on the north side are the *Red Lion Pub,* a Brit-style boozer, and the *Enigma Club*, a disco with a big screen for sports in its outdoor area. Internet facilities are available at Megabyte Internet Café (€4 per hour).

The coast beyond Tsiliví

The coast running northwest from Tsiliví conceals a number of beaches, usually a varying admixture of sand and pebbles, which are slowly being developed for tourism. They generally become more low-key the further you go until you reach the distinctive kink in the coastline that shelters the busier resort of Alykés.

First up, and only a short stroll from Plános, is **Boúka** beach, a quiet but nondescript strand, harbouring the *Old Village Taverna* just inland, the *Abra Cat Abra* beach bar and a few room enterprises such as *Adamantia Studios* (☏26950/27 396; ❹), back on the road. More appealing swimming spots are to be found a few kilometres further along. One such is **Pahýs Ámmos** – the name means "thick sand", despite the beach comprising flat stones – at the end of some verdant lanes, full of vineyards and vegetable-packed greenhouses. At the beach itself is the fine *Porto Roulis psarotavérna*, while further back along the lanes there is accommodation in the shape of the good-value *Pension Petra* (☏26950/62 140; ❷) and the more upmarket *Hotel Tsamis-Zante* (☏26950/62 962, ⓦwww.tsamis-zante.com; ❻). Contiguous with Pahýs Ámmos but reached by a different access road, **Dhrosiá** has a bit more sand and similar level of development; both the *Avouras* (☎26950/61 716; ❷) and *Drosia* (☎26950/62 256, ⓕ62 679; ❸) apartments are bright and breezy, and sustenance is available at the *Andreas* fish taverna or *Poseidon* beach bar.

A little further on, and within easy reach of the inland hamlets of Yerakári (see below), is the beach of the same name, though some signs refer to it as Psaroú. This lovely sandy stretch is perhaps the finest along this section of coast, with shallow water and relatively few visitors, though the *Psarou* taverna deserves custom for its good-value fish, meat and well-prepared salads and dips. There is not much else in the way of facilities, but only 300m back from the coast is one of the island's better campsites, *Paradise Camping* (☎26950/61 888), hidden in thick tree cover. Almost adjacent is the tiny, burgeoning resort of **Ammoúdhi**, which has a couple of tavernas, such as the old-style *Tasos*, shops, and the *Last Resort* and *Camelot* bars. The place is starting to attract package groups and has some expensive studios as well as the more reasonable *Ruassi* (☎26950/62 613 or 61 405; ❸) and *Oasis* (☎26950/44 166 or 62 847; ❹) apartments, adjacent to each other on the northwest side. From here the next coastal resorts are at Alikanás and Alykés, covered in the northeast section.

Yerakári and Tragáki

Inland from these beach resorts is a network of tiny villages that are well worth exploring on foot or bicycle. Zákynthos Town's hellish traffic dies away at Vanáto, and northwest of here lie some beautiful, traditional hamlets where tourism has barely begun to intrude. Particularly recommended are the **YERAKÁRI** "trio", 10km from Zákynthos Town and within a fifteen-minute walk of each other: hilltop **Áno** (Upper) **Yerakári**, whose Italianate campanile is visible from miles around and where great views are to be had from *O Lofos* taverna; neighbouring **Méso** (Middle) **Yerakári**; and **Káto** (Lower) **Yerakári**, where you can go horse-riding for around €20 per hour with Yianni's Horses (☎26950/62 121). Three winding kilometres to the east, off a minor road towards Plános, is **TRAGÁKI**, which boasts some surviving pre-earthquake architecture (a detailed leaflet describing a historical trail around the village is available in local shops). It's a working village with houses round courtyards, a still-functioning olive press, an ancient well and, on the outskirts, ruins of Venetian houses. Apart from a friendly *kafenío*, and two shops supplying villagers' needs, it makes absolutely no concessions to tourism.

Meanwhile, just off the road between Plános and Tragáki, the modern Avouri Amphitheatre hosts concerts and plays three times a week in summer – watch for ads or ask in Zákynthos Town. A couple of kilometres north of Tragáki is **Kypséli**, another lovely hilltop village, crowned by the attractive church of Ayía Paraskeví. A drink at the incongruously hip *Konaki* café can prove most welcome if you are walking the area.

Argási

Argási, 4km southeast of Zákynthos Town, is the closest large resort to the island capital, with hotel complexes now climbing the lower slopes of Mount Skopós. Commercialization is rampant, evidenced by the number of places advertising karaoke or Greek Nights. The beach, however, is skimpy – in parts no more than a few metres wide – and there's little of note in the village beyond a once-ruined church, now rebuilt of concrete, and, hidden away near the beach (just behind the *Life's a Beach* snack bar), a tiny but beautiful Venetian chapel. All the facilities are spread along the coast road and the thoroughfare that branches off at the main T-junction.

There is little reason to base yourself here unless you're on a cheap package or want to spend time exploring the Vassilikós peninsula to the south and yet be near the clubs at night. **Rooms** can be had at *Pension Vaso* (☎26950/44 599 or 44 207; ➋) on the main road from Zákynthos Town entering the village, and nearby *Soula* (☎26950/44 864; ➋), about 100m inland – turn off the main road opposite the church with the startling orange-and cream-coloured campanile. The seafront sports some sizeable hotels, such as the *Locanda* (☎26950/45 386 or 45 563, ℉23 769; ➎) and the larger *Iliessa Beach* (☎26950/45 345, ⓦwww .iliessa.com; ➍); both have en-suite rooms, some with sea views, as well as pools and gardens overlooking the beach.

Eating out in Argási is an indifferent affair; in fact you'd be better off heading into Zákynthos Town in the evening. The noble exception is the classy *Venetsiana*, set in a garden on the southern edge of the resort, which combines good traditional food with nightly performances of *kandádhes*. Other than that, the *Three Brothers*, which specializes in fish, is preferable to most of the main road tavernas, which serve a bland mix of Greek and international food, while, on the main side street, the *Big Plate* can offer some good vegetarian alternatives. For a complete change of scene, there's a Chinese, the *Courser*, down an alley near the T-junction in the centre of town, or the Indo-Chinese *Asia Palace* on the main road.

Argási is also home to the island's main **dance clubs**, most of which line the road in from Zákynthos Town, sporting hilarious facades that would not look out of place in Disneyland: *Vivlos* and *Barrage* are typical of these, while the *Manhattan Club* is up the hill behind them and the *Koutsis* live music club is on the southern side of the resort; entry is normally free, with prices reflected in drinks, and things rarely get going before midnight. There is no shortage of smaller bars in Argási itself, with names such as *The Wreck*, *Kiss* and *Magic Mushrooms* reflecting the attempt to create an air of decadence.

Argási is the main point of access for **Mount Skopós**, via a signposted path leaving the coast road at the first hairpin bend out of town to the south. It's a long day's hike to the summit and back, over some fairly rough terrain, and the view of the mainland and Kefsalloniá to the north, while spectacular, can sometimes be misty.

The Vassilikós peninsula

The **Vassilikós peninsula**, stretching southeast of Zákynthos Town, is the most beautiful part of the island, with untouched countryside and forest, the island's two best beaches and, for early risers, great sunrises over the Peloponnese. Most tourism in the area is through island-based companies or overseas villa companies such as Simply Ionian, and often dependent on rented transport: the KTEL **bus** from Zákynthos Town visits four times a day and there is also a free, daily, private bus from Laganás to Áyios Nikólaos in the south of the peninsula. There's usually a taverna or two within walking distance of most accommodation, but otherwise you're pretty much stranded – which makes it perfect for those seeking peace and seclusion, but not so great for those who crave company or amenities.

To add to the sense of isolation, Vassilikós, in the wake of the 1953 earth-quakes, is the most confusingly named area on the island. Officially, the name Vassilikós applies to the whole fourteen-kilometre peninsula to the southeast of Argási; the name dervies from a single village, Áno Vassilikós, located halfway down the peninsula. However, different maps of the island attribute the name Vassilikós to various hamlets on the peninsula, and haphazard road signs only add to the confusion.

Kamínia Beach and Pórto Zóro

The road south from Argási rises up through the foothills of Mount Skopós, passing, after about 2km, the *Agnadi* taverna – with great views – before a signposted turn-off for the first swimming spot on the peninsula, newly-created **KAMÍNIA BEACH**, still not marked on most maps. A wide asphalt road leads down to the small but pretty beach, slightly wider than Argási's, and backed by two adjacent accommodation possibilities: both are fine, though the friendly *Levantino Rooms* (☎26950/35 366, ⓦwww.levantino.gr; ❹) is more welcoming than the marginally plusher *Villa Fiore* (☎26950/35 204 or 35 468; ❹), whose restaurant turns out grilled and oven items. Both establishments have bars and currently allow free use of their umbrellas and sun-beds to patrons. There is also a volleyball net unusually set up *in* the gradually shelving sea.

About 3km further along from the Kamínia turning, another recently upgraded road winds down to **PÓRTO ZÓRO**. This is the first really picturesque beach on the peninsula: clean and sandy, with a fair amount of flora, although it gets pretty busy. There's a canteen and a **taverna**-cum-bar, the 🍴 *Porto Zoro* (☎26950/35 304, ⓦwww.portozorro.gr; ❸), with simple but modern **rooms** overlooking the beach, which makes Zóro an excellent place to chill out for a while. The jazz and Latin vibes played at the painstakingly landscaped *Azurro* snack-bar add to the chill factor.

Before the Pórto Zóro turning, a newly surfaced road inland leads up and over the peninsula, to the only two beaches before Yérakas on its **west side**, Sekánia and Dháfni, the latter being the more popular of the two, with the *Velouzo* snack bar and *Mela Beach* taverna, good for inexpensive fish. Neither cove is particularly spectacular though, and they both attract more crowds than you might expect. On the opposite side of the coast road from the turning to Dháfni, another road leads down to missable Voudherí beach, between Kamínia and Pórto Zóro, where the awkward rocky entry into the water is enough to deter most swimmers.

Áno Vassilikós and beaches

Back on the main road, you soon reach the small hamlet of **ÁNO VASSI-LIKÓS**, which straggles along the road above a small beach, part sand, part pebble, with deposits of sea grass. A lane running inland as you enter the settlement leads to the new **Nemoroza Folklore Museum** (summer only, daily 10am–2pm & 4–6pm; €3), where the modest collection of pre-quake photos, everyday tools and miscellaneous artefacts hardly justifies the entrance fee. The increasing number of **rooms**, shops, bars and restaurants in Áno Vassilikós constitute the only real development on the peninsula that is not down at sea level. If you want to stay, try cosy *Villa Anna* (☎26950/35 316; ❷), the somewhat larger *Vassilikos Apartments* (☎26950/35 280; ❸), or *Angelika* rooms (☎26950/35 201 or 35 221; ❷).

Among the **tavernas**, *O Gallos*, as the name suggests, provides French dishes like rabbit *gibelotte* as well as Greek cuisine, while *Dioskouri* is a more traditional, family-run place with good prices on their tasty starters such as potato croquettes. There's even an inexpensive Chinese place, named *Dynasty*, which only opens in the evenings, as does *O Aderfos tou Kosta*, a popular garden taverna with a range of succulent meat dishes plus fish and numerous veggie options, round the next bend south. A little further on, the *Logos Rock Club* lives up to its name by providing the rockiest soundtrack on the whole peninsula.

Just to the south is the longest and one of the most commercialized beaches in this part of the island, with umbrellas stretching almost all the way down to Aýios Nikólaos. There are two separate access roads, the first signposted to **Iónio Beach**; at this end of the wide strand there is the *Porto Ionion* taverna and the lushly landscaped apartment complex of Nikos Tsirikos (☎26950/35 497; ❸). The whole beach is more commonly (and mystifyingly) known as **Banana**, which is how it is signposted at the next turning. The beach has dunes and a firm, though very narrow, strip of sand. There's nowhere to stay at this southern end, but refreshment is provided by several beach bars, including the suitably laid-back *Relax* and *Kahlua*. No Fear watersports offers the usual range of marine activities.

Áyios Nikólaos

About 3km from Áno Vassilikós, **ÁYIOS NIKÓLAOS** boasts the most attractive beach on this side of the peninsula: a small stretch of sand cleft in the middle by a rock outcrop crowned with a bar. The resort is set in a rocky, almost desert-like landscape in a remote area of the peninsula, and at first sight may appear to be little more than a single complex: the ⚓*Vasilikos Beach* (☎26950/35 325–8, ⓦwww.hotelvasilikosbeach.gr; ❺), a large, modern, three-storey **hotel** set back from the beach, with restaurant, pool and bar. The enterprising hotel encourages people to come and use its beach facilities (umbrellas, watersports, scuba diving etc) by putting on a free **bus service** that connects with Laganás, Kalamáki and Argási a couple of times a day. Other accommodation options include two very modern **apartment** developments with all mod cons, the great-value *Christina* (☎26950/39 474; ❷) and *Virginia* (☎26950/35 315; ❸). Among the few village **eateries**, the *Familia* stands out for its extensive dinner menu and particularly good omelettes for breakfast. Down by the sea, the *Plaka Beach* is a reasonable fish taverna, which also does things like sausage and lamb *kléftiko*, while party-goers can boogie at the *Ammos Beach Club* by day or night. On the southern outskirts of the village, *Logothetis Farm* (☎26950/35 106, ⓦwww .logothetisfarm.gr; ❺) offers horse-riding (daily 8am–11am & 6–8pm) and has some secluded cottages for rent.

Pórto Róma and Yérakas

What some maps call Vassilikós village is in fact a barely inhabited junction in the middle of nowhere, where the bus from Zákynthos Town stops and turns. Here you'll find several tavernas, houses and villas scattered in the lush, almost jungle-like surrounding countryside. Minor roads lead off to Pórto Róma on the left and Yérakas beach on the right.

The small cove of **Pórto Róma** shelters a sand-and-pebble beach (which occasionally suffers from oil pollution), a bar and a taverna of the same name on the cliff above, but little else. There are, however, a fair few enterprises, mostly **apartments** on or just off the road down: *Katerina* (☎26950/35 456, ⓦwww.villakaterina.com; ❸), off the main road, is closest to the sea; English-run *Mimi's Apartments* (☎ & 🖷26950/35 007, ⓔmimis1@otenet .gr; ❸) has good-value modern units on the road that branches off to the north; and 1km back from the sea, the *Panorama* (☎26950/35 055, ⓔpanoramazante@mycosmos.gr; ❺) has modern studios arranged round a jacuzzi, pool and a Net Café (€5 per hour). Finally, the *Vlahos* is a simple taverna with a wide selection of wholesome traditional food, about 500m back from the beach. From the tiny harbour the Marios glass-bottom boat runs daily turtle-spotting cruises in the summer months (10am–1pm €33; 9.30am–4pm €39).

Far preferable, however, is **Yérakas**, the island's finest beach, a long, lazy crescent of golden sand and shallow waters protected from the open sea and prevailing winds by low sandy cliffs. A turtle-breeding ground (see box opposite), the beach heaves during the day in high summer, but is off limits between dusk and dawn; off-season, Yérakas is a stunning haven. An interesting **Turtle Info Centre** (Ⓦ www.earthseasky.org) with a number of colourful displays occupies an open-air booth on the road towards the car park at the back of the beach. There are also three tavernas on the road: *Gerakas* has live music in the evening, though *To Triodi* is better for its fine grilled and baked dishes, and there's one small snack bar on the sand, but as yet no other facilities. It is possible, however, to **stay** quite near the beach, and thus have it almost to yourself between curfew and crowds: *Liuba Holiday Houses* (Ⓣ26950/36 029 or 35 313, Ⓕ35 481; ❹) has a field of small and basic self-catering cabins a few minutes' walk from Yérakas.

Laganás Bay

Laganás Bay is the first glimpse of Zákynthos most tourists get from a jet coming in to land at the island's airport. **Laganás** itself is the largest single resort on the island, and the most popular, with the facilities, and problems, to match. Even in the last knockings of the season in late October, when Zákynthos can sometimes still be baking hot, Laganás continues partying around the clock while other island resorts are closing down. This is *not* a place to come for a quiet break or an early night. Its neighbouring resort to the east, **Kalamáki**, gives onto a superior section of the same beach and is much less developed – though not necessarily quieter, owing to the proximity of the airport.

At nearly 9km, the beach in Laganás Bay is the longest on the island and, in spite of the crowds, one of the best. It has slightly muddy sand (firm enough for vehicles), and the sea is shallow and clear – though usually busy with bathers and pleasure craft at the Laganás end. The beach between Laganás and Kalamáki is one of the biggest breeding grounds for the **loggerhead sea turtle** in Greece, part of a designated National Marine Park, where a number of strict rules are enforced (see box opposite). The presence of wheel tracks and used condoms on the beach suggests that not everybody is getting the message, though.

There are three **islands** in Laganás Bay, none of them inhabited and only two accessible. Boat trips to **Marathoníssi**, the largest, run every few hours from stalls on the beach (€4 per person). The island has a small sandy beach, part of which is a turtle breeding ground (so don't disturb any sticks you see protruding from the sand), and offers an escape from the crowds of Laganás – though it's sometimes exposed to prevailing winds and has absolutely no facilities. **Áyios Sóstis**, a diminutive rock islet near the main beach, houses the *Cameo* discotheque, has a small pebbly beach and can be reached by a rickety wooden walkway a few hundred metres to the south of Laganás. The third island, **Peloúzo**, near the Vassilikós peninsula, is simply a large rock.

Loggerhead sea turtles

One night in September 1995, a bomb went off in the offices of Zákynthos architect, Nikos Lykouresis, a founder of the Zakynthian Ecological Movement. No one was hurt, but the attack, believed to have been carried out by opponents of the ecology movement, took the tension between conservationists and businesspeople to a new high, though also proved to be a turning point. The subject of the tension was the **loggerhead sea turtle**, *Caretta caretta*, which breeds on two of the main beaches on Zákynthos and elsewhere on the island besides. The turtles are an endangered species, and this is one of their largest breeding grounds in Europe.

The tensions had begun in the early 1980s, just when the tourism boom was taking off. Environmentalists started a campaign to protect the turtle breeding grounds where, from May to October, the females come ashore at night to lay their eggs, bury them in the sand and return to the sea. The hatchlings usually emerge at night, burrow out and head for the water.

Environmentalists were worried about the detrimental effect of local businesses – bars and tavernas setting out tables and chairs on the sand, the sunbed franchises planting bayonet umbrellas in the sand, the watersports companies whose propellers might prove a threat to the slow-moving animals and the discos and bars whose noise and lights might deter the females from laying and disorient the hatchlings.

The two factions, represented on one side by a coalition of ecological groups – the World Wildlife Fund, Sea Turtle Protection Society of Greece, the Zakynthian Ecological Movement and Friends of the Ionians – and by local businesses on the other, battled for several more years after the bomb incident over proposals to make Laganás Bay, the main breeding ground, a protected area. Finally the ecologists won the day and on December 1, 1999, Laganás Bay was officially declared the **National Marine Park of Zákynthos** (㉅ www.nmp-zak.org).

Naturally, the bay has not been cleared completely of businesses or umbrellas and tourism in Laganás largely goes on as usual, but certain strict guidelines have been laid down, particularly regarding boat activity: no boats are allowed on the Vassilikós peninsula side of the bay, there is a strict 10kph speed limit throughout the rest of it and boats are only allowed to drop anchor down towards Límni Kerioú. In addition, there is a night-time curfew on the beaches and a limit on the number of umbrellas and areas within which they can be placed. Greece being Greece, however, the statute book is one thing, the practical reality quite another. The Greek authorities have already been hauled before the European Court for failing to implement the protective measures, so the jury is still out as to how effective they can be in saving the rare turtle.

Paradoxically, Greek tourism operators have discovered that a little anthropomorphism actually helps business, and the loggerhead has been pressed into the service of the merchandising industry: bars, restaurants, hotels and shops all borrow the name and image, and you can carry a memento of the imperilled reptile home on T-shirts, tea towels, paperweights, jewellery boxes, wall hangings, posters, matchboxes, decorative magnets and snowstorm shakers. It's possible that the animal itself might eventually die out, only to live on as a fridge magnet.

There are a few simple things you can do to avoid disturbing the turtles' breeding habits. The World Wildlife Fund has issued the following list of **guidelines** for visitors:
1. Don't use the beaches of Laganás and Yérakas between sunset and sunrise.
2. Don't stick umbrellas in the sand in the marked nesting zones.
3. Take your rubbish away with you – it can obstruct the turtles.
4. Don't use lights near the beach at night – they can disturb the turtles.
5. Don't take any vehicle onto the protected beaches.
6. Don't dig up turtle nests – it's illegal.
7. Don't pick up the hatchlings or carry them to the water, as it's vital to their development that they reach the sea on their own.
8. Don't use speedboats in Laganás Bay – a 10kph speed limit is in force.

Laganás

Prior to the arrival of tourism, **LAGANÁS** was little more than a small hamlet near the mouth of a stream emptying into the bay. Now it's a massive hive of commercialism stretching for over 1km along the beach, and a similar distance inland along its main thoroughfare and along the Kalamáki road parallel to the beach. The bulk of accommodation here is new or purpose-built and prone to dodgey plumbing and fittings. Bars, restaurants and snack-bars are all but interchangeable, although some do go out of their way to offer alternatives to what, at times, can look like an unending diet of junk food. Greek has become a second language here, which is how the predominantly Anglophone visitors like it; many businesses are in fact owned or staffed by expat or retired Brits. It has the widest range of beach amenities on the island, and provides off-beach attractions such as horse-riding and ballooning. While hotels are mostly block-booked by package companies, competition has forced many of them to open their pools and grounds to outsiders – provided you use their bars or restaurants.

The resort is constructed on a simple grid plan. Roads are nameless, but you'll soon learn to navigate using familiar landmarks. The two key thoroughfares are the main drag, which runs perpendicular to the beach, and the right-hand turning nearly 1km back from the sea, by Dennis's Bikes, where buses turn in the direction of Kalamáki. The one tourist attraction in the resort is the **Reptile House** (adults €5, children €3), on the Kalamáki road, which is supervised by a knowledgeable Greek-Australian naturalist, who leads guided tours and provides hands-on experiences with a range of creatures from turtles to Burmese pythons – you can even stroke a piranha.

Accommodation

While many of the places to stay in Laganás are monopolized by tour operators, there are still plenty of **rooms** and **apartments** to be had – but in

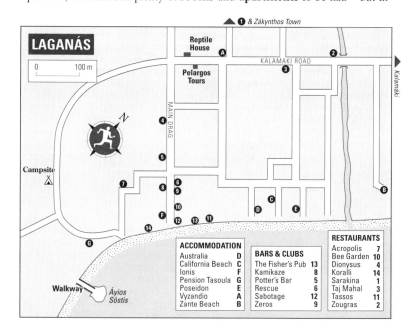

high season it can be extremely busy, and anyone heading here should phone ahead. Accommodation is often smack in the middle of the party zone, though the southwesterly end of the resort tends to be quieter; numerous private houses offering walk-up room accommodation can be found on the road that leaves the centre of the main drag, opposite the *Time Out* bar, and curves round to the beach at the hamlet of Lithákia, at the southern end of Laganás Bay. Alternatively, you can contact the Room-owners' Association (daily 8.30am–2pm and 5–8pm; ☎26950/51 515) or one of the local travel agents (see p.252), which have a range of places to stay on their books.

There's a basic **campsite**, or rather, a field with facilities, just a short distance southwest of Laganás – it's signposted in town, but the quickest route is to walk south along the beach for 200m to the first turn-off road, which leads up to the site. Vehicles should follow the road that extends from the Kalamáki road at the main junction to reach the campsite about 700m on.

Hotels

Most of Laganás's **hotels** are either on the beach to the north of the main drag, or a few minutes' walk back from it. However, an increasing number now trail back towards the airport, causing some staying "in" Laganás to have to commute to the beach by bus.

Australia ☎26950/51 071–3 ⓕ51 857. Small(ish) hotel, set just back from the beach, with a pool. Jointly managed with the adjacent *Sirene*. ❸

California Beach ☎26950/52 337–9, ⓕ52 340. Large, comfortable hotel complex with a/c rooms and pleasant grounds, just back from the beach. ❺

Ionis ☎26950/51 141, ⓦwww.hotelionis .com. Medium-sized but very friendly hotel, not far away from the beach on the main drag, with en-suite rooms, balconies, a bar and pool. ❹

Poseidon ☎26950/51 827–31 ⓕ51 199. Right on the beach and rather flashy with a pool; a/c en-suite rooms with balconies and sea views. Mostly for groups. ❺

Pension Tasoula ☎06950/51 560. Between beach and campsite, a friendly place with cosy rooms and a leafy courtyard. ❷

Vyzandio ☎26950/51 136. On the Kalamáki road, no frills but also no package groups and by far the cheapest and most traditional hotel around; basic en-suite rooms. ❷

Zante Beach ☎26950/51 130, ⓦwww.louishotels .com. The smartest hotel in Laganás, set away from the party zone nearly 1km towards Kalamáki and two blocks back from the beach. En-suite rooms, balconies, restaurant, bar and pool. Very popular with north European coach parties, so unlikely to have vacancies unless booked well in advance. ❽

Restaurants

Good **food** isn't a big selling point in Laganás. Many of the seafront and main drag businesses specialize in snacks, junk food and British staples such as fish and chips or fry-ups. These are, however, only versions of the original: fish will be a local white-meat, bonier, oilier but tastier than North Sea cod or haddock; and a Greek sausage (*loukániko*) doesn't taste anything like the British banger. At least the sheer number of competing restaurants keeps prices reasonable.

Acropolis 80m off the main drag. Garden taverna with a lengthy menu of Greek and international dishes. Also offers special themed Greek evenings with music and dance.

Bee Garden Just off the beach end of the main drag. Serves a wide range of inexpensive Chinese food in a quietish, leafy garden.

Dionysos The best of the bunch that line the main

drag but still fairly generic, bashing out all the taverna staples at competitive prices.

Koralli One of the better tavernas on the beach, serving fish, meat dishes and a fair selection of starters and salads.

Sarakina 2km inland and accessible mainly by the restaurant's own free minibus which cruises Laganás touting for trade. Offers live music and has the added attraction of being set opposite the grounds of a ruined Venetian mansion. The food is above average taverna fare, with a huge range of *mezédhes*, and not too expensive.

Taj Mahal On the Kalamáki road. Comprehensive range of favourite curries, plus Karahi, Irani and South Indian dishes, prepared by a subcontinental chef. Decent value.

Tassos Beachfront grill house, serving delicious chops, *souvláki* and some fish. More authentic and better value than most places on the front.

Zougras On the Kalamáki road before the bridge leaving Laganás. Vast menu of pan and grilled fish and meat dishes, and nightly performances of *kandádhes*. Good local wine adds to the atmosphere.

Nightlife

There's a **bar** every few metres along Laganás's main thoroughfares, with rib-tickling names such as *Sabotage*, *Kamikaze* and even *Potter's Bar*. Prices are reasonable and lengthy happy hours abundant, but the chance of enjoying a quiet drink is scarce. The nicest spot for a tipple is the seaside balcony of *The Fisher's Pub*. *Rescue* and *Zero's* are two of the most popular indoor discos, almost adjacent to each other on the main drag and both blessed with mercifully efficient air-conditioning but precious little taste in music.

Listings

Bike and motorbike rental Dennis's Bikes ⊤26950/52 997, by the Kalamáki turning at the back of the main drag.

Car rental The island-wide Ionian rental company has cars, jeeps and motorbikes (⊤26950/51 797 or 52 114, ⊕53 105).

Doctor There's a surgery, with English-speaking staff, on the main drag (daily 9.30am–2pm & 5–10pm; ⊤26950/52 252) and Zante Medical Care has a 24-hour emergency line (⊤26950/52 865).

Exchange There are no banks in Laganás, but cash dispensers are dotted around, and plenty

of travel agents will change cash and travellers' cheques. There is a big Eurocambio exchange bureau near the Kalamáki turning.

Internet Full Internet access is available at the Cyber Saloon café (€4/hr), a couple of blocks to the left of the main drag as you approach the sea from the main junction.

Travel Agent Pelargos Tours (⊤26950/52 017, ⊕51 386), on the Kalamáki road, and Smart Travel (⊤26 950/53318, ⊕24 365), on the main drag, both offer all the usual services.

Kalamáki

KALAMÁKI is basically a baby version of Laganás, offering all the good features of the bay without the drawbacks of the main resort. It has a variety of accommodation and tavernas, and its comparatively restrained nightlife is a notch more upmarket than that of Laganás. Just one street runs down to the sea, although a smattering of developments is springing up in lanes off it and the ugly US-style strip mall along the Laganás road could be a sign of things to come. Surprisingly, there is still very little building down at the beach. The biggest downside is the proximity of the airport: the drone of aircraft waiting to take off is quite audible from the centre of the village.

Accommodation

Kalamáki has a number of small, decent **hotels**, which are being increasingly monopolized by tour companies, although the places listed below keep at least some rooms for independents, as well as **rooms** owned by the proprietors of the two *Stanis* tavernas (⊤26950/26 375 or 26 374; ❸) towards the back of the village, and some small apartment complexes. Smart Travel (⊤26950/26 252, ⊕24 365), by the Laganás junction, handles a wide range of rooms, apartments and villas, and can change money.

Crystal Beach ☏ 26950/42 788, Ⓦ www
.crystalbeachhotel.info. Kalamáki's largest hotel,
approaching luxury status, is comfortable, with an
unrivalled setting overlooking the beach, at the
bottom of the main street. Two restaurants and
bars, and a pool. ❻

🏃 Katerina ☏ 26950/22 824,
Ⓔ vickylikou@mailshack.com. Behind the
beach and one of the closest options to it. Quietly
located and friendly block of modern apartments
with a rural feel. ❹

Klelia ☏ 26950/27 056 or 41 288, Ⓦ www
.hotelklelia.gr. Smart, newly built, forty-room
hotel on the main street, but a bit soulless. ❺

Mary Apartments ☏ 26950/45 660 or 45 306.
Comfortable studios, all a/c with kitchens and TV,
in a new yellow building at the start of the
Laganás road. ❹

Metaxa ☏ 26950/27 441–3, Ⓕ 27 445. Small,
stylish building on the main street with a pool and
smart rooms; excellent value. ❸

Eating and drinking

Restaurants in Kalamáki tend to be aimed at people who like to dress up for
dinner, with decor and prices to match. The two *Stanis* tavernas, one on the road
to Laganás, the other on a picturesque knoll above the beach, with its own small
menagerie loose in the garden, have extensive menus of Greek and international
dishes, although the beachside version is geared more to lunches and its sibling
more to evening meals. Worthwhile alternatives include the *Merlis*, which mixes
Greek bakes and grills with Italian cuisine, mainly pasta and meat-based dishes,
and the *Afrodite* taverna, with standard Euro-Greek fare at reasonable prices.
For a change, the *Guru*, 400m along the Laganás road, does a reasonably priced
range of Indian and some Chinese food with special menus for two.

Nightlife tends to begin in establishments such as *Fawlty Towers* cocktail bar
on the main strip, the *Rose n' Crown*, by the junction, or *Down Under*, 200m
along the Laganás road, which has video showings. The action then gravitates
towards the *Byzantio Club* on the hillside above the village, which has a garden
with breathtaking views over the bay and islands. Tucked into the foothill below,
the *Cave Club* is another popular watering hole.

Límni Kerioú

Without doubt the most attractive spot in Laganás Bay is **LÍMNI KERIOÚ**,
which is tucked into the far southwestern corner of the bay between the lake
that supplies the first half of its name and the sea. The lake is an atmospheric
patch of brackish, swampy water, home to reeds and a few wading birds; it is
separated from the sea by a small patch of land and the modest sandy beach,
around which a micro-resort has begun to grow up. Still, it is a far cry from
the excesses of Laganás and even Kalamáki, making it one of the better places
to unwind by the sea on the whole island. The settlement and lake are actually
removed by some 6km from the west coast village of Kerí (see overleaf) that is
responsible for the second half of the name. Nevertheless, it is often alternatively
known simply as Kerí beach.

As the area is still relatively undiscovered and has not caught on with the
tour operators yet, finding **accommodation** should not be a problem and is
facilitated by the local Room-owner's Association (☏ 26950/45 105). On the
beach towards the harbour the Seaside Internet Café (☏ 26950/22 827, Ⓦ www
.seaside.net.gr; ❹) offers comfortable modern apartments, as well as computer
facilities (€4/hr). Two appealing options towards the bluff at the far end of the
beach from the approach road are the cosy 🏃 *Pansion Limni* (☏ 26950/48 716,
Ⓦ www.pansionlimni.com; ❷) and the *Castello-Panorama* rooms, managed by
the adjacent *Poseidon* **taverna** (☏ 26950/48 708, Ⓔ michaela@zak.gr; ❸), which
has a great view of the bay and serves a decent range of meat, fish and salads. Of
the gaggle of beachfront tavernas by the approach road, *Psarokalyva* is best for its

wide selection of fish, meat and vegetable dishes and excellent barrelled wine. On the corner of the approach road, the *Taverna Keri* also has a fair range of staples and occasional live music. The most popular bar for a cocktail is the *Rock Café* back on the front, but don't expect it to get too animated. The beach is also home to one of Zákynthos's better **scuba-diving** operations, the Turtle Beach Dive Centre (☎26950/49 424, ⒲www.diving-centre-turtle-beach.com).

The west coast

Zákynthos's skeletal public transport service renders most of the hill villages in the west and north of the island off limits to those without transport. Local tour agencies do offer island **coach tours** in season but these are whistle-stop tours with only a few breaks for meals, refreshment and sightseeing. This side of the island is well worth making the effort to visit, however, for the pre-earthquake architecture of villages such as **Kerí** and **Kiliómeno**, the sweeping coastal vistas and sunsets (most famously at **Kambí**), two of the island's oldest monasteries and the weaving centre of **Volímes.**

Kerí

Though hidden in a fold above the cliffs at the island's southernmost tip, **Kerí** is easily accessible. The village retains a number of pre-quake, Venetian buildings, including the church of the Panayía of Kerí – who is said to have saved the island from marauding pirates by hiding it in a sea mist. Kerí is also famous for a geological quirk, a series of small tar pools mentioned by both Pliny and Herodotus, but these have mysteriously dried up in recent years. A rough path leaving the southern end of the village leads on 1km to the lighthouse, where the surrounding cliff paths afford spectacular views of the sea and tree-tufted limestone sea-arches and -stacks. The Marathiá caves, down below, can only be reached by boat.

There is no accommodation in the village, but about 2km before you reach Kerí, the recommended ⚵*Taverna Apelati* (☎26950/43 324, ⒺKiourkas@otenet .gr; ❷) has some **rooms** in a great setting amidst olive groves and vineyards, a short way off the main road – a good option for those with their own transport. As you enter Kerí, two tavernas with west-facing sea views, *The Sunset*, good for roasts like *kondosoúvli*, and *Ta Dhilina*, with home-style oven food, are ideal for sunset dinners. Further on there are just a couple of traditional *kafenía* on the village's tiny square, and there is another good taverna, *Keri Lighthouse*, shortly before the lighthouse itself.

Maherádho

Some 10km west of Zákynthos Town, **Maherádho** also boasts some impressive pre-earthquake architecture, and is set in beautiful arable uplands, surrounded by terraced olive and fruit groves. The magnificent **church of Ayía Mávra** has a free-standing campanile, and contains a splendid carved iconostasis and icons by Zakynthian painter Nikolaos Latsis. The town's major festival – one of the biggest on the island – is the saint's day, which conventionally falls on the first Sunday in June. The town's other notable religious edifice, the typically Byzantine domed church of the **Panayía**, commands breathtaking views over the central plain. The interior, however, has been denuded of most of its artwork, much of it moved to Ayía Mávra.

Kilioméno to Kambí

Ascending into the bare mountainscape of the west coast on a rough country road from Maherádho, you'll reach, after 6km, **KiliOmÉno**, the best place to see surviving pre-earthquake domestic architecture, in the form of the island's traditional two-storey, stone-built, tile-roofed houses. The town used to be named after its church, **Áyios Nikólaos**, whose impressive campanile, begun over a hundred years ago, still lacks a capped roof but features some ornate sculpture on its upper reaches. The village also boasts one of the most attractive dining options on the island. Set in a splendid 1630 stone building, the *Alitzerini* is a traditional *inomayirío* serving rare dishes such as *pantséta*, as well as stuffed spleen and *sofigadhoúra* (beef in a red sauce with cheese). Seating is in tiny ground-floor rooms or on the upstairs balcony, and an acoustic duo play most evenings during the establishment's high season opening.

About 6km past Kilioméno, a newly paved road loops down to the coast and back again at the village of **Áyios Léon**, where more standard but tasty fare is available at the *Fioro* taverna. The detour passes through farmland, cordoned off by a maze of short dry-stone walls, on its way to the jagged volcanic rock of the coast. There are two points with sea access, one below an easily visible canteen, and a little further north, the tiny inlet of **Pórto Limniónas**, topped by a taverna of the same name. On the other side of the main road just before Áyios Léon a small road leads inland to two more delightful mountain villages. The first, after 3km, is **Loúha**, a jumble of old stone houses with red-tile roofs set on a verdant valley hillside. You can get a basic snack or drink at the *Kafenio tis Louhas*, next to the squat rectangular church of Ioánnis Theológos. A further 3km uphill after Loúha, and east, **Yíri**, crowning a plateau-like hilltop, has the feel of a ghost town, with shutters firmly closed in most of the stone dwellings. There is, however, a minuscule *kafenío* with a beer garden attached and the atmospheric stone courtyard of the *Kefalo Kolona* taverna, where you can eat fine rabbit *stifádho*, beside the plain ochre church of Profítis Ilías.

Meanwhile, the main road from Áyios Léon continues climbing another 4km up into the island's highest western hills, where a left turning just beyond Éxo Hóra leads a further 4km to the tiny clifftop hamlet of **Kambí**, the destination for numerous coach tours organized to catch sunset over the sea. The village contains three cliff-top tavernas, especially built for this natural show, with extraordinary views over the 300-metre-high cliffs and western horizon, although you're likely to find yourself sharing the sunset with a sizeable crowd of fellow visitors. The best of the tavernas, especially for filling grills, is *The Cross*, named after Kambí's most striking landmark and perched just below it. On an incline above the village the imposing concrete **cross** itself is said to have been constructed in memory of islanders killed here by nationalist soldiers during the civil war – one lurid legend says that islanders were hurled from the cliffs. An alternative history of the cross claims that it was erected to commemorate those killed by the Nazis during the island's wartime occupation.

Mariés to Volímes

Five kilometres north of Kambí, following the bare mountain road north, **Mariés** is one of the few villages in the region with access to the sea. A steep, rough track leads down 7km to the small rocky cove of **Stenítis Bay**, which has a waterfront taverna and dock, while a second, paved road descends to **Pórto Vrómi**, from where small boats conduct trips to Shipwreck Bay for around €10 per head (note that this road does not link up at Pórto Vrómi with the other road down from Anafonítria). Mariés itself, protected in a wooded green valley, has an unusual three-aisled church dedicated to Mary Magdalene, who is said to have stopped here to preach en route to Provence. Tough hiking paths lead southeast up onto the slopes of Mount Vrahiónas, the island's highest mountain, with views across the island and north to Kefallonía. On the main road heading northwest, the *New Life* taverna (aka *Pergoulia*) turns out excellent cheap grills.

After this, the main mountain road veers round to the northeast to reach Volímes after 10km. A small detour to the east just over halfway takes you to **Orthoniés**, another picturesque mountain village with a fine stone gateway, some old, squat, stone-built houses and a café. A more interesting route, however, branches off east at the village of Anafonítria to the **monastery** of the same name (and then on down to the coast at Pórto Vrómi). The monastery, dating from the fourteenth century, is no longer inhabited, but recent renovations have been completed, making it well worth a peep. The main chapel contains some original fifteenth-century frescoes above the altar and a splendid wooden iconostasis. Behind it, a more recent side chapel and the cemetery beyond are also open to the public. Food, drink and gifts are available at the nearby edge of the village – try *Yiorgos* taverna.

Back on the asphalted road from Mariés to Volímes, you can continue for 4km to reach the area's other old holy retreat, the **monastery of Áyios Yióryios ton Kremnón**, the construction of which began in the sixteenth century. It still houses two monks and, apart from some of the original buildings, has two noteworthy features: a small chapel with some fine icons painted on wood and a peculiar, round lookout tower. Just north of the monastery, a newly paved road branches off to the sheer clifftop above **Shipwreck Bay**. A metal platform bracketed onto the cliff affords vertical views of a cargo ship that ran aground here in the 1960s, buried in the sand hundreds of feet below; it's quite safe, but definitely only for those with a head for heights. The beach itself is quite stunning even without its peculiar centrepiece and is easily reached by tour boats from various parts of the island if you want a closer look. A footpath near the platform leads 300m over rocky scrub to the **cave of Áyios Yerásimos**, crowned by a tiny chapel. The seasonal taverna near the clifftop only opens for a few weeks a year, so take provisions if you want to hang out at other times.

Volímes is the largest of the island's hill villages, with the exception of Katastári, and in fact comprises three smaller settlements: Káto (Lower), Méso (Middle) and Áno (Upper) Volímes, which are within a few minutes' drive of each other. Each is a small living museum of rural island architecture. **Áno Volímes**, built on a hillside surrounding the church of Ayíos Dhimítrios, whose solid stone campanile stands on the other side of the road from the sanctuary, is probably the best-preserved village on the entire island. The church of Ayía Paraskeví in Méso Volímes was rebuilt after the earthquake, using original masonry, and still has the beautiful sculpted door and window frames. Volímes is the end destination of most island tours, mainly because of its reputation for fine embroidery and farm produce, notably cheese and honey. Shops selling intricately embroidered lace and rugs of various sizes and designs, including the ubiquitous turtle-motif, line the road of the middle village. The Women's Agrotourism Cooperative here is a self-help organization established in 1988 as part of a national, government-sponsored initiative to involve rural women in tourism; its office in Áno Volímes can organize accommodation in private homes in the villages or you can try the nearby *kafenío* (☎26950/31 222; ❸), which can arrange large studios for four. The nearby *Kamináki* taverna serves good, home-style cooking.

The northeast

Around 12km northwest of Zákynthos Town, the mountains that cover the whole west of the island begin to converge on the east coast, which has a distinctive kink just beyond the small resort of **Alikanás**. The only northern resort of any size, **Alykés**, is not more than a fifteen-minute walk down from the sprawling mountain village of **Katastári**. Further on, the peaks shelve even more abruptly down to the sea, leaving only a handful of beaches, best of all Xigiá. The island tapers to an end at Cape Skinári, just below which are the famous **Blue Caves**, and a little further south, **Áyios Nikólaos**, from where Zákynthos's only ferry connection with Kefalloniá departs. The further you go towards Cape Skinári, the quieter and more attractive things become.

Alikanás

The last resort of note before the coast hooks round to Alykés is **Alikanás**, which is neatly tucked into the eastern side of the headland separating the two; in fact its inland section behind the village is beginning to blend into the encroaching southern reaches of Alykés. Alikanás has two distinct stretches of beach: a tiny northerly one with a harbour, and a longer strand below the *Shoestring* café–bar to the south – follow signs to the *Redskins* bar. Here you will find the good-value *Blue Shadows* apartments (☎26950/83 489; ❸), perched right above the sea, and the *Psaropoula* fish taverna. A short way back inland towards the village proper, the new apartment block *Velendzas* (☎26950/83 561, ℻83 519; ❹) is another comfortable place to stay. The village of Alikanás has a growing number of tourist facilities, such as the *Medoussa* taverna, good for starters and grills, and bars such as *Fever* and *Tipsy Toad*.

Alykés

The largest beach in the region is at **Alykés**, a resort that continues to undergo gradual development but is still quieter than Tsiliví. It's known for its salt pans (hence the name), which give the back of the village the appearance of a moonscape, while its long beach, perhaps owing to a steep seabed, experiences lively surf created by the prevailing winds. The beach is actually divided into two strips by a brackish canal and the quay beside its outlet. Most of the action is on the northwestern side of this dividing waterway and you can safely bypass the characterless sprawl of burgeoning development that lines the main road before it crosses the canal and runs alongside it into the resort proper.

Not too much **accommodation** of decent value is available to the independent traveller. The best deal by far is at the mildly chaotic *Eros Piccadilly Hotel* (☎26950/83 606 or 83 497, ⓦwww.erospiccadilly.com; ❷), near the main crossroads, which has adequate en-suite rooms above a restaurant. There are quite a few **hotels** behind the beach with sea views. Worth investigating are the *Ionian Star* (☎26950/83 416, ⓦwww.ionian-star.gr; ❹), a small, friendly place with its own restaurant and garden; the stylish air-conditioned ✈ *Montreal* (☎26950/83 241, ⓦwww.montreal.gr; ❹); and the huge *Astoria* (☎26950/83 533 or 83 658, ⓔastoriaz@otenet.gr; ❹). Spring Tours (☎26950/83035, ⓦwww.springtours.gr) can arrange rooms and apartments here and in nearby Katastári, the village visible on a hillside to the southwest.

The choice of **places to eat** has increased dramatically of late. Among the half-dozen or so tavernas in the village (twice as many again line the road back towards Alikanás), the *Ponderosa* has a wide range of fish and meat at good prices, and the vast *Fantasia* offers a variety of Euro-Greek dishes and free house wine with dinner. Besides these, there are three pizzerias, the *Taj Mahal*, which serves Chinese as well as Indian cuisine, and the *Bits'n'Pieces* crêperie. Several much-of-a-muchness bars such as the *Magic Mushroom* cocktail bar vie for the custom of the night owls, and *Cheers* has a big screen for sports, while *Jammin'* is a lively spot in the new southern end. The Yria café offers rather expensive Internet access (€6 per hour). The bus system more or less gives out at Alykés, but it would make a reasonable beach base for those exploring the north with their own transport. Cars and motorbikes can be rented from Alikes rental (T & F 26950/83 616). The surrounding villages of Katastári and Pighadhákia can also be visited on the summer-only toy train *To Trainaki*, which completes an 8km circuit by road for €10 per person.

Katastári and around

Straddling the main road through the northeast of Zákynthos, the sprawling village of **KATASTÁRI** is the second largest settlement on the island. There is not much original architecture to admire or anything particular to divert visitors, but precisely for that reason it makes a good place to take in some real life in a contemporary island community. It would be a shame to stay in Alykés, for example, without strolling up here at least once. The most impressive, albeit modern edifice is the **church of Iperayía Theotókos**, which dominates the lower village square on the way up from Alykés. This huge rectangular brick building boasts unusual twin belfries, and a small amphitheatre has been constructed to seat people for festival activities. There's nowhere obvious to stay, but a couple of cafeterias offer a warm welcome, and the *Vlassis* taverna and *To Kendro psistariá* serve unpretentious food at giveaway prices. A post office and several functional shops complete the amenities.

Less than 2km south of Katastári, between the main road and the mountains, the hamlet of **Pigadhákia**, whose name means little wells, harbours a couple of unexpected treats. An old warehouse has been converted into the **Vertagio Cultural Museum** (summer daily 9am–3pm & 5–7pm; €3), which is full of weaving and agricultural equipment, plus old documents, coins, photos and displays of traditional Zakynthian homes. In the yard outside a carriage and some mill equipment are on display and you may meet the resident goat. Nearby, the small chapel of **Áyios Pandeleïmon**, with brightly coloured stained-glass windows, was rebuilt after the earthquake, though the campanile survives from 1838. The chapel's unique feature is the running spring that is hidden beneath the altar. Next to the chapel, the *Kaki Rahi* **taverna** serves good traditional fare such as *tyropittákia*, *keftédhes* and beef *kokkinistó*.

North to Cape Skinári

The main road soon starts to undulate between fairly high mountainous sections and sea level – creating some major bends and hair-raising driving conditions. Some 3km north of Katastári, the *Ksigia* taverna, serving Greek staples, commands a bend at the top of a headland with splendid views. A little further on, the road dips to a point just above a diminutive, pebble beach known as **Xygiá**, which is flanked by a sheer rock wall on one side and rugged coastline on the other. An unexpected gush of colder spring water emanates from half way along the rock wall, where confident swimmers can also dive under a ledge into a small cave. To reach the beach, take a short, unmarked, motorable track off the road; it leads to a path above the beach. There is just a seasonal canteen on the bluff above.

Less than 2km further on, the road descends again to the larger pebble beach of **Makrýs Yialós**. Here pedal boats can be rented to explore the local mini-caves, while motorboats run excursions up to the Blue Caves for around €8. There's a canteen at the back of the beach, while the excellent *Pilarinos* taverna, on the hill above, rents out cheap camping plots in its shadeless grounds. A few hundred metres further on, the brand new ⚜ *Makris Gialos Apartments* (☎26950/31 558, Ⓦwww.e-zakynthos.com/makris-gialos; ❹) are comfortable and attractively built in island stone. Just to the north of Makrýs Yialós you come to a pretty promontory with a small harbour and the *Míkro Nisí psarotavérna*, beyond and above which there are a couple of places to rent rooms; try *Klímati* (☎26950/31 225; ❸) if you fancy a bit of isolation.

△ Korithí Lighthouse, Cape Skinári

6

The next settlement is the port of **Áyios Nikólaos**, not to be confused with the beach resort at the opposite end of the island. Also note that it is usually referred to as Skinári, both here and on Kefalloniá, with which it is connected by the ferry to Pessádha twice daily in summer.

Tourism is just beginning to develop here. Perhaps tired of seeing the constant stream of tourists pouring off the boat and immediately disappearing towards the south, the locals have been trying to tempt people to stay by increasing the number of accommodation and dining options and occasionally grabbing visitors before they can board their vehicle. There is also a common scam whereby northbound tourist traffic is flagged down and informed that this is the last place from where a boat trip can be taken to the Blue Caves: a bare-faced lie. If you've come this far, carry on for the cheaper and far friendlier excursions available at Cape Skinári (see below).

Although tourism is still low-key, the amount of building in progress suggests it may not remain so for long. At present, the best deal on rooms is at the *Panorama* (☎26950/31 013, Ⓔpanorama@altecnet.gr; ❸), as you climb to the south, while the *Blue Beach Bungalows* (☎26950/31 522–3, Ⓦwww.bluebeach.gr; ❺), to the north, is a huge complex with a pool and spiral waterslide that is advertised all over the island. Incredibly, some of the most classy and expensive apartments anywhere in Greece (at over €200 a night) are to be found here at the small but exquisitely decorated and furnished ⚜ *Nobelos* (☎26950/31 131, Ⓦwww.nobelos.gr; ❽), situated on a bluff above the sea. For meals, try the *La Storia* fish restaurant on the harbour, or the *Orizodes* taverna to the south. The nearby *Magica Luna* café is a very laid-back spot for a drink overlooking the sea.

Just inland from the main road further north, the village of **Askós** is the location of one of the island's newest attractions, the **Stone Park** (daily May–Sept 9am–7pm; Oct–April 10am–5pm; €7.50). Newly fashioned out of a small mountain valley, the park is supposed to show a diversity of ecosystems and biospheres but is very much a work in progress and hardly a haven for animal lovers. It's a good deal greener than when it first opened and a few more exotic creatures such as the Cambodian pot-bellied pig have been imported. Unfortunately, the free guides who accompany you round the circuit usually have to be physically restrained if they are to be prevented from poking the pig and his friends with a stick on the occasions when they are not posing for visitors.

As you near the northern tip of Zákynthos, the thick covering of olive and pine gives way to low-lying rocky scrub until the land peters out at **Cape Skinári**, crowned by the Korithí lighthouse. **Korithí** itself is more a scattered collection of buildings than a village, but it can claim to have one of the most charming and unique places to stay in the entire Ionians: the upper storeys of two old windmills have been converted into double rooms, run by the nearby ⚓ *Faros* taverna (☎26950/31 132; ❺), which also has some traditional stone houses (❹) for rent and serves a fine range of food. Advance booking for the windmills is essential for obvious reasons. The only other refreshments are at a canteen behind the windmill. Just in front of the windmill there are steps all the way down to a section of the **Blue Caves**, a splendid set of eroded recesses in the base of the cliffs where the water assumes a luminescent blue colour. The three friendly brothers whose family own the *Faros* enterprise also run the best-value trips to the Blue Caves (€7) and Shipwreck Bay (€10; combo €15). You can drive to within walking distance of the lighthouse, but it's not particularly spectacular. Otherwise, you can loop back round southwest towards Volímes to complete the northern circuit.

Travel details

Buses

Zákynthos Town to: Alykés (5 daily; 50min); Argási (9 daily; 15min); Áyios Leon (1 daily; 40min); Kalamáki (12 daily; 20min); Katastári (4 daily; 45min); Laganás (14 daily; 30min); Límni Kerioú (2 daily; 50min); Méso Yerakári (1 daily; 25min); Tsiliví (11 daily; 30min); Vassilikós/Áyios Nikólaos (4 daily; 45min); Volímes (2 daily; 1hr 30min). Services are reduced at weekends and out of season.
There are also several daily bus connections to Athens via Kyllíni and Pátra, varying in number according to seasonal variations in ferry schedules (see opposite), and three services a week to Thessaloníki via Lamía, Almyrós (for Vólos), Lárisa and Kateríni. For information call KTEL on ☎26950/22 255 or 42 656.

Ferries

Áyios Nikólaos/Skinári to: Pessádha on Kefalloniá (2 daily May–Sept; 1hr 30min).
Zákynthos Town to: Kyllíni (5–7 daily in summer, 3 daily in winter; 1hr 30min).

Flights

Zákynthos airport to: Athens (1–2 daily; 55min); Corfu (1 weekly in summer; 1hr 55min); Kefalloniá (1 weekly in summer; 25min); Préveza (1 weekly in summer; 1hr 15min).

Contexts

Contexts

The historical framework

Isolated off the west coast of Greece, perilously close to Italy, the Ionian archipelago has stood apart from the mainland and the Aegean until recent times, and its history reflects this. This section is intended just to lend some perspective to travels in the Ionians, and is weighted towards the era of the modern, post-independence nation – especially the twentieth century.

The earliest cultures

The archipelago's isolation puts it on the sidelines of the historical narrative that produced the great archeological finds at Delphi, Mycenae, Olympia and elsewhere. However, evidence in the form of tools has been found on Corfu and Kefalloniá, suggesting that the region was inhabited by Paleolithic (early Stone Age) hunter-gatherers as long ago as 70,000–50,000 BC, prior to the last great Ice Age. At this time Corfu and the other islands were still part of a dry landmass, and what is now the northern Adriatic was covered by a vast forest. These people would originally have come from the eastern Mediterranean, finding themselves "islanded" during the period 14,000–10,000 BC, when the ice thawed, raising the level of the Mediterranean by over a hundred metres. Their communities would have been agrarian and self-supporting, producing pottery and handicrafts, and worshipping earth/fertility deities, clay figurines of which can be seen in some island museums. The development of agriculture, trade and sea travel would transform this civilization into one that learnt to specialize, compete and, when it seemed advantageous, go to war.

Minoans and Mycenaeans

The Bronze Age **Minoan civilization** (2500–1100 BC) was a period of fluctuating regional dominance in the Mediterranean, based upon sea power, with vast palaces serving as centres of administration. Foremost amongst them was **Knossós** on Crete, the centre of the Minoan civilization that dominated the Aegean. Some islands in the Ionian archipelago traded with the Minoans – wood from Kefalloniá's unique fir species, *Abies cephalonica*, was used in the construction of the palace of Knossós – but on the whole they stayed apart from Minoan culture.

Also important – and closer to the Ionian – were Mycenae, Tiryns and Argos in the Peloponnese. When the Minoans went into decline, around 1400 BC, **Mycenae**, south of Corinth and 150km from what is modern-day Pátra, became the seat of power. For at least two centuries, Mycenae ruled the region – and in turn gave its name to the period – until it, in turn, collapsed around 1200 BC. This is a period whose history and remains are bound up with **legends**, recounted most famously by **Homer**. Mycenae was the home of Agamemnon, engineer of the **Trojan War**, which was the subject of Homer's *Iliad*, and it was the end of the Trojan War that started Odysseus' long voyage home in the *Odyssey*. Debate continues over the provenance of the *Iliad* and *Odyssey*, both in terms of their authorship – it's likely that they were originally oral epics – and whether they were journalism, fiction or both. They seem to have been based in fact, although the amount of detail accepted varies between rival authorities. They certainly reflect the prevalence of violence, revenge and war as part of the culture, instigated and aggravated by trade and territorial rivalry (one reading of the *Odyssey* casts Odysseus as little more than a pirate and opportunist). The few surviving examples of architecture from this period – sections of vast fortifications seen on Corfu, Itháki, Kefalloniá and elsewhere, and known, with Homeric felicity, as Cyclopean walls – give a measure of the level of political tension and aggression in Mycenaean Greece.

At this time, and for centuries after, Greece was a collection of small independent regions, divided by clan loyalties and geography, vying for power, and forming and dissolving alliances as the power structure shifted. These miniature states succeeded or failed depending on their level of military or economic strength; Corfu, for example, established itself as a powerful naval force, and Kefalloniá was perfectly situated to become a trading post between the east and west Mediterranean.

The Dorian and Classical eras

As the circulation of trade and population around the Mediterranean increased, so these communities had to cope with the sudden and not always welcome arrival of new peoples and businesses that might supplant their economic power. The most radical alteration to the balance of power was the influx of northern **Dorians**: their unseating of Mycenaean rule was traditionally viewed as an "invasion" but is nowadays thought to have been a fundamental shift in the region's economy, which wrought drastic changes among the palace cultures and their naval forces in the eleventh century BC.

The Dorians imported their own religion, the twelve gods of **Olympus**, supplanting the widespread cult of Dionysus – deity of wine, fruitfulness and vegetation, and originally a goddess – and other female earth/fertility deities. The Dorian era was also notable for the appearance of a "Greek" **alphabet**, which is still recognizable alongside modern Greek and which replaced the "Linear A" script discovered on Crete, and the later "Linear B" Minoan/Mycenaean script.

City-states: Sparta, Athens and Corinth

The ninth century BC saw the birth of the Greek **city-state** (*polis*). Citizens – not just royalty or aristocracy – had a hand in government and community activities, and organized commerce and leisure. Economic and territorial expansionism increased, as did overseas trade, and this would shortly create a new class of manufacturers.

The city-state was defined by those who lived in it, and each state retained an individual identity and culture. Consequently, alliances between them were always temporary and tactical. Athens and Sparta, the Dorian city-state in the southern Peloponnese, were the two most powerful, and pursued a bitter rivalry for centuries.

Sparta was founded and run according to a militaristic regime which some today describe as fascistic. Males were subject to military service between the ages of 7 and 30, and young women were also expected to excel in athletics. **Athens** was the place that developed the – at the time, limited – notion of democracy. Its literal meaning, recognizable from modern Greek, is "people power", but this only applied to "freeborn" males, and not to women or slaves. As many as 40,000 Athenians were entitled to vote at the Assembly. Not only

Athens, but every city-state had its **acropolis** or "high town", where polytheistic religious activity, under the aegis of Zeus, was focused.

After Athens and Sparta, **Corinth** was the next most powerful city-state, and the one that exercised the most influence on Corfu and the Ionian islands. Corinth was both a trading centre and a powerful naval force, with strong colonialist tendencies. As well as Corfu, it settled Syracuse (on Sicily) and Lefkádha, and would later seal tactical alliances with the city-states of Kefaloniá, notably Pale and Same. Affinities between regions and city-states shifted violently when it came to war: while Corfu prospered after it was colonized by Corinth in the eighth century BC, a fierce battle between the two was one of the causes of the **Peloponnesian Wars** in 431–404 BC. Similarly, Kefaloniá's city-states all took the Athenian side during that war, only to find themselves invaded by their distrustful allies, who used the island as a power base against Corinth.

Sparta emerged as nominal victors from the Peloponnesian Wars, but the years of warfare had drained all city-states of resources and commitment to the political system. The increasingly complex world of trade was subverting the older structures, and the invention and spread of **coinage** – an innovation as radical in its time as computerization today – was expanding and streamlining commercial life. A revitalized Athens, for example, was trading as far afield as the Black Sea, and Corfu had established trade links with Egypt.

Hellenistic and Roman Greece

The most important factor in the decline of the city-states was meanwhile developing beyond their boundaries, in the northern kingdom of **Macedonia** – a territory and title still fiercely contested today.

The Macedonian empire

Based at the Macedonian capital of Pella, **Philip II** (king from 359–336 BC) forged a strong military and unitary force, extending his territories into Thrace. He then pushed south to take the rest of Greece (including the Ionian islands), in 338 BC, defeating the Athenians and their allies at the decisive Battle of Chaironeia, just east of Delphi. On his assassination in 336 BC, Philip was succeeded by his son, **Alexander the Great**, whose extraordinary thirteen-year career extended his empire into Persia and Egypt and even parts of modern India.

These vast gains began to crumble almost immediately after the death of Alexander in 323 BC. The empire was divided up into the three Macedonian dynasties of the world, **Hellenistic**, though Corfu and the Ionian islands fell victim to a series of regional takeovers, including early incursions by the Romans.

Roman Greece

Corfu, fatefully positioned between the heel of Italy and the Greek mainland, was the first city-state seized by the **Romans**, in 229 BC. The Romans subdued the rest of Greece over some seventy years of campaigns, from 215 to 146 BC. However, Rome allowed considerable autonomy in terms of law, religion and language, and Greece and its overlords coexisted fairly peacefully for the next four centuries. While Athens and Corinth remained important cities, the emphasis of power shifted north – particularly to towns such as Salonica

(Thessaloníki) along the new Via Egnatia, a military and civil road connecting Rome and Byzantium via the port of Brundisium (modern Brindisi).

The Byzantine empire and medieval Greece

The shift in power towards the north of Greece was exacerbated by the decline of the Roman empire and its division into eastern and western halves. In 330 AD Emperor Constantine moved his capital to the Greek city of Byzantium, which was transformed Constantinople (modern Istanbul), the "new Rome" and spiritual and political capital of what became the **Byzantine empire**. While the last western Roman emperor was deposed by barbarian Goths in 476 AD, the oriental portion of the empire was to be the dominant Mediterranean power for some 700 years, and only in 1453 did it collapse completely.

Christianity

Although Christianity was formally introduced during the reign of Constantine, Christian preachers had been travelling in Greece since the first century AD – Corfu is believed to have first been evangelized in 37 AD. By the end of the fourth century, Christianity was the official state religion, its liturgies (still in use in the Greek Orthodox Church), creed and New Testament all written in Greek.

In the seventh century, **Constantinople** was besieged by Persians, and later by Arabs, but the Byzantine empire held, losing only Egypt, the least "Greek" of its territories. From the ninth to the eleventh century, it enjoyed a "golden age", both spiritual and political. Intrinsic in the Orthodox Byzantine faith was a sense of religious superiority, and the emperors saw Constantinople as a "new Jerusalem" for their "chosen people". This was the start of a diplomatic and ecclesiastical conflict with the Catholic West that would have disastrous consequences in subsequent centuries. As antagonism grew, the eastern and western patriarchs mutually excommunicated each other.

From the seventh through to the eleventh century, parts of **Byzantine Greece** became a rather provincial backwater. Administration was top-heavy and imperial taxation led to semi-autonomous provinces ruled by military generals, whose land was usually taken from bankrupt peasants. This alienation of the poor primed a disaffected populace for change, almost regardless of who implemented it.

Ionian and central Greece were particular vulnerable when waves of **Slavic raiders** staged numerous sorties from the Balkans in this period. At the same time, other groups moved down into the region from **central Europe** and were assimilated peaceably. From the thirteenth century on, immigrants from **Albania** fanned out across central Greece, the Peloponnese and nearby islands.

The Crusades, the Venetians and the Ottomans

With the Byzantine empire in steady decline, the eleventh century saw dramatic rearrangements of the power structure, particularly in the western parts of Greece. The **Normans** landed first at Corfu in 1081 and occupied the rest of the Ionian over the next two years. They returned to the mainland, with papal approval, a decade later on their way to liberate Jerusalem. This was only a fore-taste of regular incursions into the Ionian region by the **Crusaders** on their way to Asia Minor. Richard the Lionheart, for example, landed on Corfu in 1192, but hastily left, fearing arrest by Byzantine officials who regarded him an enemy of the Orthodox Church.

In the **Fourth Crusade** of 1204, Venetians, Franks and Germans turned their armies directly on Byzantium and sacked and occupied Constantinople. These Latin princes and their followers, seeking new lands and kingdoms, divided the best of the empire among themselves. All that remained of Byzantium were three small rival states based on Nicaea in Asia Minor, Epirus in northwestern Greece and distant Trebizond on the Black Sea.

Each of these post-imperial factions regarded itself as the rightful successor to Byzantium, and the Ionian archipelago, like the rest of Greece, passed a turbulent half-century in which they vied for power with one another as well as with the Crusaders. The islands were a part of the **Despotate of Epirus**, which had its capital at Arta on the mainland opposite Corfu. When the most powerful of the successor states, the **Empire of Nicaea**, recaptured Constantinople in 1261, the Despots of Epirus refused to recognize the revived Byzantine administration until granted considerable local autonomy.

Venice, meanwhile, had made its intentions known back in 1204, demanding the islands when the spoils of Byzantium were being shared out. In 1350 it again made an offer for the Ionian islands, but was refused. However, local lords and landowners on Corfu sensed the way power was moving in the region, and saw they would be safest with the Venetians. In 1386, Venice, taking advantage of an interregnum in the Ionians, sent an army to conquer it and was asked to "protect" the island by its leaders. Over the next century and more, Venice set its sights on subsuming the other Ionian islands and Párga – the only toehold the Venetians managed to get on the mainland – into its empire.

In the meantime, the **Ottoman empire** grew more powerful in the east. Constantinople finally fell in 1453, and a decade later most of the former Byzantine empire was in Turkish hands. Even Zákynthos was seized for a time by the Turks, as were Kefalloniá and Itháki; tiny Paxí was sacked and most of its population enslaved by the Ottoman admiral, Barbarossa. Lefkádha passed between Turkish and Venetian rule several times, before finally joining the rest of the Ionian islands under Venice in 1684.

Under what Greeks refer to as the "Dark Ages" of Ottoman rule, much of present-day Greece passed into rural provincialism, taking refuge in a self-protective form of village life that has only recently been disrupted. Taxes and discipline, occasionally backed by acts of genocide against rebel communities, were inflicted by Turkish authorities, but estates passed into the hands of local chieftains, who often had considerable independence. Greek identity was sustained by the **Orthodox Church** which, despite instances of forced conversions to the Muslim faith, was allowed to continue. Monasteries organized schools, often secretly, and became the sole guardians of Byzantine culture, although many scholars and artists emigrated west, contributing to the Renaissance.

In contrast, the Ionian islands flourished under Venice. Extensive planting of olives established an industry that continues throughout the islands today. Venice's distinctive architecture, with its signature Lion of St Mark, was transposed to the towns of Corfu, Argostóli, Lefkádha and Zákynthos. Venice sustained the lords and landowners, and brutally crushed any attempts to propose land reform. This would eventually undermine them, particularly when islanders became involved in the **Filikí Etería**, or "Friendly Society", a secret group working to build opposition against the Turks.

The struggle for independence

As the Ottoman empire itself began showing signs of unravelling, opposition to Turkish rule became widespread, exemplified by the **klephts** (brigands) of the mountains. The French Revolution of 1789 gave fresh impetus to "freedom movements" and to the *Filikí Etería*, who were recruiting on the Ionian islands as well as among exiles living abroad. Napoleon's declaration of war on Venice fired visions of independence in the Ionian, but after he had defeated the Venetians in 1797 he sent emissaries to the archipelago to establish his own authority. Nevertheless, the **French** upended the social order and freed serfs, and jubilant crowds burnt the *Libro d'Oro* (the "Golden Book" that listed those aristocrats favoured by the Venetians) in impromptu celebrations in most of the Ionian capitals. In Corfu, the French embarked on an ambitious building programme, but this was cut short by Napoleon's downfall in 1814.

Throughout the Ionians, the French were replaced by the administrators of a militarily imposed **British** protectorate. The British introduced their own judicial and education systems, and set about building roads, reservoirs and other civic projects. Despite the benefits of these innovations, British rule was marked by a high-handedness – along with a tendency to use brute force to quell dissent – that won them few friends.

The War of Independence

By 1821, the *Filikí Etería* had assembled a motley coalition of *klephts* and theorists, who launched their insurrection against the Turks at the monastery of **Áyia Lávra** near Kalávrita in the Peloponnese, where on March 21 the Greek banner was openly raised by the local bishop, Yermanos. Despite punitive resistance by their British rulers, the Ionian islands enthusiastically if surreptitiously supported the rebellion with money, weapons and manpower. While much of the detail of the ensuing **War of Independence** is confusing – with landowners believing they were fighting to regain their traditional privileges, and peasants seeing it as a means of improving social conditions regardless of who was in power – the Greeks, through local and fragmented guerrilla campaigns, managed to present a coherent threat to Turkish rule.

Outside Greece, prestige and publicity for the insurrection was promoted by the arrival of a thousand or so **Philhellenes**, almost half of them German, though the most important was the English poet, **Lord Byron**, who died while training Greek forces at Messolóngi in April 1824. Byron's connections with the Ionian islands, in particular Kefaloniá, conferred on him an abiding heroic status here as elsewhere in Greece.

Greek guerrilla leaders such as **Theodhoros Kolokotronis** were responsible for the most significant military victories of the war, but the death of Byron had an immense effect on public opinion in the West. Originally, aid for the Greek struggle had come neither from Orthodox Russia, nor from the Western powers of France and Britain, ravaged by the Napoleonic Wars. Yet when Messolóngi fell again to the Turks in 1827, these three powers finally agreed to seek autonomy for parts of Greece, and sent a combined fleet to confront the Turks, then sacking the Peloponnese. After an accidental sea battle in **Navarino Bay** destroyed almost the entire Turkish fleet, and heightened aggression from Russia, Turkey was forced to accept the existence of an autonomous Greece.

In 1830 Greek independence was confirmed by the Western powers and borders were drawn. The new country contained just 800,000 of the six million

Greeks living within the Ottoman empire, and the Greek territories were for the most part the poorest of the Classical and Byzantine lands, comprising Attica, the Peloponnese and the Argo-Saronic and Cycladic islands. The rich agricultural belt of Thessaly, Epirus in the west and Macedonia in the north remained in Turkish hands. Meanwhile, the British, despite championing the cause of Greek independence on the mainland, held onto the Ionian islands until they were finally ceded to Greece on **May 21, 1864**.

The emerging state

Modern Greece began as a republic, and its first president was a Corfiot. An aristocrat and career diplomat, **Ioannis Kapodhistrias** (1776–1831) had gained an impressive reputation negotiating with the British and Russians, and won widespread support for his defence of Lefkádha against the Albanian ruler of Epirus, Ali Pasha. Kapodhistrias concentrated on creating a viable structure for the emerging Greek state in the face of diverse protagonists from the independence struggle, though his later career was marred by unpopular acts of nepotism and autocracy. Almost inevitably, he was assassinated – in 1831, by chieftains from the Máni peninsula – and perhaps equally inevitably, the Western powers who had forced the resolution of the independence issue stepped in. They created a monarchy and installed a Bavarian prince, **Otho**.

The new king proved to be autocratic and insensitive, giving official posts to fellow Germans and dismissing suggestions by the landless peasantry that the old estates be redistributed. A popular revolt forced him from the country in 1862, and the Europeans produced a new prince, this time from Denmark. Britain ceded the Ionian islands to Greece as part of this arrangement, more or less as a sweetener. **George I** proved more capable than his predecessor: he built the first railways and roads, introduced limited land reforms in the Peloponnese and oversaw the first expansion of the Greek borders.

The Megáli Idhéa and war

From the very beginning, the unquestioned motivating force of Greek foreign policy was the **Megáli Idhéa** (Great Idea) of liberating Greek populations outside the country and incorporating the old territories of Byzantium into the kingdom. In 1878 **Thessaly**, along with southern Epirus, was ceded to Greece by the Turks. Less illustriously, the Greeks failed in 1897 to achieve *enosis* (union) with **Crete** by attacking Turkish forces on the mainland, and in the process virtually bankrupted the state. The island was, however, placed under a high commissioner, appointed by the great powers, and in 1913 became a part of Greece.

It was from Crete, also, that the most distinguished Greek statesman emerged.

△ Ioannis Kapodhistrias

Eleftherios Venizelos, having led a civilian campaign for his island's liberation, was in 1910 elected as Greek prime minister. Two years later he organized an alliance of Balkan powers to fight the **Balkan Wars** (1912–13), campaigns that saw the Turks virtually driven from Europe. With Greek borders extended to include the northeast Aegean, northern Thessaly, central Epirus and parts of Macedonia, the *Megáli Idhéa* was approaching reality. At the same time, Venizelos proved himself a shrewd manipulator of domestic public opinion by revising the constitution and introducing a series of liberal social reforms.

Division, however, was to appear with the outbreak of **World War I**. Venizelos urged Greek entry on the British side, seeing in the conflict possibilities for the "liberation" of Greeks in Thrace and Asia Minor, but the new king, Constantine I, married to a sister of the German Kaiser, imposed a policy of neutrality. Eventually Venizelos set up a revolutionary government in Thessaloníki, and in 1917 Greek troops entered the war to join the French, British and Serbians in the **Macedonian campaign**. On the capitulation of Bulgaria and Ottoman Turkey, the Greeks occupied Thrace, and Venizelos presented at Versailles demands for the predominantly Greek region of Smyrna on the Asia Minor coast.

It was the beginning of one of the most disastrous episodes in modern Greek history. Venizelos was authorized to move forces into Smyrna in 1919, but by then Allied support had evaporated and in Turkey itself a new nationalist movement was taking power under Mustafa Kemal, or **Atatürk** as he came to be known. In 1920 Venizelos lost the elections and monarchist factions took over, their aspirations unmitigated by the Cretan's skill in foreign diplomacy. Greek forces were ordered to advance upon Ankara in an attempt to bring Atatürk to terms.

The so-called **Anatolian campaign** ignominiously collapsed in summer 1922, when Turkish troops forced the Greeks back to the coast and a hurried evacuation from **Smyrna** ensued. The Turks moved in and systematically massacred whatever remained of the Armenian and Greek populations before burning most of the city to the ground.

The exchange of populations

This ensuing Treaty of Lausanne in 1923 ordered the **exchange of religious minorities** from both countries. Turkey was to accept 390,000 Muslims from Greece. Greece, mobilized for a decade and with a population of less than five million, was faced with the resettlement of over 1,300,000 Christian refugees. The *Megáli Idhéa* ceased to be a viable blueprint.

The effect on Greek society was far-reaching. The great agricultural estates of Thessaly were finally redistributed, both to Greek tenants and refugee farmers, and huge shanty towns developed around Athens, Pireás and other cities, a spur to the country's then almost nonexistent industry.

Political reaction was swift. A group of army officers assembled after the retreat from Smyrna "invited" King Constantine to abdicate and executed five of his ministers. Democracy was nominally restored with the proclamation of a republic, but for much of the next decade changes in government were brought about by factions within the armed forces. Meanwhile, among the urban refugee population, unions were being formed and the Greek **Communist Party** (KKE) was established.

By 1936 the Communist Party had enough democratic support to hold the balance of power in parliament, and would have done so had not the army and the by then restored king decided otherwise. Yiorgos (George) II had been voted in by a plebiscite held – and almost certainly manipulated – the previous year, and so presided over an increasingly factionalized parliament.

The Metaxas dictatorship

In April 1936, George II appointed a Kefallonian, **General Ioannis Metaxas**, as prime minister, despite the fact that Metaxas only had the support of six elected deputies. Immediately a series of KKE-organized strikes broke out and the king, ignoring attempts to form a broad liberal coalition, dissolved parliament without setting a date for new elections. It was a blatantly unconstitutional move and opened the way for five years of ruthless and at times absurd dictatorship.

Metaxas averted a general strike with military force and proceeded to set up a state based on fascist models of the time. Left-wing and trade union opponents were imprisoned or forced into exile, a state youth movement and secret police set up, and rigid censorship, extending even to passages of Thucydides, imposed. It was, however, at least a Greek dictatorship, and though Metaxas was sympathetic to Nazi organization he completely opposed German or Italian domination.

World War II and the civil war

The Italians tried to provoke Greece into **World War II** by torpedoing the Greek cruiser *Elli* in Tínos harbour in August 1940. The Greeks made no response. However, when Mussolini occupied Albania and, on October 28, 1940, sent an ultimatum demanding passage through Greece for his troops, Metaxas' legendary riposte to the Italian foreign minister was *óhi* ("No"). (In fact, his response, in the mutually understood French, was *C'est la guerre*.) The date marked the entry of Greece into the war, and *óhi* Day is still celebrated as a national holiday.

Occupation and resistance

Fighting as a nation in a sudden unity of crisis, the Greeks drove Italian forces from the mainland and in the operation took control of the long-coveted and predominantly Greek-populated northern Epirus. The Ionian islands found themselves on the front line, and were taken by the Italians. The Greek army, however, lost its impetus during a harsh winter fighting in the mountains, and British backup never materialized.

In April the following year Nazi columns swept through Yugoslavia and across the Greek mainland, effectively reversing the only Axis defeat to date, and by the end of May 1941 airborne and seaborne **German invasion** forces had completed the occupation. Metaxas had died before their arrival, while King George and his new self-appointed ministers fled into exile in Cairo. Few Greeks of any political persuasion were sad to see them go.

The joint **Italian–German–Bulgarian Axis occupation** of Greece was among the bitterest experiences of the European war. Nearly half a million Greek civilians starved to death as all available food was requisitioned to feed occupying armies, and entire villages throughout the mainland and especially on Crete were burnt and slaughtered at the least hint of Resistance activity. In the Ionians, even the olive crop was sequestered, driving the olive industry underground.

The Nazis supervised the deportation to concentration camps of virtually the entire **Greek Jewish population**. This was at the time a sizeable community. Thessaloníki – where former UN and Austrian president Kurt Waldheim worked for Nazi intelligence – contained the largest Jewish population of any Balkan city, and there were significant populations in all Greek mainland towns and on many islands. Over two thousand Jews were rounded up in Corfu Town alone for transportation; fewer than a hundred returned.

With a quisling government in Athens – and an unpopular, discredited royalist group in Cairo – the focus of Greek political and military action over the next four years passed largely to the **EAM**, or National Liberation Front. By 1943 it was in virtual control of most areas of the country, working with the British on tactical operations, with its own army (**ELAS**), navy and both civil and secret police forces. On the whole, it commanded popular support, and it offered an obvious framework for the resumption of postwar government.

However, most of its membership was communist, and the British prime minister, **Churchill**, was determined to reinstate the monarchy. Even with two years of the war to run it became obvious that there could be no peaceable post-liberation regime other than an EAM-dominated republic. Accordingly, in August 1943 representatives from each of the main Resistance movements – including two non-communist groups – flew from a makeshift airstrip in Thessaly to ask for guarantees from the "government" in Cairo that the king would not return unless a plebiscite had first voted in his favour. Neither the Greek nor British authorities would consider the proposal, and the one possibility of averting civil war was lost.

The EAM contingent returned divided, as perhaps the British had intended, and a conflict broke out between those who favoured taking peaceful control of any government imposed after liberation, and the hardline Stalinist ideologues, who believed such a situation should not be allowed to develop.

In October 1943, with fears of an imminent British landing force and takeover, ELAS launched a full-scale attack upon its Greek rivals; by the following February, when a ceasefire was arranged, they had wiped out all but the EDES, a right-wing grouping suspected of collaboration with the Germans. At the same time other forces were at work, with both the British and Americans infiltrating units into Greece in order to prevent the establishment of communist government when the Germans began withdrawing their forces.

Civil war

In fact, as the Germans began to leave in October 1944, most of the EAM leadership agreed to join a British-sponsored "official" **interim government**. It quickly proved a tactical error, however, for with ninety percent of the countryside under their control the communists were given only one-third representation; the king showed no sign of renouncing his claims; and, in November, Allied forces ordered ELAS to disarm. On December 3 all pretences of civility or neutrality were dropped; the police fired on a communist demonstration in Athens and fighting broke out between ELAS and **British troops**, in the so-called **Dhekemvrianá** battle of Athens.

A truce of sorts was negotiated at Várkiza the following spring, but the agreement was never implemented. The army, police and civil service remained in right-wing hands and, while collaborators were often allowed to retain their positions, left-wing sympathizers, many of whom were not communists, were systematically excluded. The elections of 1946 were won by the right-wing parties, followed by a plebiscite in favour of the king's return. By 1947 guerrilla activity had again reached the scale of a full **civil war**.

In the interim, King George had died and been succeeded by his brother Paul (with his consort Frederika), while the **Americans** had taken over the British role, and begun putting into action the Cold War **Truman doctrine**. In 1947 they took virtual control of Greece, their first significant postwar experiment in anti-communist intervention. Massive economic and military aid was given to a client Greek government, with a prime minister whose documents had to be countersigned by the American Mission in order to become valid.

In the mountains US "military advisers" supervised **campaigns against ELAS**, and there were mass arrests, court martials and imprisonments – a kind of "White Terror" – lasting until 1951. Over three thousand executions were recorded, including a number of Jehovah's Witnesses, "a sect proved to be under communist domination", according to US Ambassador Grady.

In the autumn of 1949, with the Yugoslav–Greek border closed after Tito's rift with Stalin, the last ELAS guerrillas finally admitted defeat, retreating into Albania from their strongholds on Mount Grámmos. Atrocities had been committed on both sides, including, from the Left, wide-scale destruction of monasteries and the dubious evacuation of children from "combat areas" (as told in Nicholas Gage's virulently anti-communist book, *Eleni*). Such errors, as well as the hopelessness of fighting an American-backed army, undoubtedly lost ELAS much support.

Reconstruction and dictatorship: 1950–74

After a decade of war that had shattered much of Greece's infrastructure (it is said that not one bridge was left standing by 1948), and had killed twelve percent of the 1940 population, it was a demoralized, shattered country that emerged into the Western political orbit of the 1950s. Greece was perforce **American-dominated**, enlisted into the **Korean War** in 1950 and **NATO** the following year. In domestic politics, the US embassy – still giving the orders – foisted upon the Greeks a winner-takes-all **electoral system**, which was to ensure victory for the Right over the next twelve years. Overt leftist activity was banned (though a "cover party" for communists was soon founded), and many of those who were not herded into political "re-education" camps or dispatched by firing squads, legal or vigilante, went into exile throughout Eastern Europe, to return only after 1974. The 1950s also saw the wholesale **depopulation of remote villages** as migrants sought work in Australia, America and Western Europe, or the larger Greek cities.

Constantine Karamanlis and Cyprus

The American-backed right-wing **Greek Rally** party, led by **General Papagos**, won the first decisive post-civil-war elections in 1952. After the general's death, the party's leadership was taken over – and to an extent liberalised – by **Constantine Karamanlis**. Under his rule, stability of a kind was established and some economic advances registered, particularly after the revival of Greece's traditional German markets. Health and life expectancy improved dramatically as the age-old scourges of tuberculosis and malaria were finally confronted with American-supplied food and pesticides. Less commendable was Karamanlis's encouragement of the law of *andiparohí*, whereby owners of small refugee shanties or Neoclassical mansions alike could offer the site of their property to apartment-block developers in exchange for two flats (out of eight to ten) in the finished building. This effectively ripped the heart out of most Greek towns, and explains their baleful aesthetics a half-century on.

The main crisis in foreign policy throughout this period was **Cyprus**, where a long terrorist campaign was waged against the British by Greek Cypriots who demanded self-determination with a view to achieving *enosis* (union) with Greece. Turkey adamantly opposed *enosis* and said that if Britain left Cyprus it should revert to Turkish rule. In 1959 a compromise was reached which granted independence to the island and protection for its Turkish Cypriot minority but ruled out any union with Greece.

By 1961, unemployment, the Cyprus issue and the presence of US nuclear bases on Greek soil were changing the political climate, and when Karamanlis was again elected there was strong suspicion of intimidation and fraud carried out by rightwing elements and the army. After eighteen months of strikes and protest demonstrations, during which the leftwing deputy **Grigoris Lambrakis** was assassinated in Thessaloníki in May 1963 (an event which became the subject of the Costa-Gavras film *Z*), Karamanlis resigned and went into voluntary exile in Paris.

George Papandreou and the Colonels

New elections held in February 1964 gave the **Centre Union Party**, headed by **George Papandreou**, an outright majority and a mandate for social and economic reform. The new government was the first to be controlled from outside the right since 1935, and in his first act as prime minister, Papandreou sought to heal the wounds of the civil war by **releasing political prisoners** and allowing exiles to return. When King Paul died in March and his son came to the throne as **Constantine II**, it seemed as though a new era had begun.

But soon **Cyprus** was again taking centre stage. Intercommunal fighting between Turkish Cypriots who wanted partition and Greek Cypriots who wanted *enosis* broke out in 1963, and in 1964 it was only the intervention of the United States that dissuaded Turkey from invading the island. In the mood of military confrontation between Greece and Turkey – both of them NATO members – Papandreou questioned Greece's role in the Western alliance, to the alarm of the Americans and the Greek right.

The right was also opposed to Papandreou's economic policies which were having an inflationary effect, and it feared the growing power of the Left, fears that were bolstered in May 1965 when a plot by **Aspida** (Shield), a subversive group of left-wing army officers, was uncovered – and linked, it was claimed, with Papandreou's son Andreas, a minister in his father's government. More serious were indications of rightwing plots within the army against the government, and when Papandreou moved to purge the army of disloyal officers, the Right took this as an attack on their traditional domination of the armed forces. In July, when the king would not support the prime minister in his attempts to dismiss certain officers, Papandreou resigned in order to gain a fresh mandate at the polls, but the king would not order new elections, instead persuading members of the Centre Union to defect and organise a coalition government. Punctuated by strikes, resignations and mass demonstrations, the political situation in Greece became increasingly unstable over the next year and a half until new elections were eventually set for May 1967.

It was a foregone conclusion that George Papandreou's Centre Union Party would win the 1967 poll against the discredited coalition partners. But **King**

Constantine, disturbed by the party's leftward shift, was said to have briefed senior generals for a coup. True or not, the king, like almost everyone else in Greece, was caught by surprise when a group of unknown **colonels** staged their own **coup** on April 21, 1967. In December the king staged a counter-coup against the colonels, but when it failed he went into exile.

The junta announced itself as the "**Revival of Greek Orthodoxy**" against corrupting Western influences, not least long hair and miniskirts, which hardly helped the tourist trade. All political activity was banned, independent trade unions were forbidden to recruit or meet, the press was so heavily censored that many papers stopped printing, and thousands of communists and others on the left were arrested, imprisoned and often tortured. Among these were both Papandreous, father and son, the composer Mikis Theodorakis and Amalia Fleming, the widow of the discoverer of penicillin Alexander Fleming. Thousands were permanently maimed physically and psychologically in the junta's torture chambers. The world famous Greek actress Melina Mercouri was stripped of her citizenship in absentia, and thousands of prominent Greeks joined her in exile. Culturally, the colonels put an end to popular music (closing down most of the live *rebétika* clubs) and inflicted ludicrous censorship on literature and the theatre, including (as under Metaxas) a ban on the production of classical tragedies. Meantime, the TV and radio broadcast endless speeches by chief colonel **Papadopoulos** – rambling, illiterate texts that became a byword for bad grammar, obfuscation and Orwellian Newspeak. Convinced that he had acquired the job of ruling Greece for life, in 1973 Papadopoulos abolished the monarchy and declared Greece a republic with himself as president.

Restoration of democracy

The colonels lasted for seven years, and whatever initial support they may have met among Greeks, after the first two years they were opposed by the vast majority, including a great many on the right who were embarrassed by their oafishness. Opposition was voiced from the beginning by exiled Greeks in London, the United States and Western Europe, but only in 1973 did demonstrations break out openly in Greece – the colonels' secret police had done too thorough a job of infiltrating domestic resistance groups and terrifying

△ Politics in Corfu Town

everyone else into docility. On **17 November** the students of the **Athens Polytechnic** began an occupation of their buildings. The ruling clique sent armoured vehicles to storm the Polytechnic's gates and a still-undetermined number of students (estimates range from 34 to 300) were killed. Martial law was tightened and Colonel Papadopoulos was replaced by the even more noxious and reactionary **General Ioannides**, head of the secret police.

The end came within a year when the dictatorship embarked on a disastrous political adventure in **Cyprus**, essentially the last playing of the *Megáli Idhéa* card. By attempting to topple the Makarios government and **impose enosis** on the island, the junta provoked a **Turkish invasion** and occupation of forty percent of Cypriot territory. The army finally mutinied and **Constantine Karamanlis** was invited to return from Paris to again take office.

Karamanlis swiftly negotiated a ceasefire in Cyprus, and in November 1974 he and his **Nea Dhimokratía** (New Democracy) party were rewarded by a sizeable majority in elections, with a centrist and socialist opposition. The latter was the Panhellenic Socialist Movement (PASOK), a new party led by **Andreas Papandreou**.

Europe and a new Greece: 1974 to the present

To Karamanlis's enduring credit his New Democracy party oversaw an effective and firm return to **democratic stability**, even legalising the KKE (the Greek Communist Party) for the first time in its history. Karamanlis also held a **referendum on the monarchy**, in which seventy per cent of Greeks rejected the return of Constantine II. So a largely symbolic, German-style presidency was instituted instead, which Karamanlis himself occupied from 1980 to 1985, and again from 1990 to 1995.

PASOK comes to power

"Change" and "Out with the Right" were the slogans of the election campaign that swept the socialist party, **PASOK**, and its leader Andreas Papandreou to power on October 18, 1981. PASOK won 174 of the 300 parliamentary seats and the Communist KKE, though not a part of the new government, returned another 13 deputies. The manifesto of Greece's first socialist government was to devolve power to local authorities, nationalize heavy industry, improve the skeletal social services, purge bureaucratic inefficiency and malpractice, end bribery and corruption, and to follow an independent foreign policy after removing US bases and withdrawing from NATO and the European Community.

The new era started with a bang as long-overdue **social reforms** were enacted. Peasant women were granted pensions for the first time; wages were indexed to the cost of living; civil marriage was introduced, family and property law was reformed in favour of wives and mothers; demanding dowries was forbidden (though it still continues informally); and equal rights legislation was put on the statute book. In addition, ELAS was officially recognized and was permitted to take part in ceremonies commemorating the wartime resistance. This prompted fears that the military might again intervene, especially when Andreas Papandreou, imitating his father, briefly assumed the defence portfolio himself. But he went out of his way to soothe military susceptibilities, increasing their salaries, buying new weaponry and being fastidious in his attendance at military functions.

Economically, Papandreou promised a bonanza which he must have known, as an academically trained economist, was strictly a fantasy. As a result he pleased nobody. He could not fairly be blamed for the inherited lack of investment, low productivity, deficiency in managerial and labour skills and other chronic problems besetting the Greek **economy**. But he certainly aggravated the situation by allowing his supporters to indulge in violently anti-capitalist rhetoric, which frightened off potential investors. At the same time Papandreou's government had to cope with the effects of **world recession**. Shipping, the country's main foreign-currency earner, was devastated. Remittances from émigré workers fell off as they became unemployed in their host countries, and tourism diminished. Unemployment rose, inflation hit 25 per cent and the national debt soared.

Under the slogan "Vote PASOK for Even Better Days", backed by a public spending spree intended to buy votes, and a shamelessly nationalistic "Greece-for-the-Greeks" foreign policy, Papandreou won a second term in June 1985. But by October, PASOK had imposed a two-year wage freeze and import restrictions, abolished the wage-indexing scheme and devalued the drachma by fifteen percent. In the event it was the **European Community**, once Papandreou's bête noire, which rescued him from his follies with a huge two-part loan on condition that an austerity programme was maintained. Increasingly autocratic, Papandreou responded to criticism from the left by firing trade union leaders and expelling three hundred dissenting members of his own party. Fearing that only the presence of US bases in Greece guaranteed protection from Turkish aggression, Papandreou's demand for their removal was dropped. Nor with the European Community – soon to become the European Union – propping up Greece financially would Papandreou now bite the hand that fed.

Despite Papandreou's many failings and about-turns, it seemed unlikely that PASOK would be toppled in the 1989 elections. But the collapse of Soviet rule in Eastern Europe was reflected by a shift away from the left in Greece, and then there was Papandreou's very public affair with an Olympic Airways hostess half his age, causing humiliation to his wife and family, not to mention a whole raft of economic scandals. In consequence, PASOK lost power as a trio of inconclusive elections finally resulted in the New Democracy party winning a tiny majority, its leader **Constantine Mitsotakis** becoming prime minister.

On assuming power, Mitsotakis prescribed a course of austerity measures to revive the chronically ill economy. Little headway was made, though given the world recession that was hardly surprising. Greek inflation was still approaching twenty percent annually, and at nearly ten percent, unemployment remained stubbornly high. Other measures introduced by Mitsotakis included laws to combat strikes, but these were ineffectual, as breakdowns in public transport, electricity and rubbish collection all too frequently illustrated.

The Macedonian problem and return of PASOK

The last thing the increasingly unpopular Mitsotakis needed was a major foreign policy headache. But that was exactly what he got in 1991 when one of the breakaway republics of the **former Yugoslavia** named itself **Macedonia**. Greeks felt threatened because Macedonia was a name historically associated with northern Greece, and the fear was that this new and unstable country was laying claim to a part of Greek heritage and territory. Greek diplomacy and propaganda fought tooth and nail against anyone recognizing the breakaway state, let alone its use of the name Macedonia, but Greece became increasingly isolated, and by 1993 the new country had gained official recognition from both the EU and the UN – albeit under the provisional title of the "**Former Yugoslav Republic of Macedonia**" (FYROM). Salt was then rubbed into Greek wounds when the FYROM started using the Star of Vergina, symbol of the ancient Macedonian kings, as a national symbol on its new flag, as well as having passages in its constitution referring to "unredeemed" Aegean territories.

The Macedonian problem effectively led to Mitsotakis' political demise, after the defection of a senior party figure, Andonis Samaras, and his creation of a new party, Politiki Anixi, based on the issue of Macedonia. When parliament reconvened in September to approve stringent new budget proposals, the government failed to muster sufficient support, and early elections were called for October 1993. On 11 October Papandreou romped to victory; and the youthful Miltiades Evert, ex-mayor of Athens, replaced Mitsotakis as head of the New Democracy party.

So a frail-looking **Andreas Papandreou**, now well into his seventies, became prime minister for the third time. He soon realised that he was not going to have nearly so easy a ride as in the 1980s, with the economy still in dire straits, and nor could PASOK claim to have won any diplomatic battles over Macedonia, despite a lot of tough posturing. The only concrete move was the imposition in October 1993 of a trade embargo on the FYROM, which merely landed the Greeks in trouble with the European Court of Justice – and succeeded in virtually shutting down the port of Thessaloniki. By contrast, alone among NATO members, Greece was conspicuous for its open support of **Serbia** in the wars wracking ex-Yugoslavia, ostentatiously supplying trucks to Belgrade via Bulgaria. In November, Greece lifted its embargo on the FYROM, opening the borders for tourism and trade in return for the former Yugoslav state suitably editing its constitution and removing the offending emblem from its flag. Relations, in fact, were instantly almost normalized, with only the name still a moot point.

Domestically, the emerging critical issue was the 76-year-old Papandreou's obstinate clinging to power despite obvious signs of dotage. Numerous senior members of PASOK became increasingly bold and vocal in their criticism, and in January 1996, after months in hospital intensive care, Papandreou finally resigned the premiership, which went to technocrat **Kostas Simitis**. On assuming office, Simitis vowed *not* to play to the gallery, saying: "Greece's intransigent nationalism is an expression of the wretchedness that exists in our society. It is the root cause of the problems we have had with our Balkan neighbours and our difficult relations with Europe." **Andreas Papandreou** died in June, "a common cheat", as Karamanlis called him in his tart memoirs, when it was discovered that he had accumulated a vast fortune beyond anything he could have earned legitimately as a public servant. But for the time being, Papandreou's death generated a wave of pro-PASOK sentiment which Simitis successfully exploited by quickly calling elections in September and gaining victory. Evert resigned as the New Democracy leader and was succeeded by Karamanlis's nephew Kostas.

Earthquake diplomacy and the Euro

September 1997 saw a timely boost to national morale with the awarding of the 2004 Olympic Games to Athens. Meanwhile, Kostas Simitis, who unlike Papandreou was genuinely pro-European, devoted himself to the unenviable task of getting the Greek economy in sufficiently good shape to meet the criteria for European **monetary union**. The fact that inflation stayed consistently down in single figures for the first time in decades was testament to his ability; indeed his nickname, among both foes and supporters, was "the accountant".

An unexpected and dramatic change in **Greece's relations with Turkey** came when a severe **earthquake** struck northern Athens on September 7, 1999, killing scores and rendering almost 100,000 homeless. It came less than a month after a devastating earthquake in northwest Turkey, and proved to be the spur for a thaw between the two historical rivals. Greeks donated massive amounts of blood and foodstuffs to the Turkish victims, and were the earliest foreign rescue teams on hand in Turkey; in turn they saw Turkish disaster-relief squads among the first on the scene in Athens. Soon afterwards, foreign minister George Papandreou (son of Andreas) announced that Greece had dropped its long-time opposition to EU financial aid to Turkey in the absence of a solution to the outstanding Cyprus and Aegean disputes, and further indicated that Greece would no longer oppose Turkish candidacy for accession to the EU.

With his handling of the Turkish detente and progress towards European monetary union the main campaign issues, Simitis called elections five months earlier than required, on April 9, 2000. In the event, PASOK squeaked into office for a third consecutive term by a single percentage point. But the crucial factor was voters' mistrust of Kostas Karamanlis's manifest inexperience. Simitis capped his election victory by announcing Greece's official entry into the euro-currency zone on 20 June, though it later turned out that the conditions were met only by his government falsifying its budget deficit data. Greece adopted **the euro** on January 1, 2002.

The year also saw a strange saga played out with the arrest of apparently the entire operational members of the terrorist group **Dhekaeftá Novemvríou**. This shadowy, leftist organization, named after the Polytechnic uprising against the Colonels, had been a thorn in Greece's security since 1974, killing twenty-four industrialists, politicians and NATO military personnel, and bombing the property of foreign corporations in Athens and elsewhere. As with all successful police actions, their destruction was the result of a stroke of luck, when a bomb exploded prematurely in the hands of an operative. After a nine-month trial, fifteen of the group's members received multiple life sentences.

Olympian hurdles and a new Karamanlis

In the October 2002 municipal and prefectural elections, New Democracy took substantial control. PASOK had now been in power nationally for nine-teen out of the last twenty-three years, and sentiment was growing for a change. In February 2004 Simitis stood down as party leader, signalling his belief that one of his main reforms had been effected: an end to personality-based politics, and the completed evolution of an issue-based, centrist, technocratic party. That said, both parties had familiar dynastic names in charge, with **George Papan-dreou** taking over leadership of PASOK, and fighting an election against New Democracy, led by **Kostas Karamanlis**.

New Democracy won comfortably and Karamanlis, who became prime minister, dedicated himself to negotiations over divided **Cyprus** in an attempt to get the entire island into the EU on May 1, 2004 (in the event the inter-nationally recognized Republic of Cyprus did join, but without the Turkish-occupied north). He also took personal responsibility for ensuring completion of all preparations for the **2004 Olympic Games**. In a last-minute rush all facilities were ready in August, in time for the games in Athens, but the cost rose to three times the original estimates, and as a result of poor marketing,

Greece may continue to occupy the EU's economic cellar with Portugal, but it's still infinitely wealthier (and more stable) than many of its neighbours, and this has acted as a magnet for a permanent underclass of **immigrants**. Since 1990 they have arrived in numbers estimated at 800,000 to well over a million, a huge burden for a not especially rich country of just over ten million citizens. These days your waiter, hotel desk clerk or cleaning lady is most likely to be Albanian, Bulgarian or Romanian, to cite the three largest groups of arrivals. There are also significant communities of Pakistanis, Egyptians, Poles, Bangladeshis, Syrians, Filipinos, Ukrainians, Russians, Equatorial Africans, Kurds and Georgians, not to mention ethnic Greeks from the Caucasus – a striking change in what had hitherto been a homogeneous and parochial culture.

The Greek response to this has been decidedly mixed. The Albanians, making up roughly half the influx, are almost universally detested (except for the ethnic-Greek northern Epirots), and blamed for all manner of social ills. For the first time, **crime** – especially burglaries – is a significant issue. The newcomers have also prompted the first significant anti-immigration measures in a country whose population is more used to being on the other side of such laws – Greece is a member of the Schengen visa scheme and sees itself, as in past ages, as the first line of defence against the barbarian hordes from the East. The Aegean islands regularly receive boatloads of people from every country in Asia.

In June 2001, as an attempt to cope, legal residence was offered to the estimated half-million illegals who could demonstrate two years' presence in Greece, and pay a hefty amount for retroactive social security contributions. This and a subsequent amnesty legalized about 300,000 residents. Not that the other illegals are likely to be deported *en masse*, as they do the difficult, dirty and dangerous work that Greeks now disdain, especially farm labour, restaurant work and rubbish collection. From an employer's point of view, they are cheap – thirty to forty percent less costly than native Greeks – and they are net contributors to the social welfare system, especially to pensions where Greece, like much of Europe, is seeing its population shrinking and aging. The Albanians in particular are also buoying up much of the banking system by their phenomenal saving habits and wiring of funds home.

Though there is much that is positive about immigration, it must also be said that it is having the effect of making Greece less identifiably Greek and of making the native Greeks themselves less welcoming and more self-absorbed than formerly.

jacked-up hotel prices and fears of terrorism, tourism to Greece actually fell during the year and the Games turned in a deficit.

The after-effects of Olympic spending, and Greece's joining the euro at too high a level after rigging its accounts, were felt in March 2005 when trade unions launched a wave of twenty-four hour strikes across the country in protest at high inflation and rising unemployment. In April the Greek parliament ratified the EU constitution, but it soon became a dead letter when it was rejected by referendums elsewhere. A further wave of **industrial action** followed in June over the government's plans for labour and pension reforms.

But there was at least some positive economic news, with **shipping** undergoing something of a boom; nearly a fifth of the world's merchant fleet is owned by Greek companies, and their fortunes have a significant impact on the country. And as the dust settled, the Olympics, for all their faults, showed enduring benefits to **Greek infrastructure**, particularly in the completion of the new **metro system** for Athens, which now speedily and cheaply connects a new airport with the city. These improvements should lay the foundation for the country's future development.

Wildlife

Apart from the flora and fauna blown, washed or otherwise carried here, nature on the islands has developed from what was here over 10,000 years ago, when the icecaps melted and stranded these drowned mountains out at sea off the coastline of mainland Greece. Thanks partly to the Venetian invaders – whose extensive olive-planting programmes, at a time of general deforestation in the Mediterranean basin, bound and held much of the islands' topsoil – the Ionian islands are unusually green and fertile compared to most Greek islands.

Before the inundation at the end of the last Ice Age, great forests stretched across much of Italy, what is now the Adriatic Sea and east across the north of Greece. Extensive deforestation for fuel, building and to clear land for cultivation and grazing utterly transformed this landscape on mainland Greece, far less so on the Ionian islands. The difference can be observed on any ferry journey in the region, simply by comparing the bare brown hills of the mainland with the olive groves and pine woodlands that cover most of the eastern coastlines and lower hillsides of the islands.

Modern Greece has escaped some of the worst effects of the intensification of agriculture, but there are signs that it may be succumbing. Pesticides and chemical fertilizers are now playing a larger part in farming, controversial (and possibly carcinogenic) olive sprays are gaining ground on Corfu and Paxí, despite EU regulations, and factory fishing threatens what is an already depleted fish stock, as well as the livelihood of independent fishing workers. Ugly and exploitative development has destroyed swaths of the countryside and coastline and, despite the eco-friendly soundbites of politicians and businessfolk, many Greeks (and, it has to be said, many visitors) regard the environment as little more than a convenient garbage dump.

Nevertheless, Greece's environment has yet to approach the state of parts of northern Europe; away from developed areas, it's still possible to find landscapes almost untouched by mankind. Rainy winters make the islands a great draw for botanists, especially in spring, and the vegetation in turn attracts ornithologists and their prey.

Flora

The Ionian archipelago follows a different biological clock from northern Europe or America, particularly noticeable in the development of its **flowers**. Despite being among the most northerly of the Greek islands, the Ionians see daffodils and crocuses in January, freesias and antirrhinums in March, and by Easter most woodlands and domestic gardens are in full bloom. Hot summers – not always guaranteed in this region – tend to blast most plant life, only for autumn rains to produce a second growth among some plants, such as dwarf cyclamen.

The best time to visit is spring, ideally around **Easter** – much of the plant life will have died back before most charter flights begin arriving in the region. By Easter, wild and cultivated carnations, geraniums, garlic, valerian and bush angelica are in flower, as is the slightly sinister bell-like datura. Country walks are likely to be scented with wild rosemary, oregano, thyme (parts of Lefkádha are smothered in this herb; beekeepers park hives in it to flavour the honey) and sage, as well as eucalyptus and myrtle, the last of which is used to line the streets in some Easter parades, giving off a heady aroma as the procession tramples over it.

The onset of **summer** brings yellow broom and, in flowering years, the tiny white star-like flowers of the olive tree. Scarlet pimpernels, anemones, camomile, campanula and love-in-a-mist abound. This is also the time that the region's two sturdiest blooms, the oleander and bougainvillea, appear. Wild orchids can materialize almost overnight. As summer progresses, new growth tends to be on the hills and lower slopes of the mountains. Hollyhocks, asphodel, pinks and grape hyacinths are common at high altitudes.

While the more mountainous islands are largely bare of **trees** at higher altitudes, the lower slopes of Lefkádha and Kefalloniá are notable for impressive stands of Aleppo pine, holm oak and, on the latter, the native Cephallonian fir (*Abies cephalonica*) – which can also be found at even lower levels, notably the beaches of Skála. The ubiquitous **olive tree** (*Olea europea*), unlike its pruned mainland relative, is allowed to grow to unmanageable sizes on the islands; some of those on Corfu and Paxí may be as much as 500 years old. As well as commonplace fruits such as apple, orange, lemon, lime, pear and cherry, figs and prickly pears are also found throughout the islands.

Birds

Despite the unwanted attention of thousands of Greek gun-owners, who seem to regard the Ionian skies as one big funfair rifle range, a great variety of **birds** breed on the islands and migrate through them. Greece is a natural stopping-off point for species that winter in Africa but breed in northern Europe. Visitors in May should catch some of the northbound swarms; the late autumn return journey is less concentrated.

After the sparrow, the **house martin** is probably the commonest bird in the Ionians, visiting in summer. As well as wheeling in great clouds over Corfu Town, it builds its mud nests in handy niches around the roofs of buildings, often under exposed eaves, where the parents can be observed feeding the young. Some canny birds simply nest in taverna awnings.

Blue tits, bullfinches, greenfinches and goldfinches are common in woodland and orchards, and in marshland and coastal dunes it's quite common to spot the avocet, bee-eater, sandpiper, grey heron, kingfisher and oyster-catcher. In farmland and scrub you are also likely to glimpse the woodchat shrike, Sardinian warbler, the cirl bunting and the crested skylark. The golden oriole is one of the prettiest visitors to the islands, although if Paxí is anything to go by, its commonest habitat seems to be the deepfreeze – islanders apparently consider them great delicacies. It's not uncommon to spot pelicans as well.

Most dramatically, there are a number of **predatory birds** common in the islands. Peregrine falcons can be spotted in more remote areas, often in pairs, usually turning endless circles on guard above a nest. Kestrels are a regular sight, hovering on thermals while hunting. Buzzards, griffons and Egyptian vultures and, in more solitary mountainous areas, the golden eagle, can also be seen, though rarely these days.

At night, you're likely to hear nightingales in less developed areas, as well as the tiny Scops owl; barn owls nest here, but are rarely seen.

Mammals

The Ionian islands share the more run-of-the-mill **mammals** common throughout Greece – rats, mice, voles, squirrels and foxes – but tend to lack the larger predators of the mainland's mountainous areas. The **jackal** is still said to be found in the remotest parts of Corfu, although with some difficulty, as it is shy and mainly nocturnal. On Kefalloniá, visitors to Mount Énos might possibly glimpse the dozen or so **wild horses** still at large on the mountain's slopes.

Hedgehogs are fairly common, and though shy will often forage in gardens. Similarly, pine martens and stone martens may also be glimpsed in fairly developed areas. At dusk, you're likely to spot an airborne mammal, the tiny pipistrelle bat.

The region's two aquatic mammals – the **dolphin** and **monk seal** – are very rare. The former can sometimes be seen, particularly around Paxí (early morning is usually the best time), when they race or play around ferries and other boats. Monk seals are rarer still, but are known to breed in caves around Paxí and other island coastlines. They are very shy, and should not be approached. As well as being endangered, the seal is easily scared away from its own habitat, although in breeding season it can also be quite protective.

Reptiles and amphibians

The summer heat and dry, rocky landscape of parts of the islands provide an ideal habitat for reptiles. Yet even **reptiles** avoid the intense heat; best times to catch them are mornings in spring, before the sun begins to bake.

Most of the islands have their own subspecies of **lizard**. On Corfu and Paxí, the most common is the Dalmatian algyroides, around 15cm long, with a red-brown body and dazzling blue under its lower jaw. The Balkan wall lizard, green/brown-coloured with a long tail, is seen throughout the islands, particularly Kefalloniá and Zákynthos. In the countryside south of Corfu Town, it's sometimes possible to spot the black/grey spiny agama or Rhodes dragon (this is the only place in the Ionians this resident of the Dodecanese has ever been seen).

Most dramatic of the lizards is the **Balkan green lizard**, which can be seen in open or uncultivated countryside (and sometimes the wilder gardens). This bright-green animal can grow up to half a metre in length, most of which is its tail, a crucial balance in its party-piece of running on its hind legs, from one hiding place to another. Looking like miniature tyrannosaurs, they can sometimes be spotted legging it around the gardens of the *Corfu Palace Hotel*.

A distant relative of the lizard, the **gecko**, is a common sight indoors throughout the islands, particularly at night. They cling to walls and ceilings with adhesive pads on their feet, and are both harmless and terrified of humans. Two species, the pink-tinged Turkish gecko and the brown/grey Moorish gecko, are common to the Ionians. You'll most often see them on walls or around light fittings, which attract the flies and mosquitoes on which they feed.

Tortoises can often be found on Corfu, Zákynthos and Kefalloniá. The Hermann's tortoise breeds on all three islands, and favours gentle grassy terrain. The best time to spot them is mid-morning, when they are likely to be basking between hiding places.

Two of the tortoise's smaller aquatic relatives, the European pond terrapin and stripe-necked terrapin, can be found in ponds, rivers and other freshwater environments. The European tends to be black with gold splotches, the stripe-necked grey or brown.

A somewhat larger version of the terrapin, the sea turtle, is common in the Ionians from Corfu down to Zákynthos. The **loggerhead turtle** (*Caretta caretta*) is now a protected species (see p.249), although anyone visiting Zákynthos will see that flagrant breaches of the rules regarding loggerheads are an almost daily occurrence. As with Schrödinger's cat, it seems likely that the very act of looking at the turtles endangers them. Leatherback and green turtles also breed in the region, but are rarely sighted.

Among **snakes**, there are adders on most of the islands (if you're unfortunate enough to frighten one into biting you, note that they're not poisonous). Large – up to two metres – brown snakes are probably Montpellier snakes, a slightly poisonous snake that feeds on rats and other small mammals. Grass snakes are also quite common, and harmless. The one dangerous species is the nose-horned viper, a short snake with zigzag marks down its back, and one of the most poisonous in Europe.

In springtime, the islands are alive with frogs and toads. The **green toad** announces itself with a curious throaty noise and its remarkable bright-green and grey marbled skin. Also common is the small **tree frog**, green or brown in colour – it can alter like a chameleon – and with adhesive suckers on its feet that enable it to climb. Its mountaineering skills and love of water sometimes lead it into bathrooms, where it does similar insect-catching work to the gecko.

Insects

Grasshoppers and crickets are common in Greece, but not as prevalent as the **cicada**, whose distinctive noise typifies and evokes a Mediterranean afternoon for many visitors. Whereas the grasshopper and cricket produce their sounds by rubbing limbs together, the (male) cicada produces its rasping susurrus by rapidly vibrating cavities on either side of its body. The cicada has a green, cricket-like body, hard to find in trees and shrubs, especially as they tend to fall silent when approached.

The islands are also home to over forty species of **butterfly**, best seen in spring or early summer. Migrant butterflies that will be recognized from north European environments include the red admiral, large and small whites and the painted lady. One of the largest butterflies in Greece, the orange-yellow two-tailed pasha is a rare sighting, but remarkable; some are the size of a small bird. Cleopatras, with their large yellow wings, and the green hairstreak, a small vivid-green butterfly, can also be spotted. Most remarkable, however, are the swallowtails, with their yellow and black colouring and telltale trailing wing tips.

Books and maps

Most of the books below should be available from any good bookshop, including online stores. We've given the publisher where the book is published outside the UK or US.

Travel and general accounts

Peter Bull *It Isn't All Greek to Me*; *Life's a Cucumber*. Now out of print, but well worth tracking down, British actor Bull's two books are about his love affair with Greece, in particular Lákka on Paxí. Some characters are still alive on the island today, and the tiny house he built over three decades ago stands on the cliffs overlooking Lákka bay.

Gerald Durrell *My Family and Other Animals*. Very funny anecdotal memoir of Durrell's childhood on Corfu over half a century ago. Excellent on the (now vanished) landscape and Durrell's passion for island fauna; big brother Larry also makes an appearance.

Lawrence Durrell *Prospero's Cell*. The first of his islands trilogy (which includes *Reflections on a Marine Venus,* on Rhodes, and *Bitter Lemons,* on Cyprus), this has hardly been out of print since it was published in 1945. Durrell's magical diary of his time on Corfu in the year before World War II is highly recommended for visitors to the island, and mandatory for those visiting Kalámi.

Lawrence Durrell *Spirit of Place*. Durrell's collected shorter prose pieces include recollections of Corfu and travels in the Ionians, including a return visit after the war.

Martin Garrett *Greece: A Literary Companion*. Extracts of travel writing and the classics, arranged by region. Enjoyable and frustrating in equal measure.

Edward Lear *The Corfu Years* (Denise Harvey, Athens). Superbly illustrated journals of the nonsense versifier and noted landscape painter, whose paintings and sketches of Corfu, Paxí and elsewhere offer a rare glimpse of the Ionian landscape in the nineteenth century.

Henry Miller *The Colossus of Maroussi*. The perfect companion volume to *Prospero's Cell*: writing in Paris in 1939, Miller was invited to holiday in Kalámi with the Durrells on the eve of World War II. Much of the book covers journeys elsewhere, but the stranger's view of Corfu (and the Durrells) is wonderfully over-the-top.

James Pettifer *The Greeks: The Land and People Since the War*. The best introduction to contemporary Greece, its recent history, as well as politics, culture and topics such as the impact of tourism. Having worked as a reporter in Greece and the Balkans, Pettifer eschews clichés for a complex and unsparing portrait of the modern state.

Terence Spencer *Fair Greece, Sad Relic: Literary Philhellenism from Shakespeare to Byron* (Denise Harvey, Athens). Greece from the fall of Constantinople to the War of Independence, through the eyes of English poets, essayists and travellers.

Richard Stoneman *A Literary Companion to Greece*. Extracts from the classics, but also some more modern fare, including Kavafy's famed poem *Return to Ithaca* and Wilde on Zákynthos. Over 21 pages on the Ionians, although oddly no mention of Byron's *Childe Harold's Pilgrimage*.

History and the classics

A good general history is *A Traveller's History of Greece* by **Timothy Boatswain and Colin Nicolson**, which gives a slightly dated but well-written overview of all periods Greek. The only specific history of any of the Ionian islands in English is *Old Corfu: History and Culture* by **Nondas Stamatopoulos** (KM Typografia publishers, Corfu), an incredibly detailed, labour-of-love history of the island and town, concentrating on antiquities.

The classics

Many of the classics make excellent companion reading while travelling around Greece – not least Homer's *Odyssey*, even though its geographical links with the Ionian islands have become confused rather than confirmed over the centuries. Thucydides' *History of the Peloponnesian War* should also prove illuminating for those travelling in the Ionian islands, which were embroiled in the war. The following are all available in Penguin Classic editions:

Herodotus *The Histories*;
Homer *The Odyssey; The Iliad*;
Pausanias *The Guide to Greece (2 vols)*;
Plutarch *The Age of Alexander; Plutarch on Sparta; The Rise and Fall of Athens*;
Thucydides *The History of the Peloponnesian War*;
Xenophon *The History of My Times*.

Ancient history

A.R. Burn *History of Greece*. Probably the best general introduction to ancient Greece, though for fuller and more interesting analysis you'll do better with one or other of the following.

M.I. Finley *The World of Odysseus*. Good on the interrelation of Mycenaean myth and fact.

John Kenyon Davies *Democracy and Classical Greece*. Established and accessible account of the period and its political developments.

Oswyn Murray *Early Greece*. The Greek story from the Mycenaeans and Minoans to the onset of the Classical period.

F.W. Walbank *The Hellenistic World*. Greece under the sway of the Macedonian and Roman empires.

Byzantine, medieval and Ottoman

Nicholas Cheetham *Medieval Greece*. General survey of the period and its infinite convolutions in Greece, with Frankish, Catalan, Venetian, Byzantine and Ottoman struggles for power.

John Julius Norwich *Byzantium: The Early Centuries, Byzantium: The Apogee* and *Byzantium: The Decline and Fall*. Perhaps the main surprise for first-time travellers to Greece is the fascination of Byzantine monuments. Norwich's three-volume history of the empire is a terrific narrative account, full of deranged emperors and palace coups; a single-volume abridgement, *A Short History of Byzantium*, is also available.

Timothy Kallistos Ware *The Orthodox Church*. Good introduction to what is effectively the established religion of Greece.

Modern Greece

Richard Clogg *A Concise History of Greece*. A remarkably clear and well-illustrated account of Greece from the decline of Byzantium to 1991, stressing recent decades.

Mark Mazower *Inside Hitler's Greece: The Experience of Occupation 1941–44*. Scholarly and well-illustrated history of Greece during the war, which demonstrates how the complete demoralization of the country and incompetence of conventional politicians led to the rise of ELAS and the onset of civil war.

C.M. Woodhouse *Modern Greece, A Short History*. Woodhouse was active in the Greek Resistance during World War II. Writing from a right-wing perspective, his history is briefer and a bit drier than Clogg's, but he is scrupulous with facts.

Archeology and art

John Beckwith *Early Christian and Byzantine Art*. Illustrated study placing Byzantine art within a wider context.

John Boardman *Greek Art*. A very good, concise introduction to the art of the ancient world in the "World of Art" series.

Reynold Higgins *Minoan and Mycenaean Art*. A clear, well-illustrated roundup.

Sinclair Hood *The Arts in Prehistoric Greece*. Sound introduction to the subject.

Gisela Richter *A Handbook of Greek Art*. Exhaustive survey of the visual arts of ancient Greece.

Suzanne Slesin et al. *Greek Style*. Stunning and stylish domestic architecture and interiors, including Corfu and elsewhere in the islands.

R.R.R. Smith *Hellenic Culture*. Modern reappraisal of the art of Greece under Alexander and his successors.

Peter Warren *The Aegean Civilizations*. Illustrated account of the Minoan and Mycenaean cultures.

Modern fiction

Louis de Bernières *Captain Corelli's Mandolin*. De Bernières' wonderful tragicomic epic of life on Kefalloniá during World War II and after has become almost a fashion accessory among visitors to the island in recent summers. His take on historic detail has also won praise from Greek intellectuals, which should complete the recommendation. The later narrative is telescoped wildly, but the novel deserves the plaudits plastered on the cover.

Stratis Haviaras *When the Tree Sings*; *The Heroic Age*. Although unrelated to the region, these two remarkable novels, now out of print, are recommended for their quasi-autobiographical treatment of two periods in recent Greek history: the former a magic-realist vision of the Nazi occupation of a small Aegean island; the latter a personal history

of the civil war, both seen through a boy's eyes.

Russell Hoban *The Medusa Frequency*. While much of Hoban's avant-garde mystery takes place in the circuitry of the narrator's word processor, it also involves a journey into an underworld region which can only be accessed by a rather unusual gateway: an olive tree in the hills of Paxí.

Anne Michaels *Fugitive Pieces*. Acclaimed Canadian poet's first novel tells tale of a Holocaust survivor rescued from Poland by a Greek archeologist after seeing his parents killed by the Nazis. Written in densely poetic prose, the story is told through diaries discovered by another descendant of the Holocaust, as the central character grows up in Zákynthos and later in Canada, where his mentor trains him to be a scholar and translator.

Specific guides

Lance Chilton *Walks in Northwest Corfu*. A slim, easily portable volume containing twelve routes in the Aríllas, Áyios Yeóryios and Áyios Stéfanos areas, complete with accurate and lovingly drawn maps. Also *Walks in Lefkada and Meganisi* by the same author.

Arthur Foss *The Ionian Islands*. Published in 1969, on the cusp of the region's development, this elegant and erudite guide to the islands mixes description with a comprehensive knowledge of the archipelago's history and culture. Copies fetch fancy prices in the secondhand book market, so try your library.

Noel Rochford *Landscapes of Paxos* and *Landscapes of Corfu*. Seasoned

hiker Rochford has a rather dense prose style, but these are excellent pocket guides to walks around the two islands.

Hilary Whitton Paipeti *The Second Book of Corfu Walks* (Hermes Press, Corfu). This is a more leisurely, but no less extensive, guide to walking on the island, written by a knowledgeable long-term resident. The same author has also written the *Companion Guide to the Corfu Trail* (Pedestrian Publications, Corfu) and a detailed account of places and events associated with the Durrell brothers in Corfu, titled *In the Footsteps of Lawrence Durrell and Gerald Durrell in Corfu (1935–39)* (Hermes Press, Corfu).

Flora and fauna

Marjorie Blainey and Christopher Grey-Wilson *Mediterranean Wild Flowers*. Comprehensive field guide.

Anthony Huxley and William Taylor *Flowers of Greece and the Aegean*. The best book for flower identification, an excellent general guide with good photographic illustrations.

David MacDonald and Priscilla Barrett *Collins Field Guide: Mammals of Britain and Europe*. The best guide on the subject.

Roger Petersen, Guy Mountfort and P.A.D. Hollom *Field Guide to the Birds of Britain and Europe*; **Herman Heinzel et al** *Collins Guide to the Birds of Britain and Europe*. There are no specific reference books on Greek birds, but these two European guides have the best coverage.

Tom Tolman and Richard Lewington *A Field Guide to the Butterflies of Britain and Europe*. A field guide that sorts out all the butterflies you're likely to see, although it's a bit detailed for the casual observer.

Maps

The reliability of maps in the Ionian has improved no end since the Athens-based **Road Editions** mapped the area; their individual island maps (Kefaloniá and Itháki are together) are well worth seeking out and paying a bit extra for, as older and more common rivals such as Toubi's are nothing like as accurate. Road maps are fine for finding your way around by vehicle and even for walking main footpaths, but still not much good for serious country trekking. Town maps, usually only available for the island capitals, are also limited in detail and accuracy.

Maps on a par with Britain's Ordnance Survey do exist in Greece, from the **Yeografikí Ipiresía Stratoú** (Army Geographical Service, or YIS), based in Athens. Unfortunately, you have to go there to get them, and those that cover any sensitive border areas are regarded as a military secret. This includes great chunks of Corfu, owing to its proximity of Albania, and even parts of other Ionian islands – pretty amusing when you consider the border in question is with EU partner Italy, hundreds of kilometres away across the Adriatic. Consequently, these YIS masterpieces are redundant for the Ionian until such a time as restrictions are relaxed, and the only printed help you are likely to find is in locally produced walking guides and maps, such as those by Friends of the Ionians and various enterprising individuals; such orientation aids not referred to below are mentioned in the relevant chapters of the Guide.

The most reliable general map of the Ionian region is the ***Bartholomew Corfu & Ionian Islands Holiday Map*** (1:100,000), which is as geographically accurate as possible at this scale, even on the smaller islands. Also serviceable are the AA-MacMillan and Globetrotter maps at a similar scale.

On **Corfu**, an independent mapmaker, Stephan Jaskulowski, has produced a beautiful set of hand-drawn maps to sections of the island, which should soon be available in book form. The maps detail all roads, tracks and main paths, with lines of elevation and navigational features. At the moment, each island section map costs €3 in the form of a colour photocopy. A similar island map is available on **Paxí**; produced in recent years by cartographers Elizabeth and Ian Bleasdale and sold by most tourism businesses on the island, it is chiefly a detailed walking map, but is the best, and certainly the most accurate, of any of the maps of Paxí.

Language

Language

Language

So many Greeks have lived or worked abroad in America, Australia and, to a much lesser extent, Britain, that you will find someone who speaks English in the tiniest island village. Add to that the thousands attending language schools or working in the tourist industry – English is the lingua franca of most resorts, with German second – and it is easy to see how so many visitors come back having learned only half a dozen restaurant words between them.

You can certainly get by this way, but it isn't very satisfying, and the willingness to say even a few words will upgrade your status from that of dumb *tourístas* to the honourable one of *xénos/xéni*, a word that can mean foreigner, traveller and guest all rolled into one.

Learning basic Greek

Greek is not an easy language for English-speakers, but it is a very beautiful one, and even a brief acquaintance will give you some idea of the debt owed to it by western European languages. On top of the usual difficulties of learning a new language, Greek presents the additional problem of an entirely separate **alphabet**. Despite initial appearances, this is fairly easily mastered – a skill that will help enormously if you are going to get around independently (see below). In addition, certain combinations of letters have unexpected results. This book's transliteration system should help you make intelligible noises, but you have to remember that the correct **stress** (marked throughout the book with an acute accent) is crucial to getting yourself understood.

Greek **grammar** is more complicated: nouns are divided into three genders, all with different case endings in the singular and in the plural, and all adjectives and articles have to agree with these in gender, number and case. All adjectives are arbitrarily cited in the neuter form in the following lists. Verbs are even worse, with active verbs in several conjugations, passive ones, and passive ones used actively(!). To begin with at least, the best thing is simply to say what you know the way you know it, and never mind the niceties. Even "Eat meat hungry" should get a result; if you worry about your mistakes, you'll never say anything.

Language-learning materials

Teach-yourself Greek courses

Breakthrough Greece (Pan Macmillan; book and two cassettes). Excellent, basic teach-yourself course – completely outclasses the competition.

Greek Language and People (BBC Publications, UK; book and cassette available). More limited in scope, but good for acquiring the essentials and the confidence to try them.

Anne Farmakides *A Manual of Modern Greek* (Yale UP/McGill UP; 3 vols). If you have the discipline and motivation, this is the best for learning proper, grammatical Greek; indeed, mastery of just the first volume will get you a long way.

Phrasebooks

Greek, A Rough Guide Phrasebook (Rough Guides). For an up-to-date, accurate pocket phrase book not full of *plume de ma tante*-type expressions, look no further than Rough Guides' very own; English-to-Greek is sensibly phonetic, though the Greek-to-English section, while transliterated, requires mastery of the Greek alphabet.

Dictionaries

The Oxford Dictionary of Modern Greek (Oxford University Press). A bit bulky but generally considered the best Greek–English, English–Greek dictionary.

Collins Pocket Greek Dictionary (HarperCollins). Very nearly as complete as the *Oxford* and probably better value for money.

Oxford Learner's Dictionary (Oxford University Press). If you're planning a prolonged stay, this pricey two-volume set is unbeatable for usage and vocabulary. There's also a more portable one-volume *Learner's Pocket Dictionary*.

The Greek alphabet

Greek	Transliteration	Pronounced
Α, α	a	a as in fat
Β, β	v	v as in vet
Γ, γ	y/g	y as in yes, except before consonants and a, o or long i, when it's a throaty version of the g in gap
Δ, δ	dh	th as in then
Ε, ε	e	e as in get
Ζ, ζ	z	z sound
Η, η	i	i as in ski
Θ, θ	th	th as in theme
Ι, ι	i	i as in ski, indistinguishable from η
Κ, κ	k	k sound
Λ, λ	l	l sound
Μ, μ	m	m sound
Ν, ν	n	n sound
Ξ, ξ	x	x sound, never z
Ο, ο	o	o as in box
Π, π	p	p sound
Ρ, ρ	r	r sound, slightly rolled
Σ, σ or ς	s	s sound
Τ, τ	t	t sound
Υ, υ	i/y	i as in ski, indistinguishable from η
Φ, φ	f	f sound
Χ, χ	h/kh	harsh h sound, like ch in loch
Ψ, ψ	ps	ps as in lips
Ω, ω	o	o as in box, indistinguishable from o

Combinations and diphthongs

AI, αι	e	e as in get
AY, αυ	av/af	av or af, depending on following consonant or vowel
EI, ει	i	i as in ski, indistinguishable from Ë
EY, ευ	ev/ef	ev or ef, depending on following consonant or vowel
OI, οι	i	i as in ski, indistinguishable from Ë
OY, ου	ou	ou as in tourist
ΓΓ, γγ	ng	ng as in angle; always medial
ΓΚ, γκ	g/ng	g as in goat at the beginning of a word; ng in the middle
ΜΠ, μπ	b	b at the beginning of a word; mb in the middle
NT, ντ	d/nd	d at the beginning of a word; nd in the middle
ΤΣ, τσ	ts	ts as in hits
TZ, τζ˙	tz	dz as in adze

Katharévoussa and dhimotikí

Greek may seem complicated enough in itself, but problems are multiplied when you consider that until late in the twentieth century there was an on-going dispute between two versions of the language: *dhimotikí* and *katharévoussa*, traces of which still survive.

When Greece first achieved independence in the nineteenth century, its people were almost universally illiterate, and the language they spoke – *dhimotikí*, "demotic" or "popular" Greek – had undergone enormous change since the days of the Byzantine empire and Classical times. The vocabulary had assimilated countless borrowings from the languages of the various invaders and conquerors, namely the Turks, Venetians, Albanians and Slavs.

The finance and inspiration for the new Greek state, and its early leaders, came largely from the Greek **diaspora** – Orthodox families who had been living in the sophisticated cities of central and eastern Europe, or in Russia. With their European notions about the grandeur of Greece's past, and lofty conception of Hellenism, they set about obliterating the memory of subjugation to foreigners in every possible field. And what better way to start than by purging the language of its foreign accretions and reviving its Classical purity? They accordingly devised what was in effect a new form of the language, **katharévoussa** (literally "cleansed" Greek). The complexities of Classical grammar and syntax were reinstated, and Classical words were dusted off and resuscitated. To the country's great detriment, *katharévoussa* became the language of the schools and the prestigious professions, government, business, the law, newspapers and academia. Everyone aspiring to membership of the elite strove to master it.

The *katharévoussa/dhimotikí* debate was a highly contentious issue through most of the twentieth century. Writers – from Sikelianos and Seferis to Kazant-zakis and Ritsos – all championed the demotic in their literature, as did the political Left in its rhetoric, while crackpot right-wing governments forcibly (re)instated *katharévoussa* at every opportunity. Most recently, the colonels' junta of 1967–74 reversed a decision of the previous government to teach in *dhimotikí* in the schools, bringing back *katharévoussa*, even on sweet wrappers, as part of their ragbag of notions about racial purity and heroic ages.

Dhimotikí returned once more after the fall of the colonels and it is now unthinkable it should be usurped again. It is used in schools, on radio and TV, by newspapers (with the exception of the extreme right-wing *Estia*) and in all official business. The only institutions that refuse to bring themselves up to date are the Church and the legal professions – so beware rental contracts.

This is not to suggest that there is now any less confusion. The Metaxas dictatorship of the 1930s changed scores of village names from Slavic to Classical forms, and these official place names still hold sway on most road signs and maps – even though the local people will use the *dhimotikí* form. Thus you may see "Plomárion" or "Inoússai" written on officially authorized maps or road signs, while everyone actually says Plomári or Inoússes.

Greek words and phrases

Essentials

Ne	Yes	To vrádhi	In the evening
Málista	Certainly	Edhó	Here
Óhi	No	Ekí	There
Parakaló	Please	Aftó	This one
Endáxi	OK, agreed	Ekíno	That one
Efharistó	Thank you	Kaló	Good
(polý)	(very much)	Kakó	Bad
(Dhen)	I (don't)	Megálo	Big
Katalavéno	understand	Mikró	Small
Parakaló,	Excuse me,	Perissótero	More
mípos miláte	do you speak	Ligótero	Less
angliká?	English?	Lígo	A little
Signómi	Sorry/ Excuse me	Polí	A lot
Símera	Today	Ftinó	Cheap
Ávrio	Tomorrow	Akrivó	Expensive
Khthés	Yesterday	Zestó	Hot
Tóra	Now	Krýo	Cold
Argótera	Later	Mazí	With
Aniktó	Open	Horís	Without
Klistó	Closed	Grígora	Quickly
Méra	Day	Sigá	Slowly
Nýkhta	Night	Kýrios/Kyría	Mr/Mrs
To proï	In the morning	Dhespinís	Miss
To apóyevma	In the afternoon		

Other needs

Trógo/Píno	To eat/drink	Trápeza	Bank
Foúrnos, psomádhiko	Bakery	Leftá/Khrímata	Money
Farmakío	Pharmacy	Toualéta	Toilet
Tahydhromío	Post office	Astynomía	Police
Gramatósima	Stamps	Iatrós	Doctor
Venzinádhiko	Petrol station	Nosokomío	Hospital

Requests and questions

To ask a question, it's simplest to start with the name of the thing you want in an interrogative tone.

Parakaló, o foúrnos?	Where is the bakery?	Póte?	When?
Parakaló, o dhrómos	Can you show	Yatí?	Why?
ya...? Parakaló,	me the road to...?	Ti óra...?	At what time...?
éna dhomátio	We'd like a	Ti íne/Pió íne...?	What is/Which is...?
yia dhýo átoma?	room for two	Póso káni?	How much
Parakaló, éna	May I have a kilo		(does it cost)?
kiló portokália?	of oranges?	Ti óra aníyi?	What time does
Poú?	Where?		it open?
Pós?	How?	Ti óra klíni?	What time does
Póssi or pósses?	How many?		it close?
Póso?	How much?		

Accommodation

Xenodhohío	Hotel	Krýo neró	Cold water
Éna dhomátio...	A room...	Boró ná to dho?	Can I see it?
yia éna/dhýo/tría	for one/two/	Boróume na	Can we camp here?
átoma	three people	váloume tín skiní	
yia mía/dhýo/trís	for one/two/	edhó?	
vradhiés	three nights	Kámping/	Campsite
me megálo kreváti	with a double bed	Kataskínosi	
me doús	with a shower	Skiní	Tent
Zestó neró	Hot water	Ksenónas neótitos	Youth hostel

Talking to people

Greek makes the distinction between the informal (*esí*) and formal (*esís*) second person, as French does with *tu* and *vous*. Young people, older people and country people nearly always use *esí* even with total strangers. In any event, no one will be too bothered if you get it wrong. By far the most common greeting, on meeting and parting, is *Yiásou/Yiásas* – literally "Health to you".

Hérete	Hello	Parakaló, miláte	Speak slower, please
Kaliméra	Good morning	pió sigá	
Kalispéra	Good evening	Pos léyete sta	How do you say
Kalinýkhta	Good night	Eliniká?	it in Greek?
Adío	Goodbye	Dhén kséro	I don't know
Ti kánis?/Ti kánete?	How are you?	Tha se/sas dhó ávrio	See you tomorrow
Kalá íme	I'm fine	Kalí andámosi	Au revoir
Ke esí/esís?	And you?	Páme!	Let's go!
Pos se/sas léne?	What's your name?	Parakaló,	Please help me
Me léne...	My name is...	name voïthíste	

On the move

Aeropláno	Aeroplane	Pou pas/pate?	Where are you going?
Leoforío	Bus	Páo stó…	I'm going to…
Aftokínito	Car	Thélo ná	I want to get off at…
Mihanáki, papáki	Motorbike, moped	katévo stó…	
Taksí	Taxi	Ó dhrómos yia…	The road to…
Plío/Vapóri/Karávi	Ship/boat	Kondá	Near
Podhílato	Bicycle	Makryá	Far
Otostóp	Hitching	Aristerá	Left
Me ta pódhia	On foot	Dheksiá	Right
Monopáti	Trail	Katefthía	Straight ahead
Praktorío leoforíon	Bus station	Éna isitírio yia…	A ticket to…
Stási	Bus stop	Éna isitírio me	A return ticket
Limáni	Harbour	epistrofí	
Tí óra févyi?	What time does	Paralía	Beach
	it leave?	Spiliá	Cave
Tí óra ftáni?	What time does	Kéndro	Centre (of town)
	it arrive?	Eklisía	Church
Pósa hiliómetra?	How many	Thálassa	Sea
	kilometres?	Horió	Village
Pósses óres?	How many hours?		

Days of the week and the time

Kyriakí	Sunday	Dhýo/trís iy óra	Two/three o'clock
Dheftéra	Monday	Tésseres pará	Twenty to four
Tríti	Tuesday	íkosi	
Tetárti	Wednesday	Októ ke pénde	Five minutes
Pémpti	Thursday		past eight
Paraskeví	Friday	Éndheka ke misí	Half past eleven
Sávato	Saturday	Se misí óra	In half an hour
Tí óra íne?	What time is it?	S'éna tétarto	In a quarter-hour
Mía iy óra	One o'clock		

Months and seasonal terms

Yennáris	January	Septémvris	September
Fleváris	February	Októvris	October
Mártis	March	Noémvris	November
Aprílis	April	Dhekémvris	December
Maïos	May	Therinó	Summer schedule
Ioúnios	June	dhromolóyio	
Ioúlios	July	Himerinó	Winter schedule
Ávgoustos	August	dhromolóyio	

Numbers

énas/mía/éna	1	saránda	40
dhýo	2	penínda	50
trís/tría	3	exínda	60
tésseres/téssera	4	evdhomínda	70
pénde	5	ogdhónda	80
éxi	6	enenínda	90
eftá	7	ekató	100
okhtó	8	ekatón penínda	150
enyá	9	dhyakóssies/ia	200
dhéka	10	pendakóssies/ia	500
éndheka	11	hílies/hília	1000
dhódheka	12	dhýo hiliádhes	2000
dhekatrís	13	éna ekatomýrio	1,000,000
dhekatésseres	14	próto	first
íkosi	20	dhéftero	second
íkosi éna	21	tríto	third
triánda	30		

Greeks' Greek

There are numerous words and phrases that you will hear constantly, even if you rarely have the chance to use them. These are a few of the most common.

Éla!	Come (literally) but also Speak to me! You don't say! etc.	Pedhí moú	My boy/girl, sonny, friend, etc.
Oríste?	What can I do for you? also Please repeat.	Maláka(s)	Literally "wanker", but often used (don't try it!) as an informal address.
Embrós! or Léyete!	Standard phone responses	Sigá sigá	Take your time, slow down
Ti néa?	What's new?		
Ti yínete?	What's going on (here)?	Kaló taxídhi	Bon voyage
Étsi k'étsi	So-so	Ópa!	Whoops! Watch it!
Pó-pó-pó!	Expression of dismay or concern, like French *O la la!*		

A food and drink glossary

Basics

Aláti	Salt	Katálogos	Menu
Avgá	Eggs	Kréas	Meat
(Horís) ládhi	(Without) oil	Lahaniká	Vegetables
Hortofágos	Vegetarian	O logariasmós	The bill

Méli	Honey	Thallassiná	Seafood (non-fish)
Neró	Water	Tyrí	Cheese
Pipéri	Pepper	Yiaoúrti	Yoghurt
Psári(a)	Fish	Záhari	Sugar
Psomí (olikís)	Bread (wholemeal)		

Cooking terms

Akhnistó	Steamed	Tís óras	Grilled/fried to order
Psitó	Roasted	Tis skáras	Grilled on charcoal
Saganáki	Fried in a small pan (usually cheese)	Yahní	Stewed in oil and tomato sauce
Stí soúvla	Spit-roasted	Yemistá	Stuffed (squid,
Stó foúrno	Baked		vegetables, etc)
Tiganitó	Pan-fried		

Soups, starters and sides

Dolmádhes	Stuffed vine leaves	Fasolákia	French (green) beans
Fasoládha	Bean soup	Frésko kremíyhi	Spring onions
Kolokythokeftédhes	Courgette balls	Horiátiki	Greek (literally
Kopanistí	Spicy cheese dip	(saláta)	"peasant") salad
Melitzanosaláta	Aubergine/ eggplant dip		(usually cucumber, onion, tomato, olives
Mezédhes	Starters, hors d'oeuvres		and féta cheese)
		Hórta	Greens (usually wild)
Skordhaliá	Garlic and potato dip	Kolokythákia	Courgettes/zucchini
Soúpa	Soup	Maroúli	Lettuce
Taramosaláta	Cod roe paté	Melitzána	Aubergine/eggplant
Tzatzíki	Yoghurt, garlic and cucumber dip	Papoutsákia	Stuffed aubergine/ eggplant
Tyrosaláta	Creamy cheese dip	Patátes	Potatoes
Angoúri	Cucumber	Rízi/piláfi	Rice (usually with
Bámies	Okra/ladies' fingers		sáltsa – sauce)
Bouréki	Courgette/ zucchini, potato and cheese pie	Saláta	Salad
		Spanáki	Spinach
Briám	Ratatouille	Yígandes	White haricot beans
Domátes	Tomatoes		(usually in tomato sauce)
Fakés	Lentils		

Meat and meat-based dishes

Arni	Lamb	Kokorétsi	Liver and offal kebab
Biftéki	Hamburger	Kondosoúvli	Seasoned pork roast on the spit
Brizóla hiriní/ moskharísia	Pork/beef chop	Kotópoulo	Chicken
Gourounópoulo	Spit-roast suckling pig	Loukánika	Spicy homemade
Hirinó	Pork		sausages
Keftédhes	Meatballs	Moskhári	Veal

Moussakás	Aubergine/eggplant, potato and meat pie with béchamel sauce topping	Sofríto	Beef stewed in pepper and garlic
Païdhákia	Lamb chops	Soutzoukákia	Mincemeat rissoles/ beef patties in seasoned tomato sauce
Pantséta	Pan-fried strips of pork belly		
Pastitsáda	Corfiot soup made of pasta and offal	Stifádho	Meat stew with tomato sauce
Pastítsio	Macaroni baked with meat	Sykóti	Liver
		Youvétsi	Baked clay casserole of meat and pasta

Fish and seafood

Astakós	Lobster	Glóssa	Sole
Atherína	Sand smelt	Kalamária/ Kalamarákia	Squid/Baby squid
Bakaliáros/ Vakaláos	Cod		
		Karavídhes	Crayfish
Barboúni	Red mullet	Marídhes	White bait
Bourdhéto	Fish (often cod) baked in rich red pepper sauce	Mýdhia	Mussels
		Okhtapódhi	Octopus
		Sardhéles	Sardines
Galéos	Dogfish, hound shark	Soupiá/soupiés	Cuttlefish
Garídhes	Shrimp, prawns	Tsipoúra	Gilt-head bream
Gávros	Mild anchovy	Xifías	Swordfish

Sweets, desserts and fruits

Baklavás	Honey and nut pastry	Fistíkia	Pistachio nuts
Bougátsa	Creamy cheese pie served warm with sugar and cinnamon	Fráoules	Strawberries
		Karpoúzi	Watermelon
		Kerásia	Cherries
Galaktoboúreko	Custard pie	Krystália	Green miniature pears
Halvás	Sesame or semolina sweetmeat	Lemóni	Lemon
		Mílo	Apple
Karidhópita	Walnut cake	Pepóni	Melon
Kréma	Custard pudding	Portokáli	Orange
Pagotó	Ice cream	Rodhákino	Peach
Pastélli	Sesame and honey bar	Sýka	(Dried) figs
Rizógalo	Rice pudding	Stafýlia	Grapes

Cheese

Féta	Salty, white cheese	Katsikísio	Goat's cheese
Graviéra	Gruyère-type hard cheese	Myzíthra	Sweet cream cheese
		Próvio	Sheep's cheese
Kasséri	Medium cheese	Saganáki	Fried cheese

Drinks

Bíra	Beer	Kókkino	Red
Boukáli	Bottle	Rozé/kokkinéli	Rosé
Gála	Milk	Lemonádha	Lemonade
Gazóza/sódha	Generic fizzy drink	Metalikó neró	Mineral water
Kafés	Coffee	Portokaládha	Orangeade
Krasí	Wine	Potíri	Glass
Áspro/lefkó	White	Stin yássas!	Cheers!
		Tsáï	Tea

Glossary of words and terms

Acropolis Ancient, fortified hilltop.

Agora Market and meeting place of an ancient Greek city; also the commercial "high street" of a modern town or village.

Amphora Tall, narrow-necked jar for oil or wine.

Áno Upper; common prefix element of village names.

Apókries Pre-Lentern carnival.

Archaic period Late Iron Age period, from around 750 BC to the start of the Classical period in the fifth century BC.

Arékia Italian-influenced folk ballads (see box p.238)

Astikó (Intra)city, municipal, local – as in phone calls and bus services.

Áyios/Ayía/Áyii Saint or holy (m/f/plural). Common place-name prefix (abbreviated Ag or Ay), often spelled Agios or Aghios.

Byzantine empire Created by the division of the Roman empire in 395 AD, this, the eastern half, was ruled from Constantinople (modern Istanbul). In Greece, Byzantine culture peaked twice: in the eleventh century, and again at Mystra in the early fifteenth century.

Capital The flared top, often ornamented, of a column.

Classical period Essentially from the end of the Persian Wars in the early fifth century BC until the unification of Greece under Philip II of Macedon (338 BC).

Corinthian Columns with capitals carved with acanthus leaves; a temple built in this order.

Dhiamerismata Flats or apartments, often applied to holiday rentals.

Dhimarhío Town hall.

Dhomátia Rooms for rent in purpose-built blocks or private houses.

Dorian Northern civilization that displaced and succeeded the Mycenaeans and Minoans through most of Greece around 1100 BC.

Doric Minimalist, unadorned columns, dating from the Dorian period; a temple built in this order.

Estiatório Restaurant; see "Eating and Drinking" in Basics (p.44) for fuller description.

Exoterikó International, in case of mail or phone call, literally "outer".

Frieze Band of sculptures around a temple or other building. Doric friezes consist of various tableaux of figures (Metopes) interspersed with grooved panels (Triglyphs); Ionic ones have continuous bands of figures.

Froúrio Medieval castle; also modern military headquarters.

Garsoniéra/es Studio villa/s, self-catering apartment/s.

Geometric period Post-Mycenaean Iron Age era named for the style of its pottery; begins in the early eleventh century BC with the arrival of Dorian peoples. By the eighth century BC, with the development of representational styles, it becomes known as the Archaic period.

Hellenistic period The period following Macedonian expansion under Alexander the Great to the fall of Corinth to the Romans in 146 BC during which the eastern

Mediterranean world was under Greek cultural and political hegemony.

Heptanese Old-fashioned term for the Ionian islands, including Kýthira.

Heroön Shrine or sanctuary, usually of a demigod or mortal; war memorials in modern Greece.

Ierón Literally, "sacred" – the space between the altar screen and the apse of a church, reserved for priestly activities.

Ikonostásis Screen between the nave of a church and the altar, supporting at least three icons.

Ionic Elaborate, decorative development of the older DORIC order; Ionic temple columns are slimmer with deeper "fluted" edges, scroll-shaped capitals and ornamental bases.

Iperastikó Inter-city, long-distance – as in phone calls and bus services.

Kafenío Coffee house or café; in a small village the centre of communal life and probably serving as the bus stop, too.

Kaïki (plural Ka´kia) Caique, or medium-sized boat, traditionally wooden and used for transporting cargo and passengers; now refers mainly to island excursion boats.

Kalikantzári Hobgoblins in folklore.

Kámbos Fertile agricultural plateau or plain, the latter usually near a river mouth.

Kandádhes Distinct Ionian form of song, a hybrid of Greek folk and classical Italian (see box p.238).

Kantína Shack, caravan or even a disused bus on the beach, serving just drinks and perhaps sandwiches.

Karnaváli Common term for the pre-Lentern festival.

Kástro Any fortified hill or a castle.

Katholikón Central chapel of a monastery.

Káto Lower; common prefix element of village names.

Kendrikí Platía Central square.

Kinitó Mobile phone.

Klephts Mountain brigands, infamous for lawlessness and renowned for resistance to Turks.

Kouros Nude Archaic or Classical statue of an idealized young man, usually portrayed with one foot slightly forward of the other.

Leofóros Avenue, usually included when part

of an address.

Limáni Port or harbour.

Limenarhío Port Authority.

Macedonian Empire Empire created by Philip II in the mid-fourth century BC.

Maéstro Prevailing northwesterly winds, common in the Ionians in summer.

Metope see Frieze

Minoan Crete's great Bronze Age civilization, which dominated the Aegean from about 2500 to 1400 BC.

Moní Formal term for a monastery or convent.

Mycenaean Mainland civilization centred on Mycenae and the Argolid from about 1700 to 1100 BC.

Naós The inner sanctum of an ancient temple; also, any Orthodox Christian shrine.

Narthex Western vestibule of a church, reserved for catechumens and the unbaptized; typically frescoed with scenes of the Last Judgement.

Neolithic Earliest era of settlement in Greece, characterized by the use of stone tools and weapons together with basic agriculture. Divided arbitrarily into Early (c.6000 BC), Middle (c.5000 BC) and Late (c.3000 BC).

Néos, Néa, Néo "New" – a common prefix to a town or village name.

Nomarhía The prefecture building which administers each Nomós.

Nomós Modern Greek province or county – the larger islands each constitute a separate one.

Odeion (Odhío) Small ancient theatre, used for musical performances, minor dramatic productions or councils.

Odhós Street, not usually mentioned or written in addresses.

Orchestra Circular area in a theatre where the chorus would sing and dance.

Palaestra Gymnasium for athletics and wrestling practice.

Paleós, Paleá, Paleó "Old" – again a common prefix in town and village names.

Panayía Virgin Mary.

Pandopolío Old-style grocer's shop.

Paniyíri Festival or feast – the local celebration of a holy day.

Pandokrátor Literally "The Almighty"; generally refers to the stern portrayal of

Christ in Majesty frescoed or in mosaic in the dome of many Byzantine churches. Also name of Corfu's largest mountain.

Paralía Beach or seafront promenade.

Paramoní Eve, of festival or celebration.

Pediment Triangular, sculpted gable below the roof of a temple.

Períptero Street kiosk.

Pinakothíki Picture/art gallery.

Platía Square, plaza.

Protokhroniá New Year's Day.

Psarotavérna Fish restaurant; see "Eating and Drinking" in Basics (p.46).

Psistariá Grill restaurant; see "Eating and Drinking" in Basics (p.46).

Pýrgos Tower or bastion.

Stele Upright stone slab or column, usually inscribed; an ancient tombstone.

Stoa Colonnaded walkway in Classical-era marketplace.

Tahydhromío Post office.

Taverna Restaurant; see "Eating and Drinking" in Basics (p.45) for fuller description.

Témblon Wooden altar screen of an Orthodox church, usually ornately carved and painted and studded with icons; more or less interchangeable with Ikonostásis.

Temenos Sacred precinct, often used to refer to the sanctuary itself.

Theatral Area Open area found in most of the Minoan palaces with seat-like steps around. Probably a type of theatre or ritual area, though this is not conclusively proven.

Tholos Conical or beehive-shaped building, especially a Mycenaean tomb.

Tilekárta Phonecard.

Triglyph see Frieze

Vólta Walk or ride for pleasure, often conducted in the evening.

Zaharoplastío Patisserie serving sweets and cakes.

Acronyms

ANEK Anónymi Navtikí Etería Krítis (Shipping Co of Crete, Ltd), which runs most ferries between Pireás and Crete, plus many to Italy.

DIKKI Democrat Social Movement, a party leftward of PASOK.

EAM National Liberation Front, the political force behind ELAS.

ELAS Popular Liberation Army, the main Resistance group during World War II and the basis of the communist army (DSE) in the civil war.

ELTA The postal service.

EOT Ellinikós Organismós Tourismoú, the National Tourist Organization.

FYROM Former Yugoslav Republic of Macedonia.

KKE Communist Party, unreconstructed.

KTEL National syndicate of bus companies. The term is also used to refer to bus stations.

ND Conservative (Néa Dhimokratía) party.

OTE Telephone company.

PASOK Socialist party (Pan-Hellenic Socialist Movement).

Travel store

TRAVEL

& MORE

Small print and
Index

A Rough Guide to Rough Guides

Published in 1982, the first Rough Guide – to Greece – was a student scheme that became a publishing phenomenon. Mark Ellingham, a recent graduate in English from Bristol University, had been travelling in Greece the previous summer and couldn't find the right guidebook. With a small group of friends he wrote his own guide, combining a highly contemporary, journalistic style with a thoroughly practical approach to travellers' needs.

The immediate success of the book spawned a series that rapidly covered dozens of destinations. And, in addition to impecunious backpackers, Rough Guides soon acquired a much broader and older readership that relished the guides' wit and inquisitiveness as much as their enthusiastic, critical approach and value-for-money ethos.

These days, Rough Guides include recommendations from shoestring to luxury and cover more than 200 destinations around the globe, including almost every country in the Americas and Europe, more than half of Africa and most of Asia and Australasia. Our ever-growing team of authors and photographers is spread all over the world, particularly in Europe, the USA and Australia.

In the early 1990s, Rough Guides branched out of travel, with the publication of Rough Guides to World Music, Classical Music and the Internet. All three have become benchmark titles in their fields, spearheading the publication of a wide range of books under the Rough Guide name.

Including the travel series, Rough Guides now number more than 350 titles, covering phrasebooks, waterproof maps, music guides from Opera to Heavy Metal, reference works as diverse as Conspiracy Theories and Shakespeare, and popular culture books from iPods to Poker. Rough Guides also produce a series of more than 120 World Music CDs in partnership with World Music Network.

Visit www.roughguides.com to see our latest publications.

Rough Guide travel images are available for commercial licensing at www.roughguidespictures.com

SMALL PRINT

Rough Guide credits

Text editor: Jeremy Atiyah
Layout: Pradeep Thapliyal, Dan May
Cartography: Rajesh Chhibber
Picture editor: Mark Thomas
Production: Katherine Owers
Proofreader: Madhulita Mohapatra
Cover design: Chloë Roberts
Photographers: Michelle Grant and Nick Edwards
Editorial: **London** Kate Berens, Claire Saunders, Geoff Howard, Ruth Blackmore, Polly Thomas, Richard Lim, Clifton Wilkinson, Alison Murchie, Karoline Densley, Andy Turner, Keith Drew, Edward Aves, Nikki Birrell, Helen Marsden, Alice Park, Sarah Eno, David Paul, Lucy White, Joe Staines, Duncan Clark, Peter Buckley, Matthew Milton, Tracy Hopkins, Ruth Tidball; **New York** Andrew Rosenberg, Richard Koss, Steven Horak, AnneLise Sorensen, Amy Hegarty, Hunter Slaton, April Isaacs, Sean Mahoney
Design & Pictures: **London** Simon Bracken, Diana Jarvis, Jj Luck, Harriet Mills;
Delhi Umesh Aggarwal, Madhulita Mohapatra, Ajay Verma, Jessica Subramanian, Amit Verma, Ankur Guha

Production: Aimee Hampson, Sophie Hewat
Cartography: **London** Maxine Repath, Ed Wright, Katie Lloyd-Jones; **Delhi** Manish Chandra, Jai Prakash Mishra, Ashutosh Bharti, Rajesh Mishra, Animesh Pathak, Jasbir Sandhu, Karobi Gogoi, Amod Singh
Online: **New York** Jennifer Gold, Suzanne Welles, Kristin Mingrone; **Delhi** Manik Chauhan, Narender Kumar, Manish Shekhar Jha, Lalit K. Sharma, Rakesh Kumar, Chhandita Chakravarty
Marketing & Publicity: **London** Richard Trillo, Niki Hanmer, David Wearn, Demelza Dallow, Louise Maher; **New York** Geoff Colquitt, Megan Kennedy, Katy Ball; **Delhi** Reem Khokhar
Custom publishing and foreign rights: Philippa Hopkins
Manager India: Punita Singh
Series editor: Mark Ellingham
Reference Director: Andrew Lockett
PA to Managing and Publishing Directors: Megan McIntyre
Publishing Director: Martin Dunford
Managing Director: Kevin Fitzgerald

Publishing information

This fourth edition published June 2006 by
Rough Guides Ltd,
80 Strand, London WC2R 0RL, UK
345 Hudson St, 4th Floor,
New York, NY 10014, USA
14 Local Shopping Centre, Panchsheel Park,
New Delhi 110017, India
Distributed by the Penguin Group
Penguin Books Ltd,
80 Strand, London WC2R 0RL, UK
Penguin Putnam, Inc.
375 Hudson Street, NY 10014, USA
Penguin Group (Australia)
250 Camberwell Road, Camberwell,
Victoria 3124, Australia
Penguin Books Canada Ltd,
10 Alcorn Avenue, Toronto, Ontario,
M4V 1E4, Canada
Penguin Group (New Zealand)
Cnr Rosedale and Airborne Roads
Albany, Auckland, New Zealand
Cover design by Peter Dyer.

Typeset in Bembo and Helvetica to an original design by Henry Iles.

Printed in LegoPrint S.p.A in Italy

© Nick Edwards and John Gill 2006

320pp includes index

A catalogue record for this book is available from the British Library

ISBN 13: 978-184353-617-8

ISBN 10: 1-84353-617-X

The publishers and authors have done their best to ensure the accuracy and currency of all the information in **The Rough Guide to The Ionian Islands**, however, they can accept no responsibility for any loss, injury, or inconvenience sustained by any traveller as a result of information or advice contained in the guide.

1   3   5   7   9   8   6   4   2

Help us update

We've gone to a lot of effort to ensure that the fourth edition of **The Rough Guide to The Ionian Islands** is accurate and up to date. However, things change – places get "discovered", opening hours are notoriously fickle, restaurants and rooms raise prices or lower standards. If you feel we've got it wrong or left something out, we'd like to know, and if you can remember the address, the price, the time, the phone number, so much the better.

We'll credit all contributions, and send a copy of the next edition (or any other Rough Guide

if you prefer) for the best letters. Everyone who writes to us and isn't already a subscriber will receive a copy of our full-colour thrice-yearly newsletter.

Please mark letters: "**Rough Guide The Ionian Islands Update**" and send to: Rough Guides, 80 Strand, London WC2R 0RL, or Rough Guides, 4th Floor, 345 Hudson St, New York, NY 10014. Or send an email to **mail@roughguides.com**

Have your questions answered and tell others about your trip at
www.roughguides.atinfopop.com

SMALL PRINT

Acknowledgements

The author **Nick Edwards** would like to thank everybody who helped him on the last tour, especially Maria of the Hotel Gorgona in Nydhrí, Panayiotis of the Hara in Argostoli and Kostas of the Boukari Beach. Also thanks to Andronikos of the Kyani Akti in Argostóli and Kostas of the Angonari near Ágrafi for fine feasts. Once more gratitude goes to Mariana, Petros, Orestes and Orfeas for excellent hospitality in Horepískopi. Cheers to Peter Hemming for the Lixouri tour and yiasas to Pam and all at Pub Old House. And here's to the old friends who joined in at various stages: Ann, Steve, Carol & Simon and Gordon. Finally, a huge hug to Maria for minding the homestead.

Readers' letters

Thanks to those readers of the 3rd edition who took the trouble to write in with their amendments and additions. These included Jeff Alterman, Antony Gordon, Paul Hofman, Roger Hunter, Irene Sharp, Bill Stewart, Graham Whitehouse and Lance Woodman. Apologies for any misspellings.

SMALL PRINT

Photo credits

All photos © Rough Guides except the following:

Introduction
Sunset over Corfu © Steve J Benbow/Axiom
Homeric Hunt © Terry Harris/Just Greece photo
  library/Alamy
Mountian Biking in Vassiliki © Jack Moscrop/
  Axiom

Things not to miss
01 Lefkádha Beaches © Jochem D Wijnands/
  Getty Images
08 Melissáni Cave © Mick Rock/Alamy
09 Frikes © Emile Lulder/Corbis
11 Loggerhead Turtle © David Boag/Alamy
13 Windsurfing in Vassilikí © Doug McKinlay/
  Axiom
14 Easter Procession © IML Images Group
  Ltd/Alamy
18 Cricket © Steve J Benbow/Axiom

Architecture Insert
Old Corfu Town © Derrick Furlong/Robert
  Harding Picture Library/Alamy

Beaches Insert
Mýrtos Beach © Rob Rayworth/Alamy
Touristic Beach © aophotography.com/Alamy

B&Ws
p.128 Gáïos Town, Paxos © James Davis/Alamy
p.221 Ássos, Kefalloniá © IML Images Group/
  Alamy

SMALL PRINT

Selected images from our guidebooks are available for licensing from:

ROUGHGUIDES**PICTURES**.COM

Index

Map entries are in colour.

INDEX

INDEX

315

Map symbols

maps are listed in the full index using coloured text

MAP SYMBOLS

┅┅┅	International boundary
‒ ‒ ‒	Chapter division boundary
═══	Major paved road
═══	Minor paved road
───	Unpaved road (regional maps)
┈┈┈	Unpaved road (town maps)
┄ ┄ ┄	Footpath
⊥⊥⊥⊥	Steps
▬▬▬	Pedestrianized road
─ ─ ─	Ferry route
═══	Coastline/river
───	Wall
⸸	Place of interest
✈	Airport
⸸	Church (regional maps)
⛪	Monastery
♛	Castle
∴	Ruins
⌂	Cave

▲	Mountain peak
⸷	Lighthouse
⚑	Campsite
◉	Accommodation
ⓘ	Information office
@	Internet
✉	Post office
★	Bus stop
🄿	Parking
⊞	Hospital
🍇	Vineyard
⚓	Swimming pool
⊙	Statue
▬	Building
⊞	Church (town maps)
⬭	Stadium
⊡	Christian cemetery
▦	Park
▒	Beach

Travel Insurance

Wherever you are, wherever you are going, we ve got you covered!

Visit our website at
www.roughguides.com/insurance
or call:

- UK: 0800 083 9507
- Spain: 900 997 149
- Australia: 1300 669 999
- New Zealand: 0800 55 99 11
- Worldwide: +44 870 890 2843
- USA, call toll free on: 1 800 749 4922

Please quote our ref: *Rough Guides Newsletter*

Cover for over 46 different nationalities and available in 4 different languages.

ROUGH GUIDES

TM
COLUMBUS DIRECT
Travel insurance